Islands of Agreement

Islands of Agreement

✳ MANAGING ENDURING ARMED RIVALRIES

GABRIELLA BLUM

HARVARD UNIVERSITY PRESS
Cambridge, Massachusetts, and London, England   2007

ISBN-13: 978-0-674-02446-5
ISBN-10: 0-674-02446-X

The Cataloging-in-Publication Data is available from the Library of Congress

To my mother and father, with all my love

Contents

Illustrations

Acknowledgments

My first thoughts on how parties trapped in enduring armed rivalries may also engage in joint efforts were kindled by my participation, as a young officer in the Israel Defense Forces' Military Advocate General's Corps, in the Israel-Lebanon Monitoring Group, which operated from the summer of 1996 to the winter of 2000. The Group was established to oversee the implementation of an "Understanding" reached between Israel, Lebanon, and Syria on how to conduct a war without affecting civilians. The idea of warring parties, with no mutual contacts outside the battlefield, coming together to discuss how to enhance protection for civilians, seemed to me, at first, an oxymoron; as time went by, however, it became clear that it was exactly what *should* happen when conflicts continue on end.

This book is based on my studies and research while at Harvard Law School's SJD program, under the supervision of Anne-Marie Slaughter, Robert H. Mnookin, and Antonia Handler Chayes. It is very much due to my work with them, complementing previous experience, that the idea of bringing international relations, international law, and negotiation theory closer together has emerged.

Anne-Marie Slaughter has been a pioneer in synthesizing international law and international relations, arguing forcefully and convincingly that the two strands of scholarship must be interwoven if we are ever to come up with a convincing theory on international behavior. Slaughter's book, *A New World Order* (Princeton University Press,

2004), in which she demonstrates how global networks, whether formal or informal, of judiciaries, parliaments, executives, and bureaucrats form de facto global governance, is a path-breaking study of the international system. It is largely for her study of global governance, which looked for a plethora of interstate relationships we are not always cognizant of, that I could articulate the following question: if transgovernmental networks can serve as forms of governance in peacetime, why not look for such forms of governance—or, management—in wartime?

Robert Mnookin's lifelong work on bargaining, negotiation, and barriers to conflict resolution has directed me to the other strand of this work. Mnookin's argument that legal and business disputes must be *managed*, if not *resolved* (see *Beyond Winning*, Harvard University Press, 2000), has not yet been fully developed in the literature on international conflicts. This is the main normative argument that I set out to make: Instead of being preoccupied with prevention of conflicts or with their resolution, we should shift our focus to management. Mnookin's study of barriers to conflict resolution, whether strategic, institutional, or psychological, which prevent parties from reaching mutually beneficial agreements even when ample opportunities exist for reaching them, informs my work throughout.

Antonia Chayes, together with her husband Abram Chayes, has been a leading scholar of international regimes and of states' compliance with international law. Through a rare combination of vast practical experience and academic scholarship, the Chayeses offered a thorough and comprehensive study of compliance with international regimes, arguing that overall states *do* comply with international agreements they enter into. My relationship with Toni Chayes began when I challenged the validity of the arguments she and Abe Chayes made in *The New Sovereignty* (Harvard University Press, 1995) about dealing with security regimes or with parties who are at conflict with each other. Open to the challenge, as always, Toni suggested I pursue this criticism further. I have tried to do so in this book. Many of the prescriptive components of the *Islands of Agreements* I suggest here are founded on the findings and arguments made by Toni and Abe in their seminal work on international compliance. I'll forever regret not having had the chance to meet Abe.

Beyond being an endless source of intellectual influence and guidance, Anne-Marie, Bob, and Toni have given me their utmost, in every possible way. I am deeply in their debt.

Harvard Law School has been my home away from home, during my studies and, more recently, during my time as a visiting assistant professor. I am forever grateful to the Harvard Law School faculty for its support and kindness. My conversations with many of the faculty members have significantly improved this book.

Hilit Blum has been my dedicated editor throughout the manuscript's various stages; her inspirational comments and excellent styling are apparent on every page.

Special thanks are due to friends and colleagues—Lucian Bebchuk Naomi Chazan, Ehud Eiran, Michelle Ferenz, Oren Bar-Gill, Nikitas Hatzimihail, Martha Minow, Rick Pildes, Roy Schöndorf, Ronen Shamir, Sven Spengemann, Annecoos Wiersema, and Chen Zak—for their many illuminating comments. My gratitude also goes to the Tel-Aviv University Law School faculty, to the faculty of the Lauder School of Government, Diplomacy, and Strategy at the Interdisciplinary Center in Herzliya, and to the program managers at the Conflict Management Group, Cambridge, Massachusetts, for giving me the opportunity to present and discuss my work.

Karen Tenenbaum, Panagoula Diamanti-Karanou, Cillian Nolan, and Ashim Krishna Sood, gave me invaluable research assistance, enriching my pages with both data and ideas. Aaron Haas, Kamyar Hariri, and Giddon Tikutzki helped with the chapter on Lebanon. Marilyn Uzuner, Maura Kelley, and Deborah Gallagher provided much-needed technical support.

I wish to express my thanks and appreciation for the generous financial support I have been privileged to receive from the Program on Negotiation at Harvard Law School and from the E. David Fischman Scholarship, United Jewish Fund and Council. A special mention is owed to Susan Hackley and James Kerwin from the Program on Negotiation for their ongoing care and assistance.

Michael Aronson of Harvard University Press believed in this project from its early stages and recommended it for publication by the press. I am deeply grateful to him and to Jeanine Rees who has worked with him on this project. I also thank two outside reviewers of Harvard University Press for their incisive and unsparing comments, which have forced me to rethink and refine my arguments. Any remaining mistakes are mine alone. A special thanks to Tonnya Norwood of NK Graphics who so ably chaperoned this manuscript in its transition into book form.

Finally, my deepest abiding gratitude goes to my mother and father. Without their unbounded love and encouragement, this work and much else would not have come to pass.

Islands of Agreement

✳ Introduction

> Thus it would seem that any effort to replace brute
> force by the might of an ideal is, under present
> conditions, doomed to fail. Our logic is at fault if we
> ignore the fact that right is founded on brute force and
> even to-day needs violence to maintain it . . . There is
> no likelihood of our being able to suppress humanity's
> aggressive tendencies.
>
> *WHY WAR? A CORRESPONDENCE BETWEEN ALBERT EINSTEIN*
> *AND SIGMUND FREUD, TRANS. STEWARD GILBERT*

In the summer of 1932, the League of Nations' International Institute of Intellectual Cooperation commissioned one of its members, Albert Einstein, to invite a person of his choosing to exchange views on any problem he considered worthy of public debate. Einstein's choice was a lifelong preoccupation: "Is there any way of delivering mankind from the menace of war? . . . Is it possible to control man's mental evolution so as to make him proof against the psychoses of hate and destructiveness?"[1] Implied in the question was half an answer—if war was a psychosis, what more natural than to seek its treatment in science and in scientific method. It was not surprising, therefore, that Einstein should have chosen as his correspondent the thinker and practitioner who was most vigorous in endorsing the application of scientific method to the human psyche, and with the most promising results—Sigmund Freud. But Freud's project had never been that refined form of mental eugenics—"to control man's mental evolution"—envisioned by the great physicist, who was, in general, most comfortable with human nature at arm's length. Freud was too firmly grounded in human nature in its present form to believe in any such imminent possibility.

The exchange between the two scientists encapsuled the generational enterprise in the wake of World War I (and, as Einstein foresaw—and as Freud did not—on the eve of another global crisis) to find aid in all and any scientific disciplines by which to put a rational stop to the mind-boggling phenomenon of war. Einstein, long a committed, publicly outspoken pacifist, was certain war could be abolished "not through fear" but by invoking "what is best in human nature." The solution, he thought, lay in self-knowledge: "We need to be made conscious of our prejudices and learn to correct them."

Freud refused to believe in a divisible humanity, in which the best could be neatly extracted from the worst. His inquiry into individual behavior—and, by inference, social relations as a whole—found a fatefully heterogeneous system, in which best and worst motives and impulses acted indissolubly. The phenomenon of war, in Freud's account, is therefore as endemic to humanity as its noblest impulses, essentially intractable, and in any case hardly something that may be expunged from the continuum of life.

But if history has tended to vindicate the view that war cannot be taken out of life, it has also shown that, complementary, life cannot be extracted from war. Since time immemorial, people, communities, and nations have shown themselves to be mixed-motive entities, capable of single-mindedly trading, working, and even celebrating with enemies they were, at the same time, single-mindedly killing. In ancient Greece, for example, a sixteen-day truce—*Ekecheiria* ("lift your hand")—was announced before and during the Olympic Games, every four years. The tradition began in the ninth century B.C., and survived for about twelve hundred years. In the Middle Ages, centuries of crusades and jihads saw a complex relationship of cross-Mediterranean trade and cultural influences form between Muslims and European Christians, who were otherwise, from time to time, called to fight each other to the hilt for control of the Holy Land. Their elaborate exchange of ideas, in between bloodbaths, brought, for instance, the writings of the great philosopher and medical scientist Ibn Sina into European medical schools, where they were taught until the sixteenth century. And containment arrangements have been known to materialize at the initiative of soldiers on the field and not just of governments. John Keay, telling the history of the English East Indian Company, recounts,

> "Although for much of the seventeenth century the Dutch and English were bitter rivals throughout the East, on the long voyage to and from Europe hostilities were usually suspended. At the Cape [of Good Hope] and at St. Helena ships of the London Company amicably exchanged news and provisions with those of the V.O.C. [Dutch East India Com-

pany]. Hadah was postman for both Companies, and occasionally Dutch and English ships actually sailed together." [John Keay, *The Honourable Company: A History of the English East India Company* (London, 1991), p. 94]

Today, mixed-motive interaction between nations is on the increase; as our world grows more global and interdependent, long total wars of the kind Freud and Einstein witnessed have become less probable. Countries and nations depend on one another and cooperate with each other, directly or indirectly, in myriad ways; they need each other to open and maintain channels of transportation, communication, and commerce, as well as to cooperate on those areas of common good that know no boundaries—the environment, health, science, and culture. But interdependence also breeds competition and conflict. The sets of relations nations now hold between them are increasingly multifaceted, and encompass disagreement and cooperation, discord and harmony, conflict and peace together.

Einstein had advocated global governance that would be founded on international law in its most aspiring form, as an upholder of nations' best behavior and an eradicator of their worst. Indeed, this was the path international law set out to follow after World War II, outlawing war, while resignedly allowing for very narrow exceptions and regulating it further than ever before if and when it happened. But just as domestic law had failed to rid human relations of their "baser" elements of violence, so international law was not to be successful in doing away with belligerence in international relations.

In fact, once the drive to make international law a globally regulating principle finds its full expression, the world it reflects appears not so much as the "best of all possible worlds" but rather as an admixture of complex relations obtaining between states. If we knew nothing of state behavior and, Lady of Shallot–like, looked at it only through the mirror of international law, we would find a whole spectrum of relationships accommodated simultaneously; countries are encouraged to abide by rules ensuring a cleaner and healthier environment even as the weapons they are aiming at each other are limited by type and number.

But long before the codification of modern international law, parties in conflict instinctively knew that they had a relationship outside of war and that politics could work in two worlds at once: that of conflict and that of ongoing everyday life. Over time, parties in conflict gave this acknowledgement form and expression in bilateral agreements between them. To this day, warring parties find a way to realize a potential for cooperation through a mechanism I have named "islands of agreement"—those areas in interstate relationships that remain safe or even prosperous amidst the tide of conflict. Together, the sea of conflict and the islands of agreement formed within it make up the sum of the interstate relationship.

My aim in this work is to show how, in reality, peace and war can and do coexist. My starting point leans towards the mottled Freudian perspective: rapid developments in the nature of war on the one hand and politics on the other mean that international relationships can now more rarely than in the past be reduced to either straight peace or straight war. The more interconnected our world becomes, the more peace and war tend—or at times are forced—to coalesce.

Recent years have seen an unprecedented flux of practical efforts at, and scholarship on, conflict resolution and prevention. Nonetheless, while these are of course invaluable, we must finally come to accept that while humanity is its old self, some conflicts will always be inescapable. In this work I wish to suggest that there is a need for a shift in perspective away from the constricting and essentially total notions of "prevention" and "resolution" towards the widely encompassing concept of management.

The dominant view of management has tended to restrict it to the domain of conflict, focusing on conflict's military aspect, and to judge the success of management by whether or not it had promoted resolution. My own view of management derives from my view of conflict as only a part of the whole potential of interstate relations. The drama of conflict, whether it occurs between people or nations, naturally and justifiably tends to captivate and hold our gaze at the expense of any other potential interaction the parties might have between them. But if we are willing to widen our lens, most conflictual situations, even those of armed confrontation, may be found to include some areas that both parties have in common and that can serve as a basis for cooperation, however limited. My perspective is that whatever the reasons conflicts erupt or endure, they are an integral part of a wide potential of mutual engagement, realized or not. Every relationship needs a modicum of management. Conflict may affect the kind or direction of management, but the latter still takes place within the context of a more holistic, mutual relationship.

I suggest, therefore, that by concentrating our efforts, as we have tended to do, on *conflict resolution only*, we often neglect the potential of strengthening those elements that fall outside the conflict yet inside the relationship.

Common ground is not necessarily intentional. It can exist willy-nilly; it is enough that two countries are members of the World Health Organization and share the responsibility for drafting its International Code on Marketing of Breast-milk Substitutes, for them to have some zone of potential cooperation whether or not they choose to make further use of it. Those extreme cases in which conflict is the be-all and end-all of the relationship do not mean that the potential does not exist—only that politicians or communities have chosen to reject it.

When they do not reject it is the moment islands of agreement are born. This work is dedicated to the study of islands of agreement: how they may be formed, what makes them sustainable, and what their potential impact on the relationship might be.

The book is set out as follows: Chapter 1 lays the conceptual framework to the theory, locating it within existing disciplines of conflict studies. It goes on to define the phenomenon of islands of agreement, exploring its various components and weighing its potential advantages and risks. The chapter goes on to suggest a general model for the establishment and sustainment of islands of agreement.

To test the concept, I have chosen the setting of enduring armed conflicts, i.e., conflicts that are intractable for a long period of time, immune to prevention or resolution efforts. Two reasons informed my choice: The first is that such conflicts pose the most obvious challenge to the prevention or resolution enterprise and to the modern notion that, as Primo Levi has put it, "There are no problems that cannot be solved around a table, provided there is good will, and reciprocal trust—or even reciprocal fear."[2] The second reason is that conflicts that last the longest are also those that are most visibly located within broader spheres of multidimensional relations.

Chapters 2 through 4 each contain a case study of an enduring conflict in which the method of islands of agreement has been employed, once or repeatedly. These are the conflicts between India and Pakistan; Greece and Turkey (and Cyprus); Israel and Lebanon (and Syria).

Chapter 5 concludes with a synthesis of theory and practice, reevaluating the proposed model in light of the experience gleaned from the three case studies and grappling with the normative implications of employing islands of agreement in enduring conflicts.

CHAPTER ONE

Islands of Agreement:
The Conceptual Framework

And the war began, that is, an event took place opposed
to human reason and all human nature. . . . What led to
this extraordinary event? What were its causes?
Historians, with simple minded conviction, tell us . . .

LEO TOLSTOY, *WAR AND PEACE*, TRANS. CONSTANCE GARNETT

The full, true causes of war, Tolstoy tells us, cannot be known. Nothing
that affects so many people so profoundly can truly be understood by a
single historian, even if he or she should spend a lifetime piecing together a multitude of narratives. Nor can the insistence on one point of
view, one single historical, philosophical, or psychological doctrine,
prove more than a tragically limited insight. The event drowns out the
individual voice and eye. The more perspectives, causes, and effects the
epic writer summons for our consideration, the more roundly he seems
to defy us to conclude anything about the connections that may be
made between them. And yet, being human, the great humanist tells us,
we must forever be attempting the noble failure of understanding.

But if the cataclysmic possibilities of modern war defeat even our
imagination's most epic reach, that is because the binary model of war
and peace often no longer appropriately captures what we, sometimes
dimly, grasp as the constantly changing political reality of our lives. The
darker aspects of globalization and interdependence breed—alongside
cooperation and growth—new enemies, new weapons, and new vulner-
abilities. We are no longer sure at all times when either peace or war is
occurring. Leaping out of their polarities, both war and peace are now
so intermingled with each other that even the international legal system
mirrors this conceptual murkiness; the term "war" is nowhere defined
and is rarely found in international treaties or documents of recent

decades. Instead, international law scholars increasingly favor the looser term "armed conflict." Some of those who follow and record wars place the bar of "war" at a minimum of a thousand military battle deaths.

Our general understanding of what peace might be is correspondingly meandering further and further away from clear definability. If peace is nonbelligerency, then North and South Korea may be said to be at peace with each other, however separated by the minefields of the Demilitarized Zone, and so may China and Taiwan or Israel and the United Arab Emirates, although the Chinese government does not recognize Taiwan, or the UAE Israel. Increasingly, too, the phenomenon of international terrorism by nonstate actors redefines relations between countries formally at peace.

At the same time, countries we would conventionally consider to be "at peace" experience hybrid forms of "peace with conflict"—dramatic disputes and fallings out or awakening of dormant grievances, which, thanks largely to the amplifying effect of modern media, gain high resonance worldwide. Examples abound: the political conflict between the United States and much of western Europe over the war in Iraq in 2003 brought three million people to the streets of Rome in what was listed in the *Guinness Book of Records* as the largest antiwar rally ever, and triggered a wave of "anti-American fervor" throughout Europe; a peace agreement formally ending World War II is yet to be signed between Russia and Japan, while their sovereignty dispute over the islands of Etorofu, Kunashiri, and Shikotan, and the Habomai group (known in Japan as the "Northern Territories" and in Russia as the "Southern Kuril Islands") continues. Oftentimes, countries we could not imagine as enemies at this day and age are found in surprising postures of confrontation: in August 2005 Canada sent two warships to the Nordic Sea to assert its sovereignty in the face of Danish counterclaims over the one-half square mile of Hans Island.[1] A year earlier, Britain sent Secretary of State for Defence Geoff Hoon, Princess Anne, and the nuclear-powered submarine *HMS Tireless* to Gibraltar's three hundreth birthday celebrations, by way of an eloquent signal to its Spanish rivals. Spanish Foreign Minister Miguel Moratinos remarked in response that "it is very strange that, in the European Union of the 21st century, one member state should be celebrating the military occupation of part of another member state."[2]

To define war and peace today we must rely more than ever on our intuition and common sense. We know that not every dispute is conflict and not every conflict is war. Even if, as a result of global interconnectedness, almost every dyad of countries one might pick may be found to harbor some dispute or conflict within it over some issue or another, there have been but few instances of all-out interstate war since the second half of the twentieth century and the advent of nuclear weapons. The dramatically changed nature of the modern battlefield also necessarily revises our traditional ideas of what war is. In some cases, intuition may go one way, yet the legal perspective is surprisingly ambiguous: legal scholars have been wrangling over the question of whether the Israeli-Palestinian armed clashes since September 2000 can be termed "armed conflict" in the proper legal sense, though clashes have already claimed over four thousand lives on both sides.[3]

Perhaps a more useful approach, then, would be to seek to resituate conflict theory within the spectrum of interactions between countries that may best be encompassed by the simple term "international relationships." This is in no way intended to downplay the notion of conflict, only to reincorporate it into a continuum exhibiting many gradations. Sigmund Freud, one of the first to address the causes of war scientifically, encourages us to take this integrative view; in *Why War,* his reply to Albert Einstein's address, he says,

> Conflicts of interest between man and man are resolved, in principle, by the recourse to violence. It is the same in the animal kingdom, from which man cannot claim exclusions; nevertheless men are also prone to conflict of opinion, touching, on occasion, the loftiest peaks of abstract thought, which seem to call for settlement by quite another method.[4]

Freud then goes on to explain his views on violence, both private and national, as a natural facet of human relations:

> Each of these instincts [the erotic and the aggressive] is every whit as indispensable as its opposite and all the phenomena of life derive from their activity . . . It seems that an instinct of either category can operate but rarely in isolation; it is always blended (alloyed, as we say) with a certain dosage of its opposite . . . Thus the instinct of self-preservation is certainly of an erotic nature, but to gain its end this very instinct necessitates aggressive action.[5]

My working assumption is that accepting conflict as one, however extreme, point on a curve of human relations inevitably guides us to seek its remedies within the inclusive world of a total relationship between parties. The following pages attempt, therefore, to relocate the study of conflicts within the broader field of vision of international relationships, a relocation which, even as we attempt to manage a conflict, allows us some leeway to maneuver outside its constricting fold. By this approach, which I have named "islands of agreement," I propose to complement the conflict studies' preoccupation with conflict prevention and conflict resolution, which to my mind still harks back to the binary model of war and peace, by looking at conflict management as an end in itself.

To understand where conflict literature stands today, it may be worthwhile to consider in brief its genealogy and development. As an academic discipline, conflict literature rose essentially as a product of the sea change that has occurred, in the wake of two world wars, in modern attitudes towards war. When we examine three or four decades of writing about conflict in the twentieth century, we find, trailing such spearheading volumes as Quincy Wright's *A Study of War* (1942) or Lionel Curtis's *World War, Its Cause and Cure* (1945), an array of works pragmatically titled "War as a Public Health Problem" (1965), *The War Disease* (1972), *Studies on the Contagion of Violence* (1973), "The Epidemiology of Peace and War" (1979) and so on.[6] Such titles mark, first and foremost, a decided departure from Clausewitzian thinking; war was no longer to be considered as part of normal and pragmatic politics but as a malignant pathological phenomenon, like smallpox or tuberculosis, and as such as an issue of public hygiene. Its mitigation, by inference, became a scientific duty. It is no accident that some of those who were most vehement in their condemnation of war as a deep pathology or abnormality in mankind were also the champions of advanced technology of their age; in *Flight to Arras* (1942), his record of suicide flight missions over a ravaged France, nobleman, explorer, soldier, aviator, and writer Antoine de Saint-Exupéry protests, "War is not an adventure. War is a disease. Like typhus."[7]

Once considered a fit topic for proper scientific attention, war became first and foremost *observable*. Scholars saw their first duty to be, *pace* Tolstoy, understanding and describing as fully and as systematically as possible the causes for the eruption and continuation of hostile activities and, correspondingly, the necessary conditions for peace. To understand, went their underlying assumption, was the first step towards finding a cure. And that a cure could and should be found seemed indubitable. To this end, the breadth of human capabilities deriving from new science and technology, which had been so malignantly and recklessly misapplied in warfare, now had to be redirected to the subject with the same rigor required by any scientific problem. An array of disciplines was thus brought to bear on war, ranging from mathematics to psychology, history, political science, economics, and sociology. Each attempted to establish a theoretical framework, within which it would be possible to articulate what drives countries or communities to fight one another. Each also developed a wide-ranging jargon to account for the phenomenon of conflict in general and, by application, of any one specific conflict.[8]

It must be remembered, however, that war was not always conceived as an "event opposed to human reason and all human nature." On this matter Western civilization has undergone a profound revolution in accepted norms; a revolution no older, and in many ways much younger, than the hundred and eighty years or so that separate us from the events described in *War and Peace*.[9] In the words of Bernard Brodie, a master of American strategic thought,

> while attitudes to war changed remarkably little over the millennia, they have changed quite rapidly over the last two centuries, more rapidly in the half century since WWI, and with especial force since the coming of nuclear weapons . . . Where war was once accepted as inevitably a part of the human condition, regrettable in its tragic details but offering valued compensations in opportunities for valor and for human greatness—or, more recently, in opportunities for the ascendancy of superior peoples— the modern attitude has moved towards rejection of the concept of war as a means of resolving international or other disputes.[10]

In light of this development, in 1945 the Nuremberg and Tokyo trials finally established that wars of aggression were "crimes against peace." The United Nations Charter, which was concluded that same year, justified the use of force for self-defense or collective security alone and forbade it for all other purposes. By the 1950s, ministries of defense around the world were redefining their missions in terms of deterrence instead of war.[11] International violence came to be commonly portrayed as a pathological consequence of sovereignty and nationalism—a tragedy resulting from misperceptions, faulty decision making, and poor communication, altogether a remnant of martial habits that were no longer appropriate for the age of interdependence.

As Freud had propositioned when he spoke of "progressive rejection of instinctive ends," much of our Western definition of what is "civilized" has to do with the measure of our distance from and abhorrence of war.[12] Present justifications of war are by and large confined to self-defense or to "correction of what is conceived to be blatant injustice."[13] Today's modern, "civilized" world likes to think it abominates war as much as it idealizes peace.[14] As recent examples show, when leaders from across the globe choose to go to war, they seem to accept it as an inevitable requirement that their public justification for doing so should be the need to "restore peace." Efforts to resolve conflicts are now considered a central, if not the central, function of the international community, whether through national and international representatives and resources or through numerous nongovernmental organizations and individuals who are involved in almost every conflict around the world.[15] By and large, it is the peaceful enterprise, not the violent one, which today reflects positively upon the glory and heroism of leaders.[16]

And yet, for all this much-trumpeted, much legally enshrined and institutionalized opposition, war has hardly grown scarcer in recent times. On the contrary, since the end of World War II, our world has witnessed numerous interstate and intrastate armed conflicts. Even a study conducted by researches from Maryland University, which does suggest an improvement in numbers of armed conflicts over recent years, does not, as its editors admit, make a case for overoptimism.[17] Although the study reports a drop in interstate wars, it also, like three other existing studies, records a distinct shift from interstate to intrastate conflict or towards a hybrid of the two.[18]

According to another ongoing study—the Uppsala conflict database of 2005—since the end of the Cold War, there were 118 conflicts in eighty locations, the majority of which were internal armed conflicts, at times with some international dimension.

The Conflict Studies Literature

> According to them, if only Metternich, Rumyantsev, or Talleyrand had, in the interval between a levèe and a court ball, really taken pains and written a more judicious diplomatic note, or if only Napoleon had written to Alexander . . . there would have been no war. (Tolstoy, *War and Peace*)

Beginning roughly in the 1970s, a second wave of literature on war transferred its emphasis from war and peace to conflict prevention and resolution, a shift that at once, most valuably, broadened the canvass of debate to include all manner of social and political conflict (interstate, ethnic, familial, business related and interpersonal) and made possible a more prescriptive approach. The collective endeavor of conflict studies scholarship in recent decades has been to pin down conflict to separable identifiable causes—separable, therefore manageable—and ultimately defeatable.

Methods vary: some scholars take a selective approach, focusing on one main strand of study, such as bargaining theory or social psychology, while others integrate several approaches into a working model.[20] But whether selective or integrative, the main contribution of this literature lies in its ambition not only to identify barriers to conflict resolution but also to provide negotiators and policy makers with effective, indeed enthusiastic, prescriptive guidance on how to surmount them. In fact, much of the appeal of the literature on conflict and peace derives from its potential for practical political application.[21]

The normative emphasis is on *doing away* with conflict. Recent years have seen a tidal wave of books seeking to empower us with tools for preventing conflicts—personal, collective, or national—and for resolving them if they occur.[22] The unspoken but omnipresent doctrine regarding conflict in this literature is that violence is always negative, that adversaries can almost always reach agreements without the use of force if only they get to know each other, eradicate mutual misunderstandings, and acknowledge each other's needs, and that agreements entailing win-win outcomes are waiting to be discovered.

Generally, the theoretical possibility that conflicts occur or persist simply because there can be no agreement, that "intractables" really are "intractables," is only reluctantly, even embarrassedly, recognized.[23] Implicitly, the underlying assumption of conflict studies literature is that the persistence of conflicts derives from the parties' resistance—whether by choice or constraint—to the voice of reason—a resistance that is, by any reasoned calculation, unaffordable.[24]

In a volume titled *Intractable Conflicts and Their Transformation*, the editors rejoice,

> The central message of this book is that there are no unresolvable conflicts, only conflicts in which parties stubbornly resist solutions . . . The authors of this book have broken apart the monolith of intractability, unpacked the myth of intransigence.[25]

Only teeth-grittingly do they acknowledge,

> Although we believe that in most cases reducing the intractability of conflicts is desirable, we also recognize that often one (or more) adversary believes that any likely settlement of its conflicts would be worse than maintaining the struggle.[26]

The protestation against the notion of intractability is voiced not only by scholars but also by statesmen and thinkers who wrangle with conflict. In the words of Vladimir Velebit, a Yugoslav general, statesman and a UN official, who negotiated on behalf of the then-Yugoslavia a settlement over Trieste,

> I am certain there is no such conflict in the world that cannot be settled if both sides are determined to find a settlement.[27]

Velebit does not clarify the question of whether "determined" also means "ready to forgo vital interests."

Similarly, the possibility that attempts at conflict resolution may sometimes, even if successful, lead to undesirable consequences or that there are times when violence may be the only available option runs counter to a strong and all-prevailing modern, and Western, cultural bias against all violence and in favor of peace almost at any cost. But even the international legal project of outlawing war concedes that some wars are inevitable; even the Geneva Conventions, as Michael Ignatieff, reminds us, "make no ringing claims about human brotherhood. Instead, they accept war as a moral anthropological ritual—the only way that certain human disputes can be resolved."[28]

Whether there are always other viable options and alternative paths to war is a question that exceeds the scope of this work. But even assuming that all conflicts are ultimately soluble in the best of all possible worlds, this is a difficult assumption to find comfort in, given war's devastating effects while it persists. Moreover, throughout history a significant portion of wars has involved issues of crucial importance to governments and entire societies, questions of identity, issues perceived as fundamental to national pride or even survival, and essentially irreconcilable values.[29] In such cases, as Ignatieff puts it, "war remains the ultimate arbiter of human disagreements."[30]

Ultimately, the realization must remain that conflicts are not all the result of misperceptions or hard-bargaining tactics; that, as long as human beings are human, not all conflicts can be prevented; and that prescriptions for resolution may, at times, be oversimplistic. In the words of international politics scholar K. J. Holsti, "the whole intellectual edifice surrounding theories of conflict resolution seems to be inappropriate for the diagnosis and handling of these sorts of conflicts."[31]

Enduring Conflict: The Case for Management

While it is possible that the study and practice of prevention strategies has at times been instrumental in averting conflicts or at least in mitigating them (prevented conflicts are impossible to measure of course), many conflicts persist for years, while all attempts to resolve them, either by agreement on compromise or a decisive military victory, fail. They become, in effect, intractable, moving in repeating cycles of escalation and relative calm, always on the edge of erupting into an all-out war.

Conflicts such as these, which have festered for years without resolution, have been termed by some scholars "enduring rivalries" (mainly in the interstate context), and by others "intractable conflicts" (as a looser concept). Several definitions have been offered; some political scientists suggested objective criteria, such as the number of violent interactions between the same rival states over a specific period of time; others, however, have disputed the calculative approach of these definitions, arguing that "instead of emphasizing their endurance or disputatiousness, it is the conceptualization of rivalry that needs to be stressed. . . ."[32] In this study I use the terms "enduring rivalries" and "intractable conflicts" interchangeably, leaning mostly towards the qualitative, even subjective, criteria. This is because I believe that, whether an enduring or intractable situation, a rivalry or conflict, it is these quarrels' iron grip over diverse aspects of national psyche and culture that merits special attention.

The study of enduring conflicts is particularly illuminating in our context not necessarily because of their prevalence or severity. In fact, as the end of the twentieth century has demonstrated, shorter, intrastate conflicts are more widespread and more devastating than enduring interstate conflicts (on which the enduring rivalry literature has traditionally focused). It took only a hundred days, between April and July 1994, for the Hutus to kill eight hundred thousand Tutsis and moderate Hutus in Rwanda, in which, ultimately, before much notice was taken by the outside world, over a million people died.[33] The breakup of the former Republic of Yugoslavia left between one hundred thousand and three hundred thousand (estimates vary widely) dead, in the largest death toll on European soil since World War II. In the Democratic Republic of the Congo, according to some accounts, 2.5 million people died in the civil war in the years 1998–2003. The International Crisis Group estimates that one thousand people still die every day from war-related causes.[34]

Rather, my interest in enduring rivalries as test cases derives from two qualities inherent in their nature. One is their persistence, which poses a serious challenge to the literature on conflict resolution, as it refutes the possibility, for example, that the conflict is enduring only because a certain leader at a certain point in time has been a fool or a warmonger. There are, of course, exceptions—the killing of UNITA faction leader Jonas Savimbi in 2002 brought an end to forty years of civil war in Angola. Yet the evolution of most enduring conflicts strongly suggest that not all conflicts are either preventable or resolvable (at least, in any foreseeable time), that dialogue cannot always lead to reconciliation, and that the continuation of the conflict—even when it does not promise a decisive victory, sometimes over generations—is still perceived by the rivals as offering them a better alternative to what they estimate might be a possible negotiated agreement.[35] As Gary Goertz and Paul Diehl, who have been studying the phenomenon of interstate enduring rivalries, describe them,

> many rivalries exist for decades, and they become ingrained in political life. Governments become accustomed to them, and they play a role in domestic politics and elections. This image of conflict challenges the traditional view in the scholarly literature, which characterizes international conflict as exceptional events of relatively short duration.[36]

Yet more important, a conflict, when it endures, can present to our eyes not only parties at violence but a whole relational world. While the scope of the conflict means it has probably become multifaceted and multilayered, it is also probable that the parties have some relationship outside it, so that much besides violence is likely to reveal itself to examination and to use.

Perceiving conflicts as an integral part of relationships leads me to believe in the importance of conflict management as a valuable, indeed indispensable, enterprise, set apart from the concept of resolution. Every relationship requires management, even a successful one. Naturally, a conflict setting poses special challenges for management, but it is also the situation in which management is most needed to ameliorate the sufferings and damages conflicts bring about while they persist.

Management is a familiar term in conflict literature. However, it is mostly used to denote a second-best effort; as William Zartman has put it, "management preserves the conflict for resolution another day, at a more propitious time, and may be able to forestall the self-enforcing effects of some of the characteristics. After all, freezing is better and less painful than boiling."[37] At most, the literature welcomes management as a milestone or a tool for resolution.[38]

This rigid perception of a necessary dependency between management and resolution has also meant that the traditional treatment of management has set its sights mainly upon the military aspects of the rivalry. Historically, efforts at "conflict regulation"—an older word for "management"—of the 1950s and 1960s (some surrounding the Cold War) centered only on strategies or actions directly related to the conflict.[39] This constricting outlook is still dominant today: as the editors of two new volumes on intractability published by the Washington Institute of Peace conclude, "the first lesson is that conflict management, which usually involves freezing the conflict through a negotiated and durable cease-fire and the subsequent long-term deployment of outside forces, may be the best option among bad alternatives."[40] This cryogenic logic may explain why management carries with it so little expectation and generally retains the air of an unheroic, uncharismatic exercise.[41]

In the following pages I argue that once we perceive a long-standing rivalry as a full set of (sometime unrealized) possible relations, our sense of what management may be will broaden correspondingly. Once we cease to confine management to the military aspects of the conflict, or once we give it room to work elsewhere as well—still better, once we cease to expect it to "resolve" and are happy to let it "manage"—management becomes a broadly encompassing, transitive concept that transcends the "A to Z" conflict-to-resolution spectrum. It can then set to work more freely within the broader sphere of the rivals' relationship, to include such diverse spheres as trade, environment, culture, transportation, energy, and so forth. In other words, conflict management becomes "relationship management."[42]

I believe that the current strong bias in favor of prevention and resolution puts us in peril of neglecting many potential workable, creative tools for management, especially when it comes to enduring conflicts. Considered in its own right, management relates to a total world of international relations, lying in between or outside the conflict-resolution polarities.

This is not mere semantics. If, when we enter into the thick of an interstate conflict (or indeed into any other type of enduring rivalry), we define our efforts as oriented at "management" rather than "resolution," this definition is likely to transform our perceptions and attitudes towards the management enterprise.[43] No less important, change in definition is also likely to modify the parties' expectations of management; and new expectations, in turn, may affect the parties' cost-benefit analysis with regard to it. That is to say, if in calculating payoffs, the parties were satisfied to consider only those stemming directly from the management efforts and to disregard the question of these efforts' ultimate effectiveness in promoting resolution, the value assigned to the management-only regime might be different—higher or lower, depending on the circumstances— from the value assigned to management tied to resolution only.

The parties' expectations of the management regime may also affect their level of commitment to it. On the one hand, a move defined as a step on the way to resolution may generate greater commitment than a "mere" management effort, due to the higher stakes involved in the process as a whole. On the other, where there is strong reluctance to resolve the conflict altogether, defining the boundaries of the management regime in narrower terms may actually generate greater commitment.

Moreover, management that is not explicitly tied to resolution may also allow the parties to build trust, understanding, and consideration, without fearing that this more benign approach necessarily be perceived by their rival (or by hard-line domestic constituencies) as a willingness to make more concessions on the core contested issues.

Finally, once we unleash management from tight adherence to the strictly conflictual element, more conflict management mechanisms can be contemplated and designed. Once such mechanisms are neither assessed nor tested in their capacity to bring the parties to halt belligerency or to carry them closer to resolution, the range of possible management efforts is materially extended. By exploring spheres that do not directly bear on the parties' core contested issues, indeed by sweeping our gaze across the parties' entire interaction vis-à-vis each other, we may open up opportunities for containing conflict and even for realizing mutual gains from cooperation. Thus, although a lack of cultural or educational ties between the parties does not usually belong to the inner core of the dispute, it becomes easier, within this model, to conceive of a management regime than enhances such ties without bearing on either the core dispute or the armed aspects of the conflict and that may nonetheless be mutually rewarding.

It may of course be the case that the parties themselves resist any recognition of their relationship outside the conflict. This, however, is not evidence that the relational view is wrong. The potential exists, whether or not the parties choose to realize it.

To conclude, in its fullest sense, management should be extracted from the ambitious, yet in a sense not ambitious enough, prevention-to-resolution race and repositioned within the scale of broader, hybrid international interactions. This is not in any way to say that efforts towards resolution are redundant; only that a fuller, multidimensional effort that is not limited to the conflict part of the relationship can be pursued. Consequently, the effects of conflict management mechanisms on the long-term relationship between the parties reach beyond the time and place of conflict to the charged historical space between the parties. This sort of management continues long after the core dispute has been "resolved." Diplomatic relationships, like any other relationships, require ongoing maintenance. From this perspective, the term "resolution" becomes less critical in that it no longer represents a sought-for epilogue or closure.

Islands of Agreement as a Conflict Management Tool

The Concept

Throughout history, rivals have frequently found a joint interest in limiting the scope of their conflicts, in excluding some spheres from them, and even in engaging in cooperative efforts for their mutual benefits. I propose naming these arrangements "islands of agreement."

Islands of agreement are areas of asylum from which the conflict may be excluded and within which the rivals may be able to exchange some mutual commitments and be reminded of their respective interests. The islands do not dry out the sea; large or small, they are always surrounded by the flood. But where they succeed in standing dry, peaceful relations reign at the heart of ongoing tension and even belligerency.

History abounds in such examples: In 1406 King Henry IV of England issued orders protecting fishermen of foreign states (France, Flanders, and Brittany), along with their vessels, cargoes, and crews from any assault or capture as a prize of war, and placed them under his special protection. This practice was based upon a prior agreement with the French king for reciprocal treatment. In 1521 Holy Roman Emperor Charles V and Francis I of France signed a similar treaty. These mutual agreements were normally respected.

In 1848, a treaty between the United States and Mexico stipulated that "if (which is not to be expected, and which God forbid) war should unhappily break out between the two republics . . . the merchants of either republic then residing in the other shall be allowed to remain 12 months to collect their debts and settle their affairs . . . Women and children, ecclesiastics, scholars of every faculty, cultivators of the earth, merchants, artisans, manufacturers, and fishermen . . ." shall be protected.[44] In 1875 a treaty between the United States and Prussia adopted similar provisions.[45]

Early in its war with China in 1894, Japan added to the class of protected enemy people and vessels "boats on a voyage of scientific discovery, philanthropy, or religious mission."[46]

The mechanism I suggest differs conceptually from "management" or "regulation" efforts heretofore explored by scholars. While islands of agreement are essentially limited agreements, which are not in themselves novel in the literature, once we transpose their emphasis unto the whole spectrum of interstate relationships, they grow broader in scope and aspiration—becoming a "relationship management" tool.[47] We are liberated to use islands when we have resisted the instinct to reduce the parties' relationship to that of "conflict" merely.

Islands of agreement may be established to contain or resolve parts of the conflict, create regimes of interstate cooperation, and potentially evolve into broader agreement. In their containment function, they carve out pieces of the conflict and attempt to sustain an equilibrium of more-limited hostile engagement, thereby mitigating destruction and preventing further escalation. Examples of containment include the exclusion of certain areas or certain structures from the sphere of combat, such as the successful creation by the International Committee of the Red Cross of neutralized zones and protected areas during the conflicts in Bangladesh (1971), Cyprus (1974), Vietnam and Cambodia (1975), and Nicaragua (1979) (although a similar attempt by the UN to do the same in Bosnia proved a dismal failure); the declaration of a temporary cessation of belligerency during shared holidays; the imposition of limitations on the use of certain weapons, such as the U.S.-Soviet Anti Ballistic Missile Treaty, etc.[48]

In their cooperative function, islands can also generate regimes of joint venture, in which the parties realize mutual gains from reciprocal or interdependent efforts. These cooperative endeavors are not limited to the conflict but may extend to any facet of the interstate relationship, such as culture, trade, environment, civil aviation, telecommunication, water sharing, etc. Cooperation islands create value, develop relationships among rival actors (governmental, nongovernmental, individual), and increase the costs of escalation, even if the conflict continues.

Ideally, islands may work in a cumulative process, building brick by brick into broader agreements and moving the parties towards a more peaceful existence.

Though islands of agreement are by no means limited to enduring conflicts, I have chosen to concentrate on their workings in these contexts. For reasons I give below, long, intricate quarrels between states pose the most challenging—and at the same time, often the most promising—scenarios for the operation of islands of agreement as a conflict management tool.

Armed or potentially armed conflicts may sometimes arise out of a single issue. More commonly, though, persistent conflicts tend to evolve around a knot of interrelated issues, such as land, religion, ethnic tension, national hostility, ideology, natural resources, or human rights. Moreover, even where conflicts erupt over a limited dispute, which could theoretically be reduced to a few core contested issues, their persistence over long periods of time is likely to extend to other spheres of the relationship. As noted by Edward Azar, "these conflicts appear to start with one set of stated goals, primary actors, and tactics, but very quickly acquire new sub-actors, new goals, and new types of resources and behaviors."[49] Indeed, conflicts may develop to a point where they shape identities, as peoples, nations, and countries define themselves in opposition to their rivals, making it harder and harder to differentiate between core contested issues and issues that are ostensibly outside the scope of the rivalry.

When several issues exist in conjunction, they create a multidimensional conflict, which then stands a high chance of continuing, irresolvably, for years. Such were the Hundred Years' War between England

and France in the fourteenth and fifteenth centuries; the series of conflicts between Britain and Russia between 1877 and 1923; the recurring territorial disputes between Russia/the Soviet Union and Japan between 1895 and 1976; the twentieth century arch-rivalry of the Cold War between the United States and the Soviet Union; and the ongoing conflicts between Israel and its Arab neighbors.[50]

As far as conflict management is concerned, this multidimensionality is Janus-faced in value: while the breadth and complexity of an enduring conflict are often what make agreement more difficult to achieve, they are also what may open up opportunities for value creation.[51] Through the separation of and linkage between contested issues, some trade-offs may be found, both within and across spheres, so that the interests of both rivals are met through package deals.[52]

Thus, for example, a relatively simple dispute over a maritime boundary that is not accompanied by deep-seated historical animosity (on such grounds as ethnic or religious tensions) is less likely to produce a violent, enduring conflict; at the same time, its possible solutions are also relatively limited in scope, as they may include only one of three options—acknowledging the existing boundary, acknowledging an entirely new boundary, or making several adjustments to the existing one to meet the contesting parties' claims. Negotiations would therefore be limited to the distributive aspects of the boundary dispute: namely, who gets what out of the fixed territorial unit.

In multidimensional conflicts, conversely, the opportunities for trade-offs and agreements are exponentially increased: rather than being confined to one or two spheres, the possibilities of trading both within and across spheres allows exchanges between such diverse issues as water rights and territory, movement of people and security measures, trade benefits and refugee resettlement, more-limiting rules of engagement, and third-party intervention, etc. While reaching agreement on all these issues simultaneously is likely to prove impossible (at least at a certain point in time), it may nevertheless be feasible to convince the parties to reach more limited, local, or focused agreements, simply because there are more issues to choose from (this is true for same-sphere trade-offs as well). Such limited agreements do not nullify the distributive tension, but they do potentially increase the overall surplus. In this way, limited agreements may serve as islands within the ongoing conflict, their purpose being to create a zone of limited peace alongside one of a limited war.

Beyond assuming a given rivalry to be multidimensional, we must also assume it to be intractable, at least in the near future, based on repeated failure of previous attempts to resolve it. And while external or internal shocks that may eventually break up the rivalry are always a possibility, they cannot be relied upon or expected within any specific time frame.

In persistent armed conflicts, while resolution is unattainable, a decisive military victory is equally unachievable. Whether the rivals are possessed of equal force or the intensity of preferences compensates for an asymmetry in power, previous interactions between the rivals attest that neither can defeat the other in the near future. Again, changes in technology, capabilities, global political constellations, regional alliances, preferences, or leadership may all change this equation; and yet again, these cannot be relied upon in the short run.

Consequently, the parties are trapped between their ongoing interest in maintaining the rivalry and avoiding a compromise resolution, and their inability to impose a favorable outcome on each other.

However, the parties' capabilities and resources are not unlimited. Even the strongest powers in the world are subject to resource constraints such as manpower, money, military equipment and capabilities, energy resources, etc. Rivals may face strong domestic and international pressures acting as a check on their ability to divert resources—even when they are otherwise available—to promote the rivalry. Of course, there may be cases in which the domestic constituency has no effective voice or influence over the leadership, as in dictatorships. It is even possible that the purpose of the continuation of the rivalry is to suppress opposing domestic actors. In such cases, domestic pressure does not effectively block the ability of leaders to invest in the rivalry. But even then, and perhaps more so, international pressure is expected to play a restraining role.

Given the resource constraints, countries trapped in an enduring rivalry often face financial crises due to the huge expenses involved in the rivalry's continuation. Domestic needs remain unmet, as the means required to provide for them are dedicated to the rivalry. Since both rivals face the same problems, both have an interest in cutting back on their investment in the conflict, "investment" being both direct expenditures and indirect losses incurred by the opportunity costs of noncooperation in areas of mutual interest. In some spheres, such as joint water resources, noncooperation may threaten survival.

Alongside the incentive to cooperate, there are real barriers and obstacles to cooperation. As the basic prisoner's dilemma model demonstrates, these exist in every mixed-motive interaction, but are further aggravated in the context of an enduring rivalry. When an interaction is a rivalry, in which a party is interested not only in saving itself the costs of cooperation but also in inflicting further costs on its rival, stable cooperation is rendered that much more difficult to sustain. Moreover, a concern that the rival might benefit more from cooperation, coupled with fundamental and pervasive suspicion and distrust, cloud the possibility of reaching agreement or of sustaining it once reached. The following pages are dedicated to showing how despite these difficulties, enduring rivals can nonetheless succeed in taking potentially lucrative gambles together.

Notably, for islands of agreement to be employed in a given rivalry, we need not make any assumption with regard to the rationality—in the formal sense of utility maximization—or irrationality of the actors involved. While it may seem that rational actors would want to save costs by engaging in bilateral management efforts, it may be equally rational for one party to prefer an "all-or-nothing" approach and refuse to interact with its rival in any way other than combat. There were no reported islands of agreement in the eight years of conflict between Iraq and Iran; indeed, in a war in which nonconventional weapons were employed and thousands of young children sent to battle, it may be assumed that the preference of the two countries' leaders remained victory at any cost. This, in itself, does not tell us anything about the rationality of the parties involved.

The opposite is also true: the existence of islands of agreement in the relationship does not necessarily imply that the parties are both rational. It could be that an irrational party has entered into a series of limited agreements under a miscalculation of their benefits and effects, where an accurate calculation would have dictated not to do so.

Only when psychological barriers and an entrenched tradition of conflict and animosity prevent parties from fully realizing the extent of benefits that may arise from limited cooperation with their rivals could we argue that the lack of such cooperation is the result of irrationality.

To better define the conceptual and analytical framework of islands of agreement, we must first distinguish them from four closely related yet different concepts: confidence-building measures (CBMs), phased peace agreements, status quo, and limited war. While many islands of agreement in fact fall within the scope of each of these categories, they are conceptually as well as practically more ambitious than any of these concepts.

CBMs

The term CBM (confidence-building measures) has been used by scholars in various ways, ranging from ad hoc goodwill measures to broad, institutionalized agreements. However, in this latter form CBMs have, for the most part, been narrowed down to arms control or other military aspects of the conflict. Throughout this work, to accentuate the idea of islands of agreement as a broader relational concept, I employ the term CBM in its narrower sense, to denote transitory gestures employed by parties to a conflict with the intention of fostering a positive atmosphere, promoting trust, and reducing tensions. CBMs tend to be ad hoc by nature, at times unilateral and mostly informal. They are not intended to create a new regime but only to bear a temporary and usually minor effect on the existing one. Typically, they include releasing of prisoners, allowing an occasional movement of people across borders, extending medical assistance to accident victims, etc. Such were the unilateral release of seventy-one captive Ethiopian soldiers by Eritrea in 1998, during the two countries' border conflict; the U.S. government's approval of Illinois State Governor George Ryan's 1999 visit to Cuba, intended to protest against the U.S.-imposed embargo on Cuba; and the letter sent by the British prime minister, Margaret Thatcher, to the Argentinean president, Raul Alfonsin, congratulating him on his 1983 election, during the Falkland conflict.[53]

The islands of agreement I study here may include such CBMs but are generally more formal, wider in scope, more institutionalized, bilateral, and continuous. Their intention is to create a new operational regime under which the rivals might interact. In addition, islands usually cover a broader subject matter, are forward looking, and involve an ongoing expectation on both sides for reciprocal compliance with the undertaken provisions.

Nonetheless, there may be instances in which it is harder to tell islands from CBMs: for instance, in April 2002 North and South Korea announced that they would renew the family reunification program, halted fifty years earlier, under which families divided by the cease-fire line would be able to reunite in either of the two states.[54] Whether such a step should be seen as an ad hoc CBM or as an island of agreement depends on its specific characteristics: the longer an arrangement operates, the more people it requires for its operation, the more people it directly affects, and the more interstate cooperation entailed in its execution—the more it would be appropriate to characterize it as an island of agreement.

PHASED PEACE AGREEMENTS

Phased peace agreements are limited accords reached as part of a chain of conscious successive moves towards a comprehensive resolution. Negotiations are thus staggered, producing a series of smaller contracts along a precharted course. Such (in theory) was the Israeli-Palestinian Oslo peace process, begun in 1993, which accumulated interim arrangements between Israel and the Palestinian Liberation Organization and was meant to culminate in final status agreement.[55] Another example is the 1995 Dayton Accords, intended to design a multifaceted, phased peace process in the Balkans.[56] By contrast, islands of agreement are reached precisely with the understanding that a comprehensive solution is unattainable. They are not consciously part of a peace process. The motivation for their conclusion is not that they are a brick in the wall of peace; they may end up as such a brick but are not explicitly designed to be. In comparison, the failed U.S. efforts (known as the Mitchell, Tenet, and Zinni Plans) to stop the renewed violence that erupted between Israel and the Palestinians with the second intifada in the fall of 2000 and to provide for a series of exchanges of mutual, limited commitments were in effect islands of agreement, in that they were not intended as a comprehensive peace plan.[57]

STATUS QUO

Some islands may be status quo agreements, which, although not meant to bring about a formal peace, do stop the use of force or threat of it by the rivals. Such stabilizing arrangements are truce, armistice, and status quo or unlimited cease-fire agreements. If and as long as they are observed long term, such agreements do not altogether dry out the conflict but create for a while a space free of violent interaction.

Islands of agreements, however, are more interesting when they stand amidst an ongoing conflict in which violence is always on the simmer. Also, while status quo agreements limit themselves to the armed aspects of the conflict, islands of agreement may pertain to each and every sphere of the conflict or, indeed, more broadly, to the entire span of the interstate relationship.

LIMITED WAR

Finally, every conflict around the world is limited in some way, or we should be living in Armageddon. It may be that the battleground is confined to certain areas, with very few military exchanges occurring elsewhere. Certain weapons might not be introduced into the fighting. Some installations might not be targeted, etc. This limitation of the conflict to certain boundaries has sometimes been termed "a limited war."[58] Often the war is limited not because the two parties have agreed not to expand it but simply because an independent preference for limiting the war exists on both sides. For instance, both parties may decide not to target structures erected in projects run by the World Bank or other third parties, not as a concession to each other but rather because of their independent preference not to extend their rivalry to include third parties, especially parties that might be beneficial to them in the future. In such cases, the limitation of war, to follow Robert Keohane's distinction, is not the result of "cooperation" but rather of "harmony, i.e. of identical action taken for independent self-interest reasons."[59] To give a different example, when economists argue for unilaterally liberalizing trade by abolishing tariffs and other trade barriers, they often do so because they believe such a policy would be most beneficial to a state's economy whether or not other states immediately follow.[60] Trade liberalization then is the result of harmony of interests, not cooperation. In other cases, limitation of war can simply be the result of mutual deterrence.

My interest lies, instead, in cases of calculated undertakings to further contain the conflict between the parties rather than in cases in which the war is limited because of aligned independent interests or through a balance of threat.

The distinction between instances of a limited war and the presence and effect of islands of agreement is, in many instances, hazy and difficult. This is even more so when dealing with implicit or tacit arrangements than when the understanding is explicit. A signed agreement between the United States and the Soviet Union banning all intermediate-range nuclear missiles is easier to identify as an island of agreement than the undeclared decision by the two countries not to bomb each other with nuclear weapons from airplanes.[61]

Cooperative arrangements, which the parties are required to take active steps to implement, are also easier to classify as islands of agreement than containment arrangements, in which the parties are required only to omit certain actions. Thus, the agreement between the United

States and the Soviet Union to set up a Hotline, by which they could communicate directly with one another (a lesson learnt from the effects of poor communication during the Cuban missile crisis), is easier to define as an island of agreement than a case in which parties refrain from mobilizing forces into certain areas.[62] Similarly, when dealing with tacit agreements, if certain actions were previously taken by the rivals and were then ceased, we would be quicker to recognize the cessation as part of an island of agreement than had such actions never been part of the conflict to begin with.

In summary, the question of whether a limitation of the conflict between two rivals should be classified as an island of agreement or simply as part of the concept of "limited war" is context dependent. Ultimately, we should look for a calculated mutual decision rather than unilateral independent actions, however much the latter may amount to a similar outcome.

Characteristics of Islands of Agreements

Drawing on international relations theories, negotiation models, and international law makes it possible to suggest some preliminary models for the workings of islands of agreement.[63] The challenge here is to articulate general principles that apply to the establishment and sustainment of islands of agreement, as independently as possible from the characteristics of any specific conflict in which they might operate.

DIVISIBILITY

Perhaps the most fundamental principle of islands of agreement is that the management arrangement must be such that it does not prevent the rivals from exercising their continued interest in maintaining the conflict. That is to say, the topography of the system must be formed so as to ensure that the conflict does not perpetually spill over to the island and that the peace on the island does not interfere too much with the conflict elsewhere.

Note that Thomas Schelling argues that

> if we ask, then, where we might draw a line if we wished to limit somehow the size of weapons, the means of conveyance, the situations in which or the targets on which they can be used, the answer is that we are—in a purely technical sense—free to draw a line anywhere we please. There is no cogent reason for drawing it at any one particular gradation rather than another. But that is precisely why it is hard to find a rationale for any particular line.[64]

My argument here is that while we might not find an intrinsic rationale based on fairness or morality, practical considerations do delineate a principle of sectioning—namely, the divisibility of the regulated sphere from the core conflict.

This prerequisite derives from the primary assumption that the conflict is, for the time being, insoluble. As long as the parties' interest in continuing the conflict persists, any attempt to tie their hands and force them to relinquish their basic positions on the core controversies is doomed to fail. Thus we adhere to this principle outlined by Montesquieu in *The Spirit of the Laws:* "the law of nations is naturally founded on the principles that the many nations ought to do to each other, in times of peace the most good, and in times of war the least bad, that is possible without injuring their genuine interests."[65]

It must therefore be assumed that the "divisibility principle" stands to be violated whenever the island of agreement attempts to assert dominion over one of the core controversial spheres, such as the allocation of rights in a disputed territory or the access of worshipers to a contested holy site. Any such attempted regulation is likely to be immediately susceptible to violations as a most penetrating disturbance of the status quo of the conflict. In fact, if such arrangements ever do succeed in generating a new, stable, and peaceful status quo, this may mean that the strong initial assumption regarding the refusal to compromise over the core controversies has been miscalculated in that particular case.

The divisibility principle applies within each regulated sphere as well as between different spheres. History shows us that islands of agreement can touch the very core of the conflict successfully (and thus, perhaps, revert to the traditional "conflict regulation" effort). Actions that seem essential to the parties must remain permitted under the regulatory regime. During the First Anglo-Dutch War of 1652–1654, England, incongruously, remained an important customer of the Dutch arms market. In 1653 England was allowed to buy 150,000 pounds of match in Amsterdam. The reasoning was that, as Dutch arms makers were the finest in the world, the States-General permitted weapons to be exported rather than allow skilled craftsmen to migrate.[66] In general, when an island concerns trade in munitions, there must be enough people on both sides to keep commerce going so that war can go on and to keep war going so that commerce may thrive.

Similarly, during the Dutch Revolt from Spain (1568–1648), Dutch supremacy of the sea forced Spain to send its troops over land: "and the same cause reduced her to such straits for necessaries that, by a mutual arrangement which seems very odd to modern ideas, her wants were supplied by Dutch ships, which thus maintained the enemies of their country, but received in return specie which was welcome in the Amsterdam exchange."[67]

A SYMMETRY OF COSTS AND BENEFITS

Oftentimes what induces countries to violate or defect from cooperative endeavors is the will to spare the necessary costs entailed in complying with them. For example, countries may enter into an agreement on cooperation in environmental protection, with a real and genuine interest in reducing global pollution. And yet they might violate the agreement just the same because the costs of compliance prove too high. Their purpose in violating the agreement, in this case, is not to increase pollution; that may be the end result but not the motivation, which is simply to save the costs of compliance.

In a situation of ongoing conflict, however, we must assume that there is an underlying interest not only in minimizing one's own costs but also in inflicting additional costs on the rival.[68] This is why, in war as in football, parties play offense as well as defense. Incidentally, such an interest is not unique to political conflict setting: in economic competition it exhibits itself in many business strategies, as in the practice of predatory pricing.

The same concern makes parties especially sensitive to the respective costs and benefits entailed by any island of agreement.[69] Imbalance is perceived as substantial on any one side. The disadvantaged rival might fear that the surplus of gains would be translated into material advantage for his adversary. This fear would be further accentuated by both parties' interest in harming their rival.

The concern about relative gains has been extensively addressed by international relations theorists, who have grappled with the question of the degree to which this concern actually obstructs cooperation.[70] Some studies by institutionalist scholars have shown that the concern of relative gains is less likely to have much impact on cooperation when the expected gains from cooperating are considerable for both sides.[71]

As the subsequent case studies show, while the relative gains concern can never be dismissed outright, it does not hinder cooperation altogether. Instead, by and large, it comes to generate a parallel concern about *asymmetry*: meaning that arrangements must be *perceived* as entailing equal costs and benefits for both parties more than they must actually entail them.

Given the multidimensionality of an enduring conflict, it is possible to think about arrangements under which the obligations imposed are neither identical nor even in the same sphere. For instance, the right of use of airspace may be granted in exchange for the removal of certain trade barriers. In such cases, the difficulty would be to translate the costs and benefits accrued in the different spheres into some kind of measurable utility units, so that they could be compared.[72]

PRACTICALITY

Related to the divisibility and balance requirements is the principle entailing that islands of agreement must be designed and applied in a practical fashion; in other words, that the obligations they impose must be ones the parties can reasonably meet.

Islands of agreement should be only as politically ambitious as the relationship between the two rivals permits. By aiming too high, an agreement might run the risk of becoming counterproductive. An over-ambitious agreement entailing impractical obligations stands likely to be constantly violated—and soon thereafter widely ignored. As the basic relationship between the rivals is one of distrust and suspicion, renegotiating more practical terms is a less viable option than it may be in other settings. Thus, the agreement regime is likely to collapse and unlikely to be quickly replaced by another.

Assessing the appropriate level of ambition is a difficult task. The height of ambition may depend on the characteristics of the political leaders of the rivals at a certain point in time, on whether they are more forthcoming and conciliatory or more belligerent and distrusting. It is also likely to depend on the peoples of both rivals—on the degree of animosity and suspicion they feel and express towards each other, as on recent levels of violence they have experienced.

For example, in June 1998 the United States brokered an agreed moratorium on air raids between Ethiopia and Eritrea, entrenched at the time in a bitter border conflict. The agreement stipulated that the moratorium "will continue indefinitely or until such time as either party concludes that any prospect for a peace process has come to an end and provides a formal, advance notice to the United States Government that it will no longer respect this moratorium." While it might have been more ambitious to try for a regime that would outlast the peace talks, it was probably the broker's estimation, in this case, that the moratorium stood a chance only so long as the parties still believed that the peace process was viable.

Finally, present endeavor is of necessity subject to consciousness of past experience. Therefore, when designing a new regulatory regime, we should take into account former attempts, failed or successful, to regulate or agree on certain issues.

When we consider practicality, we must also work in the uncertainty factor, which means that any action taken by the parties has some unforeseeable consequences. Uncertainty derives not only from lack of information but also from mistakes or malfunctions, or what is known as the "trembling hand" effect, which a practical regime must be able to factor in, at least to some degree.

FORMALITY

Islands of agreement can be formal, that is, written, legislated, publicized, monitored, etc., or informal. Although some empirical research done in the 1980s has found that "degrees of formality tend to have relatively little to do with the effectiveness of regimes measured in terms of the probabilities of participants' compliance," this is not necessarily the case in the context of enduring rivalries, where informal or tacit arrangements raise a series of problems.[73]

First, as indicated earlier, when an agreement is tacit, it is almost impossible to determine whether there was indeed a mutual exchange of commitments and undertakings or whether the parties, independently of each other, simply chose to refrain from certain actions or perform others. In the latter case, an observer may infer a mutual agreement where none actually exists, only because the rivals have chosen to behave in a similar manner. Here, the concept of limited war better accounts for the parties.

Second, informal agreements seem to be inherently more ambiguous, therefore exposed to different interpretations. Indeed, that is often their purpose. As the context of enduring rivalries necessarily presumes high levels of mistrust, an informal arrangement might be more susceptible to competing recollections and interpretations of its exact undertakings and commitments. This is doubly true when an agreement aims not only to contain the conflict but also to create cooperative arrangements, requiring active steps from both parties.

Third, the more formal the agreement, the easier it is to monitor compliance with its provisions: leaders, experts, bureaucrats, domestic constituencies, and international actors are naturally better able to monitor compliance when the agreement is set down for scrutiny than when it is informal and open to mutual contestation.[74] This, of course, is true only if the agreement is not only formal but also publicized. Publicity and formality serve to enhance the credibility of the commitments undertaken by ensuring greater supervision over compliance levels, by a larger number of spectators.

To this final point are added the symbolic effects islands may have on the perceptions and attitudes of the rivals' constituents as well as on outside observers.[75] In the context of an ongoing conflict, even an agreement which might appear to be redundant is of importance.[76] For instance, in February 2001, more than a year into the second intifada, the two parties concluded a joint declaration, to which they still adhere, on keeping water infrastructure out of the battle zone.[77] It is highly plausible that even without such a declaration neither party would have targeted the other's water installations, because such action would have outraged public opinion, invited potential retaliations, and so forth. Nevertheless, the conclusion and announcement of the declaration was a ray of light in an otherwise bleak scenario.[78] In this instance, it was the mere formality of the agreement that turned the protection of water installations from a limitation of the war into an island of agreement.

But islands of agreement may be effective even if informal. In fact, there are easily apparent advantages to informal arrangements, which allow agreement to be reached even when there are structural barriers, such as opposing domestic forces or previous commitments by leaders to a different policy. In such cases, the informality of the understanding may give one or both parties the necessary cover needed to save face as well as to avoid sensitive questions of representation.

It is even conceivable for an island of agreement to stem from a tacit exchange that is never made explicit.[79] But such an agreement, like all informal arrangements, would only be feasible if its subject matter were relatively simple and straightforward. That is because the first precondition for compliance is that the parties agree on what had been agreed.

In 1990, for example, the United Nations High Commissioner on Refugees (UNHCR) began using existing distribution centers in Sri Lanka "to provide a relatively safe environment" to internally displaced persons and others seeking relief. These safe havens, called Open Relief Centers, were established when the UNHCR signed a formal understanding with the government of Sri Lanka in 1993, specifying there will be no interference with the centers by military forces without prior consultation with UNHCR. No such agreement was reached with the Liberation Tigers of Tamil Eelam (LTTE), however, except for "an apparent consensus that humanitarian efforts should be respected." But although the neutrality of the shelters was often challenged, no one who sought relief there is known to have died from attack.[80]

That safe havens and other protected areas must be established with the consent of all sides in order to work goes without saying. Equally salient is Sophie Haspeslagh's observation that "the operation has to be clearly defined and understood by all parties."[81]

CLARITY AND AMBIGUITY

For any agreement drafter, there is a constant tension to be surmounted between the will to design clear rules, which would leave as little room as possible for future disagreements, and practical considerations, which necessitate using some ambiguity to gloss over current disagreements.[82] When greater ambiguity is incorporated, the assumption is that consultation and dialogue would later enable the parties to go on and resolve any dispute arising from the implementation of the agreement. The right balance between clarity and ambiguity varies according to the type of agreement concerned. Thus, when aiming for a peace agreement, it may be wiser to allow for greater ambiguity and have faith in subsequent renegotiation. When dealing with a management agreement, in contrast, and bearing in mind that the conflict continues overall, the drafters of the agreement should lean towards greater clarity. Abram Chayes and Antonia Handler Chayes describe how, in the series of arms control agreements between the United States and the Soviet Union during the Cold War, the protagonists moved from concise agreements—the first being the 1963 Limited Test Ban Treaty (LTBT), which consisted of five articles spanning two to three pages altogether—to very elaborate ones in order to reduce interpretive leeway, so that the 1989 Strategic Arms Reduction Treaty (START) grew to be "the size of a telephone book."[83]

Still, we must assume that no agreement can possibly anticipate all the potential disagreements arising over its implementation and that some room for developing a subcodex of rules should be allowed for. This understanding is closely related to the two following characteristics of islands of agreement: the lack of enforcement mechanisms and the requirement of a substitute in the guise of institutions.

ENFORCEMENT MECHANISMS

Most islands of agreement are likely not to include any real enforcement mechanism to ensure compliance. As Chayes and Chayes observe, "compulsory means of authoritative dispute resolution—by adjudication or otherwise—are not generally available at the international level."[84] We should expect this to be particularly true in the context of enduring rivalries—it is hard to imagine that the parties would agree in advance to compensate each other for a breach of the agreement or to subject themselves to material sanctions imposed by a third party. As the parties remain rivals outside the scope of the accord, they would be reluctant to risk the possibility of being "punished" for defecting from the regime created by it. Even more problematic is the prospect of self-subjection to enforcement when the issue is not an outright defection from the regime but rather a different interpretation of its rules.

All this might be somewhat mitigated in a multilateral framework, in which the rivals are only two among many members. Thus, it is feasible that parties would submit themselves to the World Trade Organization's compulsory dispute resolution system, in the knowledge that it does not address itself uniquely to their dispute but might nonetheless address it as well as any other.

In a bilateral setting, a mutual interest in the preservation of the regime on the one hand and deterrence maintained by a balance of power on the other are the factors most likely to ensure compliance with the agreement.[85] On the whole, such mutual interest would depend on a continued favorable assessment of costs and benefits deriving from it. Deterrence can be maintained as long as there is no significant change in the power relations or in the readiness to exercise power on both sides.

Nevertheless, material enforcement mechanisms may sometimes be replaced by "softer" measures, such as reporting, monitoring, or verification, which serve not only to disperse information and monitor compliance, enhancing the parties' reputation concerns, but also to threaten the parties, if necessary, to the sanction of "shaming" for instances of noncompliance.[86] In the Sri Lankan case, Karen Landgren suggests that the Open Relief Centers established by the UNHCR created a space in which the government and to a certain extent the guerillas were "conscious of the impact of international opinion on human rights questions and this may have played a role in concern for civilian casualties."[87]

INSTITUTIONS

I introduce the "institutional" facet in the present context to mean any kind of monitoring, verification, or consultation mechanism that is incorporated into the regime designed by the island of agreement. It is important to stress that I employ the term "institution" here in a different sense from its traditional application in international relations scholarship as a synonym for "regime." When "institution" means "regime," it is defined as consisting of "rules, norms, principles and decision making procedures."[88] No distinction is therefore made between an explicit or implicit agreement forming a regime and any mechanism set up to oversee or implement it. Both are viewed as components in the sum total of the regime. In the present context I wish to make this distinction and use "institutions" to refer only to the regime's second component, namely, a monitoring, consultation, or implementation mechanism. My reason for making this distinction is that the role of institutions in the manner I refer to them, is independent from the role of the agreements associated with them. In fact, similar agreements supplemented by different institutions would in all probability yield different regimes. The effectiveness and endurance of a regime, I argue, depend in part on the institution it establishes to oversee an agreement.

An institution is first and foremost a substitute for enforcement mechanisms. When a monitoring or verification mechanism is in place, the parties may find greater confidence that the balance of costs and benefits under the agreement is being preserved. Such a mechanism serves to keep both sides informed about compliance and noncompliance as about any possible exploitation by either side of the arrangement in a way unacceptable to its rival.[89] Since asymmetry in information is considered one of the greatest impediments to cooperation, an effective monitoring or verification mechanism is of crucial importance.[90] In fact, institutionalist international relations scholars have noted that if an agreement can operate without any monitoring, detection, or enforcement mechanism, this means that the parties are in harmony, in which case an institutionalized cooperation regime is unnecessary for the fulfillment of mutual interests.[91]

Where the institution includes a joint consultation mechanism, it makes available to the parties a forum in which they can discuss implementation, account for incidents of noncompliance, and develop a subcodex of rules to supplement the island of agreement. Such were the Standing Consultative Commission created by the United States and the Soviet Union under the Strategic Arms Limitation Treaty (SALT I) and the Special Verification Commission created under the Intermediate Nuclear Force Treaty (INF), both intended to serve as the official dispute-resolution fora and to facilitate the adaptation of the treaty to changing circumstances.[92]

By establishing channels of communication and generating a continuous dialogue, working relationships between diplomats, military personnel, bureaucrats, experts, and even private actors emerge, creating a language and culture of cooperation. As Robert Keohane and Joseph Nye have noted, "when the same officials meet recurrently, they sometimes develop a sense of collegiality, which may be reinforced by their membership in a common profession . . . Transgovernmental elite networks are created, linking officials in various governments to one another by ties of common interest, professional orientation, and personal friendship."[93]

Moreover, institutions established to oversee or monitor one agreement may be used to facilitate negotiation of others within the same sphere. Thus, institutions created by SALT I contributed to the negotiation of the SALT II and later the START treaties. Similarly, the Committee on Security and Cooperation in Europe (CSCE) established a process that expanded disarmament regimes beyond the 1975 Helsinki Final Act, to include the 1986 Stockholm Agreement on Disarmament in Europe, the 1990 Paris Accords, and the 1990 and 1992 Vienna CSCE documents on East-West CBMs in Europe.[94]

When successful, the developed culture of cooperation may diffuse across other spheres of the rivalry, encouraging further efforts at dialogue and collaboration. To borrow the terms of the constructivist school of international relations, the language and norms of cooperation may become part of the prevailing discourse in society, reshape public preferences and attitudes, and ultimately affect the parties' self-perception as well as their view of each other and of the conflict as a whole.[95]

REPRESENTATION AND ACCOUNTABILITY

In a classic interstate conflict, problems of representation seldom arise, as it is usually clear who represents whom. The problem begins with the involvement in the conflict of nonstate actors and third parties.

Enduring rivalries often contain some component of nonstate actors' involvement, even when the primary rivalry is among governments. But agreements between governments tend to leave nonstate actors out in the cold and unrepresented. In part, this may be the result of a state's refusal to confer recognition or legitimacy on an enemy nonstate actor. It may also be in the interest of the government related to such nonstate actor to present itself as the ultimate and sole empowered organ of representation, and keep the nonstate actor out of formal negotiations.

Whatever the motivation for not dealing directly with nonstate actors may be, it is crucial that the government that undertakes to limit such actors' activities be willing and able to do so in conformity with its undertakings. Where no such accountability can be exacted, the commitments undertaken by the leadership are bound to be violated, impairing the leadership's credibility as a reliable partner for future dealings. In the most extreme cases, it may be unclear who controls whom—the government controlling the nonstate actor or vice versa.

An example of such a case was the relationship between the Afghan Taliban regime and the Al-Qaida terrorist network. After the 1998 Al-Qaida attacks on the United States embassies in Nairobi and Dar-A-Salaam, the United States government was reported to have negotiated with the Afghan Taliban government the capture and extradition of Al-Qaida leader Osama Bin Laden.[96] The negotiations proved to be futile, as the Taliban government was unable and/or unwilling to account for Bin Laden's—or Al-Qaida's—actions. After the September 2001 attacks on the United States, the recognition that the Taliban could not and would not account for Bin Laden's terrorist activities brought the United States to refuse to negotiate with the Taliban any further and, instead, to topple the regime.

Problems of representation and accountability are bound to intensify when islands of agreement are established in the context of an ethnic conflict or a nontraditional international conflict (such as "the war on terror") in which one or both parties are nongovernmental factions. In such instances, it may not be altogether clear who represents the faction, what the scope of the representative's popular support is, or to what degree the representative is able to control or account for actions of members of the faction. Former Senate majority leader George Mitchell faced this problem in his efforts to negotiate a decommissioning arrangement between the warring factions in Northern Ireland in 1995: one of the tallest obstacles arose as the leadership of the Sinn Fein nationalist party denied any linkage to the Irish Republican Army, thereby refuting its accountability for the decommissioning of the IRA.[97] Although the IRA has later announced it was decommissioning its weapons, it never publicly clarified what degree of authority Sinn Fein had to negotiate on its behalf.

A similar difficulty arises where the actions of a state party to a conflict are heavily prescribed by the interests of allied states not directly part of the rival dyad. Any management regime must be designed so as to take these lateral interests into account and ensure that they do not act as a barrier to the subsequent implementation of the agreement. With regard to the United States attempts to negotiate with the Taliban in 1998, observers noted that any such negotiations would have to include Pakistan, Afghanistan's neighbor and one of only three countries to have recognized the Taliban regime.[98]

INTERGOVERNMENTAL, SUBGOVERNMENTAL, AND NONGOVERNMENTAL COOPERATION

Islands of agreement can emerge within the framework of intergovernmental organizations—such as the UN, the Organization for Security Cooperation in Europe, the African Union, the Organization of American States—that are oftentimes useful in harnessing to a cooperative effort additional parties beyond the rivals themselves. One example is the cooperation struck among the various members of the Association of Southeast Asia Nations (ASEAN), first established in 1967, in the various fields of trade, investment, regional security, agriculture, environment, labor, culture, science and technology, transnational crime, and more, despite many ongoing conflicts between its members.[99] Another is Mercosur, the "Southern Common Market," which was founded in 1991 as a trading zone between Brazil, Argentina, Uruguay, and Paraguay, and which has been instrumental in promoting the rapprochement between Brazil and Argentina in the early 1990s. Mercosur set the stage to enhanced economic ties, greater infrastructural integration, and expanded cross-border ties.[100]

Subgovernmental cooperation takes place among bureaucrats and local government officials working under "technical" or "professional"— rather than political—colors. This allows the governments to enjoy the gains from cooperation without losing political capital, domestically or internationally, as the rivalry continues. Anne-Marie Slaughter has demonstrated how the intensifying ties between substate-level officials in recent years have created forms of de facto global governance, led by ministers, parliamentarians, judges, bureaucrats, and even NGOs.[101] Islands of agreement can play a similar role, albeit much more constrained, even within an enduring rivalry.

NGOs can play a double role in affecting policy: they can establish cooperation themselves, as when trade chapters decide to enhance industrial relations or universities promote joint educational programs. At the same time, peace networks, humanitarian organizations, or environmental advocacy groups can press key decision makers to reach formal agreements and understandings with their counterparts in the rival country; in such settings, NGOs become "'enablers' of increased state cooperation."[102]

Media organizations have a special role to play in the creation of regional islands of agreement, by virtue of their broad power bases and immediate access to audiences across borders as well as to raw, unprocessed information. In the nexus of conflicts in the Caucasus, for example, the Yerevan Press Club, a nonprofit nongovernmental association of journalists established in 1995 for the support and development of independent and professional media in Armenia, has sponsored several regional projects: The MediaDialogue Web site, for instance, was established to "create a virtual hub of information relevant to the region, provide first-hand information, and facilitate the dialogue between the media and the public of the countries of the region." The Web site features newspaper pieces from Armenia, Azerbaijan, Georgia, and Turkey on issues of mutual concern, including the 1915 Armenian genocide—a particularly sensitive subject in Turkey—and the current conflict in Nagorno-Karabakh.[103]

Another media-sponsored island in the same region emerged through the collaboration between three radio stations in Armenia, Azerbaijan, and Georgia—the South Caucasus Radio Bridge—dedicated to facilitating regional cooperation and integration through a regular exchange of news and information across the borders. Sponsored by the Eurasia Foundation South Caucasus Cooperation Program (SCCP) grant for a partnership of radio stations from each country, the Radio Bridge offered listeners a forum for discussing regional common problems, such as corruption, compulsory military service, poor medical care, and the like. The program, airing in the Russian language in Tbilisi, Baku, and, Yerevan, also featured hard-hitting interviews with public figures, followed by a question-and-answer session with the audience.[104] Under the terms of the grant, first awarded in 2001, the partner stations were to arrange for exchanges of journalists and host a conference for the program's guests to discuss possibilities for new regional initiatives.

In general, nongovernmental initiatives for islands of agreement enjoy greater freedom than governmental or government-related initiatives. Thus, while islands between officials cannot emerge without the explicit support of the respective governments, privately sponsored schemes can exist so long as there is no explicit opposition by the government. The ability of nongovernmental or private parties to succeed in such schemes would vary from state to state and would hinge on the political system of government, the scope of individual freedoms and liberties, and the overall strength of civil society. In some cases there may be legal or practical barriers—such as a law prohibiting any trade with the enemy or visa requirements for any visitation of enemy nationals—the removal of which would necessitate some governmental involvement.

Needless to say, the role of domestic constituencies in facilitating, blocking, or otherwise influencing the formation of islands of agreement depends on their ability to influence the political process in general. In Syria, Iraq (under Saddam Hussein), or Iran domestic constituencies enjoy only limited political power to influence choices made by their leaders. In such instances, there is almost no two-level diplomacy in play. Rather, the decision on whether to enter into dialogue with the rival rests with the leader alone.

THE ROLE OF THIRD PARTIES

One of the most important aspects of islands of agreement is that they are created by the rivals themselves. Third parties may propose them, help to keep them balanced, or altogether urge, tempt, browbeat, and cajole the parties into sticking to them. Ultimately, however, it is at the will of the rivals that islands are formed—and dismantled. In this they differ radically from coercive external intervention efforts by others, whether through military power or through legal adjudication. This difference is ultimately material to the characteristics of islands of agreement and to what benefits or potential risks they may entail.

The most obvious role for third parties to play is that of intermediaries, a channel of communication opened up where none other exists, when the mere dialogue with the enemy implies some recognition of it and may confer (or at least may be perceived as conferring) a degree of legitimacy on its "rivalrous being."[105] Mediation is also important for alleviating fears and suspicion on both sides, as each party's fears and concerns are channeled through the mediator and "translated" by him or her into a more palatable address. The mediator may count, as the adversary cannot, on being received with a more attentive ear, even when what he or she has to voice is less than welcome.

Acting as middle man the mediator often assumes an all-important face-saving capacity, helping concessions to appear as if they have been made towards himself or at least under his pressure. At his or her best, a mediator acts as a "third eye," a seemingly impartial or more-objective referee, on whom the parties may rely for an external assurance that the regime designed under the agreement is indeed a balanced one in terms of the costs and benefits it entails.[106] While the rivals may not be eager to substitute their own assessment for that of a third party, the latter's judgment may compensate for their deficiency of information on what is happening on the other side. When they have earned the privileged position of well-informed confidantes, mediators can go further and identify possible areas of containment or cooperation.

Third parties answer both psychological and political needs. They may act effectively to remove barriers erected by the more skeptical or reluctant domestic constituencies on either side.[107] It is sometimes enough for a third party simply to get involved to reassure hardliners that a regime is "safe" to enter into. In other cases, a third party may act to mobilize domestic support for concessions required by the leadership, force a political leadership to disregard objecting constituencies, or give a more-willing leadership sufficient political cover for its more-reluctant public.[108]

Third parties may also offer the parties vital material incentives to enter into an agreement. If either of the parties perceives itself to be at a disadvantage in terms of costs and benefits, a third party may be able to rectify the imbalance through a side payment—some form of compensation by which to even out the difference and mollify domestic opposition.[109] Another contribution may be an investment in a joint project, without which such a project would be unfeasible. Contributions of this kind are frequently made by the World Bank in joint mine-clearing and water projects between rival states.[110]

Finally, an ongoing involvement of third parties in the regime created under the island of agreement works to stabilize it, by making any defection from it no longer a strictly bilateral matter between the rivals themselves but also a defiance of the relationship with the third party. Reputation concerns, mentioned earlier in the context of peace settlements between enduring rivals, are thus enhanced, as the outsider on the scene makes known an ongoing expectation of compliance from both rivals.[111]

THE ROLE OF INTERNATIONAL LAW

In many if not most instances, the regime designed by the island of agreement concerns a sphere that is already addressed by existing international law, whether conventional or customary. Possible spheres include the conduct of warfare, the legality of the use of certain weapons, the sharing of transboundary watercourses, environmental protection, the delimitation of land and sea boundaries, the exploitation of joint reservoirs of natural resources, the protection of ethnic minorities, and limitations on international commerce such as trade barriers.

At the same time, however widely recognized and accepted these rules are seldom useful in resolving disputes.[112] First, one or both rivals may still contest the validity of a certain international legal norm, either because they were not parties to the convention under which it was established or because they challenge its status as binding customary law. Second, even when the validity of the norm is acknowledged, its interpretation or application in certain circumstances may be open to competing claims. Moreover, in numerous instances it would be possible to cite different international norms of equal validity and strength in support of opposing positions. Finally, countries may agree to a certain rule in principle but explicitly object to its applicability to rivalries in which they are involved. For this reason, countries often add explicit reservations, understandings, or declarations to multilateral treaties or other agreements in which the rule is prescribed. Thus, Syria, Libya, and Yemen often add reservations to treaties, stating that ratification shall in no way signify recognition of the state of Israel. The United Arab Emirates added a reservation to its accession to the 1977 Additional Protocol to the Geneva Conventions, not only denying recognition of Israel but also stating that the provisions of the Additional Protocol are inapplicable in respect of Israel."[113] In the same vein, the United Kingdom has stated that it would not apply the provisions of several conventions in its relations with Southern Rhodesia "until the Government of the United Kingdom inform the depositary that they are in a position to ensure that the obligations imposed by the Protocol in respect of that territory can be fully implemented."[114]

Even when the validity and theoretical applicability of an international norm go unchallenged by either of the rivals, that norm's usefulness as a trump card in the dispute is highly restricted. There are few international adjudication bodies to which one rival could subject the other against its will, such as the European Court of Justice or the World Trade Organization Dispute Settlement Body. The few that do exist have jurisdiction over a limited set of issues or countries. Disputes that do not fall within the purview of these adjudicatory bodies remain largely irresolvable absent consent by both rivals to submit them to third-party arbitration or adjudication. Thus, the International Court of Justice, which has subject-matter jurisdiction over most international disputes, can only adjudicate matters brought before it with the consent of both disputants.[115] Absent the ability to enforce the legal rule on a defiant party, the mere existence of the rule does not in itself suffice to promote the interests of the party wishing to rely on it. It may add rhetorical force to the claims of the rival wishing to forward it as a basis for staking a claim or else help to shore up domestic and international support in favor of a certain position.[116] However, while these are not insignificant contributions, rarely do they succeed in forcing the contesting rival to concede. From this perspective, Robert Mnookin and Lewis Kornhauser's paradigm of negotiations taking place "in the shadow of the law," whereby out-of-court settlements tend to mirror in-court judicial decisions, is of questionable applicability in the international arena.[117]

Notwithstanding this analysis, international law fills a potentially powerful presence in the formation and sustainment of islands of agreement. It creates a basis for mutual dealings, in feeding divergent positions with a common formal language to borrow from and build on.

International law does not suffer from tautology; in a sense, it can never be repeated enough. Parties desiring to tailor an agreement to their needs can pick and choose from several available accepted rules or norms, and by reaffirming to each other what has been generally affirmed by the international community—themselves included—reinforce their pledge to their, however limited, bilateral relationship. By explicitly agreeing to undertake certain commitments vis-à-vis a particular rival in the here and now, the rivals commit themselves more weightily than when their commitments are assumed abstractly in a multiparty setting without explicit reference to any rivalry or scenario. Reaffirmed, these commitments become, in effect, a declaration addressed to the rival, to domestic constituencies, and to the international community of the signatory's willingness to allow its commitments to govern the rivalrous relationship. A repetition between rivals of the widely recognized international legal obligation to respect diplomatic and consular immunities carries more weight than the two respective acceptances of the multilateral Vienna conventions on diplomatic and consular relations.[118]

Islands of agreement may also depart from the general international rules that regulate a certain sphere, fashioning instead an ad hoc legal arrangement for a given circumstance. This arrangement may be intended to solve an outstanding dispute or merely to redesign and improve a regime already in place. Whatever its purpose, the new arrangement may refer to existing international rules as a benchmark but need not be bound by them. It may be more restrictive or less, choose one interpretation of the rule and disregard another, prefer one valid rule over another, design verification or monitoring mechanisms that do not exist under the applicable international norms, or even design a cooperative regime in a sphere not at all regulated by existing international instruments.

In time, islands of agreement may themselves become a source of general international law.[119] Often, they pour content into vague or general treaty provisions in the form of a specific arrangement, which could at a future instance be relied upon as an example of how a certain provision is to be interpreted or applied. More broadly, islands of agreement may be used as evidence of state practice, which could, in turn, form part of customary law making.[120] During the Spanish-American War, for example, two Spanish fishermen operating in and out of Havana challenged the capture of their fishing vessels—the *Paquete Habana* and the *Lola*—by the United States Navy. In accepting their appeal, the United States Supreme Court ruled that the accumulation of state practice regarding the protection of fishermen at times of war, including a series of bilateral agreements to this effect between warring parties, had culminated in a customary international norm.[121]

Potential Perils

So far I have tried to show that management is a worthy effort in its own right in many situations of conflict. I have suggested islands of agreement as an operating model through which we might implement management, in its wider sense. The exercise, however, is not risk free. The fundamental choice to reinforce relationships by limiting the conflict, as well as some out-of-conflict spheres, alters the relationship, for good or ill.

Whereas the potential benefits arising out of islands of agreement are relatively easy to predict, the risks of applying this method are not all visible at first sight. Yet recognizing and weighing these risks intelligently against the benefits is critical for sizing up the method's potential and advisability at a given moment. Risks must be taken into account both in the decision to resort to this method of conflict management as a whole, and in the specific design of the individual limited agreements.

By their very nature, islands of agreement are used when the judgment is that no comprehensive resolution is attainable in the near future. Yet the decision to employ them in the relationship may not only be a derivative of this judgment but also a universal affirmation of it. When one is announcing a "limitation which enables conflict to continue," one is as good as announcing to the world and—what is worse—to one's self that the rivalry is indeed unending. Whatever else it does, as a concept with a name an island of agreement serves, first, to anchor the rivals' belief in the intractability of their conflict and reinforces their notion that what it would take to transform their relationship is fundamentally unattainable. If we choose to use this method we must therefore be aware of the danger that it might be driving away any potential challenge to the notion of the present situation extending ad infinitum. We must therefore be alert and try to keep the system itself as mobile and as open to further additions as possible.

A second risk of islands of agreement is that they are bound to be perceived as a litmus test of trustworthiness.[122] For the two rivals who conclude a limited agreement, the success or failure of this experiment in little serves as a crucial indicator to the potential success or failure of broader peace efforts. At the same time, since the underlying relationship is one of deep suspicion and hostility, we can expect instances of violations of the agreement to draw more attention than instances of compliance, to be more often than not regarded as intentionally malevolent, and to carry greater weight of perceived significance than if they occurred in a different setting.

The heightened importance attached to violations of islands of agreement becomes in itself an escalator of tensions, since naturally violations are more likely to occur in the setting of enduring conflict than in a more stable equilibrium between the parties. As earlier noted, the setting of enduring rivalries dictates that islands of agreement be designed in an especially careful manner: when this design is imperfect, and even when it is flawless, some violations should always be expected, as with any international arrangement. When they do occur, they then increase the gulf of mutual wariness which the agreement was designed to lessen.[123]

In its containment form, a third risk that accompanies this tool of conflict management lies in what I term "the pressed balloon effect." When an inflated balloon is squeezed at one point, the air locked inside does not disappear. Rather, it expands the remaining area of the balloon outwards. Containment often works in the same way; once the rivals are prevented from carrying out certain belligerent operations under the management regime, those actions that remain permitted may actually be exacerbated.

In addition, any agreement short of a comprehensive peace treaty addressing all issues in dispute is bound to be unstable to some degree, with underlying tensions always simmering below. The instability of the agreement is not risk free. As enduring rivalries are by nature prone to violence, and as any, even minor violent interaction increases the risk of future escalation, the collapse of even a limited agreement may put the match to an already flammable situation.

Finally, even when islands are perfectly designed and implemented, and even in the most optimistic scenario in which they accumulate in an evolutionary process, their operation may pose some risk to a final settlement of the dispute. While the concerns previously mentioned may be equally applicable to other management models, this specific risk is a direct derivative of the concept of islands of agreement:

The negotiation literature emphasizes the importance of value creation in bargaining. Value creation is essentially an increase of the possible surplus generated from the exchange of commitments by the two negotiating parties. The way to create more value is to add exchanges to the agreement, with each exchange generating a certain positive surplus. This method has been termed by the literature on bargaining the "integrative approach."[124] Exchanges do not have to be symmetrical—goods, services, or commitments can be reciprocated in and across different spheres, depending on the interests of the parties. The more items added to the negotiation table, the more opportunities for value creation open up. The distribution of the generated surplus from one exchange can be matched by the distribution from another. Thus, in an international contest, if one party calculates that it had gained less from the allocation of water rights than its counterpart, it may be compensated by the opening up of certain trade relations. Or, if trade relations are not an issue on the negotiation table, the counterpart may offer a unilateral commitment to clear mines from a border area.

When the method of islands of agreement is employed, the rivals carve out pieces of their relations and regulate them, distributing the surplus arising from the regulation. The agreement on the core contested issues is deferred to a later, then to a still later, stage. But when several islands of agreement are in place, already covering most of the treatable spheres of the bilateral relations, opportunities for value creation at the final negotiation stages of the dispute dry up. The rivals are hence faced with having to distribute their rights in the core contested issues, with much more limited ability to compensate for losses with surplus from other exchanges. The multidimensionality of the dispute is thus reduced back to a single-issue (or few-issues) contest. The division of a contested territory can no longer be compensated for by a positive surplus from the removal of trade barriers, since those have already been removed under a previous trade agreement; for example, water sharing is no longer an incentive to comprehensive peace, as it has already been allocated. In fact, many of the material incentives arising from a comprehensive peace agreement may already have been distributed under preceding islands of agreement.

Moreover, when islands accumulate, and even when they accumulate effectively yet without developing further into broader agreement, a status quo may be created in which the situation becomes tolerable to both sides. Despite the ongoing suffering of some civilians or soldiers, who continue to carry the burden of conflict, the two rivals might well be lulled into thinking their situation falls within the bounds of "acceptable existence." Under such conditions it would be extremely difficult to reawaken in either or both a sense of urgency.

All these concerns converge into one greater normative question: By employing islands of agreement, are we not merely creating a more bearable status quo that allows the parties to maintain the conflict? In other words, are we not deferring a final settlement? And would it not be better just to let the rivals "fight it out"?

I will return to this question, after testing the model in three case-studies, in the concluding chapter.

Testing Theory in Practice

The concept of islands of agreement is not a novelty in practice. As I have shown, it has been employed in conflicts around the world for centuries.

In the following chapters I wish to test this concept within the scope of three case studies, which involve islands of agreement within decades-old enduring conflicts: India-Pakistan, Greece-Turkey-Cyprus, and Israel-Lebanon/Syria. These cases show how islands of agreement work within three scenarios on the scale of optimism: one being a "classic," limited but still-varied collection of islands, which hold their ground despite the continuation of hostilities outside them; the second, a near-optimal picture, where the islands have gradually congealed into more peaceful relations all round; and the third, an example of a minimal arrangement within ongoing belligerence, an island that has remained isolated throughout its existence, to be overrun, repeatedly, by conflict.

The three cases greatly vary in terms of their conflicts' histories, intensity, and prospects for peaceful resolution. They also differ across the range of parameters dictating what may be termed the "culture" of their conflicts: geographical setting; the number and political nature of rivals; the rivals' power relations; religion, ethnicity and culture; systems of government and representation; relative economic strength; and so forth.

India and Pakistan are engaged in an interstate rivalry, which has erupted into four major wars in the past six decades, leaving hundreds of thousands dead, injured, and homeless; its ceaseless skirmishes, mainly in Kashmir, continue to inflict numerous casualties and destruction. The conflict also contains some component of nonstate actors in the form of insurgent groups operating in and from Kashmir. The two South Asian countries' overt nuclear arms race puts a quarter of the world's population under immediate threat. Yet for decades, since the creation of both as independent states, the relations between them have been knotted, defined, and to some extent normalized by numerous islands of agreement.

Greece and Turkey are entrenched in an even longer national conflict-turned-rivalry, which has, over time, projected itself onto the island of Cyprus. The island now lies at the heart of the dispute, alongside the competition over control of the Aegean Sea, adding an intrastate dimension to the interstate rivalry. Since the mid 1970s the conflict has been "mild," claiming almost no casualties, although up until the last decade, tensions still ran high. Today, Greek-Turkish relations exemplify a best-case scenario of what may happen when islands of agreement coagulate into broader accord. But I have chosen it not only as a near-optimal case but also as an international contest vis-à-vis the West, which, in its stubborn continuation over many decades as well as in its present "second life" as competition over the right to belong to Europe, seems to pose a fascinating challenge to Western notions of conflict and resolution, of what it means to be Western and civilized.

Shifting to the Middle East, Israel's conflict with Lebanon is not a purely bilateral feud; actual fighting goes on between Israel and nonstate Lebanese armed groups, but it is fueled by all-important veiled state actors in the figure of Syria and Iran. The conflict, which began in the 1970s, has throughout its history and various incarnations inflicted thousands of casualties, caused untold destruction, and put the inhabitants in the adjacent border areas in constant peril. The 1996 Understanding and its nearly four years' existence affords us a unique opportunity to probe in depth the experience of one stand-alone island of agreement within ongoing belligerence, to study its various components, and to gauge its effect on the rivalry. While the two former cases show islands of agreement evolving across a broad historical spectrum, the latter, which existed within a limited time frame with a sole aim of containment and was extensively monitored and documented, gives us a fascinating glimpse of the fine details and inner workings of this conflict management mechanism.

The only feature common to all three case studies is their rivalries' long endurance despite numerous attempts at resolution. Historically, all meet both the more "technical" criteria for enduring rivalries, as suggested by the literature, as well as the more intuitive ones. All present an excellent, although by no means complete, setting in which to examine how the model suggested here can be fleshed out. And in all three, islands of agreement have been employed at one point in time in some form or another, although their character—the manner of their employment, the types of regimes created, their numbers, duration, spread over time, and concerted effect on the rivalry—all differ considerably.

Testing the analytical framework offered here raises a number of methodological challenges. First, although my materials are historical, I am not a historian by training. The purpose of this study is not to give a full account of each feud but to focus attention on its multidimensionality and the sometimes counterintuitive coexistence of war and peace.

Second has been the problem of sources: the study relies on historical reviews, documents, observers' reports, studies by analysts, and media accounts. It is by no means a complete data set; far from it. For the most part, I relied on information available to the public and in English. In the Israel-Lebanon case, I relied also on my own private notes concerning the Israel-Lebanon Monitoring Group. This necessarily excluded some invaluable sources, the absence of which may have affected my judgment regarding the whole spectrum of views and feelings on either side of each conflict—from the deep sources of rivalry to the challenges of cooperation.

The next challenge was in evaluating history: in coming to judge the characteristics of islands of agreement as promoting the "success" or "failure" of the regime they design—how was "success" or "failure" to be measured? In part, I used compliance levels as indications for success, though keeping in mind that compliance with a regime does not necessarily ensure an effective promotion of its goals.[125] Where it was possible to measure tangible benefits, such as lower levels of violence or generation of surplus from trade, I turned to these benefits as indicators. Where positive effects were more intangible, such as improvement in communications or relations or the possible sparing of human lives, I compared the period of the regime with the situation before and after; prevention, in general, is a difficult thing to measure. To assess successful prevention, one can only build on past experience and hope to show some causation that moves beyond chance. In other cases, I referred to evidence of improved channels of communication, ongoing meetings between officials, relationships developing between nonstate actors, or positive comments by stakeholders as yardsticks for success. The sustainability of a created regime was another marker.

Assessment became even harder when "success" or "failure" were looked for not in the immediate sense but with a longer-term view to the influence on the overall rivalry. Any claim to be made for islands of agreement as potentially promoting or inhibiting resolution is by definition valid only ex post facto, that is, either once the island has ceased to be or once the relationship has passed on to a different stage.

The final methodological problem, which cuts across the attempt to draw conclusions from the data offered here, is perhaps the hardest to resolve: the "success" or "failure" of any regime must be weighed against alternatives. Weighing alternatives necessitates a counterfactual examination, which is always imaginary and inevitably speculative. This hurdle presents itself with full force when we attempt to evaluate the overall effect that islands of agreement might have had on the relationship between the rivals: have the islands promoted rapprochement, or have they delayed a material change in the relationship? Here too, while some "independent" criteria may be available, any answer must ultimately remain a possible suggestion, though as probable as possible. It must be left open to challenges based on other counterfactual exercises.

While counterfactual exercises are impossible to prove or disprove altogether, they are essential to this project. I have tried to make them as explicit and as defensible as I could.[126]

Last but not least is the question of objectivity. No human narrative can hope to be neutral in the telling. Even such a seemingly simple decision as where to begin telling the story makes, as I have discovered, for some bias. I have tried to do justice to each side of each dispute, but complete justice cannot be hoped for. Naturally, I had to be especially careful in the Israel-Lebanon case, as I am an Israeli and a former participant in the Israeli-Lebanon Monitoring Group. If I have nonetheless misrepresented any detail of political action or motivation, I hope I may be forgiven.

CHAPTER TWO

India and Pakistan:
Islands of the Subcontinent

The affair . . . ended with the spectacle of two nations
in violent opposition, not for the first time nor as yet
for the last because they were then still locked in an imperial embrace of such long standing and subtlety it
was no longer possible for them to know whether they
hated or loved one another, or what it was that held
them together and seemed to have confused the image
of their separate destinies.

PAUL SCOTT, *THE JEWEL IN THE CROWN*

To begin with, India and Pakistan were never really given the luxury of
noncooperation. For some years after the imperial embrace was finally
over, they were still locked painfully together, their separate destinies,
whether self-sought or thrust upon them, still very much confused. So
intermingled were their populations, so traumatic and artificial was
their partition, that almost every step towards nation building now required some sort of organized cooperation: to enable the movement of
people across borders, to transfer their bank accounts with them as they
went, to protect places of worship whose worshippers had been forcibly
evicted, never to return, or to share what precious water could be found
between long-settled and newly formed communities.

The conflict between India and Pakistan, easily the largest in scale
among the three treated here, in terms of the very size of the populations involved, has destroyed, blighted, shifted, and shaped many
millions of lives and continues to do so today. Its history has been fre-
netically written and rewritten on both sides of the border, not to mention elsewhere, and will be rewritten many times over for as long as it
goes on; indeed, histories offered by both sides seem not only parts of
the conflict but also of its extensive body of agreement and management
documents. India and Pakistan have fought each other in four large-

scale wars, the first soon after gaining their independence from British rule in 1947 and undergoing the trauma of partition; the second in 1965; the third—which led to the creation of Bangladesh—in 1971; and the fourth in 1999. All told, these wars have claimed the lives of tens of thousands of combatants, as well as numberless civilians. And all but one (1971) were fought, at least ostensibly, over control of the territory of Kashmir. The sixty-year old territorial dispute feeds an ongoing low-intensity conflict in which lives on both sides of the border are still lost as a matter of course. Over the years and outside the wars the conflict has already spiraled into several crises of varying magnitude and, given the nuclear capabilities of both countries, keeps the threat of doomsday looming large over the subcontinent's 1.25 billion people.

Surprisingly, however, this potentially deadliest of all global conflicts has also bred more or less successful regulation in nearly all aspects of the rivals' relationship. Indeed, among enduring rivalries it stands perhaps as a sole example in which potential islands of agreement being so fully and so broadly realized alongside an active armed conflict of many decades. It may be inconceivable to us that Indians and Pakistanis should compete against each other in a full-fledged cricket series while their compatriots are killing each other along the Line of Control (LoC) in Kashmir. Yet it is nonetheless true and communicates much that, to an outsider, may seem strange or even incomprehensible: the sheer scale of the conflict, which is large enough to involve many and exclude many, the uncertain alignment between governments and their citizens, the possibility of cooperation even within the bloodiest feud, and perhaps most counter-intuitively—a bilateral relationship that cannot be reduced to conflict alone.

I will therefore tell the story twice: first, as a tale of an enduring rivalry; then, as a record of a positive bilateral interaction that approximates normal interstate relations.

"Vivisect India," was Gandhi's sardonic cry over the two-nation theory that was to divide his country. To him, the idea of partition was unthinkable, a disastrous perpetuation of all the subcontinent's ills. For his opponent, Mohammad Ali Jinnah, however, as for the Pakistan he bequeathed, this theory was the only foundation possible for a new national existence for Muslims. This conceptual antagonism has, over time, come to a head over the issue of Kashmir: "If Kashmir goes, the ideology of Pakistan goes. The liquidation of Pakistan as a state may then only be a matter of time."[1] Such repeated proclamations by Pakistani statesmen and historians leave no doubt as to the nature of the core conflict between the two countries. The fight over Kashmir runs deeper than territory; it is a symptom, and a symbol, of the Pakistani struggle for recognition of the two-nation theory—the very basis for the creation of Pakistan—as right and valid. This goes to the heart of Pakistani feelings of national insecurity vis-à-vis the Indian giant, five times in size at the time of the partition, who has never, in Pakistani eyes, truly accepted Pakistan's right to self-determination. In the words of former Pakistani Prime Minister Zulfikar Ali Bhutto,

> one of the dominant urges for Pakistan has been to dispel the notion of seniority or superiority of Hindu India over Muslim India by creating a Muslim State equal and sovereign to the other State.[2]

For some if not most Indian politicians and historians, especially those who went through the catastrophic events which accompanied partition, "the homeland for the Indian Muslims was a Utopia; a territorial division was bound to leave many millions of them out, in a very delicate position of being regarded as aliens, suspected of disloyalty to the land they must live in."[3] Indeed, there are more Muslims in today's India than there are in Pakistan.

But the sense of rivalry and competition is by no means only a religious or ethnic-based issue. In the words of Indian political scientist, Manorama Kohli:

> a feeling of insecurity which is almost germane to Pakistan can also be explained in Geographical realities which Pakistan inherited . . . Pakistan suffered from an inhibition the source of which was not only her limited size and resources but added to which was the constraint of building up of a new sense of identity and tradition distinct from that of India. On top of all this Pakistan's rulers had a physical handicap of governing the two wings of Pakistan divided by more than a thousand miles of Indian territory.[4]

But despite appearances, India too is not immune to feelings of insecurity. For it to even consider the legitimacy of Kashmir's accession might mean the beginning of the end—a questioning of the entire federation of former princely states. For if Kashmir can secede from the federation, why not Punjab or Assam?

The international focus on the issue of Kashmir thus often serves to mask the true multidimensionality of the Indo-Pak collision: the deep-running ethnic and religious divide, the competition over resources, over regional hegemony, over powerful alliances, and subjectively or not, over survival.

The Origins of Conflict

Partition, Independence, and War

British rule over the subcontinent ended when Pakistan was granted independence on August 14, 1947, followed by India's independence the next day. Some have argued that the most momentous failure in British imperial history was the partition of India into two nations: one a Muslim Pakistan; the other a secular, predominantly Hindu India. According to some historians, partition was an inevitable consequence of a long-standing British policy of divide and rule, by which "the people of India had been divided into two in a very competitive psyche."[5] In every way, partition was a human cataclysm: between five hundred thousand and one million people were killed in clashes and intercommunal massacres, and over 12 million people were uprooted from their homes and stripped of their property.[6] As early as November 29, 1947, K. C. Neogi, Indian minister of relief and rehabilitation, remarked,

> The magnitude of the refugee problem has been such that there has been no historical parallel to it. Nowhere in history has a transfer of population of such dimensions taken place in such a short time and under such circumstances . . . The problem itself is not really one problem, but literally scores of problems, each one having an importance and an urgency of its own.[7]

The Muslim population in preindependence India was primarily concentrated in two separated areas: the Punjab, Land of the Five Rivers, in the west; and East Bengal in the east. Under the terms of partition, the newborn Pakistan was conceived—in some ways fatally—as two noncontiguous political units: East Pakistan and West Pakistan, a divided territory separated by a thousand miles of Hindu India.

The rancor and violence of partition left an indelible scar on the newborn nations and set a tremulous ground for any future interaction between them. Sentiments of communalism, entitlement, and hostile competitiveness, already rife between the two main religious communities, were all reminded with a vengeance during this period of turmoil partition, but their ramifications reach well into the present—clouding all attempts at interstate normalcy. And, of all the demons partition has unleashed, none has been more vicious than the Kashmir dispute.

The British rule over India was partly direct and partly conducted through the native princes aided by advisers ("residents"). One of the largest princely states was Kashmir, in northern India, which was predominantly Sunni Muslim in composition, but with a significant Hindu minority in its southwest province of Jammu. The Maharajah of Kashmir, a Hindu descendant of a British ally, was given the throne as a reward for his loyalty. The Maharaja entertained his own hopes for independence in 1947, but as an irregular army of Muslim tribesmen supported by Pakistan infiltrated Kashmir in an attempt to seize control, he hastened to sign a treaty of accession to India in October 1947. Kashmir thus became the sole Muslim-majority state to accede to India.

This was the instigation for the first India-Pakistan war. India sent its own troops into Kashmir and after fierce fighting, which continued for fourteen months, managed to hold onto most of the state. Although well positioned to do so, the Indian army refrained from carrying its offensive further into other parts of Pakistan. The portion of Kashmir occupied by Pakistan during the war and held thereafter was divided into two distinct units—a thin strip of 5,135 square miles was named "Azad" (Free) Kashmir and became nominally autonomous. The remaining portion, a much larger area of around thirty thousand square miles termed the "Northern Territories," was administered directly by Pakistan's federal government. This area was predominantly Muslim, and India showed little interest in occupying it.[8] In part, this was due to India's expectation that the matter of Kashmir would eventually be resolved through the UN and to its consequent estimation that it would not be worthwhile to risk a broader offensive to capture Kashmiri territory, the future status of which was unclear.[9] India retained control over thirty-nine thousand square miles of Kashmir, today containing 70 percent of Kashmir's 13.6 million people.

For Jinnah as well as the Muslim League the matter of Kashmir was more than a territorial competition; Kashmir had to be part of Pakistan because it was overwhelmingly Muslim. As Jinnah reminded the viceroy when the issue first arose, "Kashmir" was what the K in Pakistan stood for. For the Indian prime minister, Nehru, India's promise of secular government would be enhanced through the incorporation into India of a principally Muslim-majority state. He also believed this was what the Kashmiris themselves wanted.[10]

The UN was called upon to intervene in the matter of Kashmir as early as January 1, 1948, when India, invoking Chapter VI of the UN charter, referred the question to the UN Security Council, accusing Pakistan of actively participating as well as supporting local tribesmen in acts of aggression in Kashmir.[11] Pakistan countered by accusing India of genocidal targeting of the Muslim population in Kashmir and denied direct Pakistani assistance to what it argued was a local tribesmen's uprising. It also questioned the validity of the accession to India by the Maharaja. This controversy over the *legality* of Kashmir's initial accession to India was to underlie the parties' positions on the dispute—as well as on the mechanisms of resolving it—from that time on.

After reviewing the parties' mutual complaints, the Security Council decided to establish a three-member United Nations Commission for India and Pakistan (UNCIP) to investigate and mediate in the dispute.[12] Mediation efforts all failed. Three months later, in April, the Security Council enlarged the membership of UNCIP and recommended the use of observers to stop the fighting.[13] On August 13, 1948, the UNCIP adopted a Resolution on Jammu and Kashmir calling on both parties to agree to a cease-fire, which would be supervised by the UN. Pakistan was called upon to withdraw all its forces, including Pakistani officials and tribesmen, from Kashmir. The area evacuated was to be administered by local authorities under UN tutelage. Following the Pakistani withdrawal, so the resolution stipulated, India was to withdraw its own troops from the area. Finally, the resolution summoned the parties to reaffirm their commitment to a free and fair plebiscite, in which Kashmiris would determine whether they prefer accession to India or to Pakistan.[14]

The idea of holding a plebiscite in Kashmir was agreed on, at the time, by both governments. The controversy arose instead over the sequencing of the steps required from both countries under the resolution: while India demanded that the first step in the implementation of the resolution must be a Pakistani withdrawal from Kashmir, Pakistan claimed that the plebiscite must come first.

After further discussions with the parties, on December 11, 1948, UNCIP proposed another resolution, later adopted by the Security Council, constituting an elaboration of its August resolution on the plebiscite procedures.[15] It also urged the parties to declare a cease-fire, beginning January 1, 1949. The two governments accepted the cease-fire proposal. However, the plebiscite plans were never executed, as the two parties remained adamant on their opposing sequencing demands.

The cease-fire line (CFL), about 480 miles long, was formalized with the signing of the Karachi Agreement, in July 1949.[16] A United Nations Military Observers Group for India and Pakistan (UNMOGIP) was established to monitor it. With the delineation of the CFL, Pakistan retained control of approximately one-third of Kashmiri territory. However, neither country has ever recognized a status quo, and both continued to lay claim to all of Kashmir. That same year, the UNCIP report concluded: "The roots of the Kashmir dispute are deep . . . strong undercurrents, political, economic, religious—in both Dominions have acted, and do act, against an easy and prompt solution."[17]

In view of the fragile situation in Kashmir and its predominantly Muslim population, India confirmed the region's special status in Article 370 of its constitution in 1950, allowing India-administered Kashmir more autonomy than other Indian states and limiting India's jurisdiction in it to matters of federal interest, such as defense, foreign affairs, and communications. In 1951 the Security Council adopted Resolution 91, determining that UNMOGIP should continue to supervise the cease-fire.[18] From that time on, the force has been functioning as an autonomous operation, directed by its chief military observer, albeit with very little actual force.

Throughout 1949 and the early 1950s, bilateral talks were held between Prime Minister Nehru of India and Prime Minister Bogra of Pakistan, with a view to reaching some agreement over Kashmir at first and—when no such agreement could be concluded—to creating a no-war pact. In the course of these talks, an important agreement was reached on the treatment of minorities, stipulating that both governments should ensure to the minorities throughout their territory complete equality of citizenship, security, freedoms, and liberties.[19] This was, in fact, one of the very first islands of agreements reached between the parties.

Bilateral talks continued throughout the early 1950s. In 1956, when Nehru suggested Kashmir be partitioned along the CFL without a prior plebiscite, the Pakistani reaction was so furious that all bilateral negotiations ceased. In the years to come, other attempts by Pakistan to reinvolve the UN actively in the dispute were all vehemently rejected by India; in time, this encouraged Pakistani strategic plans for taking control of Kashmir by force.

The 1965 War

In October–November 1962, India suffered a disastrous defeat in its war with China, along the Himalayan frontiers. While it was making efforts to recover its heavily damaged military infrastructure, Pakistan, who was keeping a wary eye on India's growing armament, saw an opportunity to fulfill its aspiration of seizing all of Kashmir. At the last moment, the United States, wishing to leverage the Indian defeat on the Chinese front to make leadway on the Pakistani front, sponsored bilateral talks. At the same time, however, Pakistan announced that it had reached an agreement with China to cede over two thousand square miles of Pakistan-administered Kashmir to China, and a few months later, in March 1963, the two countries formalized their joint border.[20]

India protested that the agreement violated the Security Council resolutions, which forbade the parties from unilaterally changing the status quo in Kashmir. Pakistan rejected the claim and argued that India had already violated the resolutions when it adopted a new Kashmir constitution, in November 1956, which reaffirmed that the "state is and shall be an integral part of the Union of India" and added that this included the whole state of Jammu and Kashmir, i.e., including Pakistan-administered and Azad Kashmir.[21] Beginning in January 1957, however, most of the provisions of the General Indian constitution were made applicable to the state of Kashmir as well, thereby depriving Kashmir of most of the special guarantees previously accorded to it to preserve its unique status. Subsequent bilateral negotiations continued until May 1963, but with little progress.

In April 1965, what began as a minor dispute between the parties over the waters of the Rann of Kutch—a large tidal area on the west coast, consisting mainly of marshland and trackless waste, where the border was poorly demarcated—developed into a wide-scale border war that spread into Kashmir. In June the British brokered a cease-fire, and India agreed to refer the dispute in the Rann to an international tribunal.[22] This tribunal announced its verdict on February 19, 1965: it gave 350 square miles in the northern part of the Rann area to Pakistan and the rest to India.

At the same time, Pakistan embarked on "Operation Gibraltar," in which it inserted guerrillas into Kashmir with the purpose of provoking a local uprising against India. The guerillas were successful in occupying several positions in the area, but India regained the lost posts in August and, in early September, fought off an attack in the Chamb sector of southwest Kashmir. On September 6, India launched a counterattack, invading Pakistan through the frontier in the Punjab area, between Lahore and Sialkot. Seventeen days later, after thousands had already been killed, a UN-ordered cease-fire was accepted by both sides. In January 1966, following strenuous mediation efforts by the Soviet

Union, the two countries signed a permanent cease-fire agreement known as the Tashkent Declaration.[23] The declaration affirmed the parties' commitment to good neighborly relations and stipulated that neither side would resort to force to resolve the Kashmir dispute. With its authors cognizant of the state of affairs, the Tashkent declaration did not attempt to resolve the dispute itself.

The 1971 War and the Creation of Bangladesh

East Pakistan had a majority of Bengali Muslim population. As a distinct ethnic group, in a geographically remote area, the Bengalis felt alienated from West Pakistan and accused the Pakistani government of discrimination against and neglect of East Pakistan. As the Bengali demand for independence intensified, the Pakistani government sent its army to suppress Bengali rebels. Over 10 million Bengalis fled to India in the course of 1971. In November 1971, declaring the need for humanitarian intervention but driven by the ulterior wish to have a friendlier neighbor in the northeast and a weaker Pakistan in the northwest, India invaded East Pakistan and defeated the Pakistani forces, taking ninety-three thousand Pakistani soldiers as prisoners of war.[24] East Pakistan was renamed Bangladesh and was proclaimed a new independent state. On December 17, a cease-fire was reached. The war this time did not spread into Kashmir.

Conceptually, the great significance of the 1971 war was in refuting—in Indian eyes—the Pakistani justification for its claim to all of Kashmir, or in other words for the division of territory along religious lines. The dismemberment of Pakistan and the creation of independent Bangladesh proved that a nation could not be established in south Asia solely on the basis of a common faith. Culture, ethnicity, and language were no less vital than Islam to the Bengali population's sense of identity and seclusion, which led, in turn, to its rebellion. Indeed, some Indian historians have clung to the creation of Bangladesh as proof that the two-nation theory has finally been "exploded."[25]

The most important offshoot of the 1971 war, as far as future Indo-Pak relations are concerned, was the Simla Agreement, which was signed by the two countries in July 1972, following a series of postwar bilateral talks.[26] The preamble to the agreement included an "end to the conflict," but did not declare a state of peace. Rather, it stipulated that the parties agree to "work for the promotion of a friendly and harmonious relationship and the establishment of durable peace in the subcontinent, so that both countries may henceforth devote their resources to the pressing task of advancing the welfare of their peoples." The agreement sought to lay down the principles that should govern the two countries' future relations. It also envisaged steps to be taken for further normalization of bilateral relations. Most importantly, it bound the two countries "to settle their differences by peaceful means through bilateral negotiations." Observers noted that given the clear Indian superiority in the aftermath of the war, Indira Gandhi could have achieved any political solution she wanted. The peaceful tone of the Simla Agreement, so it has been argued, was accompanied by a tacit Indian understanding (the actual existence of which is still debated) that Pakistani Prime Minister Zulfikar Ali Bhutto, upon his return home from Simla, would prepare the ground for a settlement in Kashmir, which would anchor the status quo as permanent.[27]

Simla was in fact a cluster of agreements. One of them created the Line of Control to replace the 1949 CFL, with some minor alterations.[28] The change of terminology was part of the Indian strategy to deny the UNMOGIP any future role in the conflict, by arguing that the new LoC was distinct from the cease-fire line and that the monitoring mission of UNMOGIP did not apply to the new LoC. Pakistan, however, did not accept this position. It was supported in its stance by the UN secretary general, who agreed that UNMOGIP's mandate could be terminated only by a decision of the Security Council.

Other sections of Simla dealt with the restoration of normal relationship, repatriation of all prisoners of war and civilian internees, and the reinstatement of diplomatic relations.[29] It further stipulated that neither side should seek to alter the LoC unilaterally, irrespective of mutual differences and legal interpretations, and that both parties would undertake to refrain from the threat or use of force in violation of the line. The lack of any mention of a plebiscite in the one paragraph dedicated to the issue of Jammu and Kashmir was counted an Indian achievement.

In conjunction with Simla, a series of subject-specific agreements in the areas of trade, telecommunication, postal services, visas, shipping services, and more were also concluded. In essence, Simla was an archipelago of islands of agreement that sought to establish a more normalized relationship in key areas of interstate relationship, despite the absence of any resolution on the core dispute over Kashmir.

Simla became the reference point for all subsequent bilateral talks between India and Pakistan. India insisted that the Kashmir dispute could be resolved only in accordance with the terms of the Simla Agreement. Pakistan, on the other hand, maintained that Simla did not supersede the previous UN resolutions, which called for a plebiscite by the Kashmiris. The appropriate role of the UN in mediating the dispute has remained another contentious point between the parties, surfacing even with regard to the role played by the UNMOGIP: as part of its strategy of internationalizing the Kashmir dispute, Pakistan to this day continues to submit complaints of cease-fire violations to the UNMOGIP; India, opposing internationalization, ignores them.

In 1974 the government of the state of Kashmir reached an accord with the Indian government, reaffirming its status as a "constituent unit of the union of India."[30] Pakistan, predictably, rejected the accord.

Kashmiri Insurgency

The next crisis in the Indo-Pakistani relationship was sparked by the outbreak of violent insurgency in Kashmir in December 1989, as a number of militant Muslim groups launched an armed campaign to gain independence for Kashmir or else to cede Kashmir to Pakistan. The insurgents were supplied and funded by Pakistan and Afghanistan, and received their training in Pakistan and Azad Kashmir, in camps set up by Pakistan's Inter Services Intelligence (ISI). In January 1990, the Indian federal government sent in troops to maintain order and violent clashes ensued. In the following months, both countries mobilized their forces for heavy deployment along the LoC. War seemed a stone's throw away.[31]

Although the parties managed to avoid going to war this time, relations remained tense throughout the decade. India accused Pakistan of interfering with its internal affairs, while Pakistan claimed India was abusing Kashmiris' human rights, including their right to self-determination. Pakistan also denied providing material support to the militants. The issue of Pakistani support for Kashmir militants remains the most contentious matter between the two countries.

Meanwhile, the armed militancy in Kashmir underwent significant changes: it increased in strength to include thousands of members, reinforced by mercenary Islamic fighters from countries such as Uzbekistan and Armenia who had fought in Afghanistan against the Soviet Union in the 1980s; its ideological emphasis correspondingly shifted from secular nationalist to Islamic. Increasingly, the targets of the insurgents became ordinary civilians rather than the Indian state. A concerted effort was made to attack Kashmiri Pandits, a Hindu community of Kashmiri ethnicity. This was in contrast to the previous pan-Kashmiri policy of the insurgents, which sought to harness all groups of Kashmiri ethnicity, irrespectively of religion.[32]

There are currently about two dozen armed groups claiming to be operating within Indian-held Kashmir. Most of these groups are part of the United Jihad Council (UJC) alliance, based in Azad Kashmir. Some, like the Lashkar-e-Tayeba (which is on the U.S. State Department's List of Designated Foreign Terrorist Organizations), are based in Pakistan. Within Jammu and Kashmir, the separatists are politically organized under the All Parties Hurriyat Conference (APHC), which formed out of the 1993 wave of Kashmiri insurgency. Despite the majority of Kashmiri activists being pro-Pakistan Muslims, the APHC is divided from within on the two most important issues: whether violence should be an inherent part of their struggle and whether their struggle should be for independence, for unification with Pakistan, or for accession to India.[33]

To keep the militants in Kashmir under check, India regularly deploys heavy troops in the Kashmir valley and its surrounding areas. The reported number of troops and paramilitaries operating in India-administered Kashmir is around five hundred thousand. Clashes between the Pakistani-backed paramilitaries in Kashmir and the Indian forces are almost a daily occurrence. Ongoing belligerence has generated tens of thousands of refugees and internally displaced people. India's aggressive counterinsurgency measures result in widespread human rights violations and the breeding of anti-Indian sentiments. The local Kashmiri government has been accused of corruption and incompetence, although the 2004 elected government is considered an improvement. Harsh living conditions are exacerbated by deficient infrastructure and poor access to healthcare and education.[34] Ironically, the large presence of security forces with purchasing power, alongside vast direct economic assistance from New Delhi, make Jammu and Kashmir the state with the lowest poverty rate in India.[35]

Insurgency and Strife Outside of Kashmir

In addition to interstate wars and the ongoing skirmishes in Kashmir, there has also been constant guerilla activity by separatist groups along the northeastern borders of India, in the areas adjacent to Bangladesh. These guerilla groups consist of immigrants from Bangladesh, local tribes seeking autonomy, and others disgruntled with what they perceive to be governmental apathy to their states. The conflicts between the government and a number of the tribes were settled in agreements initiated by Rajiv Gandhi, after he took office as prime minister in 1984. Other rebellions and disturbances continue, especially in the largest northeast state of Assam.[36]

Of the internal insurgency in India, the one conducted by the Sikhs was by far the gravest. The majority of the 15 million Sikhs in India live in the northern state of Punjab, which borders on Pakistan. Violent confrontations between Hindus and Sikhs, which reached their peak after the assassination of the Indian prime minister, Indira Gandhi, in 1984, left more than a thousand Sikhs dead. General Muhammad Zia-ul-Haq, Pakistan's president at the time (who came to power through a bloodless coup d'état), sought to exploit this insurgency to Pakistan's favor, covertly supporting and abetting the insurgents.[37]

In the last months of 1986, India launched a wide-scale military exercise, code-named "Brasstacks." The operation was ostensibly intended to test the readiness of the Indian army and its conventional deterrence strategy. Beyond that, it was meant to send a clear, strong message to Pakistan to cease its support for Sikh insurgency in the Punjab.

The size and formation of the exercise were unprecedented. When inquiries by Prime Minister Mohammed Khan Junejo of Pakistan remained unanswered by his Indian counterpart, Pakistan moved to bolster its own scheduled military exercises. After the completion of the exercise, Pakistani forces remained in battle-ready formation near the border, which caused considerable unease in India. By January 1987, India reacted by deploying its own troops along the border, moving closer to possible confrontation.[38]

Both leaders summoned each other's diplomatic representatives—the high commissioners—to convey their concerns. These initial contacts brought the prime ministers to agree, in a telephone conversation, to scale down the deployments and diffuse tensions.[39]

Additional Disputes

Most of the 1,809 miles of the India-Pakistan border is an internationally recognized boundary.[40] But apart from Kashmir and the route of the LoC, there are three more territories in dispute between the two countries: the Siachen Glacier, Sir Creek, and the Arabian Sea maritime boundary. There is also a more-recent quarrel over India's construction of a barrage over the Jehlum River and a dam over the Chenab River. All four disputes have been the subject of extensive discussions and negotiations between the parties, as yet with no agreement.

THE DISPUTE OVER THE SIACHEN GLACIER

The Siachen Glacier is situated in the Karakoram Mountains, near the Indo-China border, north of Kashmir. Approximately 3,860 square miles across, it runs from sixteen thousand to twenty-one thousand feet in altitude and is of no economic or social importance whatsoever. It is for this reason, as well as for the area's impossible terrain and weather conditions (with a surface temperature below minus forty degrees Celsius and wind speed running as high as 150 knots, for which the region has earned the nickname the "Third Pole"), that the original CFL under the 1949 Karachi Agreement did not cover the area of "the glaciers" but provided only that the line would pass "north to the glaciers."[41] In 1972, when the original CFL became the mutually accepted LoC under the Simla Agreement, its depiction stopped south of the glaciers and was left blank in the north. Ironically, "siachen" means the "land of wild roses."

In the 1970s and early 1980s, Pakistan permitted several mountaineering expeditions to the glacier. India, concerned by this development, launched a clandestine operation—"Meghdoot"—and established permanent posts on the glacier. In the winter of 1983–1984, the two countries engaged for the first time in violent clashes near the Siachen Glacier. Since then, the ongoing competition over the area places an onerous burden on both sides in terms of money and manpower.[42] Several thousands of men have been killed, over the years, in violent incidents and accidents in the area. On average, one Pakistani soldier is killed every fourth day, while one Indian soldier is killed every other day. Most of the casualties, however, are inflicted by the difficult weather and terrain conditions rather than by direct clashes.[43]

The significance of the Siachen Glacier to India derives from its location as the dividing line between Azad Kashmir and Aksai Chin, the Chinese-administered Kashmir. Holding the glacier would help India defend the Ladakh region in Jammu and Kashmir against a Pakistani or Chinese threat. Indeed, in some Indian strategists' eyes, the main obstacle to the resolution of the Siachen Glacier dispute is the prevalent perception of a strong linkage between the problems of Kashmir and the glacier.

This strong linkage also accounts for Pakistan's interest in the glacier. And yet Pakistan has been careful to argue that the Siachen dispute is separate and distinct from the issue of Kashmir, insisting that Siachen is a regional matter while Kashmir is an international one.[44]

Following earlier back-channel discussions on the issue, a 1989 joint statement between the Indian and Pakistani defense secretaries proclaimed that the two countries would "work towards a comprehensive settlement, based on redeployment of forces to reduce chances of a conflict, avoidance of the use of force and determination of future positions on the ground so as to conform with the Shimla Agreement and to ensure durable peace in the Siachen area."[45]

On the basis of this understanding, nine subsequent rounds of negotiations have included the Siachen issue on their agenda, but with no resolution. In 1992 the two countries reached another agreement, this time on the disengagement of forces; the idea was for both sides to withdraw from their positions on the glacier, maintaining the area as a demilitarized zone. However, due to mutual suspicion and arguments over the sequencing of withdrawals, the agreement was not formalized, remained in a draft form, and was never implemented.[46]

The Siachen Glacier has remained on the agenda of bilateral negotiations ever since, including within the composite dialogue formulated in 2004. In September 2005, the Indian defense minister stated that the two sides had now agreed in principle to withdraw troops from the glacier and that only a few modalities remained to be worked out. Pakistan on its part denied that such an agreement had been reached and insisted that major differences persisted in the two sides' view of the matter. Pakistan did, however, express its willingness to sign an agreement with India on a mutual withdrawal based on the 1989 understanding. A week later, the foreign ministers of the two countries met and released a statement that "India and Pakistan will strive to arrive at a 'common understanding' on demilitarisation of the Siachen Glacier before the next round of the composite dialogue [in January], 2006."[47]

The main obstacle, at the moment, seems to be a lack of agreement on the modalities of mutual withdrawal and, in particular, on monitoring and verification measures that would ensure that neither party reoccupies positions vacated.

THE SIR CREEK DISPUTE

Sir Creek is a sixty-mile-long estuary situated in the marshes of the Rann of Kutch, which lies on the border between the states of Gujarat (in India) and Sind (in Pakistan), at the opposite end of the border from the Siachen Glacier. The dispute originally evolved around the Rann itself. Following the armed clashes of 1965, Pakistan claimed title to half of the Rann along the twenty-fourth parallel, while India asserted that the boundary ran along the Rann's northern edge. The Indo-Pakistani Western Boundary Tribunal, to which the matter was referred for arbitration, accepted India's position in the main, conceding only small parts of the Rann to Pakistan. However, the tribunal excluded from its consideration the boundary along Sir Creek, as the parties agreed to focus their dispute on the part of the boundary that began at the head of the creek.[48]

The significance of the Sir Creek, for both parties, lies in its linkage to the delineation of the Indo-Pakistan maritime boundary, which is itself still a site of contention. While India wishes to focus discussions on the maritime boundary, Pakistan insists that the Sir Creek issue must be resolved first, so as to establish the land point from which the maritime boundary can be plotted. Meanwhile, reports of the presence of oil and natural gas in the area have raised the stakes for both parties.[49] At least six negotiation rounds have addressed the Sir Creek issue, but with no meaningful change.

Some headway has more recently been made in talks between the foreign ministers of India and Pakistan in October 2005, when the two countries agreed to undertake a joint survey of the marshy land of the Rann of Kutch off the Gujarat coast and consider options for the delimitation of the maritime boundary.

THE MARITIME BOUNDARY

The dispute over the delimitation of the maritime boundary is not only a source of political or military tensions but also of humanitarian concerns. The respective coastguards or navies habitually apprehend fishermen, who allegedly cross the boundary from the other side and who then languish in prisons for years without any contact with their families. On several occasions, imprisoned fishermen have been released as goodwill gestures, but hundreds more have remained in custody. In July 1997, for example, in the course of bilateral negotiations, the two countries exchanged 194 prisoners as a confidence-building measure, leaving over 300 still imprisoned.[50] More recently, the two sides agreed to release all fishermen and civilian prisoners who have served their sentences and whose nationality was recognized.[51] In addition to the humanitarian issue, the lack of agreement on the delimitation of the boundary also inhibits cooperation between the two navies in combating piracy, smuggling, and drugs and arms trafficking.

Between 1997 and 1999, top Pakistani naval officers believed in the importance of naval cooperation with India. They exchanged suggestions for naval exercises and other forms of collaboration. Both naval chiefs expressed a desire to meet with each other. The Indian chief of naval staff also conveyed to his counterpart the idea that the two naval headquarters may serve as a channel for their respective governments through which to negotiate a solution on Sir Creek. Without political support, however, these initiatives fell through.[52]

WATER-RELATED PROJECTS

The bilateral relationship is further strained by water-related disagreements on the interpretation and application of the 1960 Indus Waters Treaty.[53] Two projects that have attracted considerable attention and debate are the Wullar Barrage/Tulbul Navigational Project and the Baglihar Dam. Other contentious plans are the Sawalkote Hydroelectric Project and the Kishanganga Hydroelectric Project. All these disputed constructions are in Jammu and Kashmir.

At the center of the Wullar dispute lies a barrage that is to be constructed by the Indian Jammu and Kashmir government on the Jhelum River, below the Wullar Lake. The river flows into the lake from the south and exits from its west. The lake itself is an obstacle to the free flow of the river, hence the name "Wullar," which derives from the Sanskrit word "woll," meaning "obstacle."[54] According to India's contention, from October through February, the lake suffers from a severe water shortage, which imposes limitations on the navigational use of the river and lake. The Tulbul Navigation Project is intended to solve the problem through the construction of a barrage at the intersection between the river and the lake, which would regulate the water flow year-round.

Pakistan is concerned that the construction of a barrage at the foot of the Wullar would obstruct the flow of the Jehlum River into Pakistan. It might also cause a severe shortage of electricity once water is withheld over extended periods, and endanger Pakistani military infrastructure in the area if inundated.[55] As a result, claims Pakistan, the Tulbul project is not really a "navigation project" but, in fact, a water-storage project. As such, it violates the Indus Waters Treaty of 1960, which assigned the Jehlum River to Pakistan and which permitted India only nonconsumptive use of the part of the river within its territory.

The Tulbul water project is thus a classic controversy arising out of a treaty interpretation: is the project about the control or use of water for navigation, in which case it is permitted under Articles I and III of the treaty, or is it rather a water-storage project, in which case it is prohibited under Article IV?

Negotiations over the dispute first took place in the mid-1980s at the level of the two Indus water commissioners, as provided for in the 1960 Treaty. When no agreement was reached, the matter was referred to the respective governments. At that time, Pakistan suspended its plans to approach the International Court of Justice on the issue, while India halted any construction work until a settlement was found, proving that both parties expected an imminent resolution of the dispute. In March 1989, a first round of bilateral negotiation over the Wullar Barrage was conducted at the political level. At least nine rounds of negotiation have since addressed the controversy, but with little progress. The last secretary-level talks, in June 2005, were inconclusive, with each side reiterating its position.

Some commentators believe that Pakistan is not interested in any negotiated compromise, as that would mean legitimating the Indian violation of the Indus Waters Treaty. As the Wullar is only one of several water-related disagreements, Pakistan wishes to avoid any compromise that would seem to weaken its legal case under the treaty and to give India an incentive for future violations.[56]

The $1 billion, ninety-five-mile Baglihar Dam project was launched by India in June 1999, on the Chenab River, in India-administered Kashmir. Pakistan raised fierce objections, claiming a dam would affect the Chenab's downstream flow into Pakistan and so impinge on the country's exclusive rights to the Chenab waters under the 1960 Indus Waters Treaty.

Pakistan's case relies on Article III of the treaty, which states that Pakistan shall receive all those waters of the western rivers which India is under obligation to let flow. Besides this, Article IV of the treaty states that each party will "use its best endeavours to maintain the natural channels of the rivers, as on the effective date, in such condition as will avoid, as far as practicable, any obstruction to the flow in these channels likely to cause material damage to the other party." India's case is based on the words "restrictive use" of the western rivers, which is substantiated in Annexure D, of the same treaty. This stipulates that India can store water on the Chenab for generating hydroelectric power. According to India, the storage is a nonconsumptive use that does not affect the water flow.

In early 2005, Pakistan approached the World Bank with the request that the Bank appoints a neutral expert to determine the issue, as provided for in Annexure F of the treaty. The Bank accepted Pakistan's request and, after consultation with both parties, named a Swiss civil engineer as the neutral expert. The expert, accompanied by Indian and Pakistani teams, is now conducting on-site investigations and hearings in the matter. This was the first time in the treaty's forty-five years of operation that Annexure F was invoked and a neutral expert appointed. The degree to which the parties will bind themselves by his decision shall be of great interest to observers, as it will be the first time since the Rann of Kutch dispute that the parties agreed to abide by a third party's decision. The issue may be more important than it seems at first glance; in February 2005, newspapers reported a Pakistani minister as stating that war may be the only option to resolve the Baglihar dispute.[57]

The Nuclear Dimension

After China conducted its own first nuclear test in 1964, India launched its own nuclear weapons program, in part to meet the Chinese threat and in part to promote its national status as an actor-to-be-reckoned-with on the world stage. In 1974 India became the sixth country in the world to detonate a nuclear device. Pakistan followed suit with its own nuclear program. Pakistani fears intensified after its 1971 defeat and its consequent territorial dismemberment. In the decades that followed, nuclear programs of both countries were augmented by the development of short- and medium-range missiles capable of carrying nuclear warheads.[58] In April 1998, Pakistan tested its new Ghauri medium-range nuclear missile. A month later, India announced it had conducted five underground nuclear explosion tests. The tests were widely condemned by the international community, and Pakistan was urged not to retaliate. Nonetheless it did, with a similar series of explosion tests. What was previously only a potential capability now became an overt power display. In reaction, several countries, including the United States, imposed economic sanctions on both countries, which were lifted only in 2001, primarily as a U.S. gesture towards Pakistan, in gratitude for the latter's assistance to the United States in its new war on terrorism.[59] Despite strong American pressure, neither country has so far signed the Comprehensive Test Ban Treaty.[60]

To what extent the two countries' nuclear capabilities make the region more prone to war is unclear. For the most part, the international community, and the United States in particular, believes it does. Thus, in January 2002, the Central Intelligence Agency published its news report "Global Trends 2015," which projects that a threat of a nuclear war between India and Pakistan will be a "most serious issue in the next 15 years."[61] However, Indian and Pakistani officials have argued that the probability of an all-out war between them is rendered lower precisely because of the nuclear threat, which in fact serves as a powerful deterrent. To support their argument, they point to the classical rivalry between the United States and the Soviet Union, kept in check through the mutual assured destruction (MAD) equilibrium during the Cold War. But just as in the Cold War, the potential for nuclear war lies not only in the deliberate employment of a nuclear weapon but also in the accidental detonation of one. This danger necessarily casts its shadow on any benefit a MAD equilibrium might have in terms of preventing future escalation.[62] And whichever the greater source of danger, war or accident, the nuclear dimension of the conflict urges the need for conflict management mechanisms that would avert the risk of escalation.

The Kargil War

In 1998 Prime Ministers Vajpayee and Nawaz Sharif met in Colombo, Sri Lanka, in July and again in New York in September of that year, in an attempt to resume peace talks. The modalities of the dialogue process were approved and the first round of the composite dialogue process was held in October 1998, with a meeting of the foreign secretaries in Islamabad. The subjects of "peace and security," including security CBMs (confidence-building measures) and other cooperative efforts, as well as Jammu and Kashmir, were all discussed.

Among other things, the parties also agreed to establish a bus service between Delhi and Lahore beginning February 1999. In a historic gesture, Prime Minister Vajpayee of India said he would travel to Pakistan on the bus's inaugural run and meet Prime Minister Nawaz Sharif of Pakistan. Vajpayee traveled to Pakistan on February 19, 1999, and on the next day the two leaders met and signed the Lahore Declaration, perceived at the time as a revolutionary step towards peace. The declaration's preamble stated that the parties were "convinced that durable peace and development of harmonious relations and friendly cooperation will serve the vital interests of the peoples of the two countries, enabling them to devote their energies for a better future."[63] The declaration itself stressed the two leaders' commitment to refrain from intervention in each other's internal affairs, to intensify their dialogue, and to take immediate steps towards reducing the risk of accidental or unauthorized use of nuclear weapons.

The declaration was complemented by a joint statement and a memorandum of understanding.[64] The joint statement called for periodic meetings of the foreign ministers for discussion of topics of mutual concern, including World Trade Organization issues, nuclear-related commitments, visa and travel regulations, information technology, civilian detainees, and POWs. The memorandum included a series of notable mutual arrangements in the sphere of nuclear weapons. Immediately following the signing of the declaration, some prisoners from both sides were released and repatriated, and visa-granting policies to nationals of the other country were relaxed.

It all seemed like the beginning of a beautiful friendship. It was not.

On April 10, 1999, less than two months after the Lahore Declaration, India conducted a successful test firing of the extended range Agni II missile, adding to its nuclear delivery capability. The test firing was greeted with surprise, suspicion, and heightened guardedness on the Pakistani side. The ensuing instability may well have contributed to the events that were to follow.[65]

In the first week of May 1999, Indian forces detected hundreds of intruders, entrenched in the mountaintops of the Kargil sector of India-administered Kashmir. The intruders were an amalgam of Kashmiri militants, foreign mercenaries, and soldiers from the Pakistan army's North Light Infantry Regiment. Soon thereafter, infiltrations from the Pakistani side were reported along more than one hundred kilometers of front in the Mashkoh, Drass, Kargil, and Batalik sectors.[66] When the Indian director general of military operations (DGMO) contacted his counterpart, he was told Pakistan had nothing to do with the infiltration and that any activity in the area was wholly devised and executed by local militants.[67] Later, Nawaz Sharif claimed the entire operation, which was to become known as the Kargil War, was concocted by a group of powerful army generals in Pakistan, headed by the chief of army staff, General Pervez Musharraf, who wanted to derail the Lahore peace process without the knowledge of the Pakistani government. Musharraf, for his part, claimed that Sharif did know.[68] Whichever the case, commentators noted that the military takeover of the government by Musharraf a few months later was "written on the walls of Kargil."[69]

The Pakistani infiltrators managed to occupy some seventy positions on the Indian side within the month of May. Due to clashes in the area, the local population of the township of Drass was evacuated. The Indian army, relying heavily on air force for the first time since the 1971 war, moved to drive back the Pakistani infiltrators from the LoC in the Kargil sector. Pakistan then threatened to retaliate if its airspace was violated by Indian aircraft across the LoC in Kashmir. At least two Indian air force planes and one helicopter were shot down by Pakistani forces. India later alleged that the pilots of the aircraft who had ejected safely into Pakistani territory were tortured to death by Pakistani forces.[70]

Both sides were now digging their heels into their positions along the border. In an effort to reduce tensions, Nawaz Sharif used the hotline established between the two prime ministers back in 1989, to urge Vajpayee to refrain from employing the Indian Air Force. But air strikes continued. Rejecting the Pakistani-proclaimed linkage between the Kargil War and the problem of Kashmir, the United States refused to serve as mediator, showing no support or understanding for the Pakistani moves. But its attempts to put pressure on Pakistan to withdraw its forces from Kargil, were unsuccessful. Pakistani officials hinted ominously that if the war continued, nuclear weapons might be employed.[71] While official reports put the numbers of casualties of the Kargil War at hundreds on each side, the actual numbers are estimated to be much higher.

On July 25, the Indian DGMO announced that the eviction of Pakistani intruders was complete. Nevertheless, skirmishes persisted, while India rejected Pakistani proposals for an East Timor–type of referendum in Kashmir. At that time, India's government was strongly criticized from within for its inept handling of the Kargil crisis. On October 12, a military coup overthrew the Nawaz Sharif government in Pakistan, and Army Chief General Pervez Musharraf—chief architect of Kargil—was installed as chief executive.

On August 10, 1999, just as the Kargil War seemed to be waning, the Indian air force shot down a Pakistan navy Atlantique plane in the Rann of Kutch. All sixteen officers on board were killed.[72] India claimed that the Pakistani aircraft had violated Indian airspace. Pakistan denied the allegations and sought reparations.

Then, on December 24, 1999, an Indian Airlines aircraft carrying 187 passengers was hijacked by Islamist militants. The plane was taken to Kandahar, Afghanistan, where negotiations began with the hijackers. In exchange for the release of the passengers (one of whom had been killed by the hijackers), India agreed to free three Kashmiri terrorists incarcerated in Indian jails, who, upon their release, were given refuge by Pakistan. Prime Minister Vajpayee publicly accused Pakistan of masterminding the hijacking.[73]

If the Lahore Declaration had drawn the two countries one step closer to peace, the Kargil War surely pushed them many paces back. The revelation that an invasion of Kargil was planned even as the Lahore Declaration was being signed was fatal to the peace process initiated the previous year and extinguished any trust hitherto existing between the two peoples and their governments. The schism would continue to deepen as incident followed incident over the next few years and the two sides drew nearer the brink of a full-fledged war. The bilateral relationship has never since resumed to being quite what it was right before Kargil.

In the following weeks and months, India and Pakistan severed most of their communication channels. Pakistan was on the verge of denouncing the Lahore Declaration, and the situation in Kashmir deteriorated to its lowest ebb since the early 1990s.

The Aftermath of Kargil, 9/11, and Beyond

Efforts to prepare the ground for the resumption of peace talks gradually gathered pace over the next two years. Throughout 2000, Pakistan made several attempts to resume negoiations and even offered a no-war pact. India, however, demanded as a precondition for any resumption of contacts that Pakistan first cease to support the insurgents in Kashmir.

To encourage talks, both countries agreed to withdraw large portions of their forces deployed near the LoC. On November 19, 2000, India declared a unilateral cease-fire in Kashmir for the duration of the holy Muslim month of the Ramadan, a cease-fire which it then extended for the succeeding seven months. But levels of violence in Kashmir showed few signs of diminishing. Pressured by strong conservative opposition at home, Vajpayee called off the cease-fire in May 2001.

Nevertheless, soon thereafter India became one of the first countries to recognize Musharraf as the new self-proclaimed president of Pakistan, even as most countries were reluctant to recognize a leader taking office by force of a military coup. In July 2001, Prime Minister Vajpayee invited Musharraf to a peace summit in India. Musharraf accepted the invitation, and amidst much fanfare, a three-day summit took place in Agra, India. Drafts were exchanged on the two countries' positions on various bilateral issues, most notably nuclear arms and Kashmir. But despite the initial optimism, at the end of the three days, the leaders were unable to issue even a joint declaration, having reached a deadlock over the question of the "centrality" of Kashmir in such a declaration. Another source of Pakistani vexation was Vajpayee's announcement that the All Party Hurriyat Conference (APHC) in Kashmir would not be a party to the bilateral talks, as India refused to recognize or legitimize the Kashmiri militants as partners for dialogue.[74]

The attacks on the World Trade Center and the Pentagon on September 11 transformed the relationship of the two countries with the United States. They also, concomitantly, intensified domestic opposition to appeasement efforts on both sides. Pakistan's cooperation with the United States in its declared war on the Afghan Taliban regime brought the United States to lift the sanctions it had earlier imposed on Pakistan for its nuclear testing, and to offer it, instead, real economic incentives. At the same time, however, Musharraf met strong domestic opposition to his government's intensifying ties with the United States.

India, for its part, expected that the "war on terror" would echo in Pakistan and wield more pressure on it to crack down on militant and militant outfits within its territory. Initially, though, these expectations remained unfulfilled, and attacks by Kashmiri insurgents continued. In October 2001, an attack on the Kashmiri legislative assembly in Srinagar (capital of India-administered Kashmir) left thirty-eight people dead. The chief minister of India-held Kashmir, Farooq Abdullah, called on the government to target militant training camps in Pakistan.

In December, an armed attack on the Indian parliament in Delhi killed fourteen people (including the five Pakistani perpetrators). India again accused Pakistani-backed Kashmiri militants. The flagrant assault on India's symbol of democracy, just a few months after the Agra summit, was for many Indians reminiscent of the betrayal they felt when the Kargil war broke out so soon after the Lahore Declaration. It also gave fresh fodder to many who had constantly advocated a hawkish policy towards Pakistan. A substantial build-up of troops began along the border, leading to exchanges of fire.[75] All high-level bilateral ties were cut and many cooperative arrangements suspended. A wide-scale conflict seemed to loom again

To diffuse tensions, and under strong U.S. pressure, Musharraf gave a public address in January, pledging that his country would not permit terrorists to operate from within its territory. For the first time, Pakistan arrested around two thousand militant leaders, and outlawed several Islamic organizations involved in sectarian violence in Pakistan. It was not long however, before most militants were released, and the banned organizations re-emerged under different names.[76] On May 14, 2002, militants attacked an Indian army residential complex near Jammu, killing more than thirty people, a dozen of whom were women and children.[77] Pakistan condemned the attack and denied any connection with the assailants. India, rejecting the denial, expelled the Pakistani High Commissioner. Both countries intensified their forces along the LoC and heavy clashes ensued.

Almost a year later, on April 18, 2003, Vajpayee invited his counterpart to resume bilateral ties, and diplomatic relations were restored. In November, a cease-fire was declared along the LoC and on the Siachen Glacier. By January 2004, all transportation links, halted following the attack on the Indian parliament, were resumed. On January 6, the two leaders, meeting on the margins of the twelfth South Asia Association for Regional Cooperation (SAARC) in Islamabad, agreed to resuscitate their dialogue and to resolve all contentious issues, including Kashmir, in a peaceful manner. The respective foreign secretaries met the following month and committed themselves to a composite dialogue on all bilateral issues. That same month, Vajpayee met for the first time with the APHC representatives, whom he had so far steadfastly refused to engage with.

In May 2004, the Indian Congress Party, presided over by Sonia Gandhi, won the national elections and ousted Vajapyee's Bharatiya Janata Party–led government. Gandhi gave up her place to Manmohan Singh, and he was sworn in on May 22, 2004, as the first Sikh prime minister of India.

Despite the change of government, there was no letup or even significant alteration in the composite dialogue process. In fact, the Pakistani prime minister, Mir Zafarullah Khan Jamali, asserted that the change would not upset the peace process as it was in the interest of both nations to resolve outstanding issues through composite dialogue. By the same token, India's incoming prime minister Singh also pledged to drive the dialogue forward and hold talks with all parties over Kashmir.

To date, however, despite this bilateral commitment and the ongoing high-level discussion, the composite dialogue has failed to produce significant headway on any of the core disputes—Kashmir or any of the other territorial and water disagreements.

I have thus far attempted to present the Indian-Pakistani relationship in the traditional manner, that is, by recounting the two countries' history of war. I will now turn to tell the story as it is more seldom told, exploring the history of bilateral cooperation and partnership.

Spheres of Bilateral Cooperation

A History of Bilateral Cooperation

Throughout the many years of conflict—and alongside the failure of numerous attempts at formal peace negotiations—ad hoc confidence-building measures (CBMs) as well as more-institutionalized methods of cooperation have been implemented by the parties in nearly every area of state life—from security cooperation, through water and environmental protection, to trade and aviation. Among the arrangements reached, some were intended to increase communication and transparency; others have gone further to establish mutual consultation and even active collaboration in problem solving.

Some spheres of bilateral cooperation have existed from the very beginning of the Indo-Pak relationship. Others were created in the course of its continuation. In the first few years following independence, the two countries set out to resolve many urgent matters that arose from the partition, the great loss of life, and the upheaval of millions. Despite deep-seated animosity and distrust, the two countries managed to conclude a series of bilateral arrangements to deal with the mass movement of people across borders, the protection of minorities, the protection of places of worship and water allocation.[78] None of these agreements were intended to resolve the conflict but merely to meet the most urgent needs of the populations involved when there was a mutual interest in doing so. Thus, the 1948 Inter-Dominion Agreement for Preventing Mass Exodus of Minorities, one of the very first islands of agreement between the parties, concluded,

> Whereas the Governments of the two Dominions agree that mass exodus of minorities is not in the interest of either Dominion and they are determined to take every possible step to discourage such exodus[79]

Many of the provisions of these islands of agreement were unique in the sense that they were not provided for in existing international agreements or treaties but were tailor-made, designed by the parties themselves to meet the specific needs and conditions of their situation. Indeed, anything else would have been impossible given the degree of interdependence existing between the populations. Perhaps nothing quite conveys the irony of interdependence as much as the fact that the current Indian prime minister, Manmohan Singh, was born in Gah, today in Pakistan, while the current Pakistani president, Pervez Musharraf, was born in Delhi.

In addressing the Indian parliament in February 1950, Prime Minister Nehru explained the Indian motivations in its foreign policy towards Pakistan:

> The partition of India was, from every point of view, a very unnatural thing. Well, we accepted it, we continue to accept it and we will act accordingly. But as the President said in his Address, it inflicted such wounds on the vast masses of people in India and Pakistan as would take sometime to heal . . .
>
> Whatever policy Pakistan may follow, we should not follow a crooked policy. I say that, not merely on grounds of high principles but from the point of view of sheer opportunism . . . I, therefore, submit that, in our relations with Pakistan, we have first of all to follow a policy of firmness and adequate preparation but always to maintain a friendly approach. Again, there can be no doubt that India and Pakistan, situated as they are geographically and otherwise and with their historical background, cannot carry on for ever as enemies. If they do, catastrophe after catastrophe will follow.[80]

In the late 1950s, further agreements were reached on trade (subject to frequent modifications in the following years) and on border relations, including even some exchanges of territory. The border agreements indicated that their purpose was to remove "causes of tensions" and create "peaceful conditions along the Indo-Pakistan border areas." They provided for the submission of disputes that could not be resolved by negotiation to "an impartial tribunal" and established consultation mechanisms for sharing information relevant to the implementation of the arrangements. The border agreements were generally observed—not least, because they did not address the issue of Kashmir or the route of the boundary in that area.[81]

In 1960, with the extensive assistance of the World Bank and a number of countries, India and Pakistan concluded the Indus Waters Treaty, thereby resolving years of tensions and disputes over the use of the waters of the Indus Basin. In the years to follow, however, and the intensification of the Cold War, the two countries grew more distant from one another. India became a founding member of the Non-Aligned Movement and moved closer to the Soviet Union, ultimately signing the Treaty of Peace, Friendship, and Cooperation with it in August 1971. At the same time, Pakistan joined U.S.-sponsored pacts, such as the Central Treaty Organization and the Southeast Asia Treaty Organization. Cooperation in these years was limited to some channels of communication and to the implementation of previous agreements. No new agreements were concluded.

The cluster of the Simla agreements which followed the 1971 war covered a great number of spheres, including trade, border relations, aviation, telecommunication and postal services, and more. It was the first attempt of its kind to normalize the interstate relationship in a comprehensive manner.

In 1982 a joint Indo-Pakistani commission, headed by the two countries' foreign ministers, was established for the first time "to promote bilateral relations in various fields such as trade, education, culture, health, tourism, etc."[82] The joint commission was to submit mutually agreed-upon reports and recommendations to the two governments. It was to meet once a year, with additional subcommittees to convene and report, as necessary. Through the operation of the commission and the subcommittees set up under its auspices, agreements were reached in a number of areas, including improvement of telecommunication facilities; reduction of postal rates; technological coordination and exchange of scientific literature, archives, and libraries; encouragement of visits by professionals, academics, businessmen; and more.[83] As the implementation of these arrangements depended on the broader context of the political atmosphere between the two countries, some of them were ultimately not implemented or were poorly pursued.[84] By 1989, however, the commission dissolved altogether, as no significant development emerged from its discussions.

In 1990, following strenuous efforts by the United States, Pakistan and India engaged in bilateral talks at the foreign secretariat level. Pakistan suspended the talks in early 1994, after negotiations failed on the issue of Kashmir and again with Pakistani allegations of Indian misconduct in Kashmir. As one precondition to the resumption of talks, Pakistan demanded a dilution of the Indian forces on the Indian side of the LoC.[85] At that time, the Indian negotiators submitted to their Pakistani counterparts six "nonpapers" of suggestions for new prevention and cooperation regimes. Among these were a mutual commitment not to wage nuclear war on each other; a mutual withdrawal of forces from the Siachen Glacier without relinquishing territorial claims; better communication between the military commanders of both sides; and a proposal to resolve the Sir Creek dispute.[86]

Procedural controversies delayed further discussions until October 1998, several months after the two rivals' respective nuclear tests, when the process of dialogue was revived through eight joint working groups, established to deal a variety of subjects: Kashmir, peace and security, the Siachen Glacier, the Wullar Barrage, Sir Creek, terrorism and drug-trafficking, economic and commercial cooperation, and a promotion of friendly exchanges in various fields.[87] The Lahore summit was expected to push forward the talks between the foreign secretaries, but the Kargil War brought them to a halt. Officially, the framework of the joint working groups still exists today, but is yet to be actively resumed.

In the aftermath of the Kargil War and the more recent crises over Pakistani-backed militants' attacks in India, cooperation in almost all spheres was damaged, although not destroyed; in one spectator's words, "India-Pakistan interactions have gone into a deep freeze."[88] A thaw began to emerge in mid-2003, and most bilateral links were restored by early 2004. The composite dialogue, formulated in 2004, spans all contentious issues, including peace and security, Kashmir, the Wullar Barrage, the Siachen Glacier, Sir Creek, terrorism and drug trafficking, and a host of other issues of bilateral interest. In September 2004, the two foreign ministers met and signed a joint statement reviewing the status of the composite dialogue. They agreed on thirteen points, indicating a future "road map" for a comprehensive peace process. They also discussed a bus service between the two Kashmiri capitals, Srinagar and Muzaffarabad, as well as improvements in bilateral tourism and visa regimes. Follow-up meetings took place later that year to review progress on all issues.

That same month, the two leaders—Musharraf and Singh—met on the sidelines of the UN General Assembly for the first time since the latter's taking office. They agreed that accords should be implemented with practical solutions in mind. They also addressed the issue of

Jammu and Kashmir and agreed that possible options for a peaceful, negotiated settlement of the issue should be explored in a "sincere spirit and purposeful manner."[89]

In April 2005, President Musharraf visited India. He received a painting of his childhood home in Delhi and gave Singh a photo of the latter's own home village, Gah, in Pakistan. During the visit, the countries agreed to further cooperation, including opening the borders for trade across the LoC, operating the Jammu-Rawalakot bus route, reopening consulates in Karachi and Mumbai, and taking steps to facilitate meetings of families divided along the LoC. Further joint statements and agreements were announced in August 2005 (at the secretarial level), in September 2005 (with foreign secretaries and later Musharraf and Singh in New York) and in October 2005 (with the foreign ministers).

Formally, the two countries have never moved away from an intention to talk peace or at least to give a more coherent narrative to their peace moves. Times of crisis push them apart; relative calm, peaceful gestures, and third-party intervention draw them closer together. The thread is never quite cut off. Even a month following the attack on the Indian parliament in December 2001, when Indo-Pakistan relations reached an all-time low and the two countries were teetering on the brink of war, President Musharraf, in a much-publicized gesture, crossed the podium in a SAARC summit to shake hands with Prime Minister Vajpayee.

The following sections describe in detail islands of agreement between India and Pakistan in various spheres of their bilateral and regional relationships. Not surprisingly, in the security area, arrangements have tended to focus on communication and transparency, with the purpose of preventing further escalation, where the more "benign" spheres of environment protection and civil aviation arrangements allowed for actual collaboration and real mutual gains. Many of the agreements, both those intended for prevention and those intended for cooperation, state their contribution also in terms of promoting a positive atmosphere to allow for a more peaceful relationship overall.

Cooperation on Security

LAND, AIR AND NAVAL FORCES

Security cooperation between the two countries began in the 1970s, chiefly as an attempt to improve communications, increase transparency, and avoid misunderstandings that might have led to a dangerous escalation. Following the 1965 war, the two countries agreed to form a direct channel between their respective DGMOs.[90] This "hotline" is reminiscent of the one formed by the United States and the former Soviet Union at the height of the Cold War, but with an important variation; since 1990, it was agreed that it would be used not only in times of crisis but also on a regular basis, as a mechanism for exchange and dialogue. Accordingly, the two directors conduct a weekly phone conversation every Tuesday, alternating between them in initiating the call.

The effectiveness of the DGMO line has been widely questioned.[91] Critics have claimed that at times when it was needed most, as in the 1990 crisis in Kashmir or during the Kargil War, this channel was used only perfunctorily, if at all.[92] Moreover, exchanges were not always useful: as India's army chief reported following the attack on the Indian parliament in December 2001, "the DGMOs were still talking, usually on Tuesdays. Pleasantries are exchanged and sometimes clarifications are provided. There've been very little talk [sic] except the exchange of pleasantries in the last fortnight."[93]

Even more worrisome were the effects of half-truths or limited disclosures on the general levels of trust: soon after the September 11 attacks on America, Pakistan mobilized some of its strike forces to forward positions, ostensibly for an exercise. Pakistan's DGMO informed his Indian counterpart of these alleged exercises only after he was specifically asked about the observed troop movement. Reports noted that no information was volunteered at the weekly telephonic conversation. In reply, India deployed precautionary "trip-wire forces" in position.[94]

This is by no means to say the DGMO hotline is devoid of value. Analysts do acknowledge that "some skirmishes and stand-offs have been diffused by contact over this hotline."[95] Even during the heated periods in 2002, following the Kashmiri insurgents' attacks, when the Indian defense minister ruled out any additional contacts with the Pakistani army, he nonetheless stated that the DGMO line would remain operational.

The concept of a "hotline" was replicated in other bilateral contacts as well. In 1989 a hotline was established between Prime Ministers Benazir Bhutto and Rajiv Gandhi, though it was disconnected and reconnected several times. Used mostly to convey political messages, such as commitment to the process of dialogue or interest in developing bilateral ties, it was nevertheless also utilized during periods of grave escalation, such as the 1997 skirmishes in Kashmir or the Kargil War. A direct communication link has likewise been established between the sector commanders on both sides of the LoC.

The memorandum attached to the 1999 Lahore Declaration stipulated that the two sides should review the existing communication links with a view to upgrading and improving them and to provide for fail-safe and secure communication. But the upgraded hotlines are not operational, as like most other arrangements concluded at the Lahore summit, they were circumvented by the Kargil War.

Another effort to enhance transparency was made in 1991, as one of the lessons learned from the 1990 crisis in Kashmir, which brought the two countries to the brink of another war, when the two concluded the Agreement on the Advance Notice on Military Exercises, Maneuvers, and Troop Movements.[96] Under the terms of the agreement, both sides undertook to refrain from holding major military maneuvers and exercises in close geographical proximity to one another. The agreement defined the permitted size of land, air, and naval forces in the adjacent areas on both sides of the international boundary and the LoC. When exercises were to be conducted despite these limitations, the parties undertook to ensure that the strategic direction of the main force being exercised would not be the other side.

The agreement further required prior notice when moving military formations with defensive roles to operational locations for periodic maintenance of defenses or when scheduling major exercises. In addition to the planned date for the forces' deployment, the notifying side must, under the agreement, specify the type and level of the exercise, the general area of operation, its planned duration, the number and types of formations participating, and any move of strategic formations of military significance.

Finally, the agreement stipulated that naval ships and submarines from both sides were not to come nearer each other than three nautical miles, "so as to avoid any accident while operating in international waters," and that military aircraft would keep a specified distance (depending on the type of aircraft) from the other country's airspace.[97]

Critics of the Agreement on Military Exercises claim that the threshold set by the agreement, to apply only to forces at the division level and above, substantially limits its utility. Notifications of exercises have been circumvented in the past by the would-be notifying party moving the elements of the divisions separately, so as not to meet the division threshold and be required to give notice.[98]

On the same day on which the Agreement on Military Exercises was concluded, the parties also signed the Agreement on Prevention of Air Space Violations And for Permitting Over Flights and Landings by Military Aircraft. Its preamble noted the parties' hope "of promoting good neighborly relations between the two countries." The agreement called on both parties to ensure that air violations of each other's airspace do not take place. It further stipulated mandatory distances that aircraft of both countries must keep from each other's airspace and provides for procedures of notification and information transfers when aircraft violate the mandatory distances for purposes of "aerial survey, supply dropping, or mercy and rescue missions." The "no-fly zones" under the agreement are periodically violated.[99]

Other provisions dealt with the conduct of air exercises and operations near the border and incorporated the parties' undertaking to use the telephone line established between the army headquarters of the two countries to contact each other on matters of safety and air operations in emergency situations.

Surprisingly for two countries in an active conflict, the agreement did envisage possible flights of military aircraft through each other's airspace, when it stipulated that "military aircraft may fly through each other's airspace with the prior permission of the other country and subject to conditions specified in Appendix A to this Agreement."[100]

The Atlantique affair, at the wane of the Kargil War, exemplified some of the shortcomings of the agreement. As earlier noted, an unarmed Pakistani naval surveillance and antisubmarine warfare aircraft was shot down by the Indian air force in August 1999, killing all sixteen officers on board. A controversy arose as to whether or not the Atlantique had in fact crossed the border into Indian airspace. The Indian authorities claimed that the plane had violated their airspace and was shot down over Indian territory. Pakistan claimed the plane had never crossed the Indian border at all. Chunks of the plane fell in both territories. Analysts cited the lack of a joint consultative or dispute-resolution forum in which to address such incidents as a major flaw in the agreement on airspace violations and an omission that further contributed to escalation following the incident.[101] Not surprisingly, an attempt by Pakistan to seek reparations from India through the International Court of Justice failed, as the court accepted India's contestation that the court lacked jurisdiction over the matter.[102]

With regard to naval forces, all in all, skirmishes between the navies have been minimal. It is for this reason that naval islands of agreement between India and Pakistan have tended to focus on safety and humanitarian issues more than on conflict containment. Thus, at the Lahore summit the two leaders undertook to conclude an agreement on prevention of incidents at sea, "in order to ensure safety of navigation by naval vessels, and aircraft belonging to the two sides."[103]

In July 2001, newspapers reported that the Indian defense ministry had proposed to set up a hotline between the Indian and Pakistani directors of naval operations (DNOs) to prevent detention of fishermen who may have strayed into each other's waters and to tackle emergencies at sea.[104] In any case, Vajpayee had, already, prior to this proposal, directed the Indian navy not to detain Pakistani fishermen who had strayed into Indian waters. The reports also suggested that the proposed hotline between the DNOs would be beneficial in minimizing the possibility of either country inadvertently shooting down the other's aircraft, should any venture too near to an adversary's warship.

Although a hotline between the DNOs has not yet been put up, talks held in August 2005 led to a memorandum of understanding establishing a hotline between the respective coast guards, with the primary purpose of speeding up the repatriation of stray fishermen in the Arabian Sea.[105]

ARMS CONTROL

The first formal security agreement between India and Pakistan was concluded on December 31, 1988, in conjunction with the fourth SAARC Summit. Its subject was the prohibition of attacks against nuclear installations and facilities.[106] The agreement was initiated after the 1984 crisis, when it was believed that India was planning an attack on Pakistan's nuclear facilities at Kahuta, and was pressed forward following the Brasstacks military exercises in late 1986. In fact, the 1988 agreement was a formal incorporation of the verbal commitment made as early as December 1985 by then–Pakistani President Zia Ul-Haq and the then–prime minister of India, Rajiv Gandhi, not to attack each other's nuclear facilities.[107]

The preamble to the agreement notes the two governments had reached agreement while "reaffirming their commitment to durable peace and the development of friendly and harmonious bilateral relations; conscious of the role of confidence building measures in promoting such bilateral relations based on mutual trust and good will."

The agreement consists of only three provisions, which order both nations to refrain from any attack (direct or indirect) on the nuclear installations and facilities of their adversaries. It further orders both sides to provide each other, on January 1 of every year, with an update on the exact location of any nuclear facilities within their territory. This provision is interesting as it is framed in a way that is not intended to ensure compliance by the reporting party itself but rather to provide information that would ensure better compliance by the other party.

Shortly after the first mutual exchange of lists of nuclear facilities, the two countries became suspicious about the accuracy of the information provided. As no mechanism was set to ascertain the truth or inclusiveness of the submitted reports, both resorted to accusing each other of noncompliance.[108]

On August 19, 1992, India and Pakistan signed the brief yet comprehensive Declaration on the Complete Prohibition of Chemical Weapons.[109] In the declaration, the two countries pledged to become parties to the Chemical Weapons Convention (CWC), which was being negotiated, and they fulfilled this pledge when the convention came into effect on April 29, 1997. They further undertook to forego the development, production, acquisition, stockpiling, and the direct or indirect use of chemical weapons. Both countries also declared that neither possessed or intended to acquire or use chemical weapons.

However, when the CWC entered into force, India amended its non-possession statement and admitted to the existence of Indian chemical weapons stockpiles and production facilities. The amended declaration "came as a rude surprise to Pakistan," said Muhammad Siddique Kanju, Pakistan's minister of foreign affairs. He warned that "to now discover that the Indian declaration was untrue . . . has placed Pakistan in a quandary," adding that Islamabad "must now seriously question all of India's declarations, including those relating to non-development of nuclear weapons."[110] Subsequently, India began to reduce its chemical weapons arsenal, although indications are that it still has stockpiles and production capabilities. Pakistan has also signed and ratified the CWC. It has no publicly known chemical weapons program or stockpile, although it probably has the capability to develop them.[111]

After the nuclear tests in 1998, the Indian government proposed that both sides would sign a "no-first-use" pledge and also declared it would follow some provisions of the Comprehensive Test Ban Treaty, including a moratorium on nuclear tests, without, however, becoming a party to the treaty.[112] While Pakistan has not yet pledged no first use, it has, however, joined the moratorium on nuclear tests. The memorandum of understanding accompanying the Lahore Declaration stipulated that "the two sides shall continue to abide by their respective unilateral moratorium on conducting further nuclear test explosions unless either side, in exercise of its national sovereignty, decides that extraordinary events have jeopardised its supreme interests."[113] In incorporating the respective unilateral moratorium declared by both countries into a formal bilateral agreement, the memorandum lent the undertakings extra political force and significance.

The memorandum further elaborates on the Lahore Declaration's general statement that both sides "shall take immediate steps for reducing the risk of accidental or unauthorized use of nuclear weapons and discuss concepts and doctrines with a view to elaborating measures for confidence building in the nuclear and conventional fields, aimed at prevention of conflict."[114] Accordingly, the memorandum stipulated that the parties would notify each other immediately of any such accidental or unauthorized use, which may inadvertently lead to hazardous fallout or an outbreak of nuclear war between the parties. The memorandum further stated that the two parties have undertaken to give each other advance notification on ballistic missile tests and shall conclude a bilateral agreement in this regard.[115] The Indian government did inform Pakistan prior to the Agni II missile test of April 1999.

In June 2004, in a joint statement issued at the end of two days of talks between experts on nuclear CBMs, both countries claimed that their nuclear capabilities, based on "national security imperatives," constituted a "factor for stability." Pursuant to this, they agreed to put in place a "dedicated and secure" hotline between their foreign secretaries to prevent misunderstandings and "reduce risks relevant to nuclear issues." Improved utilization of the existing military hotline was also discussed.[116]

In a dramatic move in October 2005, the two sides signed an agreement to prenotify ballistic missile testing, as was prescribed for by the Lahore memorandum.[117] Under the accord, each country will give the other at least seventy-two hours' notice before conducting a ballistic missile launch test. The countries also agreed not to allow trajectories of tested missiles to approach or land close to either the border or the LoC. The agreement does not apply to cruise missiles (which Pakistan tested in the preceding August) or to surface-to-air missiles (which India tested on the day of the signing of the agreement).

No other substantive nuclear arms control agreement currently exists between the parties. The general perception is that it is too sensitive an issue, one too close to the heart of national security interests of both sides, especially when joint monitoring and verification mechanisms are involved. Pakistan has, over the years, offered to discuss arms control initiatives, but these offers have all been rejected by India. India's concerns about arms control are threefold: its own security vis-à-vis Pakistan, its own security vis-à-vis China, and its self-perceived role as a major player in world affairs, which extends its security and foreign policy interests far beyond the south Asia region.[118]

Commenting on the arms control agreements, Indian defense analysts argued that "Pakistan has traditionally equated power with military power, military power with arms acquisitions, and arms acquisitions with external political support" and that for India, on the other hand, "security of a country, particularly a developing country, can neither be built up with dependence exclusively on military power nor by depending on military aid from the external sources. The best guarantees of security are internal stability, economic development and thorough cooperation between the close or distant neighbours."[119]

As earlier noted, commentators differ in their analysis of the effect of nuclear weapons on the stability in the region.[120] Either way, neither India nor Pakistan is willing to forego their nuclear capabilities. Their arms control agreements aim instead to reduce the risk of inadvertent or accidental nuclear attack, as a more practical and attainable target. However, a primary drawback is a lack of effective monitoring mechanisms, a lack which can only be exacerbated by the heightened levels of mistrust between the two rivals.

LOCAL BORDER AGREEMENTS

Following the 1958 Nehru-Noon Agreement, a series of border agreements were concluded, mostly to finalize the location of the border in several disputed areas: a 1959 accord called for the resolution of border disputes through negotiation or arbitration and envisaged the conclusion of detailed ground rules to be observed by the border security forces of both sides. Among other things, the agreement provided that no border outpost would be located within 150 yards of the border.[121]

In a 1960 agreement, the two countries resolved certain border disputes along the India–East Pakistan border. In 1963 demarcation of the West Pakistan border along the Indian states of Rajasthan and Punjab was completed by the joint teams of surveys of India and Pakistan. Various border arrangements were also concluded following the 1965 and the 1972 wars.

In accordance with this series of agreements, India's Border Security Forces (BSF) and Pakistan Rangers hold biannual meetings to discuss issues relating to security along the border, including the use of fire, the building of fences or other security structures, illegal border crossings, and drug smuggling.

A review of media reports indicates that local and less-institutionalized understandings between regional commanders along the border are not uncommon.[122] Thus, in November 1999 it was reported that an agreement had been reached between Pakistan Rangers and Indian BSF, according to which no attempt would be made by either side to change the status of the working boundary unilaterally by the erection of fences or other defensive structures. The two sides further undertook not to fire across the border or target innocent civilians. There were also discussions on cooperation in joint patrolling, combating drug trafficking, and preventing illegal border crossing. A truce during the May harvest season was likewise concluded.[123] None of these agreements, however, pertained to the LoC in Kashmir. It is obvious that such local arrangements could not have been made or sustained without political approval or, at the very least, acquiescence.

Following the October 8, 2005, earthquake, which devastated large parts of Pakistan-administered Kashmir, the two countries in an unprecedented gesture, opened the LoC to facilitate relief efforts. Relief items were permitted to be sent in both directions and families were allowed to cross—but only on foot. Immigration, customs, and foreign currency exchange facilities were set up along with public telephones and a mosque. India, however, imposed some restrictions on passage, as it considered the opening of the LoC virtually an invitation for militants to infiltrate into its territory from Pakistan-administered Kashmir.[124]

TERRORISM AND LAW ENFORCEMENT

Unsurprisingly, the issue of terrorism has been a heated source of friction and hostility rather than a fruitful area of cooperation. Accordingly, no material improvement has been noted since terrorism was put on the agenda of the foreign secretariats' talks in June 1997. In December 2001, following the attack on the Indian parliament, and under U.S. pressure, Musharraf pledged to join the war on terrorism. But in his address, the Pakistani president stopped short of defining what he considered to be a terrorist act and whether his pledge included Kashmiri insurgents, to whom Pakistan mostly refers as "freedom fighters."[125]

Somewhat better progress was made in the area of law enforcement when in December 1998, in conjunction with the New Delhi talks between the prime ministers, the two leaders decided to set up a mechanism for consultation and information exchange between the Central Bureau of Investigation in India and the Federal Investigation Agency of Pakistan, for mutual assistance in combating crime. Emphasis was laid on counterfeiting and cyber crimes.[126]

With the revival of the composite dialogue, law enforcement and terrorism were again put on the table in discussions between the home and interior ministries. The parties agreed to strengthen cooperation in tackling drug trafficking, among other efforts, through increased contacts between narcotics control authorities and the designation of officials in the high commissions to liaise on drug control issues. In June 2004, the parties announced their decision to share information and operational intelligence to curb narcotics trafficking. To enhance information sharing, "focal points" within the relevant agencies were identified and a calendar of periodic meetings between experts on both sides was finalized.[127]

The topic of terrorism, however, proved thornier, as controversies arose over the definition of terrorism and, hence, over how to deal with it. It is quite clear that, at this time, there can be no real cooperation to combat terrorism. Pakistan is backing Kashmiri militants as a means of pressuring India into engaging in a substantive political dialogue over Kahsmir, while India demands, as a precondition to any such dialogue, that Pakistan first stop supporting anti-Indian violence. Being a significant component of the conflict, terrorism is an indivisible part of the core conflict and thus extremely difficult to regulate by agreement.

Water Agreements

South Asia is one of the most populous and thirsty regions of the world. Its main watercourses, such as the Indus, the Ganges, and the Mahakali, flow through several countries in the region, bringing controversy and conflict, as well as water, along with them. One of the main potential sources of friction was the Indus Basin, shared between India and Pakistan, which contains six major rivers and one of the oldest and largest integrated irrigation systems in the world.[128]

Disputes over the allocation of water between Punjab (in today's India) and Sind (in today's Pakistan) remained unresolved under British rule. The 1947 partition left Pakistan as the water-short lower riparian, according most of the plentiful headwater to India, since five of the six rivers have their upper reaches in India or Indian-held Kashmir. In addition, the complex, centuries-old irrigation system, developed between the rivers first by the Mughals and then during British rule, which helped to turn deserts and marshlands into fertile fields, was also partitioned. Pakistani historians are still bitter about this high-handed 1947 division by the law lord Sir Cyril Radcliffe, to whom it fell to divide the former provinces of Punjab:

> In [Radcliffe's] optimism he allowed India to put its strong hand on the jugular vein of West Pakistan. Others, too, in an anxiety to settle the immediate political issue, hardly gave a second thought to the canals waters system as a whole and the implications of its divisions. Indeed it was a great folly.[129]

The water problem is also closely linked with the Kashmir dispute, as two of the system's rivers, the Jhelum and the Chenab, flow into Pakistan from within that disputed territory. India's having physical control over these waters is a perennial source of anxiety for Pakistan, who considers the matter as threatening its national security, its social and economic safety, and its very political independence; the economic life of about 80 percent of Pakistanis and of all of Pakistan's great cities, depend on acress to these waters.[130]

In March 1948, India cut off the water supply to some of the canals, affecting 5.5 percent of Pakistan's irrigated area, at a time when hundreds of thousands of refugees from the 1947 war had to be fed. Negotiations and interim agreements to resolve the life-threatening situation continued for thirteen years, but it took the active intervention and involvement of the World Bank to negotiate the Indus Waters Treaty.[131] When finally concluded in 1960, with World Bank brokerage and sponsorship, the treaty was hailed as a groundbreaking achievement by both countries.[132]

The treaty consists of twelve articles, covering seventy-nine paragraphs in length, in addition to eight detailed annexes spanning over 102 pages. It creates a complex and calculated arrangement, which takes into account differences in the flow of water in each of the Indus rivers, the needs of the riparian states, possible water usages, and the necessary constructions of waterworks. Most strikingly, the treaty does not contain identical rights and obligations but instead seeks to create a balanced share for the benefit of both sides.

In essence, the treaty divides several rivers between the parties, giving Pakistan principal rights to the western Indus, Chenab, and Jhelum systems and awarding India similar rights in the eastern rivers (the Ravi, Sutlej, and Beas), and according each the power to veto projects, on the rivers allotted to them, by their counterparts.[133] Each party is allowed three kinds of uses of the rivers designated to the other party: domestic use (drinking, washing), irrigation for agriculture, and "nonconsumptive use (mainly, hydroelectric power)."[134]

The arrangements under the treaty required the construction of a complex system of linking canals on the western rivers in Pakistan, to replace the water flow from the eastern rivers. This construction was expected to be a lengthy and expensive enterprise. To make it a worthwhile endeavor for Pakistan, the World Bank sponsored a $900 million assistance fund, by which Australia, Britain, Canada, Germany, New Zealand, and the United States and—notably—India, all donated funds to assist the country in developing the necessary infrastructure for the better allocation and delivery of its share of water under the treaty.[135] In addition, the World Bank remained a guarantor of the treaty. This international participation and guarantee not only made the conclusion of the treaty feasible in the first place, but has also operated to stabilize the cooperative regime in the long run.

Under Article VI of the treaty, the two countries were to exchange river and canal data regularly. Under Article VIII, they undertook to establish the Permanent Indus Commission, comprised of two commissioners of Indus water, one Indian and one Pakistani, who should each be a "high-ranking engineer competent in the field of hydrology and water reuse." The commission meets once a year, alternating between India and Pakistan. Its stated purposes include establishing and promoting cooperative arrangements for the treaty's implementation, encouraging cooperation in the development of the waters of the Indus system, examining and resolving by agreement any question which may arise from the interpretation or implementation of the treaty, and submitting an annual report to the two governments.[136] Under Article IX of the treaty, if the commission is unable to resolve a specific problem, the problem is to be referred to a neutral expert; if the neutral expert fails to resolve it, a court of arbitration may be convened.[137] The treaty itself stipulates that neither party can backtrack from, modify, or terminate the arrangement unilaterally and that any changes are only viable through the conclusion of a subsequent treaty, provided it is modified by both countries.[138] To date, disputes have either been resolved through negotiations between the commissioners or have remained unsettled. As earlier noted, the issue of the Baglihar Dam is the first contentious case for which a neutral expert has been appointed, and it remains to be seen how the two parties would react to his ruling.

Despite their enduring enmity, the two countries have, for the most part, remained faithful to their undertakings. True, there have been periodical allegations of violations of the treaty, raised mainly by Pakistan, concerning India's withholding of waters from the eastern rivers.[139] Moreover, in late 2001 and early 2002 Indian officials were reported to have threatened Pakistan with the unilateral abrogation of the Indus Waters Treaty, declaring, "When Pakistan cannot honour the Simla agreement and the Lahore Declaration, then why should we honour the Indus Waters Treaty?"[140] On February 16, 2002, Pakistan even claimed a "virtual suspension" of the treaty by India two months earlier, when it prevented inspection by Pakistani engineers of its Baglihar hydroelectric project on the Chenab. In addition, the Jammu and Kashmir Legislative Assembly also called for a review of the 1960 agreement; its stated grievance was that being limited in the use of the Jehlum and the Chenab waters, the State had suffered substantial losses in power and water and should therefore be compensated.[141]

But despite these mutual threats and allegations, the Indus Waters Treaty has, on the whole, been widely respected and has not been affected by any of the India-Pakistan wars or the ongoing skirmishes. Even in times of heated armed conflict, the parties respected the treaty, refraining from any attack on the water-sharing and distribution facilities.[142] Present disputes over water usage—such as those over the Baglihar project and the Wullar Barrage dispute—take a nonbelligerent form and are not very different from any great number of international disputes on the use of international watercourses.[143] A previous (somewhat similar) disagreement over the design and construction of a hydroelectric plant on the Chenab River was resolved in 1978 in an agreement reached with reference to the Indus Waters Treaty.[144] In fact, after the last round of bilateral negotiation over the Wullar Barrage dispute, in 1998, the parties both reaffirmed their commitment to the 1960 treaty.[145] The parties' consent to submit the Baglihar question to a neutral expert is another sign of their commitment to the regime.

Should we view the Indus Waters Treaty as unique? On the one hand, it is a remarkable example of a successful resolution of a major international river-basin conflict among warring parties.[146] As one senior officer of the World Bank has noted, "had the treaty not been concluded, it would have remained another major contentious issue between India and Pakistan, and massive economic aid for subsequent development might have been wholly or partially withheld."[147]

It is equally possible, however, that apart from the wisely, calculated design of the regime and its monitoring component, there is something special about water: that the parties could afford to fight over many issues but not over something so essential to their survival.

Trade Relations

For India and Pakistan, agreements in the sphere of trade were never a matter of choice, only one of greater or lesser choice, according to the reigning political climate; the economic partition of India into two sovereign states could not be as abrupt and complete as the political partition, since under British rule the subcontinent had been developed as a single, integrated economic unit. After the partition, "the economy of [the] Indian empire was violently vivisected," leaving two split economies, much dependent on each other, with Pakistan particularly dependent on India's broader economic base.[148] The "divided psyche" was also marked by complementary economies, with India being at the time Pakistan's most important buyer, consuming 60 percent of Pakistan's total exports.[149]

Immediately upon their inception in 1947, both countries became parties to the General Agreement on Trade and Tariffs (GATT) concluded that year. Under the GATT system, as well as its successor—the World Trade Organization (WTO)—member parties are prohibited from discriminating among other members and are required to treat each other according to the most favored nation (MFN) principle, which is to grant each member the best treatment granted to any other member. However, given the unique circumstances of the two new countries, Article XXIV(11) of the GATT stipulated that "measures adopted by India and Pakistan in order to carry out definitive trade arrangements between them, once they have been agreed upon, might depart from particular provisions of this Agreement, but these measures would in general be consistent with the objectives of the Agreement."[150] This provision has never been amended since, effectively barring any WTO intervention against Pakistan.

After years of repeated violations and terminations of trade agreements whenever political crisis struck—a series of failures amounting to what has been termed by some "economic warfare" or "economic war of attrition"—there came, in 1975–1976, in the wake of the Simla Agreement, a series of new agreements, which were developed throughout the next two decades.[151] These envisioned open trade relations, stipulating that the two countries accord each other's commerce MFN status. They also detailed the commodities available for export from India to Pakistan and vice versa and ordered the two countries to explore all possibilities for expansion of trade between them on the basis of mutual advantage. An agreement on shipping services was also concluded, as well as the Agreement for Avoidance of Double Taxation of Income Derived from International Air Transport, which was reached the following decade.[152]

India, in keeping with its undertakings, granted MFN status to Pakistan in 1995, but Pakistan has not yet reciprocated this gesture— although Nawaz Sharif himself acknowledged that "once businessmen underwrote a relationship, it was guaranteed to be stable."[153] Indeed, it was due to the increased interest of Pakistan's business community that the 1980s saw enhanced economic interaction, encouraged by the competitive character of Indian goods. This was also the period during which the two countries were engaged in efforts to found a regional grouping of south Asian countries, eventually to become SAARC.[154] Initially organized on a governmental and subgovernmental level, SAARC allowed trade to become more liberalized and private initiatives multiplied.

While businesspeople and Track II diplomats of both countries are in agreement that enhanced economic cooperation would significantly benefit both countries, some Pakistani businesspeople, especially small and medium-sized manufacturers, oppose increasing trade ties, which they perceive as facilitating what amounts to an Indian economic invasion of Pakistan. Their concerns derive from the fact that India, with its larger industrial economy, would enjoy a much more favorable balance of trade than its counterpart. As the Pakistani commerce secretary openly stated in 1998, "we cannot afford free trade with India as it would badly hurt our industry."[155] The words of the Pakistani minister of finance twenty years earlier exemplify just how confrontational and entangled with the body of the conflict, rather than "benign," trade issues are perceived to be by Pakistan: "India's economic offensive could endanger the very existence of Pakistan. It threatens our industry, trade, and all levels of our employment . . . The moment the floodgates of trade with India are allowed to be opened, the Pakistani industry would be swept out of the market."[156]

While the economic concern seems to be the driving one, Pakistani security forces and other officials have not made matters easier by insisting that any enhancement of trade with India must correspond with progress on the issue of Kashmir.[157]

On April 10, 1999, the two countries signed a memorandum of understanding in New Delhi to set up the India-Pakistan Chamber of Commerce.[158] However, at present, India still has no separate commercial office in Pakistan but only a commercial wing attached to the High Commission. At the same time, Indian trade bodies and commerce chambers do exchange visits and views with their Pakistani counterparts.

Following the Kargil War and the subsequent crises over Pakistani-backed militants' attacks in India, cooperation in the sphere of trade, as in most other spheres, was severly damaged. In the Seattle WTO summit in 1999, the Indian delegation refused even to talk to the Pakistani one until Pakistan agreed to sever all links with the Kashmir militants.[159] However, contacts were not rescinded altogether. In December 2000, representatives of the textile industry of both countries highlighted the need to exchange information and reach understandings on the production and pricing of textile products.[160] More recent bilateral discussions addressed further trade relaxations with respect to certain items. Pakistan, in particular, has since allowed the import from India of vaccines and medicines for AIDS and cancer. Pakistan also agreed to the importation of poultry and agricultural commodities such as garlic and potatoes.

Today, due to Pakistani trade barriers, there are still only about a thousand items that may be imported into Pakistan from India. Official trade between the countries amounts to around $600 million a year, less than 1 percent of their export volume. Unofficial trade (through third countries) is worth around $2 billion annually. Alongside the unofficial trade, there is also illegal trade, mainly in tires, cement, tea, dry fruits, and chemicals. Estimates are that the removal of trade barriers could generate trade volume of about $6 billion a year.[161] Meantime, trade volumes have been growing, with a recent agreement on direct maritime shipping expected to increase them further.[162]

It is generally assumed that trade relations would never be truly normalized until the political disputes, chiefly Kashmir, are settled. Otherwise, "the vested interests who oppose trade with India would have an easy opportunity to politicize the issue. No Government in Pakistan can, therefore, take the step of liberalized and free trade with India under the prevailing circumstances."[163]

This, however, does not stop the two nations from looking to each other in times of special need: As recently as October 2005, during a domestic shortage, India contracted to import 650 tons of onions from Pakistan. In the past, Pakistan has sought to meet domestic sugar shortages by importing sugar from India. More recently, it has decided to import Indian cotton to offset a shortfall in its own textile industry.

In the final analysis, India and Pakistan are still far from economic normalcy. Trade interaction at the moment is limited and relates only to issues of trade volumes and lists of importable and exportable items. Growth and development-oriented economic activities such as bilateral investments and partnerships in infrastructure, industry, manufacturing, and agriculture are mostly absent, though of late there have been reports of the countries allowing each other's banks to open branches in their respective territories. There is also a possibility that a couple of Indian companies will open outlets in Pakistan.[164]

Infrastructure

India has been negotiating for years the purchase of natural gas from Iran. One Iranian proposal was to lay down a gas pipeline to connect Iran's South Parks offshore fields with terminals in the Indian Gujarat state, through Pakistani land. Pakistan agreed to the plan, which would have been economically beneficial to it, but India refused for security considerations, preferring instead a much costlier sea route. The Pakistani prime minister Musharraf has repeatedly announced his willingness to explore options that would allay Indian security fears, such as involving international companies and making them shareholders in the project.[165] Possibilities of cooperation in the sphere of energy were explored in the Agra summit of July 2001, but with no apparent significant change.[166]

Recently, pipeline talks have been revived. In August 2005, the two countries agreed to set a timetable for the project and to conduct a cost study towards its implementation. This was a surprise development, given the continuing American pressure on both parties to abandon the project. The United States wishes to isolate Iran as part of its strategy in its conflict with Iran over the latter's nuclear program. At one point, the United States even threatened to impose sanctions if the pipeline project were pursued. Negotiations between India and Pakistan on the one hand and the United States on the other have so far failed to find common ground.

While interdependence and cooperation in the sphere of infrastructure may serve as a strong stabilizer of the relationship and a disincentive to escalation, it is at the same time, and perhaps for these exact reasons, a difficult goal to achieve.

Diplomatic Relations

The respective diplomatic delegates of both countries are the Indian high commissioner to Pakistan and the Pakistani high commissioner to India. During the 1965 war, the two commissioners were recalled to their home countries. They resumed their office after the 1966 Tashkent Declaration, which appealed for a restoration of the normal functioning of the diplomatic missions. Under the declaration, both governments pledged to observe the 1961 Vienna convention on Diplomatic Relations.

In August 1992, the two countries agreed on the Code of Conduct for Treatment of Diplomatic/Consular Personnel.[167] The code, like the Tashkent Declaration, did not add to the Vienna Conventions on diplomatic or consular relations; rather, it was a bilateral political reaffirmation of the internationally recognized norms. Occasional allegations of violations of the code are voiced by both sides.[168]

In February 2000, India expelled three Pakistani High Commission staff members for "indulging in activities incompatible with their official status." Pakistan, in response, protested against the "uncivilized and inhuman treatment meted out to the Pakistani High Commission Officials" by Indian intelligence operatives.[169]

After the December 2001 attack on the Indian parliament, India once again recalled its high commissioner in Islamabad and reduced the staff at the High Commission in Pakistan by half. Following the attack on the Indian army base in Kashmir in May 2002, India moved to expel the Pakistani high commissioner in New Delhi. Observers noted that these sanctions were an encouraging sign that India was ready to employ diplomatic measures in lieu of military ones.[170]

Diplomatic spats are regular occurrences between the two countries. In the not-too-distant past, these incidents tended to be graver in nature, with diplomats on either side claiming that they had been assaulted by local police of the other country. With each political crisis, diplomatic personnel of both countries were termed persona non grata and expelled, with the usual retaliatory expulsion following soon after. But diplomatic relations are resumed as regularly as they are severed. In May 2003, the two countries again appointed high commissioners, with the composite dialogue being renewed some months later.

Movement of People

As part of the post-Simla cluster of agreements, one regarding visas was concluded in 1974.[171] The agreement details the various types and terms of visas that may be accorded visitors from the other country, as well as the checkpoints for entry and exit in each country.

During the 1999 Lahore summit, the two prime ministers pledged to relax visa and travel procedures further.[172] Subsequently, the two sides discussed the opening of additional visa offices in the respective countries. In the weeks leading to the Agra summit of July 2001, India surprised Pakistan by announcing a unilateral relaxation of visa requirements on its end. Pakistan refused to reciprocate the gesture, regarding India's unilateral move not as a sign of goodwill but rather as a devious attempt to influence international attitudes in preparation for the summit.[173] This incident was another proof of the importance of bilateralism in the conclusion—and implementation—of islands of agreement, showing how unilateral measures may be interpreted with suspicion, even if prima facie benevolent.

To allow for movement of people from one country to the other, several transport links have been set up between the two countries in the form of air services, trains and buses. Private vehicular traffic is not allowed at all across the border. Activity on the transport links is a good barometer of interstate relations, to the extent that in times of hostility it is almost always suspended. Thus, after the attack on its Parliament in 2001, India immediately stopped the Delhi-Lahore bus and train services and also air services to and from Pakistan. Pakistan was also denied overflight rights in Indian airspace. After a de-escalation of tensions, all services were restored.

In general, transport links are an important relational issue and feature in most peace talks. Of late, the countries agreed to establish a railway service between Kokhropar in Pakistan and Munabao in India. The most significant development in this regard came in April 2005, when India and Pakistan decided to set up a bus route from Srinagar, capital of India-administered Kashmir, to Muzzafarabad, capital of Pakistan-administered Kashmir. Deepening the symbolism is the fact that India conceded to Pakistan's demand that the bus passengers should carry neither visas nor passports, but only locally issued identity documents. Pakistan, in turn, dropped its insistence that the service be limited to Kashmiris alone and that the papers to be carried from Srinagar should not bear a government of India stamp. India, too, agreed to respect papers issued by the government of Azad Kashmir, which it does not politically recognize.[174]

The "bus diplomacy" between the two countries continues as two more routes have now been added—the first from Amritsar (India) to Lahore (Pakistan), and the other from Amritsar to the Sikh pilgrimage center of Nankana Sahib in Pakistan. Another route is planned between Rawalakot in Pakistan and Poonch in India.

As earlier noted, in the aftermath of the devastating earthquake in Kashmir on October 8, 2005, India and Pakistan opened the Kashmir border to civilian crossings for the first time since 1947, so as to allow quake survivors to visit their friends and relatives on either side of the border and assist in survivors' rehabilitation. The new bus links will now allow for ongoing crossings of the LoC by Kashmiris on both sides.

Civil Aviation

Since 1976 India and Pakistan have maintained an open-skies policy with regard to commercial flights of each other's airlines in their respective airspace. This is a somewhat unusual policy, given the armed conflict in which the two countries have since been engaged in.

The attack on the Indian parliament in December 2001 took its toll on cooperation in the sphere of civil aviation too, as India quickly announced a ban on Pakistani commercial overflights. Nevertheless, within six months, following Musharaff's pledge to end all terrorist incursions in Kashmir, the ban was lifted and overflights resumed. Direct flights between India and Pakistan were restored only in January 2004.

Pakistani journalists downplayed the Indian conciliatory move, claiming that India stood to gain much more from the use of Pakistan's airspace than Pakistan of India's. Indian officials have not refuted this but only stressed the importance of any "de-escalatory move."[175] On the whole, it seems that although the agreement on civil aviation favors India in terms of the benefits it entails, this advantage has not been substantial enough—or else threatening enough—to frustrate cooperation.

Telecommunications and Postal Services

As part of its efforts to normalize relationship in all spheres, the Simla Agreement called for the resumption of telecommunication and postal services. Accordingly, in 1974 India and Pakistan concluded two pacts to cover these areas of cooperation.

The Agreement on Telecommunications is a detailed arrangement, laying out available services, alongside their rates, and stipulating the principle under which the technical and operational aspects of the telegraph and telephone services shall be decided by mutual consent of the respective telecommunication administrations of the two governments.[176] The agreement also established the Committee of Technical Experts, including experts from both countries, which should meet twice a year to discuss and resolve all outstanding problems relating to operational issues and settlement of accounts. In the event of the committee being unable to resolve a dispute, it shall be resolved through consultations between the two governments.[177]

A corresponding professional consultation mechanism was established under the postal agreement, with a similar method of dispute resolution in place.[178]

Both agreements refer to the international conventions and agreements on telecommunications and postal services as the documents governing their relations wherever the specific arrangements do not deviate from them.

Cultural Cooperation

In 1988 India and Pakistan concluded the Cultural Cooperation Agreement, "to promote Contacts between the peoples of the two countries in order to develop mutual understanding and appreciation."[179] The agreement encourages cooperation in art, culture, archeology, education, mass media, and sports and envisages reciprocal visits and exchange of people and information in the various spheres of art and culture.[180]

Moreover, under the agreement the two governments pledge to endeavor to provide facilities and scholarships to students and researchers of each other's country to study in its institutions of higher education and to participate in practical training programs. They also commit to represent each other faithfully in their official publications.[181]

To fulfill the objective of the agreement, an India-Pakistan joint commission was established, with the role of formulating cultural and exchange programs and reviewing the implementation of the accord.

Currently, the two nations share extensive cultural cooperation, which extends to film, theatrical performances, concerts, cricket matches, and more, although not without impediments or difficulties. Oftentimes, performances encountered strong domestic opposition and even threats. Pakistan has raised obstacles, mainly through visa regulations, for Indian performers; in India, extremists from the Shiv Sena Party were accused of disrupting a Pakistani singer's concert in 1998 and vandalizing a cricket pitch to stop a Pakistani team from playing there. And although Indian movies are very popular in Pakistan, the Pakistani government does not allow them to be screened publicly, in an effort to protect the Pakistani film industry.

Despite the difficulties, the importance of cultural cooperation in enhancing trust and understanding between these closely related rival societies remains uncontested. The governments recognize this and have frequently intervened to suppress domestic opposition and allow for cultural exchanges, as when the Indian government publicly assured safety and public protection to a Pakistani cricket team, earlier threatened by the Shiv Sena chief.[182] Cricket, in general, seems to be an important island of agreement: India and Pakistan have twice been joint hosts of the Cricket World Cup. Pakistan actively supported India in the latter's successful bid to host the 2010 Commonwealth Games. In elections within sporting bodies, especially in cricket, where on-field rivalry is markedly intense, the two countries regularly vote for and support one another.

People-to-People Initiatives
People-to-people initiatives are organized both through long-term institutionalized mechanisms and through short-term, less-institutionalized CBMs. The latter consist of such diverse measures of goodwill as the release of prisoners by one or both governments; the participation of senior military officials and civilian decision makers with their counterparts in

various joint seminars, or the surprising assistance extended by Kashmiri militants who donated blood and a Pakistani army plane, rushing tents and blankets to earthquake survivors in Gujarat, India.[183] Similarly, during the October 2005 Kashmir earthquake, which left more than eighty-seven thousand dead, India was quick to offer help to victims on the Pakistani side of the border. Pakistan extended its assistance to India in the wake of the tsunami the previous year. As these goodwill steps are taken mostly while active hostilities continue, they serve as a striking example of how management should be addressed in its broadest sense.

Alongside such makeshift CBMs, there are some more institutionalized people-to-people fora. One example is the Pakistan-India Peoples' Forum for Peace and Democracy (PIPFPD), which brings together several hundreds of Indians and Pakistanis every two years to address existing challenges and issues a joint invitation to both governments to participate in its discussions. The conferences of the PIPFPD address a wide range of topics, including the denuclearization of the conflict, the demilitarization of the Siachen Glacier, the situation in Kashmir, women and children status, discrimination and human rights abuses, corruption, democratization, agricultural strategies, environment, and trade.[184]

Even more striking is the institutionalized Track II diplomatic channel, named the India-Pakistan Neemrana Initiative, in honor of the Neemrana village in Rajasthan, in which its inaugural meeting was held in 1991. The Neemrana Initiative group was first founded by the United States as an alternative to a Track I Indo-Pakistani dialogue, but has over time grown to be an independent forum—in fact, an unofficial sounding-board for the two governments. The dialogue is conducted between eight members on each side, all of whom are prominent figures in the Indian and Pakistani public arena. Over the last decade there were times in which the Neemrana Initiative was the only channel of formal communication open to the two governments. Commenting on the importance of this exercise, reporters noted that

> smooth personal equations, established in the process, facilitated mutual communication. And the two sides could convey harsh, unpalatable points without causing offence. At times, they appreciated each other's compulsions and appeared to muster the will to find a way out or evolve a common position.[185]

And others add,

Track Two negotiations have no Government imprimatur. They involve serious engagement between influential writers, analysts and former decision-makers on problems of mutual interest for India and Pakistan. Ideas generated in the Track Two process certainly find their way into the popular debates in both countries and occasionally feed into the policy-making process.[186]

The experience of Neemrana as well as other people-to-people initiatives confirms the benefits inherent in institutionalized frameworks, within which ongoing stable relationships can evolve to form a healthy foundation from which disputes and friction may be dealt with.

Regional Cooperation

The South Asian Association for Regional Cooperation

The South Asian Association for Regional Cooperation (SAARC) comprises the seven countries of south Asia: Bangladesh, Bhutan, India, the Maldives, Nepal, Pakistan, and Sri Lanka, with China and Japan enjoying an observer status. While preparations for establishing the organization began as early as 1980, the SAARC's charter was first adopted in December 1985, at the first SAARC Summit of the Heads of State or Government of the seven nations.[187]

The SAARC objectives are to promote the welfare of the people of south Asia through economic growth and collective cooperation and collaboration in the economic, social, cultural, technical, and scientific fields. It is also designed to strengthen the member states as a group in international fora. Bilateral and contentious issues are explicitly excluded from the deliberations of the association.

Seven technical committees operate under the SAARC auspices, dealing with agriculture and rural development; communication and transport; social development; environment, meteorology, and forestry; science and technology; human resources development; and energy. In addition, specialized ministerial meetings are held to address matters of common concern, women and children matters, disabled persons, poverty, housing, tourism, information, environment, and more.

The SAARC runs several regional centers, which serve mainly as cooperation and information exchange centers, in the fields of agriculture, tuberculosis, documentation, meteorological research, and human resources development. Since 1987 it has also been operating a food security reserve of food grains for meeting emergencies in member countries.

It also incorporates a number of professional associations, which bring together professionals from the member countries.

In the course of time, SAARC adopted conventions on the suppression of terrorism and on narcotic drugs and psychotropic substances; in 2002 it finalized additional conventions on trafficking in women and on child protection (both now ratified by all members). Pakistan has not yet incorporated these conventions into its domestic legislation. As the SAARC has no enforcement mechanism of its own, it largely depends on its members' own implementation procedures.

SAARC has also created the Meteorological Research Centre and the Coastal Zone Management Centre for environmental purposes, in which both India and Pakistan partake.

In the 1999 Lahore Declaration, both countries reaffirmed their commitment to the goals and objectives of SAARC and pledged to concert their efforts towards a realization of the SAARC vision. Nevertheless, cooperation is less than perfect; thus, in July 2001, India stood out as the only SAARC country that did not send a delegation of children to participate in the South Asia Girl Child Symposium, which was held in Islamabad, a fact which made front page news in Pakistani newspapers.

SAARC's greatest challenge may lie in the area of regional trade. On April 11, 1993, the SAARC member states concluded the South Asian Preferential Trade Agreement (SAPTA) at the SAARC summit in Dhaka.[188] The SAPTA provided a broad framework of rules for a phased liberalization of intraregional trade, based on principles of overall reciprocity and mutuality of advantages. The agreement also provided for periodic rounds of trade negotiations among the member states, to discuss mutual concessions of tariffs and other barriers to trade.[189]

In its eighth summit in 1995, the SAARC decided to establish a South Asian Free Trade Area (SAFTA), along the lines of the European Free Trade Area, to further liberalize regional trade. In the most recent SAARC summit, the members' leaders agreed that SAFTA would enter into force on January 1, 2006.

In all of these activities, India and Pakistan are meant to collaborate as equal members of SAARC. In fact, under the terms of SAFTA, Pakistan would have to accord India better treatment than under an MFN rule, which it has not yet applied vis-à-vis India. Yet the tensions arising from the two states' actual inequality are evident. India aspires to act as the hegemonic leader of the region, claiming that its ability to project its power throughout the region is the best guarantee of south Asia's security and stability. Pakistan, naturally, is averse to the idea of an India-dominated regional power structure.[190] The introduction of the bilateral conflict into the regional instrument necessarily inhibits the latter's success.

Judging from its record, SAARC has been successful in promoting some bilateral cooperative efforts in several social and economic spheres. SAARC summits also serve as a convenient and natural venue for bilateral meetings and discussion between high-ranking Indian and Pakistani officials.[191] It was the SAARC summit that set the stage for Musharraf's dramatic handshake with Vajpayee, a much-needed conciliatory gesture after the shock of the attack on the Indian parliament. Given the setting of a regional cooperative endeavor, Vajpayee, who was caught a little off-guard, could not publicly resist the proffered hand.

The operation of SAFTA remains a crucial test for SAARC's ability to overcome bilateral obstacles. It has already had one proven success, with the conclusion of the Limited Agreement on Avoidance of Double Taxation and Mutual Administrative Assistance in Tax Matters, which is intended to apply among all SAARC members, even though India and Pakistan have not been able to come to a similar agreement bilaterally.

SACEP—Environmental Cooperation

India and Pakistan are both signatories to several international conventions on the protection of the environment.[192] Some of these conventions call for regional mechanisms of cooperation and monitoring.

The main established regional environmental organization is the South Asia Cooperative Environment Programme (SACEP), established through the initiative of the United Nations Environment Program (UNEP) in 1982 and composed of Afghanistan, Bangladesh, Bhutan, India, Maldives, Nepal, Pakistan, and Sri Lanka. The principal organs of SACEP are the Governing Council of Ministers, the Consultative Committee of Representatives of Member States, and the Secretariat, which is based in Colombo, Sri Lanka.

SACEP's large objective is to foster subregional cooperation in the areas of sustainable development. Through close work with the UNEP, SACEP has addressed a wide array of issues, including capacity building and institutional strengthening, conservation and sustainable use of biodiversity, management of conservation and ecosystems, assessment of environmental information, and education and enhancement of awareness of environmental matters.

Among other things, SACEP is responsible for implementing the South Asia Seas Action Plan—a subregional mechanism established under the United Nations Convention on the Law of the Sea—to which Bangladesh, India, Maldives, Pakistan, and Sri Lanka are all parties. The plan was adopted at a meeting of plenipotentiaries in New Delhi in March 1995 and came into force in January 1998.[193]

One of the plan's main goals is to encourage regional cooperative efforts in the area of marine pollution. Following the United Nations Convention on the Law of the Sea's provisions on the prevention, reduction, and control of marine pollution from land-based activities, Annex IV of the plan includes the Regional Program of Action for the Protection of the Marine Environment of the South Asian Seas from Land-based Activities. The plan's stated goal is the "Development of Regional Program for Monitoring of Marine Pollution in the Coastal Waters of the South Asian Seas and the Regular Exchange of Relevant Data and Information." The implementation of the plan is still in incubation.[194]

Cooperation in environmental protection should not be lightly viewed. In fact, in some respects, it is even more unusual than cooperation in the security sphere, as its derived benefits are not immediately apparent in terms of easing the resource constraint. Envrionmental protection is also not devoid of security considerations; in fact, researchers of the field observe that parties involved in environmental cooperation efforts are often conscious and wary of their possible security implications. Thus, with regard to possible maritime cooperation plans, researchers from the Sandia Corporation noted, "In South Asia, oceanography projects with foreign collaboration are often viewed with suspicion because of their bearing on national security."[195]

To illustrate this point, the researchers describe the suspicion that the Indian Ministry of Defense has exhibited towards a mission carried out by the Indian Department of Ocean Development (DOD). The mission had the stated purpose of gathering atmospheric radiation and aerosol data to improve general weather circulation models, and was to be carried out at sea, with the collaboration of eight American scientists on board the ship. Even though the mission was cleared by Indian naval intelligence, the Ministry of Defense was concerned that the data collected could be "crucial for underwater and submarine navigation." The researchers then note that if such was the reaction towards a marine scientific project carried out with American collaboration, any collaborative effort with Pakistan is bound to be viewed with even greater suspicion.

COSCAP—Civil Aviation

Formed in 1999, the Cooperative Development of Operational Safety and Continuing Airworthiness Programme of South Asia (COSCAP) is a cooperative agreement between India, Pakistan, Bangladesh, Bhutan, Nepal, the Maldives, and Sri Lanka. COSCAP is an International Civil Aviation Organisation project, which aims at improving the safety and efficiency of air transport in the region by sharing resources and providing expertise in training qualified flight operations and airworthiness inspectors.[196]

SAHR—Human Rights and People-to-People Initiatives

In the regional sphere too, alongside the formalized institutions of regional cooperation there are initiatives by civil society for cooperation in South Asia. One such initiative is the South Asians for Human Rights (SAHR), which in July 2000 brought together more than a hundred delegates from recognized human rights organizations in South Asian countries. Delegates represented civil society in Bangladesh, India, Nepal, Pakistan, and Sri Lanka. The SAHR describes itself as a democratic regional body, with a large membership base of people committed to addressing human rights issues at both national and regional levels.[197] The former Indian prime minister Shri Inder Kumar Gujral was quoted as saying that the SAHR "can develop as a track two initiative at pursuing government policies by non-governmental organizations."[198]

Analysis

The conflict between India and Pakistan has drawn much of the world's attention for the past fifty-eight years. Since 1998 it has been viewed with growing concern, as the parties' nuclear capabilities now endanger not only the population of the rivals—which, compounded, amounts to a quarter of the world's total population—but to the world at large. To date, even after the 1947 war, it has taken the lives of tens of thousands of civilians and combatants on both sides. In the 1990s alone, not including the Kargil War, approximately six thousand civilians and around fifteen hundred militants and members of the security forces were killed in Kashmir.[199]

India and Pakistan are, without doubt, a classic case of enduring rivalry. Identity issues, both sectarian and national, dating back to pre-partition days play a decisive role in the Indo-Pakistani relationship and to a large extent lie at the heart of the impasse on the disputed territorial issues.[200] The necessity of generating, as it were, instant national identities has forced the two nations to define themselves in opposition to one another: India, a democracy in a mostly undemocratic region, founded on the principles of secular government, prides itself on encompassing vastly different ethnic, religious, and linguistic populations. Pakistan is also ethnically and linguistically diverse; but its founder, Muhammad Ali Jinnah, wanted to establish a one-nation state in the hope that the universal name of "Muslim" would allow it to transcend ethnic differences. Since its inception, Pakistan has been torn between an unclear democracy and Islamic extremism, which has bred several military coups throughout its history and continues to wield considerable military influence over its political life. As former Indian Foreign Secretary (and later national security adviser), S. N. Dixit, has expressed it,

> both countries achieved independence at the same time. While India, despite all its diversities, tensions and problems, has gradually consolidated its democratic and administrative institutions, Pakistan has gone through a roller-coaster ride of constantly changing political arrangements. Political institutions have no coherence and stability. Armed forces remain the ultimate centre of authority . . . [Pakistanis] even assert that being different from India in respect to practising democracy is necessary for Pakistani identity.[201]

The conflicting notions of identity, ethnicity, religion, and political structures all feed into the dispute over Kashmir, which continues to be the most contentious tangible issue of the conflict and a perpetual low-intensity conflict zone. Far exceeding mere territorial significance, Kashmir has long attained a symbolic status, not as the source of the rivalry but as its epitome, a testament to the dual process of decolonization and nationalization. In the words of Khan Zaman Mirza of the Institute of Kashmir Studies in Azad Kashmir,

> With its military occupation of Jammu and Kashmir, India . . . wants to negate and falsify the "Two-Nation Theory" . . . the very basis of the creation of Pakistan and that of the historic struggles of the Kashmiri Muslims for freedom and accession with Pakistan. It can therefore be said that Jammu and Kashmir state is a battle ground, where the national ideologies of India and Pakistan are being tested.[202]

And Indian political scientist Manorama Kohli offers a counter-opinion,

> Thus the happenings on the question of Kashmir seem to have further strengthened the urge for security for which the [Pakistani] interpretation given was "a struggle for existence and survival" and the blame was put on India as her "inability to reconcile herself to our existence as a sovereign independent state."[203]

On the other side of the border, where partition is largely conceived as the primal sin that has shaped the bilateral relationship irrevocably as conflict, Kashmir is a "lost limb" of a once whole body.

At the moment—and for the past six decades—the parties' positions remain entrenched. India ultimately seeks the fixing of the LoC as the international boundary (despite some public announcements that favor repossession of Pakistan-administered Kashmir), the end of all militancy, and the integration of Jammu and Kashmir into the Indian Union. Pakistan, in contrast, insists on the implementation of UN resolutions and the holding of a plebiscite, hoping the popular vote would support full accession to Pakistan. Pakistani as well as Kashmiri leaders have often announced that they would object to any peace agreement in which Kashmir would be divided along the LoC or, in other words, to agreements under which the LoC becomes the permanent border. India, conversely, challenges the validity of the UN resolutions on Kashmir and holds that the plebiscite requirement is no longer relevant, given the significant demographic changes that have occurred in the population of Kashmir since 1948. Both rivals quell Kashmiri aspirations for independence.

The parties cannot even agree on a mechanism through which the conflict should be discussed: India perceives the dispute as a bilateral issue, which should be resolved by the two parties themselves, while Pakistan wishes to internationalize the dispute and repeatedly calls for third-party intervention.[204] Not surprisingly, reliance on international legal principles, such as territorial sovereignty or the right to self-determination, has done little to promote resolution.

The remaining territorial disputes—the maritime boundary, Sir Creek, and the Siachen Glacier—all seem to be breathing the troubled air of Kashmir. The Siachen Glacier is geographically and strategically tied to Kashmir; the other two less so, but their resolution depends on the overall relationship between the parties. In addition, these disputes are intertwined amongst themselves, as without resolution of the Sir

Creek controversy there would be no agreed land point from which to demarcate the maritime boundary.

Of the other outstanding bilateral disagreements, those that are water related, such as Baglihar and the Tulbul project, loom most threateningly. Much will depend on how the current arbitration process over Baglihar develops.

A 2004 report by the International Crisis Group observed that "it is hard to overstate the level of mistrust between India and Pakistan . . . The governments have developed a mindset in which they are willing to suffer immense losses to score minor points."[205] India's official rhetoric on Kashmir warns against any change, forecasting a wave of secession that would lead to the breakup of the Indian Union and a wave of anti-Islamic violence across the country. Pakistani policy on Kashmir is dominated by the military apparatus, which fuels a Muslim versus Hindu sentiment and fear.

To what extent this rivalry between the governments is also a rivalry between the people is hard to determine. Polls conducted in India have shown that popular perceptions are sensitive to fluctuations, supporting hard-line policies in times of crisis and peace initiatives in times of relative calm; on the whole, the issue of Kashmir is not high on the agenda of most Indians, who are more concerned about pressing domestic problems, such as inflation, unemployment, or law and order.[206] Some Pakistani commentators have gone even further, arguing boldly, that "it seems like having the problem has been more advantageous to the rulers of both countries than truly solving it."[207]

As one Pakistani lawyer and commentator summarized it—

> the most attractive view of India among the Pakistani elite and decision makers is that of a hegemonic and a bully. The Indian view of Pakistan is that of a theocratic and militaristic state. An objective view would probably disagree with both of them. While there are many factors and developments that have contributed towards the formation of both perceptions and misperceptions as well as self and adversary's images, three factors seemed to have contributed relatively more than the others; history, media, weak and irrational leadership.[208]

Whoever the dominant forces perpetuating enmity, the conflict has endured despite the high level of communication, which has accompanied its history in the shape of numerous meetings, consultations, and negotiations, both direct and mediated. This is surely proof that its persistence is not due to any scarcity of efforts at resolution. In a speech delivered during his visit to Washington in September 2000, then Prime Minister Vajpayee succinctly expressed his frustration with the insistence of the U.S. leaders that dialogue would end all conflict:

> We are continuously told to talk to Pakistan. Even here I was told that India should show its neighbors that democracy is about dialogue. Ok, I say, let's talk, but what will we say to Pakistan? Will we say, "How is the weather" or will we say, "How are your wife and children?"[209]

At the same time, the parties seem to be in agreement that neither side would be able to force a solution to its favor militarily.[210] Dr. Moonis Ahmar of the Department of International Relations at the University of Karachi has noted that "As compared to the Indo-Pakistan wars, another round of hostilities between the two countries is conceived suicidal. In the last 23 years, the art of war has changed and the two countries have accumulated billions of dollars of sophisticated weapons. Given the situation, any future war in the sub-continent will be a zero-sum game."[211]

Neither India nor Pakistan is a rich country; both must deal with extensive poverty, malnutrition, disease, and lack of education. The need to keep the conflict going thus exacts a heavy price from both governments.[212] In figures: India's military expenditure for the year 2005 was almost $19 billion, 2.9 percent of its GDP. Its infant mortality rate is 5.6 percent, its illiteracy rate 40.5 percent. One quarter of its population lives below poverty line. Pakistan's military expenditure was $3.8 billion, or 4.9 percent of its GDP. Its infant mortality rate is 7.2 percent, illiteracy 51.3 percent. One third of its population lives below poverty line.[213] Nonetheless, the two countries continue to engage in a resource-draining and destabilizing military competition, in which the ever-turning sword of potential war (and even a nuclear one) hovers above.

And yet, if one examines other conflicts around the world, then shifts back to the Indian-Pakistani scene, one cannot avoid the surprising observation that although the parties are engaged in one of the gravest of enduring armed conflicts, they somehow also manage to maintain a seminormal relationship in most important spheres of their interstate relations. Trapped between the perceived need to invest in the conflict and the very real resource constraint, the two throughout their history have found mutual interest in limiting the scope of their hostility and creating regimes of active and ongoing cooperation.

The phenomena of free civil aviation, movement of people (even if restricted and monitored), official cross-border trade (albeit limited), water sharing, regional environmental cooperation, postal and telecommunication services, shared culture and sports, as well as some of the security arrangements I described above—are anything but typical of what we conceive of as a "normal" relationship between parties to an armed conflict. In a way, these phenomena challenge us to redefine our view of what is indeed normal.

Building Islands of Agreement

To be able to exercise containment and collaboration while maintaining their commitment to the conflict, India and Pakistan must limit agreement to spheres unconnected—whether physically or politically—to the core dispute over Kashmir.

It is for this reason that issues such as the Siachen Glacier and the Sir Creek have not yet been resolved and that fighting in both locations continues. Both areas, as well as the maritime boundary, are geographically connected to the fundamental dispute over borders, especially in the LoC area. Hence, to extract them from the conflict and resolve them separately would be more difficult. As Ashutosh Misra of the Institute for Defence Studies & Analysis in New Delhi notes,

> the biggest challenge for the leadership is to minimize the "linkage politics." All the pending disputes between India and Pakistan are victims of this linkage politics, as all these disputes are in one way or the other related to the larger dispute of Kashmir . . . In other words, the disputes are pending not because they are intractable, but because they are linked to a larger one.[214]

The Tulbul and Baglihar water projects, in contrast, are relatively separable from other issues, and water allocation in general is a sphere intuitively and institutionally kept out of armed conflict's way. It is a controversy maintained at the political level and around which neither party allows violent clashes to evolve. At least in the case of Baglihar, the parties have even agreed to submit their positions to the scrutiny of a third-party arbitrator.

The ability to shield water from war is no mean achievement. Under different reasoning, the joint watercourses flowing through Kashmir could easily have been made the linchpin of the territorial feud. One need only consider the recent threat by a Pakistani minister's that Pakistan may have to resort to war to resolve the issue of Baglihar.[215] Equally, the high stakes involved in the control of water resources might have made cooperation over water resemble the more-obstructed cooperation in the security sphere. Instead, it appears that these high stakes are what drove the parties to exclude the sphere of water from their conflict in the first place.

Water, in general, seems a peculiarly agreement-prone sphere; as international law scholar Joseph Dellapenna has written, "no matter how violent conflict between states sharing a common water source might become, and especially when water itself has played a central role in the conflict, water facilities have remained off limits to combat, cooperative water arrangements have been negotiated, and pre-existing arrangements have remained intact."[216]

It is therefore probable that the essentiality of water resources places targeting of water facilities outside the scope of acceptable military activities, somewhat like weapons of mass destruction.

The Indus Waters Treaty is especially commendable, as its function is much more than merely limitation. Besides preventing the targeting of water facilities or the allocating of water shares, it also creates an ongoing interdependency in which the parties enjoy various water usages (consumptive and nonconsumptive) and are required to cooperate continuously in its implementation.

There is little doubt that the crucial role played by the World Bank in mediating and securing the Indus Waters Treaty, as well as in raising the substantial necessary side payments to Pakistan from other countries, has been an indispensable stabilizing factor, as well as a kind of ongoing monitoring mechanism, and remains so today.

The ability to exclude certain kinds of weapons—namely, chemical (and, to a much more limited extent, nuclear)—from the sphere of combat is attributable to two main characteristics connected with their use: first, the clear distinction between these weapons and conventional weapons; and second, the material disincentives to use them—they are largely inessential (in a sense that war can go on perfectly well, and for longer, without them), potentially suicidal, and carry a fiercely condemnable public and international image. Their incorporation into the battlefield would therefore only unnecessarily impose higher costs on both sides, without much probable gain.

While the decision to exclude unconventional weapons from the battlefield might well have been a harmonious decision taken unilaterally on each side, the parties nevertheless chose to formalize it bilaterally and explicitly, adding some monitoring mechanisms, with a view to reinforcing this containment effort.

In the sphere of free trade, the worry over relative gains, which is less apparent in the other nonmilitary spheres of the relationship, still inhibits greater cooperation. Pakistan's reluctance towards freer trade with India derives from its concern as to India's higher prospective gains from such an enterprise. Higher relative gains may in time be translated into more power, which would, in turn, jeopardize Pakistan. As Pakistan perceives India's economic superiority primarily in security terms, it links any further cooperation in trade to progress on the core issues. It remains to be seen whether the regional SAFTA agreement will be successful in removing this obstacle to bilateral trade.

In spheres where relative gains have seemed minimal, as in the cases of postal, telecommunications, or even air services, agreements that entailed identical obligations were complied with even though it is highly unlikely that they did entail equal costs and benefits. High level of compliance in these spheres may have been due to the relatively minor inequalities of gains or losses and to the fact that, unlike trade, reciprocation of such innocuous services were unthreatening to domestic constituencies.

One unique sphere of cooperation is that of cultural exchanges and sporting events. Cultural sharing is singularly intimate as well as diffused cooperation. It touches people's lives directly and without mediation, through the television screen, movie theaters, or the pages of a book or a newspaper. A sensitive barometer of relations, it is also highly susceptible to fluctuations in the political atmosphere. A cricket match or a rock concert carry as much symbolic force when they happen as when they are cancelled.

Indo-Pak islands have varied not only in subject matter but also in form. One variable has been the degree of formality with which an agreement was concluded, which in turn informed the degree of compliance attained. On the whole, informal agreements were more susceptible to the effects of political mood swings; the 1992 agreement on disengagement in the Siachen Glacier was never formalized and thus had never really come into effect. While the influence of the general political atmosphere was apparent in the more formalized agreements too (such as the ones on cultural cooperation or security), it is nevertheless true to say that arrangements that were incorporated into formal and institutionalized agreements have proved more resilient. In some cases, as in the moratorium on nuclear tests or the prohibition on attacking nuclear installations, previously verbal undertakings were formally incorporated into a mutual, signed agreement, adding to their political clout.

The Indus Waters Treaty is an exceptional regime, which includes a formal arbitration mechanism, now put to the test of the Baglihar dispute. Most islands of agreement have incorporated no enforcement or dispute resolution mechanisms, but only enabled deliberations through joint commissions or other joint monitoring and consultation bodies. It is very likely that the ongoing collaboration between specialized bureaucrats (as in the fields of water, telecommunication, trade, etc.) has been useful in preserving the agreements and ensuring compliance. In fact, analysts have noted that those agreements that were not accompanied by a formal consultation or dispute resolution body, such as the agreement on airspace violations, were more susceptible to violations and suspension in times of crisis (though it is questionable whether such disparate spheres as military flights and telecommunication are entirely comparable).[217] By the same token, the full implementation of the arms control agreements, such as the Agreement on the Prohibition of Attack against Nuclear Installations and Facilities, were impeded by the absence of verification measures. As previously noted, the agreement required both sides to exchange lists of all nuclear facilities. However, as one Indian commentator has told the story,

> immediately after the two sides exchanged lists, suspicion grew over whether the lists were complete. Neither India nor Pakistan had the means to ascertain the accuracy of the lists; hence, each accused the other of concealing certain nuclear facilities (a significant omission at a time when neither country admitted to conducting nuclear tests). The absence of verifiability might have been overlooked if the two countries already had a record of trust-building measures, but without such a record, India and Pakistan remained mired in mistrust.[218]

In spite of these impediments, there is no doubt that dialogue remains vital to both sides; even the direct dialogue between the respective DGMOs, via the existing hotlines, has been regarded with respect by both the parties and observers, regardless of its poor record of effectiveness in times of crisis. Moreover, since the establishment of the DGMO hotline, other hotlines have materialized and more agencies (the navies, for example) have been considering setting up lines of their own.

Bilateral efforts have been complemented by regional ones; that its two most powerful members are also engaged in an armed conflict is no doubt a challenge to the SAARC. So far, however, SAARC has been successful in generating cooperation on several social and economic issues, as, for example, on the avoidance of double taxation, even though India and Pakistan have never agreed on this issue bilaterally. SAARC's greatest test is still to come, when it attempts, through SAFTA, to force Pakistan to remove its barriers to trade with India. The organization has recently reached an agreement on the establishment of an arbitration council, with the purpose of providing a legal framework for the settlement of commercial, investment or other disputes referred to the Council by agreement through conciliation and arbitration. To what extent India and Pakistan would make use of this arbitration council remains to be seen.

Finally, while international law has been ineffectual in settling any of the core disputes—both parties citing the principles of territorial integrity, the right to self-determination, or the prohibition on the use of force to reinforce their positions—it has nevertheless had a role to play in the building of islands of agreement. In several cases, such as the code of conduct for the treatment of diplomatic or consular personnel, general norms of international law were incorporated into bilateral, explicit commitments. The agreement on the prohibition on the use of chemical weapons was much facilitated by the concurrent efforts to create an international multilateral treaty banning such use. And the Indus Waters Treaty was founded on one internationally accepted principle of transboundary water sharing, namely, the joint management of transboundary watercourses. In all these cases, international law served to strengthen the political and legal force of the bilateral islands of agreement.

The Way Ahead

The large number of islands of agreement between India and Pakistan does not appear to impress many of the south Asian scholars, who remain largely skeptical as to their effectiveness. To them, such limited agreements act more as crisis prevention tools (or, as they are sometimes known in the literature, conflict avoidance measures) and mostly failed ones at that.[219] As proof, they remind us of the ease with which crises recur in the area, emphasizing the Kargil War as a violation of the Simla Agreement (under which both sides agreed to respect the LoC) as well as of the agreement on military exercises (which calls for advance notice on troop movement). Similarly, they claim, the agreement on airspace violations and the DGMO hotline have both proved ineffectual in preventing the shooting down of the Pakistani airplane in the summer of 2000. The skeptics also direct our attention at the unilateral pledge taken by India in November 2000 not to launch aggressive operations against the militants: though the cease-fire was extended beyond the initial plan, violence seemed only to rise, and the killing of civilians and security forces by Pakistani-backed militants was unabated.[220]

Quite apart from the fact that others involved in the process challenge this evaluation, it is more to the point that those who view the process negatively have tended to focus their attention almost exclusively on agreements in the security sphere. To reach a fair assessment of the situation, however, one must develop a more stereoscopic outlook on the total bilateral relationship, with its myriad facets. To be reminded of the Simla Agreement solely in the context of its border regulations is to miss the cluster of other issues Simla, as well as its predecessors and successors, have successfully managed.

There is also an optical illusion that causes onlookers to pay less attention to agreements that are observed and maintained, or even to the fact that those violated were, in fact, adhered to for long periods before and after the violating acts. When the critical spotlight is invariably turned upon incidents of noncompliance as the irrefutable confirmation for the futility of any future resolution, this cannot fail to bring the parties further apart than need be.

But a fair assessment is not just a question of past or even present achievement; it must also involve some appraisal of the cumulative effect of islands of agreement and their power to shape the future.

Given the diffusion of agreements across time and spheres, it is safe enough to conclude that even in bulk they were not instrumental in advancing a comprehensive resolution. More poignantly still, one must also take on board the possibility that this largely successful relationship management has in fact been detrimental to the chances of a broader agreement precisely because it has rendered the status quo not quite unbearable. Put another way, once the benefits of peace have already been reaped by some measure or another by people on both sides, what incentive remains for making further concessions? For example, had water not been regulated by the Indus Waters Treaty, it is entirely possible that water shortage would have impelled the parties to compromise on Kashmir, as a source or intersection of regional water.

One possible answer may be that the two nations have already faced many unbearable situations vis-à-vis each other, the culmination of which has been the partition and four wars. To let them "fight it out" a fifth time may mean a nuclear catastrophe, when there is no indication that either side is that inclined. In fact, with each crisis, the instincts of Indians and Pakistanis seem to tend towards immediate rapprochement.

Another answer may lie in the sheer dimensions of the two rivals, in terms of land, population, and resources. It is conceivable for the conflict in Kashmir to continue indefinitely without a single island of agreement in place (excluding, perhaps, the allocation of water). The fact is that even the loss of a thousand lives in Kashmir is too small and too remote to be much noticed in New Delhi or Karachi. On such a scale, barring a cataclysm, it is difficult to imagine an event dramatic enough to transform the rivals' fundamental positions on the conflict. If so, it would be fair to conclude that the islands of agreement already in place are not to blame for the conflict's continuation.

At the same time, when we come to consider the number and range of the islands in place, we may well ask why they have not functioned more dramatically to generate broader accord. Beyond the obvious answer that the rivals' underlying interests are too intensely divergent to be harmonized by partial agreements, another is the problem I have identified in Chapter 1 regarding the role of islands as a "trustworthiness test."[221] If the limited agreements the parties have managed to reach were also to become, for them, a test of each other's future trustworthiness in a more comprehensive settlement, then any breach by one side becomes an eagerly pounced upon indication that nothing broader could ever be maintained. Pakistan's violations of the Simla Agreement and the agreement on military exercises on the one hand, and India's violations of the agreement on airspace violations on the other, are declared by India and Pakistan, respectively, to be the ultimate proof of their rival's real intentions being other than peace seeking. India's flagrant untruthfulness in its 1992 declaration on chemical weapons is a striking case in point. What, then, each side might ask, is the use of assuming self-limitations if those are exploited by the other side to its own advantage? What is the use of lines of communication if they are used to disperse disinformation? And what is the benefit in an arms control agreement if there is no telling whether the other party cheats?

While it is safe to assume that as long as all agreements are respected and abided by, trust and understanding are increased, intuition must lead one to conclude that violations of agreements contribute more to distrust and suspicion than other comparable belligerent acts. In his remarks concerning the failure of the Lahore and Agra summits, India's deputy high commissioner in Islamabad blamed Pakistan, and stated,

"The experience has eroded the trust and confidence that Pakistan would be ready to work with India for the betterment of our people. India today is naturally cautious and is no longer willing to take Pakistan's declaratory statements at face value."[222]

Remarking on the resumption of civilian flights between the two countries, after their suspension in 2001, he then added—

"Some recent comments suggesting that Pakistan was backtracking on its commitments have no doubt delayed the possibility of further measures and also resurrected concerns about reliability and trust."[223]

While the danger of failing the litmus test for future reliability is a genuine one, the solution is not to eliminate islands of agreement, but to increase their number and range. Indeed, one of the most prevalent criticisms leveled against the two governments by observers of the conflict on both sides is that they do not do enough to bring people together. If the governments make human interaction easier, through enhanced cultural and educational cooperation, expanded trade and less restricted movement of people, this would greatly contribute to the building of trust between the two societies and to the ability of domestic constituencies to influence, or at the very least question, their governments' hard-line positions. As one Indian scholar has remarked, "due to restricted people-to-people interaction and limited exposure, people largely rely on the government's information."[224] The governments, in turn, portray their hard-line stance on Kashmir as an achievement.

In order to assess with any validity the influence of the existing islands of agreement on popular perceptions, one would have to imagine what these popular perceptions might have been, had no agreements been concluded at all—no civil aviation, movement of people, exchange of students and scholars, any kind of official trade or the world cricket series. It takes no great counterfactual effort to surmise that the ongoing contacts at various levels, as provided for or encouraged by the different agreements, help, at the very least, to press home the importance and benefits of cooperating with the enemy.

At this time, however, existing contacts are insufficient to generate a bottom-up movement that would reshape the leaderships' political entrenchment. One must only regard the degree of suspicion with which some original ideas, voiced by Musharraf in October 2004, on the need to look at new possible solutions for Kashmir, were greeted on both sides: Musharraf's premise, in what he called his offer of "food for thought," has been that the two nations must now exclude the plebiscite on the one hand, and the internationalization of the LoC on the other, as unacceptable principles to both. He proposed, instead, that Kashmir be divided up into seven regions based on geography and ethnicity—and not necessarily on religion; next, that both countries should withdraw troops from these mini-regions, in a phased process. It would then be left up to the Kashmiris, he suggested, along with India and Pakistan, to decide whether they would prefer an Indo-Pak joint administration of the territories or to be placed under UN governance.

The immediate Indian reaction, voiced by a Foreign Ministry spokesman, was to reproach Musharraf for first presenting his proposal in public before discussing it bilaterally, at first, through diplomatic channels. Newspapers reported that senior Indian officials have said they would never consider substantially re-drawing India's boundaries, as Musharraf's proposal would suggest. Former Indian Foreign Minister Jaswant Singh said: "Mapmaking has to stop in South Asia. Such attempts would not be acceptable [even] in disguise."[225] One of India's leading journalists even suggested the proposals were "intellectually unsettling" and "politically hazardous."[226]

In Pakistan itself, Musharraf's address caused an uproar: political parties, religious groups, jihadis and right-wing intellectuals, all accused the president of making a U-turn on Kashmir. Only four days after his public presentation, the Pakistan Foreign Ministry issued a statement, claiming Musharraf had not made any actual proposal for resolving the problem of Kashmir but had merely solicited the media to conduct a public debate on the issue.[227]

It is possible that it is this resistance to any fundamental change that makes islands of agreement an easier refuge for both sides. Still, if we honestly face the two alternatives—"a war to end all wars," possibly with a nuclear dimension or a hopeless local feud grinding on for generations with no abatement—islands of agreement easily show themselves to be the most hopeful course.

CHAPTER THREE

Greece and Turkey: Archipelagos of Agreement

So the many nations of men from the ships and the
  shelters
Along the front of the deep sea beach marched in order
By companies to the assembly . . .
And the place of their assembly was shaken, and the
  earth groaned . . .

HOMER, *THE ILIAD*, TRANS. RICHMOND LATTIMORE
(BOOK II, LINES 91–95)

On the eve of the new millennium, the earth surrounding the Aegean Sea "groaned" once more; this time, not for the rumblings of the tread of armies. An earthquake estimated at 7.4 on the Richter scale struck the city of Izmit in northwest Turkey in the early morning hours of August 17, 1999, in thirty seconds, and in the aftershock of the days to come, more than eighteen thousand people lost their lives, more than forty-four thousand were injured and three hundred thousand were made homeless. On November 7, another earthquake struck the region of Athens, leaving 143 Greeks dead, 200 injured, and 100,000 homeless. Nature had thus ravaged the two countries' largest cities in less than a month. Whether or not this was a signal from the gods, the quakes were to become the starting guns for a dramatic shift in Greek-Turkish relationship.

Mutual help was at once offered and accepted. For weeks and months, Greek and Turkish rescue teams, the first to appear on each other's scenes, doctors and humanitarian workers labored shoulder to shoulder in the rubble, hospitals, and makeshift shelters. In the meanwhile, the two foreign ministers, George A. Papandreou of Greece and Ismail Cem of Turkey, seized on the opportunity and initiated widescale cooperation on various related issues, able to claim that they were acting on a "popular mandate."[1] Mayor Dimitris Avramopoulos of Athens declared, "Athens and Istanbul responded to the conspiracy between history and nature in order to promote rapprochement between Greece and Turkey."[2]

Down the ages, history and nature have certainly been "conspiring" around the shores of the Aegean as hardly anywhere else. Human politics have always had to pay their dues to the fortunate-fatal geography of the region: in a statement to the U.S. Senate Committee on Foreign Relations on January 15, 1952, as the Committee was considering the accession of Greece and Turkey to the North Atlantic Treaty, General of the Army Omar Bradley, Chairman of the Joint Chiefs of Staff, commented on the two countries' geopolitical advantages:

> From the military viewpoint, it is impossible to overstate the importance of these two countries . . . Greece and Turkey occupy strategic locations along one of the major east-west axes . . . Located as they are—and allied with the free nations—they serve as powerful deterrents to any aggression directed towards Southern Europe, the Middle East, or North Africa. The successful defense of these areas—any one or all of them—is dependent upon control of the Mediterranean Sea. Greece and Turkey block two avenues to the Mediterranean . . . Greece . . . presents a barrier along the overland route from the Balkan States located to her north. Turkey, astride the Bosporus and Dardanelles, guards the approach by water from the Black Sea to the Mediterranean and to the Suez Canal and Egypt farther south. Turkey, too, flanks the land routes from the North to the strategically important oil fields of the Middle East.[3]

This prized crossroads location, as well as the natural advantages of a jagged coastal geography, have made both lands, at one point in time or another, ideal power bases for empires. But the need to share their riches has often set the two peoples in competition over these gifts of the gods—not the slightest of which has been the embrace of those "free nations" to the West. And while the West has often conceived of the two countries together—Greece and Turkey have more often than not defined themselves in opposition to one another.

Today, the two ancient-new sovereign states eye each other with more or less peaceful wariness. But their feud has lasted a long time and has had, over the course of its existence, wielded some catastrophic results— not so catastrophic, perhaps, as those engendered by the fitful birth of India and Pakistan, but grave enough for those affected by them. And perhaps the rivalry should be measured less by any material advantages it ever held in store for an ascendant party, still less by its present chances of erupting into widescale warfare, and more by the degree to which it still fuels a sense of national identity in both countries. Also, perhaps, by what may be called a vocabulary of aggression it has instilled in its participants, as they continue to spend billions of dollars on rearmament, in constant muscle flexing across the Aegean.

Both Greece and Turkey are the state-children of former empires, the Byzantine and the Ottoman. As empires and as nation-states they have emerged from under each other's cloaks, ethnically and territorially. To a large extent, the two countries' modern identities are a construct of the animosity between them: most of the present Greek territory had been under Turkish rule for at least four hundred years. Modern Greece emerged as a sovereign state at the end of a national independence struggle, supported by European forces, against Ottoman rule; it was the culmination of the educated Greek elite's long aspiration to achieve a modern statehood through popular revolution. But centuries of Ottoman domination had made it inevitable that, by now, the national identity that led to irredentist Greek nationalism would be defined by the difference from and opposition to the Turk: occupied as opposed to occupier, Christian as opposed to Muslim. Anti-Turkism was inculcated through the educational system and the official rhetoric of most of the nineteenth and twentieth centuries. Turkey, on the other hand, heaved itself pretty much unaided into modern statehood after World War I and at the end of an armed struggle against the occupying and invading Greek army.[4]

"On top of a denied common past," writes Turkish historian Sükrü S. Gürel, "the two peoples, in order to hold on to the best defined part of their identity—their nationhood—have to continue recalling their 'national liberation struggles.'"[5] Though some, mainly Greek, historians now tend to date the Greek-Turkish conflict in its relevance to the present day only as far back as 1974 (the year of the Turkish invasion of Cyprus), the persistence of national insecurities well into the here and now attests to the length of the two nations' entangled history. The more so that in the age of a united Europe power is more than ever relative and disjointed, played off across several fronts.

In both the traditional scales of area and population Greece is much the smaller of the two countries and, in popular lore, tends to regard itself as a David to the Turkish Goliath—one-sixth the size in terms of territory, population and military force, facts frequently emphasized by Greek politicians.[6] As Greek politician Fanny Palli Petralia has put it, "Turkey represent[s] a real threat to [the] Aegean islands while Greece represents no threat to Asia Minor."[7]

However, among the two it is Greece who is Europe's preferred child. For one thing, if west of the Bosphorus is Europe and east of it is Asia,

Greece is a recognized part of Europe, whereas only a fraction (about 3 percent) of Turkish territory belongs to Europe proper. For another, Europe remembers it is Europa's daughter: ethnically, culturally, and religiously, to the Western mind Turkey is still very much an "other": a too-open economic and cultural passageway between East and West, still uncomfortably militaristic—to balance the degree to which it is uncomfortably Muslim—with a poor record on human rights and an underdeveloped economy. For the Turks, therefore, small Greece is really an offshoot of the larger continent whose relation to Turkey continues to be ambivalent from the days the West dubbed the Ottoman Empire "the sick man of Europe."[8]

The European Union (EU) membership enjoyed by Greece since 1981 has stopped for the moment, short of the Turkish borders, and Greece has several times exploited its EU membership to counteract Turkish objectives. Meanwhile Turkey, being the largest force in NATO after the United States, has many times leveraged its NATO veto power against Greek ambitions in Cyprus, in the Aegean Sea, and within NATO itself.

A wide economic disparity likewise unbalances the Aegean Basin. The Turkish GDP is only $7,500 per capita to Greece's $21,300. Twenty percent of the Turkish population lives below the poverty line. Yet this disadvantage does not deter Turkey from spending over $12 billion yearly—5.3 percent of its GDP—on its 600,000-strong military. Nor does Greece fall far behind with a military expenditure of almost $6 billion, 4.3 percent of its GDP, on about 110,000 military personnel.[9] Altogether, in terms of percentage of GDP, Turkey and Greece rank first and second, respectively, in military expenditure among European NATO countries.

This is the story of a conflict that has mostly turned into competition. It is also a story of how islands of agreement, coming thick and fast together, eventually came to be a terra firma for a more peaceful coexistence.

The History—Years of Conflict

In April 1920, six months after the Armistice of the Great War, the defeated Ottoman Empire finally succumbed to the terms of a peace agreement with the Western Allies. The agreement was signed at San Remo, Italy, and its terms were later incorporated into the more comprehensive Treaty of Sevres, concluded the following August.[10] The new empire borders were decided among Britain, France, and Greece; the latter, acting under authorization from the Supreme Allied War Council, had, during the summer and fall of 1919, already gained control of Eastern Thrace up to a vertical line drawn from the Black Sea down to the Sea of Marmara, as well as of the major cities Izmir, Edirne, and Bursa, and was still advancing.[11] But the treaty was destined never to be fulfilled, as events in Turkey were unfolding rapidly.

As foreign hands were busy cutting the centuries-old empire down to size, a Turkish nationalist movement was forming under the leadership of Mustafa Kemal, better known as Kemal Atatürk. The nationalists' objectives included the renunciation of claims to the Arab provinces, the unification of areas inhabited by a Turkish-Muslim majority into an integral independent Turkish state, a guarantee of minority rights, control of the Turkish Straits, and, most significantly, rejection of any foreign restriction on the rights of the nation. Atatürk's ideal was a Westernized Turkey, in which Islam no longer exercised a hold on politics, culture, and society. The Grand National Assembly in Ankara defied the fading Ottoman regime and, expressing its alignment with the nationalist movement, elected Atatürk its president in April 1920.

Under Atatürk's leadership, the Turkish nationalist forces reassembled themselves to retaliate against the Greeks and, in a series of battles between 1920 to 1922, managed to fend off the advancing army and recapture lost territory, most notably the strongholds of Ankara and Izmir. Thousands on both sides were killed in the fighting as well as in the chaos that accompanied the city's capture. Greek soldiers and refugees were rescued from Izmir by Allied ships. To avoid a confrontation with the Allies around Istanbul, Atatürk accepted a British-proposed truce, which ordered the withdrawal of Greek troops from some of the land they had occupied.[12]

The status quo between the Ottomans, the nationalists, and the Allied forces remained in place until the end of October 1922, when the Allies invited both the nationalist and Ottoman governments to a conference at Lausanne, Switzerland. In November 1922, the Turkish Grand National Assembly announced the final abolition of the Ottoman Empire, accepting Atatürk's position that the nationalist government should be Turkey's sole representative.[13]

After months of negotiations, the Treaty of Lausanne was concluded in July 1923.[14] The treaty delineated the border between Turkey and Greece, which holds to the present day, and in the process sanctioned a form of ethnic cleansing, through a mandatory and rapid exchange of populations involving nearly 2.5 million people. Turkey accepted approximately five hundred thousand Muslims, who were forced to emigrate from the Balkans, in exchange for nearly 2 million Greeks, who were forced out of Anatolia.[15] This massive, forced population transfer was deeply traumatic for both peoples and to this day continues to inform notions of national identity. Ironically, the architect of this scheme, Norwegian Fridtjof Nansen, was awarded the Nobel Peace Prize.

The Republic of Turkey was announced by the Grand National Assembly on October 29, 1923. Atatürk was named president, and Ankara the capital. Throughout the ensuing wranglings of the two countries, the Treaty of Lausanne, for all its shortcomings, has remained the chief document of authority. Even during the dramatic relationship overhaul of recent years, it has still been relied on and clung to by both nations to a surprising degree, on several fronts of their conflict, including the treatment of minorities and the competition over the Aegean Sea. As the treaty contains provisions that are sufficiently vague to support opposing positions, this reliance on its stipulations—as on other subsequent treaties—has done little, over the decades, to move the parties closer to resolution.

After the signing of the Treaty of Lausanne, the two countries entered into what is usually described as the most harmonious era of their relationship, which was to last until the 1950s. Whether any real harmony existed is doubtful, but the respective leaderships certainly exerted great pressures to avert open hostilities. In 1930, the two national leaders—Mustafa Kemal Atatürk and Eleuthérios Venizélos—signed the Convention on Establishment of Commerce and Navigation. Under its terms, Greece and Turkey officially recognized each other's existing territorial boundaries and acknowledged naval equality in the eastern Mediterranean.[16] The convention further stipulated that the lands abandoned by Greeks and Muslims were to be considered an exchange without compensation.

In 1953 the two countries, together with the Federal People's Republic of Yugoslavia, concluded the Treaty of Friendship and Collaboration.[17] The treaty noted the intention of the parties to pursue their mutual efforts for safeguarding peace and security in their region and their commitment to resolve any differences by peaceful means. The treaty also provided for collaboration in defense matters, through the general staffs of the contracting countries, as well as collaboration in economic, technical, and cultural spheres.

However, as tensions between the Greek and Turkish communities on the island of Cyprus mounted during the 1950s, the relationship between the two mother countries likewise began to deteriorate. In September 1955, while the foreign ministers of Britain, Turkey, and Greece met in London to discuss the fate of Cyprus, a bomb exploded on the premises of the Turkish Consulate General in Salonica, near Kemal Atatürk's birthplace. That evening, a Turkish mob raided the Greek population of Istanbul, killing, injuring, and raping, destroying shops and desecrating churches. The raids drove thousands of Greeks out of Istanbul, reducing the number of Greek inhabitants of the city from 120,000 to 2,000, at which rough number the population stands today. Evidence suggests that the Turkish government instigated and encouraged the riots, to divert popular criticism from domestic problems.[18]

In 1964, again in response to a crisis in Cyprus, Turkey unilaterally denounced the 1930 Convention of Establishment of Commerce and Navigation. Twelve thousand Greek citizens were deported from their homes in Turkey within hours of receiving notice.[19]

A recurring pattern was thus initiated in the relations of the two countries, in which conflict has often been intentionally diffused into or alternately activated in various fronts, geographical or issue based, according to each country's political expediency at any given moment.

In the years to follow, the relationship remained tense, with the core conflict revolving around the issues of Cyprus and the Aegean Sea, breeding—and bred by—ethnic frictions in the mainlands.

The Mainlands—Ethnic Frictions

The 1923 Lausanne treaty provided for the respective recognized minorities in Greece and Turkey and is still the governing legal regime of this issue.[20] While only a few thousand Greeks remain in Turkey today, the Muslim minority in Greece consists of around ninety-eight thousand people, mostly of Turkish origin, and is concentrated in the province of Thrace, just west of the Turkish border. The treatment of the Turkish minority in Greece and the Greek minority in Turkey has been a continuous source of aggravation in Greek-Turkish relations, especially during times of trouble in Cyprus.[21]

In Greece, the Muslim minority has, especially until recently, suffered various forms of administrative and institutional discrimination and deprivation of rights, such as rights of citizenship, property rights, and rights of speech and association. In 1955, more than sixty thousand ethnic Turks lost their Greek citizenship under a Greek law stipulating that the Ministry of Internal Affairs could revoke the citizenship of non-ethnic Greeks on the basis that they had in fact left the country with no intention of returning.[22] Although the law was reversed in 1998, some of those wishing to reapply for citizenship have since been denied.

To this day, there is a conflict regarding the Muftis of the Turkish minority. Accusations are coming forth that the minority is still barred from choosing its own Muftis. Muftis that have been chosen by the people without appointment by the Greek government are prosecuted for "impersonating a clergyman."[23] The Greek taxation system also discriminates against the religious institutions of the Turkish minority.

On the economic front, the rate of employment of Muslims in the public sector and in state-owned industries and companies is significantly lower than their percentage in the population. Infrastructure in Western Thrace is one of the least developed in Greece; houses, schools, and other buildings occupied by the Turkish minority are among the poorest in the land.

Over the years, many non-Turkish Muslims in Greece (Pomaks and Roma) have come to view Turkey as their protecting power against Greek oppression. The government in Ankara has always been a vocal and active supporter of the Muslim minority in Greece, arguing it had a "Turkish identity" and accusing Greece of breaking up the minority into groups to weaken their original Turkish character. Since the 1980s, Greek authorities have been vehemently denying the Turkish identity of the Muslim minority. Greek law prohibits the use of the terms "Turk" or "Turkish" in titles of organization, and, according to the Turkish minority claims, even the use of these terms in names of individuals is strongly discouraged. Several Muslim-Turkish activists have been convicted and civic organizations have been dissolved for using the term "Turkish." Recently, in January 2005, the Greek Supreme Court has dissolved the Xanthi Turkish Union for this same reason, ruling that

> the association's aim is illegal and contrary to Greek public order, since it is in contradiction with the international treaties signed in Lausanne, as it is attempted openly to present that in Greece (the area of Western Thrace) there is a national Turkish minority, while according to these treaties only the presence of a religious Muslim minority is recognized in the area. The reference to the Turkish identity does not reflect some remote Turkish origin but a current quality as members of a Turkish minority that would exist in Greece and would pursue the promotion within the Greek state of state interests of a foreign state and specifically Turkey. The association

with its actions . . . gravely endangers Greek public order and national security . . . and raises a non-existent minority problem of "Turks."[24]

The Xanthi Turkish Union has recently brought its claim before the
European Court of Human Rights (ECHR).

Turkish literature and schoolbooks are still scarce and subject to governmental restrictions. Education in the Turkish schools is inferior to
that found in Greek schools. Turkish teachers are frequently harassed
and sued for calling their schools "Turkish."[25]

Greece, for its part, is particularly sensitive to a dialogue with Turkey
on these issues, as they resonate too uncomfortably of the reverse intercommunal relationship on the island of Cyprus.[26]

The previous Greek government, under EU pressure and the more
forthcoming leadership of Prime Minister Costas Simitis and Foreign
Minister George Papandreou, had made some efforts to bring its minority laws into greater conformity with EU norms. In 1999 Papandreou
launched an unprecedented campaign for changing the traditional position of the government, by which religious—but not ethnic—minorities
were recognized. Nevertheless, allegations of discrimination against the
Thrace populations persist. The prosecution of elected Muftis continues, as does harassment of secular Turkish minority leaders. Athens'
proclaimed efforts to encourage greater political participation by the
Muslim minority have also been met with some skepticism on the part
of human rights monitors.[27]

In Turkey, out of more than the two hundred thousand Greeks permitted to remain under the Treaty of Lausanne, only less than two thousand are left. Beginning in the 1930s, the Turkish government actively
encouraged Greeks to emigrate, and thousands, in particular the educated
youth, did so. The Greek Orthodox community has been persecuted by
the Kemalist regime and deprived of its privileges. In 1942 it was subjected to a discriminatory tax, the *Varlik*, which resulted in the massive
transfer of wealth from the Orthodox minority to the emerging Turkish entrepreneurial class.[28] In 1955, coinciding with intercommunal
strife in Cyprus, the Greek minority was further subjected to destruction
of its property, and in 1964 to expatriations, after which most of its remaining members left Turkey. Nevertheless, though the Greek community is declining in size, it remains one of the wealthiest communities in
the country.[29]

The Greek Orthodox Church patriarch in Istanbul is under growing pressures from the Turkish government, as the latter feels itself threatened by the patriarch's personal influence and responsibilities extending well beyond the Turkish borders. The Turkish government, like its Greek counterpart, cites the Lausanne treaty, which provides that the patriarch is to serve only the spiritual matters of the Greek Orthodox congregation in Turkey. The Turkish government is also involved in the elections for the patriarchate, thus effectively putting a check on the elected person. In 1971 the Turkish authorities shut down the Orthodox seminary in Helbeliada, near Istanbul, which was the only local teaching and training center providing the patriarchate with new clerics. To justify this act, the government relied on Turkish law, under which private religious education at the academy level is not allowed, for any religion.[30]

GREEK SUPPORT FOR KURDISH SEPARATISTS

A major stumbling block in the Greece-Turkey relationship has been Greece's alleged assistance or acquiescence to the activities of terrorist organizations opposed to the Turkish government, including the Armenian Secret Army for the Liberation of Armenia (ASALA) organization. But it was Greece's support for the struggle of Kurdish separatists against Ankara that has aroused most Turkish resentment.

The Kurdish Workers' Party (PKK) was founded in 1974 as a Marxist-Leninist insurgent group, with the goal of establishing an independent Kurdish state in southeast Turkey, where the population is predominantly Kurdish. In the early 1990s, the PKK escalated its operations beyond rural-based insurgent activities to include bombing and other forms of urban terrorism. The PKK was also added to the U.S. State Department List of Designated Foreign Terrorist Organizations.[31]

Turkish suspicion turned into flagrant anger when in February 1999 it became known that Athens was assisting Abdullah Öcalan, leader of the PKK, to flee from the Turkish security forces. This was considered by Turkey as the ultimate proof of Greece's malevolent intentions to undermine Turkish security from within.

In the wake of the Öcalan saga, Turkey was again swept by a wave of anti-Greek sentiment, encouraged by the Turkish government, which took no account of Greece's refusal to grant Öcalan permanent asylum. Greek forces were put on high alert.[32]

The Dispute over Cyprus

BACKGROUND

Empires have always converged on the island of Cyprus. Situated at the strategic maritime intersection of three continents, the legendary birth-place of the goddess of love and beauty has proved, over its history, rather a perpetual apple of strife rolling across the tables of competing, alternating regional powers. Egypt, Greece, and Rome have all, at various periods in ancient times, taken their turn at occupying its 3,562 square miles.[33] Cyprus, an invaluable pied-à-terre for any advancing army, lying right across from the Turkish shore and in close proximity to the Holy Land, was later seized upon, successively, by the crusading English (under Richard the Lionhearted), the Templars, Franks, Venetians, Turks, and British.

The island's recent history still displays the dependence on and objectification by external powers that have plagued its past. In some respects, title to the island still signals, in the eyes of both Greeks and Turks, a strategic and territorial superiority in this volatile region, as well, perhaps, as vestiges of imperial aspiration. Close attention to the way the conflict on Cyprus has developed vis-à-vis the "main" country-to-country conflict of Turkey and Greece reveals a not altogether innocent interplay, including more than one form of exploitation by the mainland countries of the offshore territory.

The Ottoman Turks captured Cyprus in 1571 and were prompt to transfer to it Turkish peasants and artisans from the mainland, who soon formed a substantial part of the island's population. True to their practice elsewhere in the empire, the Ottoman Muslim rulers treated the island's indigenous Greek Orthodox community as a self-governing religious group (a *millet*). For about 250 years, the Turkish and Greek populations lived side by side peacefully, yet separately, without assimilation.[34]

Serious frictions between the Ottomans and the Greek Orthodox leaders in Cyprus arose in 1821, as Greece was struggling for independence from Ottoman rule. The Greek Orthodox leaders were accused of conspiring with the mainland Greeks to launch a Greek-Cypriot rebellion on the island and were executed. There was also widespread looting of churches and Greek houses.[35]

Greece's victory in its war of independence ignited Greek nationalistic sentiments within the Greek population in Cyprus, whose imaginations were already fired by extremist groups bandying about the age-old *Megali*

Idea—the dream of a reunification of the Hellenic world. Their hopes seemed to receive a promising boost when, under the 1878 Cyprus Convention, in exchange for British assistance to Turkey in its war with Russia, Britain assumed administration of the island (which formally still remained part of the Ottoman Empire).[36] With Britain's assistance to Greece during the latter's war of independence still fresh in their minds, Greek Cypriots revived their aspiration for *enosis*—unification with Greece. The British did not reject the idea but thought that the Greek Cypriots might be content under British rule, at least for some time.[37]

When World War I broke out in 1914, the Ottoman Empire fought on the side of the Germans. In retaliation, Britain annexed Cyprus. In 1923, under the terms of the Treaty of Lausanne, both Turkey and Greece relinquished all rights to Cyprus and recognized British sovereignty over the island. Two years later, Cyprus was declared a British Crown Colony. Throughout this period, and for many years after, the Turkish minority on the island found itself subject to a new master, disliked and even despised by the Greek majority, which, being closer to the British rulers in culture and religion, was the clear favorite. In Cyprus, then, was staged a scene in little of a power imbalance still separating Greece from Turkey as regards Europe: though British favoritism declined throughout the 1930s as the Greek *enosis* cry intensified, enough imbalance remained to bring about the havoc that is likely the result of the politics of exclusion.[38]

Within two decades, the Greek Cypriots were successful in harnessing not only the support of Greece, which after its civil war became a vocal and persistent advocate of *enosis,* but also some U.S. support in the struggle against Britain. Greece's participation on the side of the victorious Allies in World War II (as opposed to Turkey, which maintained a German-prone neutrality) rekindled Hellenic aspirations on the island and led Greek Cypriots to believe that *enosis* was now inevitable.

But the British government, who considered Cyprus vital for defending its interests in the Middle East, was staving off any demand for self-determination or *enosis.* Turkey, in contrast, claimed that a Greek-ruled island just fifty miles off its coast might prove a fatal threat to its security (even though a clear power imbalance already existed in Turkey's favor). The Turkish Cypriots, on their part, feared that an *enosis* would result in the expulsion of the Turkish population from the island, as was the case when Crete was freed, decades earlier, from Turkish rule. In response to the demands for *enosis,* the Turkish Cypriots began campaigning for the partition—*taksim*—of the island. At this point the Greek Cypriot inhabitants made up approximately 82 percent of the population and Turkish Cypriots the remaining 18 percent.[39]

In 1950 a four-year violent campaign against the British authorities on the island was launched in Cyprus by Greek Cypriot extremists, organized under the National Organization of Cypriot Fighters (EOKA). Confronted by mounting violence and the undeniable support its perpetrators received from Greece, Turkey began to demand the return of the island to their own rule in the event of British retreat, or at the very least a *taksim*. As part of their struggle to regain control, the British authorities encouraged a violent Turkish Cypriot countercampaign against the Greek *enosis* demand. The campaign was unsuccessful in suppressing the growing strength of Greek Cypriot but instead deepened the already growing rift between the two communities.[40] Cyprus and its population thus became a battleground for five competing powers, three of which had, at one time or another, been its imperial rulers.

In 1956, the Greek Cypriots declined a British offer for a substantial self-government, which included the principle that the Turkish community be given the freedom to decide their future status for themselves.

In 1959, in the face of the spiraling intercommunal tensions and their spillover to the mainlands, the prime ministers of Greece and Turkey met in Zurich and drafted a series of three agreements: the Basic Structure of the Republic of Cyprus, the Treaty of Guarantee and the Treaty of Alliance.[41] The Basic Structure was a constitutional framework for a bicommunal sovereign republic, with the Treaty of Guarantee and the Treaty of Alliance providing assurance and protection from both internal and external threats. The president was to be Greek and the vice president Turkish. In a meeting in London, the representatives of Britain, Greece, and Turkey were joined by representatives of the two Cypriot communities, and the Zurich agreements came into effect.

The Republic of Cyprus thus became an independent state on August 16, 1960. All three governments retained the right to intervene, singly or together, to reconstitute the arrangements agreed upon in the Basic Structure, in case they collapsed. The British, under the terms of the Treaty of Guarantee, retained two sovereign bases on the island. Both *enosis* and *taksim* were expressly forbidden, and Britain, Greece, and Turkey all undertook to guarantee the independence, territorial integrity, and security of the republic. It seemed as if the proxy war conducted by Greece and Turkey in Cyprus had come to an end.

But peace was not long lived. The newly formed government, led by Archbishop Makarios, was biethnic and ultimately too delicately balanced to be capable of action. The constitutional structure, while it purported to accommodate the differences between the two communities, in fact maintained and fortified the separation.[42] Numerous disputes arose around questions of representation, authority, allocation of civil service positions, and general misgivings between the two communities. Social and cultural division intensified. By December 1963, all Turkish Cypriots quit their governmental and parliamentary positions. The envisioned biethnic government disintegrated. Vicious intercommunal fighting broke out, driving Turkish Cypriots into ghettolike enclaves.[43] Greek and Turkish forces deployed outside of Nicosia joined the clashes. Turkish warplanes flew low over Cyprus, and around twenty thousand Greek regular troops infiltrated the island. Turkey prepared to intervene with its own troops, but was stopped by the United States. UN observers reported hundreds of casualties on both sides; massive damage to villages, mostly Turkish; and thousands of people being driven out of their homes.[44]

Efforts by the three guarantor governments to restore the peace by diplomatic means failed. With the permission of the government of Cyprus, the guarantors then sent peacekeeping forces under a British command. At the end of December 1963, a neutral zone known as the "Green Line" was created between the areas occupied by the two communities in Nicosia. In its Security Council Resolution 186 of March 4, 1964, the UN, with the agreement of the Greek Cypriot government, decided to deploy a multinational peacekeeping force—the United Nations Peacekeeping Force in Cyprus (UNFICYP)—along the dividing line.[45] UNFICYP's mandate was to prevent the recurrence of the fighting, help restore law and order, and contribute to the restoration of normal conditions. The UN Secretary General also appointed a personal representative to observe the progress of the peacemaking operation. Both UNFICYP and the special representative are still performing their tasks in Cyprus today.[46]

To the Turkish Cypriots, the complete disregard exhibited by the UNFICYP mandate towards the unconstitutional character of the now-wholly Greek Cypriot government in power was a gross injustice. Until 1974 they remained a disadvantaged minority in Cyrpus, subject to economic discrimination and violent outbursts from EOKA members.[47] Renewed intercommunal clashes in 1967 generated international pressure for negotiations, but all efforts at mediating or negotiating a new constitution failed. In the aftermath of the clashes, Turkish Cypriots established the Provisional Cyprus Turkish Administration, a self-governing administration of the Turkish community.

On July 15, 1974, a right-wing Greek faction, supported by the ruling military junta in Athens at the time and advocating EOKA's earlier demand for *enosis*, staged a coup to overthrow the government of Archbishop Makarios in Nicosia. Within five days, after its offer to Britain to act jointly to restore the previous biethnic Cypriot government had been declined, Turkey purportedly invoked its role as a guarantor under the terms of the Treaty of Guarantee and sent in its military, which, in a series of operations, succeeded in taking over more than a third of the island, including parts of the capital. As a result, "the UN buffer zone became a virtual Berlin wall, with a complete separation of the populations."[48]

The Turkish invasion was universally condemned as a flagrant violation of international law and the UN charter. The United Nations General Assembly unanimously adopted Resolution 3212, calling for the respect of the sovereignty, independence, territorial integrity and nonalignment of the Republic of Cyprus, and the speedy withdrawal of all foreign troops.[49] International organizations around the world, including the European Parliament, the Council of Europe, and the Commonwealth of Nations, all called for the urgent return of the refugees to their home and the full restoration of the human rights of the population of Cyprus. On the second day of the invasion, the Athens military government collapsed and a civilian government was established. In Cyprus, Makarios reassumed the presidency.

The invasion exacted a heavy price. As in 1963, a wave of demographic dislocation wrested society apart. According to the Cypriot government, about 142,000 Greek Cypriots—then almost a quarter of the population of Cyprus—living in the northern parts of the island were expelled from their homes by the invading Turkish forces. Around forty-six thousand Turks fled from the south. An additional twenty thousand Greek Cypriots were gradually forced out of the area later on and, to date, are still unable to return to occupy their homes—though as of 2005 they can visit the north.[50] Only about six hundred Greek Cypriots reside in northern Cyprus today. Approximately fifteen hundred Greek Cypriot civilians and soldiers disappeared during the invasion and its aftermath; the fate of only a handful of them is known. Demonstrations along the Green Line still take place regularly, especially during the July and August anniversaries of the Turkish invasion.

An American-brokered cease-fire put an unquiet end to the fighting, and the Green Line now separated the two parts of the island, leaving around 36 percent of the island in the hands of the Turkish population. The ethnic division of Cyprus was completed when the two communities agreed, under the auspices of the UN, to a large-scale population exchange between the northern and southern parts of the island.[51] The reinstated Greek Cypriot government was recognized worldwide, with the exception of Turkey, as the legitimate government of Cyprus.

Turkish Cypriots refused to partake in the Greek administration and in 1975, under the leadership of Rauf Denktash, proclaimed the northern side of the Green Line to be the Turkish Federated State of Cyprus, offering to reunite with the Greek south as part of a larger federal Cyprus. The offer was rejected by the Republic of Cyprus, the UN, and the international community at large. In 1983, as efforts to create a federal structure failed, the Turkish Cypriots declared the Turkish Republic of Northern Cyprus (TRNC) as their own state, creating, in effect, an island within an island.[52] The UN Security Council denounced the declaration as "legally invalid" and called on all states not to recognize any Cypriot state other than the Republic of Cyprus.[53] The resolution has been interpreted as prohibiting direct trade with the TRNC and thus legitimizing an economic embargo imposed by the Greek Cypriots on the north. As Turkey has remained the only country to recognize the TRNC, all Turkish Cypriot trade with the outside world has since been conducted through Turkish ports.

The events of 1963 and 1974, stirred by interested powers from without, tore apart communities that have existed more or less at peace for centuries. As the mainland rivals competed over the fate of their ethnic communities on the island, it was unclear whether the conflict in Cyprus incited their competition or whether they were making a conscious and deliberate effort to project their conflict onto Cyprus.

While an island's isolation necessarily locks its conflicts within, so that any potential violence is aggravated, it also allows its controlling powers from without to prolong its function as a "place of war" located outside the safety of their own borders and involving a population who has no vote in their respective governments' elections. To an extent, then, the prospect of islands of agreement has, where Cyprus was concerned, long been taken hostage by the indefinite prospect of interdependency entailed by "island politics."

Furthermore, islanded isolation has, in time, grown powerfully symbolic for the Turks, as both they and the Turkish Cypriots they represent have come to feel themselves increasingly isolated and discriminated against by the UN and Western world opinion.

To a large extent, this experience has made both Turkey and the TRNC wary of any subsequent efforts by the UN or the United States to mediate in the dispute; it has also led to Cyprus's still-increasing militarization, especially by Turkey.[54] According to the Cypriot government, in the thirty-two years since the invasion, Turkey has imported around 115,000 Anatolian settlers into the Turkish-controlled area. The large influx of settlers has had an adverse effect on the standard of living in the area, generating unemployment and poverty. As a result, the strategy backfired, and over fifty-five thousand Turkish Cypriots consequently emigrated out of the island, reducing their ethnic group to a mere 12 percent of the approximately eight hundred thousand native population today.

Since the invasion, Turkey has deployed around thirty-five thousand well-equipped soldiers in the area under its control, making it, in the words of Boutros Boutros Ghali, the UN secretary general at the time, "one of the most densely militarized areas in the world." The Cypriot government claims that the Turkish administration in northern Cyprus is "deliberately and methodically trying to eradicate every trace of the ancient culture and historical heritage of the island as part of a policy to erase all evidence of its Cypriot character and Turkify the island."[55]

Towards the end of 1993, the governments of Cyprus and Greece announced the establishment of the Joint Defense Area, under which, as long as Turkey maintained a force of more than thirty thousand troops in Cyprus, Greek and Greek Cypriot forces would remain in a state of joint defense. Pursuant to the joint defense doctrine, any attack on Cyprus would be considered casus belli for Greece.[56]

These proclaimed military ties between the mainland countries and their island communities have done much to reinforce the role of the conflict in Cyprus as that of a proxy war between Greece and Turkey, by now far removed from any prospect of isolation as a limited intrastate ethnic conflict.

FAILED EFFORTS AT MEDIATION

Soon after the Turkish invasion of Cyprus, the UN began mediation efforts in the dispute, which continue to this day. A first round of UN-sponsored negotiations took place in 1975 but failed to lead to agreement, as the two Cypriot communities had differing positions on the appropriate constitutional framework of the proposed Cypriot federation. In 1977 progress was made when Makarios and Denktash agreed to four-point "guidelines" for negotiations towards "an independent, non-aligned, bi-communal Federal Republic."[57] The agreement on a federal structure was a departure from the 1960 constitution, and thus a meaningful concession on the Greek Cypriot part.[58] However, negotiations on the practical details, left open by the guidelines, soon reached a stalemate. On May 19, 1979, the UN-brokered Ten-Point Agreement was signed between Denktash and the new Cypriot president, Spyros Kyprianou.[59] The agreement endorsed the principles set earlier by the guidelines and added that individuals could choose to live in their own ethnic communities under a bizonal division of the island. Subsequent UN Security Council resolutions adopted the principles of the Ten-Point Agreement. But negotiations again failed to translate these principles into a specific state structure.

Both sides have raised concerns as to the implementation of the agreement: The Turkish minority emphasized the need for political equality in the federal government and the assumed security of its members. The Greek majority, enjoying a four-to-one population advantage, demanded the immediate withdrawal of all Turkish forces from the island, a full democratic government, and the transference of territory from the north to the south. Other claims pertained to the fate of those missing in the 1974 campaign, compensation for lost property, and the legal status of Turkish settlers in the Turkish part of Cyprus.[60]

During the 1980s, the UN sponsored proximity talks, as the Greek Cypriots refused to hold a direct dialogue with their Turkish counterparts. The parties made some progress in 1985, when a UN draft agreement proposed a federal structure with two autonomous states, but the Greek Cypriots retracted, contesting the allocation of voting rights under the federal system, the lack of a specific timetable for the withdrawal of Turkish troops, and the absence of a solution to the problem of 180,000 Greek Cypriot refugees wishing to return to the north.[61]

In 1992 UN Secretary General Boutros Boutros Ghali offered a new negotiation plan consisting of the "Set of Ideas." This plan extended over a hundred paragraphs and addressed the issues prescribed in the Ten-Point Agreement, including political arrangements, property division and compensation, social and economic safeguards, treatment of displaced persons, and security guarantees. The Set of Ideas provided for the demilitarization of Cyprus, alongside the restoration of the 1960 Treaty of Guarantee. It also outlined a projected division of the island into two initial ethnic zones under one sovereign entity.[62]

Negotiations to put the Set of Ideas into a comprehensive and elaborate agreement seemed promising at first. But the attempt to translate the ideas agreed upon in principle into detailed practical and formally stipulated arrangements once again exposed underlying disagreements. The Turkish Cypriots raised a series of reservations, ranging from the projected division map to the political structures of the future federation (in particular, their demand for equal sovereignty for the TRNC in the federation), as well as possible future accession of the federation to international organizations.[63] Talks eventually failed. In its Security Council resolution of November 12, 1992, the UN pointed to the Turkish Cypriots as the party to blame for the failure.[64] In March 1993, Glafcos Clerides was elected as president of Cyprus, an office he held for the following decade, under a platform of a tougher stance on the dialogue with the Turkish Cypriots. He subsequently rejected the Set of Ideas.[65]

While a comprehensive peace agreement receded from sight, attempts to design some islands of agreement on the island of Cyprus remained equally elusive. As the Set of Ideas initiative collapsed, the UN secretary general proposed a new confidence-building plan, short of a peace agreement, which included the reopening of the Nicosia international airport and the return of Varosha, an eastern coastal town, to the Greek Cypriot hands. But although both sides agreed in principle to the proposed plan, the need to settle details again proved fatal.[66]

These repeated failures are directly attributable to the multiplicity of actors with irons in the Cypriot fire. For the most part, it was the distrust felt throughout by the Turkish Cypriots, as the weaker party, of any arrangement that would better the Greek Cypriots' position without ensuring that their own interests were safeguarded in full. At the same time, the feud between the mainland countries continued to feed into the relations of the two island communities and contributed further to the political stalemate. Without the active support and encouragement of the mainland rivals, no agreement on Cyprus was possible.

Effectively, up until the rapprochement, the war was happening—and peace or war was being determined—in four places at once, including Greece, Turkey, Cyprus, and the Aegean Sea. The hostility between the mainland countries was not hot enough at the time to call for any limited measures, nor was it cold enough to motivate comprehensive measures. In other words, no divisibility was called for at all—on the contrary. It was in both Greek and Turkish interests to keep the conflict intertwined and going, so long as it was off their shores—on an island, and an island within an island, rather than an island of agreement.

The Dispute in the Aegean

The hostilities in Cyprus in the first half of the 1970s brought a change in Greek foreign policy, especially with regard to the Aegean Sea, when Turkey and Greece each lay claim to the waters and continental shelf in the area.

The Aegean is an eighty-thousand-square-mile sea lying between the Greek and Turkish mainlands. There are around twenty-four hundred Greek islands and islets in the Aegean, about a hundred of which are inhabited. There are also some sixty Turkish islands, primarily situated within three miles off the Turkish shore.

Even before 1970, Greece and Turkey were engaged in a long-standing dispute over the Aegean territorial waters, the continental shelf, and the airspace above. These disputes intensified with the opening in 1972 of the Third United Nations Conference on the Law of the Sea and the discoveries by Greece of gas and oil in the Aegean continental shelf. The parties were also, as they continue to be, at odds over the question of the demilitarization of the Aegean islands.[67]

DEMILITARIZATION OF THE AEGEAN

The Treaty of Lausanne, alongside the appended Convention Relating to the Regime of the (Dardanelles) Straits, provided for the demilitarization of the Bosphorus and Dardanelles straits, as well as of numerous Greek islands in the Aegean.[68] A subsequent treaty—the Montreux Convention of 1936—created a defensive system in the straits, which lifted some of the demilitarization restrictions imposed by the Lausanne Treaty.[69] With the end of World War II, the 1947 Paris Peace Treaty, which ended the state of war between Italy and the Allies, awarded Greece title to the formerly Italian Dodecanese Islands, which lay in close proximity to the Turkish coast.[70] The award, however, stood only under the condition that the islands remain demilitarized.

Following the 1974 Turkish invasion of Cyprus, Greece remilitarized the islands. In response, Turkey established the Army of the Aegean, whose size approached that of the entire Greek army. Further Greek militarization of the islands has since continued.

To this day, Greece and Turkey maintain conflicting stances on the scope of the remilitarization allowed under the Montreux Convention, on the exact limits imposed by the Treaty of Lausanne, and on whether the remilitarization of some of the islands by Greece in response to the 1974 Turkish invasion of Cyprus is a justified invocation of Greece's right of self-defense.[71]

TERRITORIAL SEA AND AIRSPACE

States, including islands, have sovereign rights over their territorial waters. These rights accord the coastal state or island control over the waters, the seabed below, and the airspace above. Any passage of a foreign vessel in territorial waters has to be in the form of "innocent passage," which imposes substantial limitations on it. Until 1972, when the third United Nations Convention on the Law of the Sea (UNCLOS) conference convened, territorial waters were usually declared for three or six nautical miles. A 1936 Greek law fixed the territorial sea at six miles from the Greek shores. Turkey followed in 1964. The respective six-mile regime proved a stable modus vivendi. However, the third UNCLOS conference addressed the possibility of allowing states—including islands—to extend their territorial sea to twelve miles. This option, which became the rule under the 1982 UNCLOS (which came into force in 1994), invited a new set of problems into the already taut Greece-Turkey situation.[72]

a) Territorial Waters: Extending title from the current six miles to the full twelve miles of territorial sea around the islands, as the UNCLOS now permitted, would have accorded Greece control over almost all the Aegean Sea, turning it effectively into a "Greek lake," thereby cutting off Turkish air and sea vessels from international courses they enjoy today. In contrast, splitting the territorial seas between the two countries, as Turkey demanded, would put several of the Greek islands under effective Turkish control.[73]

In support of its claim, Turkey has been relying on the UNCLOS's additional provisions for areas of special circumstances, where factors such as particular history or geography may be taken into account.[74] Turkey also claims that there are "gray areas" in the Aegean, where the surface boundary or sovereignty over the islands is indeterminate.[75] Despite the extensive literature on the Aegean conflict and the UNCLOS, it is doubtful whether there is a clear-cut legal determination in favor of either the Greek or the Turkish claims in this regard. On the political level, after the ratification by Greece of the UNCLOS in 1995, the Turkish Grand National Assembly passed a resolution authorizing the Turkish government to use all means, including military, in the event Athens extended its territorial waters to twelve nautical miles, in effect threatening Greece with war.[76]

b) Airspace: In the 1970s, in conjunction with the dispute over territorial waters, Turkey began contesting Greece's declared air regime around Greek islands in the Aegean. This regime began in 1931, when the Greeks declared a ten-mile airspace around the islands, a declaration to which both Turkey and the United States objected, under the contention that legally, the territorial airspace should correspond to the territorial sea.[77] Greece's position was that, given the high speed of modern aircraft, it could not adequately defend its islands with a perimeter of only six miles.[78] In 1960 Greece agreed to a six-mile definition of its airspace for NATO purposes, but following the 1974 Turkish invasion of Cyprus, objected to Turkish planes flying within the ten-mile range. As tensions mounted, Greece deployed military units on several islands off the Turkish coast. Turkey, on its part, deployed a "training army" on the Aegean coast. Turkish and Greek aircraft still occasionally engages in mock aerial dogfights in the four contested miles. The most recent one, in May 2006, resulted in the death of a Greek pilot in a collision between Turkish and Greek F-16s.

The dispute over airspace use is not limited to the territorial airspace alone. Another controversy relates to the flight information region (FIR) regime in the area. In 1952 the International Civil Aviation Organization concluded that the airspace over the Aegean would be part of the Athens FIR. However, between 1974 and 1980 Turkey unilaterally extended its own FIR to include parts of the Aegean airspace, as part of its suit for the continental shelf. Today, Turkey still contests the need to submit flight plans of military aircraft to the Athens FIR center.[79]

THE CONTINENTAL SHELF

The continental shelf includes the seabed and its subsoil in an area stretching up to two hundred miles from the coastal state. Title to the continental shelf, under international maritime law, accords the owner rights to the exploitation of natural resources in it and thus brings with it a significant economic potential. Islands too have a continental shelf.[80]

From the Turkish point of view, the Aegean continental shelf is a natural extension of the Turkish coast and thus should be divided at a midway point between itself and the Greek coast. If this Turkish position is accepted, most of the major Greek islands fall within the Turkish continental shelf. The Greek assertion, in contrast, is that since Greek islands have a continental shelf too, the dividing line should fall at halfway between the Turkish coast and the Greek islands, substantially limiting the Turkish continental shelf.[81]

The UNCLOS provides that "the delimitation of the continental shelf between states with opposite or adjacent coasts shall be effected by agreement on the basis of international law . . . in order to achieve an equitable solution."[82] It thus does little to resolve a dispute in which both sides can claim their positions to express the most equitable solution.

The controversy over the boundaries of the continental shelf has led to a series of intense incidents, usually referred to as "hot episodes," beginning at the time of the Turkish invasion of Cyprus, which escalated the conflict on all fronts. In 1974 and again in 1976, the two countries came a stone's throw from violent confrontation, when Turkish oceanographic vessels were sent to search for mineral resources just outside Greek territorial waters. Greece approached both the UN Security Council and the International Court of Justice (ICJ) on the matter, claiming Turkey had violated Greek rights in the continental shelf, but received little support from either. The Security Council merely called on the parties to resume direct negotiations in an effort to resolve the dispute.[83] Greece also requested interim measures of protection from the ICJ but was unsuccessful, as the court held that it lacked jurisdiction to accept the Greek application.[84]

To prevent future incidents that might lead to violence, the parties reached the Berne Declaration of 1976, which lay the ground for future negotiations on the delimitation of the continental shelf. However, the status quo was tested again in 1987, when a similar incident occurred with another Turkish vessel on an oil exploration mission. Both militaries were put on high alert. Effective American intervention averted an armed escalation.[85]

As for the hope of a future agreement, the critical point is this: whereas Greece contends that the continental shelf is the only legitimate dispute in the context of the Aegean question and that it should be solved strictly through legal mechanisms, Turkey maintains that the continental shelf is only one part of a more comprehensive political controversy which should thus be resolved through bilateral negotiations.[86] It is for this inability to separate the issue of the continental shelf from the rest of the Aegean dispute, that the Berne Declaration could never have been effectively implemented.

In addition to being a constant point of friction, the continued disagreement over the continental shelf has also hindered valuable cooperation in exploitation of oil and other natural resources in the Aegean, to the detriment of both sides.

THE IMIA/KARDAK DISPUTE

The feud over the Aegean intensified in 1996, when a related quarrel arose over the control of two uninhabited rocks (called "Imia" by the Greeks and "Kardak" by the Turks) off the Turkish shore in the eastern Aegean waters. In January 1996, some Turkish journalists took down a Greek flag placed on one of the islets by Greek citizens from a nearby island and replaced it with a Turkish flag. A few weeks later, Greek naval forces reinstated the Greek flag, taking down the Turkish one. Viewing this act as a threat to its vital interests in the Aegean, Turkish vessels landed on the islets. In Athens, this act was perceived as yet another sign of Turkish expansionist aspirations in the Aegean, threatening the security and territorial integrity of Greece. The crisis escalated to the brink of war. Only U.S. intervention succeeded in preventing an armed confrontation, and the two countries withdrew their forces from the islets.

The problem, however, still defies resolution:[87]

Greece relies on the 1923 Lausanne treaty, which accorded Turkey sovereignty only over those islands situated within a three-mile zone off the Turkish coast. As the Imia/Kardak islets are 3.8 miles off the coast, they fall outside Turkish sovereign control. Greece also points to a 1932 protocol, signed between Italy and Turkey, which specified that the rocks belonged to Italy—who, under the Paris treaty, was succeeded by Greece.

While Turkey has so far stopped short of explicitly claiming title to the islets, it has nonetheless argued that the provisions of the Lausanne treaty on this matter are too vague and that the validity of the 1932 protocol is at best questionable. According to the Turkish stance, there are thousands of rocks and small islets in the Aegean, the sovereignty over which is not governed by any valid legal document and is thus open to negotiation.[88]

The dispute in the Aegean is vivid proof of the shortfalls of international multilateral and even bilateral treaties in resolving disputes: ambiguity, accommodation of competing claims, and the lack of mandatory dispute resolution and enforcement mechanisms mean, in the context of rivalries, that often treaties are used as a rhetorical weapon more than anything else.

The Fight Over the European Union

The European Union, whom many have hoped might act as an effective catalyst for a Greek-Turkish settlement, has for many years failed to come up with a consistent and persuasive policy towards the conflict and its own role within it.[89] In part, this failure stems from European embarrassment regarding the need to think of the Balkans as part of Europe; and within that zone of uncertainty, from Greece's closer ties to the European culture it gave birth to and to whom it largely owes its nationhood, in comparison with the more pronounced otherness of a largely Muslim Turkey.[90]

In fact, rather than contributing to rapprochement, the ambiguity of the EU's position has often turned it into yet another battleground between the two states—the more so for its consistent submission to Greece as the latter repeatedly has leveraged its membership status to promote its own interests in the conflict. This submission has often caused the EU to lose, in Turkish eyes, its status as a fair and impartial third party.

For Greece, the EU has been a useful vantage point from which to extract concessions from Turkey, still excluded from the club, in exchange for the latter's being granted permission to join in. To begin with, Greece's steady conditionality strategy has been to threaten a block on Turkey's accession to the EU—as well as any other EU enlargement effort—as long as Cyprus was barred from membership. Later on, when Greece had come to accept Turkish accession as a fact, it shifted its pressure to the TRNC. Whenever Greece saw the need to reinforce the bargaining power of Greek Cypriots vis-à-vis the TRNC, it threatened to support Greek Cyprus's accession to the EU, leaving the TRNC out. Furthermore, Greece would condition any progress in the EU-Turkey discussions on improving its own bargaining power on the Aegean dispute.

Turkey, on the other hand, has fought throughout to unlink its own accession from that of Cyprus. By threatening that it would not "sit still" in the event that the Greek Cypriot government acceded to the EU without settling the matter first with the TRNC, Turkey had sought to deter the EU from accepting the Greek conditionality and to apply pressure on the EU to accept Turkey as a member regardless of Cyprus.

The EU, on its part, had been unsuccessful in untying this Gordian entanglement until December 1999, following the earthquakes, when the knot was cut off by Greece itself. In the meantime, wary of the Turkish threat, the EU was reluctant to accept Cyprus as a member prior to a political settlement on the island. Eventually, however, despite Turkish objections, Cyprus became a member of the European Union in 2004, and a solution to the Cyprus issue remains a decisive factor in the progress of Turkey's entry negotiations with the EU.

The concern displayed by the two mainland countries for the accession of their ethnic Cypriot communities to the EU, with its attendant linkage politics, was manifested throughout two states' intricate relationship with the EU. Greece won associate status in the European Community (EC) in 1962, with the promise of full membership in 1984; eventually it became a full member as early as 1981. For decades, Turkey, like the TRNC, had drawn the short straw.

While the original 1963 association agreement between Turkey and the European Economic Community envisioned a full Turkish membership in the community at an unspecified date in the future, beginning with the establishment of a customs union, the EU–Turkey Customs Union was finally established only in 1995. In exchange for its willingness to refrain from employing its veto power over the customs union, Greece received the EU's commitment to begin accession negotiations with Cyprus.[91] The conclusion of the customs union agreement was at first thought to put Turkey in the same proximity to accession as the new eastern and central European independent states. But this was not the case.

In July 1996, after the crisis in the Aegean and under Greek pressure, the European Council adopted a declaration, stating that the relationship between the EU and Turkey should be based "on a clear commitment to the principles and respect of international law and agreements, and that disputes created by territorial claims should be referred to the International Court of Justice."[92] This wording later appeared in almost every EU document addressing Turkey. Greece was thus successful in influencing the EU to accept its own preference for a judicial resolution of the Aegean conflict as the EU's official stance and to tie it to Turkey's accession. Greece also managed to block a financial protocol, which was intended to accompany the EU-Turkey Customs Union regime and which vouchsafed Turkey financial guarantees on the part of the EU.

In July 1997, the EU Commission published its "Agenda 2000" report on enlarging the Union. The report singled out Turkey to disadvantage from the other candidates for membership and used harsher language to set out its own prerequisites for Turkish membership.[93] In December 1997, the Presidency Conclusions of the European Council summit in Luxemburg explicitly excluded Turkey from the following round of accession negotiations, while including Cyprus alongside five other central and eastern European countries. The conclusions added in no uncertain terms that future strengthening of ties with the EU depended on Ankara's support for UN negotiations on Cyprus.[94]

The Turkish reaction was vociferous and harsh. Officials in Ankara and Turkish Cyprus announced the suspension of all political dialogue with the EU, accusing the latter of building "a new cultural Berlin Wall" with the intention of shutting Turkey out. In response, they announced their objection to the EU's acting any longer as a political channel.[95] Turkey also argued that a Greek-Cypriot application for accession was illegal under the terms of the 1960 Treaty of Guarantee, which conditioned the participation of Cyprus in any international organizations on the participation of both Greece and Turkey in the same organization. In a joint declaration, Turkish and TRNC leaders deplored the EU-Cyprus ongoing accession negotiation as a "historic mistake" that "will speed up the integration process between the TRNC and Turkey."[96] There were even implicit threats that Turkey would annex Turkish Cyprus if Greek Cyprus joined the EU without Turkish Cypriot agreement. Enhancing the threat was a subsequent association agreement signed between Turkey and the TRNC, encouraging future integration in economics, defense, security, and foreign policy.[97] Greece, for its part, threatened that if the Cyprus accession were somehow barred, it would veto any expansion of EU membership.

EU officials were quick to exclaim that Turkey had overreacted to the Luxemburg conclusions, and that Turkey will naturally be admitted to the EU, just as soon as it completes several necessary steps to bring it closer to the Union.[98]

The deadlock was finally broken during the European Council meeting in Helsinki in December 1999, when the EU managed to uncouple the accession processes of Turkey and Cyprus: Turkey was finally admitted, with Greece's blessing, as a candidate for future membership; and Cyprus could gain accession without first reaching a political settlement.[99] The thorny issues of a settlement in Cyprus and the Aegean were dodged, using carefully worded adjustments to existing documents. The European Council summit in Nice, in December 2000, centered on the eastward enlargement of the EU and endorsed the Helsinki formula, paving the way for the admission of both Cyprus and Turkey (alongside Malta and central and eastern European countries) to the EU.[100]

Among the conditions set for Turkey's candidacy were the requirements that both it and Greece strive to settle outstanding disputes in accordance with the UN Charter and that in case negotiations fail to produce agreement, the two countries would submit their disputes to the International Court of Justice by the end of 2004. Turkey was also called on to withdraw from its stated position that any unilateral Greek extension of the territorial waters in the Aegean would be considered a casus belli. Numerous other requirements addressed Turkish economic performance as well as human rights policies.[101]

These demands continue to set the tone for Turkey's interaction with the EU.

The First Attempt at Islands of Agreement: The Davos Process

In his brief study of the Davos process, Mehmet Ali Birand recognizes the efforts of Prime Minister Turgut Özal of Turkey towards cooperation as islands of agreement in all but name. The leader of the Motherland Party came to power in December 1983, replacing a military government that had aroused vehement opposition throughout Europe. Turkey was then in dire economic straits. Its foreign relations with its neighbors, with the West, and last but not least with Greece had reached their lowest ebb in years. Greek Premier Andreas Papandreou was quick to seize the opportunity and raise the issue of the "Turkish Threat" in NATO and other international institutions. He also acted to reduce Turkey's relations with the European community as far as possible. According to Birand,

Özal believed that the only solution would be to use a new impetus in order to pull relations with Greece away from a system of fossilised bureaucracy and a rigid establishment . . . Rather than trying to solve old problems through the customary official channels, he believed that it would be far easier to discard any ill feelings between the two societies by setting up new fields of co-operation in areas ranging from tourism to commerce . . .

Another point that made Özal different from other Turkish leaders was that he did not keep Greek-Turkish relations stagnant within the framework of "military security" and since he had no experience on these issues he had no preconceived ideas.[102]

These initiatives set in motion what came to be known as the Davos process, which lasted from 1985 to 1988. During this three-year period, Özal centered his efforts on enhancing trade. His goal was to increase the volume of trade from $60 million to $2 billion. In addition, he softened the traditional official stand on the problem of how to resolve the issue of the continental shelf, expanded further commercial channels with Greece, and reduced the number of military flights so as to reduce tension around the Greek airspace issue. At least part of the Turkish bureaucracy was excited, at first, at the prospect of some movement forward in Greek relations, with the conclusion of the Athens Memorandum of Understanding on Confidence-Building Measures and the Istanbul Guidelines for the Prevention of Incidents on the High Sea and International Airspace. However, excitement wore off when it became clear that Özal was deliberately deferring settlement of key issues such as Cyprus and the Aegean.

Greek bureaucracy, too, wanted Papandreou to pull out of the 1988 talks when it was discovered that the issue of Cyprus was to be left out. Despite the fact that the two leaders established a good rapport between them and even had what has been called "a meeting of minds" during their Davos meeting, Özal's visit to Athens that year failed in its primary mission, to soften mutual attitudes and images; the Greek public expected some concessions from the Turkish prime minister regarding Cyprus and was thus disillusioned. Interestingly, Birand, unlike others who have studied the Davos process, analyzes this failure as a failure of conceptualization:

> Both leaders have tried and failed to override the old values of their own establishments . . . Neither the Turkish nor the Greek public could understand precisely what was happening . . . Neither leader was able to explain to his people or to the press just what they had planned on doing and the philosophy behind their plans. There is a good chance that they were not able to form their own philosophy because they did not know exactly what they wanted to achieve. That is why they could not give a proper explanation even to their own bureaucracy, even to the point of not being able to give proper orders . . . They could not create a new and proper mechanism to carry out these reforms through."[103]

The Davos process demonstrated, yet again, how the power of bureaucracy could frustrate frontline politics and how an attempt to fly in the face of established views without adequate backing from the bureaucracy was likely to suffer defeat in the long term. If we accept this analysis, here is also a perfect example of how conceptualization of the process as a *management* rather than as a *resolution* effort, as the public and the bureaucracy tended to view it, might have yielded different results.

Diplomatic Efforts: 1989–1999

The end of the Cold War and the disintegration of the Soviet Union created considerable expectations that the Greek-Turkish conflict would finally come to an end. With the threat of an East-West war eliminated and related regional conflicts contained, limitless opportunities for regional and bilateral joint ventures in nearly every sphere emerged. By any rational consideration, passing over such opportunities might have seemed simply implausible.[104]

What is more, there was real danger in refusing to cooperate; the end of the East-West equilibrium maintained by the Cold War set fire to a chain of nearby regional conflicts, from the Balkans through the Caucasus and Central Asia, all of which harbored menace to vital Greek and Turkish interests alike and which could spread out at any time so as to threaten their respective security. By working together, Greece and Turkey could have asserted a strong regional presence by which to exert power and influence over the newly emerging independent states, now free from Communist rule.

Once again, however, reality was to fly in the face of theory. What happened in the 1960s was now repeated with full force: the ethnic strife and nationalistic claims, which surrounded the two rivals from east and west, rekindled ethnic tensions within and between the two countries and deepened their animosity. The old nuts of Cyprus and the Aegean resurfaced with vigor, and fresh rivalries arose over political influence in the Balkans and control over oil transport routes from the Caspian to the Mediterranean Sea.[105] Both countries were rearming with vigor.

Expectations by some for NATO intervention at this point in the conflict were disappointed. Not surprisingly, perhaps, as once again, "the Western question"—an ambivalent attitude towards the West—was resurfacing in both countries, just as it did in the 1960s. Moreover, instead of NATO working to reduce the level of militarization in the area, it was under NATO programs of arms reductions and transfers from central Europe that Greece and Turkey received munitions and battlefield equipment from western European countries from 1991 onwards.[106] It seems then, that like the EU, NATO had played into the hands of its two rival members, unable to surpass their equal veto power and pressure them into resolving their differences.

How may this wide-scale failure be accounted for?

Reflecting on the two more harmonious periods in Greece and Turkey's relations, the 1930s and the first half of the 1950s, historians perceive a common denominator: In the first pre–World War II period, both countries sensed a growing Italian threat and were encouraged by Britain to cooperate. In the second both felt threatened by the Soviet Union and were encouraged to come together by the Western Alliance, mostly the United States. Thus, Şükrü S. Gürel writes, "if it were possible to deduce definite rules concerning the bilateral relations of states by evaluating historical evidence, we could summarize thus: Turkey and Greece can/could only develop their relations in harmony when and only when they mutually perceive(d) threat and are/were at the same time encouraged by an extra-regional power dominant in the region to cooperate against this threat."[107] If this is indeed the case, it is clear that no agreement depending on such brittle, purely external conditions, with no real internal drive, can have a hope of being maintained over time. In fact, each period of "enforced" harmony eventually resulted in a nationalistic backlash.

A similar pattern informs the cadences of the two nations' relation to the West; so long as the Western Alliance survived, Turkey and Greece could contain their problems within it. But as Cold War conditions began to change during the 1960s, the "Western connection," with its negative aspects and limitations, began to be underlined and questioned in both countries.

George McGhee, former U.S. ambassador to Turkey, who recorded Turkey's initial struggle to become a NATO member in the late 1940s and early 1950s, writes from a 1990's perspective:

Turks . . . tend to feel isolated—loners in a hostile Middle Eastern world. . . . Even the US appears to the Turks to have turned against them (for example in the case of the arms embargo), as a result of the political power of the hostile US-Greek minority. Europeans, Turks feel, although they once took millions of Turkish workers and accepted Turkey in NATO, now close their doors, reject Turkey's application for full membership in the European community and discriminate against Turkish exports.[108]

Later developments fully demonstrated the uselessness of international pressures in the absence of any real motivation by either party. In the summer and fall of 1996, the disputes in the Aegean and over Cyprus's accession to the EU sparked off renewed violence in Nicosia, leaving three Greek Cypriots and one Turkish Cypriot dead, the first fatalities of the Turkish-Greek dispute since 1974.[109] Both Athens and Ankara, hard-pressed by the West to diffuse tensions and resolve their differences, came up with several largely palliative agreements, all ultimately fruitless. Turkish Prime Minister Yilmaz's "Aegean Peace Initiative," which for the first time expressed a willingness to consider third-party mediation over the Aegean disputes, failed, however, to specify under which conditions and in exchange for what this in-principle willingness might be realized in action.[110] Similarly, in July 1997, at the NATO summit in Madrid, Greek Prime Minister Simitis and Turkish President Süleyman Demirel publicly endorsed six points to advance peaceful relations.[111] The points were declaratory in essence, and led nowhere.

In September 1997, the United States brokered a deal by which Greece would release EU funds for Turkey, in return for which Turkey would accept third-party mediation over the Imia/Kardak islets. If successful, this deal would have proved the potential of cross-issue trade in multidimensional conflicts. The Turks, however, so claim American diplomats, backed off at the last minute. Two subsequent bilateral initiatives at direct dialogue brokered by the Dutch were also truncated.[112]

By now, frustration had long become the prevailing sentiment, not only in the context of the Greece-Turkey negotiations, but also in those conducted in Cyprus. A further round of talks was brokered by the U.S. ambassador, Richard Holbrooke. Holbrooke's efforts brought the two leaders of the Cypriot communities, Clerides and Denktash, to meet in New York in July 1997, where a creative solution was proposed: the Republic of Cyprus would become the State of Cyprus, with a single sovereignty and territorial personality, which "emanates equally from the Greek Cypriot and Turkish Cypriot communities."[113] At the same time, the EC confirmed that accession talks with Cyprus would begin soon thereafter, while again rejecting Turkey's application for membership. This both diminished the Greek Cypriots' incentive to compromise and infuriated Turkish Cypriots. In consultation between the Cypriot communities and their mother countries, negotiations collapsed.

Throughout this period there was only one notable occasion on which international pressure proved itself successful in influencing outcomes.

On January 6, 1997, the Cypriot government announced its order of S-300 antiaircraft missiles from Russia. The missiles were to be deployed at a specially built airport at Paphos, in western Cyprus. The government claimed that the missiles were a legitimate defensive measure against the threat posed by the Turkish Air Force, which had easy access to Greek Cypriot targets on the island. Turkey, on the other hand, insisted on regarding the government's procurement plan as a belligerent move.[114]

A meeting between Denktash and Turkish President Demirel produced a joint declaration on January 20, in which they promised to "take the necessary measures" to address the missile problem, a declaration interpreted by some to mean a preemptive strike.[115]

Attempts in the summer of 1997 to diffuse tensions by agreeing on a moratorium on military flights over Cyprus failed a few months later, when Greece was conducting joint military exercises with the Greek Cypriot government. During the exercises, Greek and Turkish aircraft confronted each other over Cyprus, but neither fired. Greece claimed that Turkish warplanes also buzzed a military cargo plane carrying the Greek defense minister. Later in October, Turkey conducted its own exercises in northern Cyprus, which included the mock destruction of missile launchers.[116]

But strong and unrelenting international pressure, as well as fear that missile deployment might harm the negotiations over accession to the EU, brought the Cypriot government to cancel its missile program at the end of December 1998.[117]

A Surprising Rapprochement: Islands of Agreement

The failure of efforts to reach agreement on the Imia/Kardak dispute, growing tensions over the S-300 missile deployment, and Turkish frustration following the EU Luxemburg summit all contributed to a political stalemate between the mainland countries, which reached its tautest point during the Öcalan affair and lasted until the middle of 1999.

In May 1999, a surprising development occurred. Foreign Minister Cem approached his Greek counterpart, Papandreou, in a letter, suggesting a Turkish-Greek agreement on combating terrorism. In his words, "resolution of this issue would permit us to approach our known differences with greater confidence." Cem further suggested, that "Parallel to the signing and implementation of such an agreement, we could also initiate a plan for reconciliation."[118]

Papandreou's reply, a month later, seized on the Turkish initiative and broadened it further: "I strongly believe that we must adopt a realistic approach which will allow outstanding issues to be dealt with in sequence, creating thus both a strengthening sense of confidence in our relations and a perspective of further steps along the way." Papandreou moved on to elaborate on the various spheres of potential cooperation between the countries, including trade, tourism, environmental protection, and law enforcement. Security issues as well as the core conflict spheres were left out.[119]

In December 1999, an exhibit on modern Turkish history was brought to Thessaloníki and Athens aboard the personal railway car of Mustafa Kemal Atatürk. The so-called "Friendship Train," which carried journalists, railway workers, and emergency rescue personnel, arrived in Greece just as the Turkish consulate in Thessaloníki was marking the sixty-first anniversary of the death of Atatürk, who was born in the northern Greek city when it was still under Ottoman rule.[120]

In January 2000, the foreign ministers of the two countries paid respective visits to one another. Greek Foreign Minister Papandreou became the highest-ranking Greek official to pay a state visit to Turkey in thirty-eight years. His was the first direct flight between Athens and Ankara in twenty-five years, as flights were halted due to the Aegean airspace dispute. This visit, the climax of six months of intensive contacts between the foreign ministries, culminated in the signing of several bilateral agreements covering tourism, promotion of foreign investments, the Aegean environment, as well as terrorism, organized crime, and illegal immigration.[121]

Five additional agreements were signed by the two foreign ministers in a reciprocal visit by Ismail Cem to Athens—the first state visit of a Turkish foreign minister to Greece in forty years. These agreements covered economic cooperation, science and technology, culture, education, maritime transport, and the avoidance of customs violations. Several other initiatives for cooperation were also discussed. The Greek-Turkish Directive Committee was created to monitor the implementation of the agreements and to coordinate the activities of the six joint committees formed to promote bilateral relations. Papandreou described his visit as a "breakthrough in relations," while Cem declared that the accords marked "a successful beginning toward a new era in relations."[122]

In May 2000, Turkish combat aircraft landed in Greece for the first time in history, and in June Turkish marines landed on a Greek beach in the course of a NATO exercise. In September 2000, the Turkish military's chief of staff attended NATO talks in Athens. At the same time, a senior Greek banker was in Istanbul, finalizing a substantial private equity fund for investment in Turkish companies.[123]

The 2000 agreements have since led to further joint protocols and arrangements in various spheres and numerous cooperative efforts.

How can this sudden rapprochement be explained? In an article published by the Western Policy Center, Papandreou named three factors that, in his mind, induced the sea-change in Greek foreign policy towards Turkey: "Political forces engulfing the region in the post–Cold War period, new realities of the 'globalized' world, and a re-evaluation of Greece's national interests." He further argued that

> the harrowing war in Kosovo brought home to the Greek people the importance and necessity of good, neighborly relations. Fear and suspicion have long since given way to a policy of regional cooperation, based on mutual understanding and common interest. Globalization, the expansion of Europe, and the seamless multicultural world in which we live are but a few of the influencing elements that compelled Greece to reassess its foreign policy . . . We sought to develop a fully balanced and comprehensive regional policy founded upon principles of internationalism, pluralism, humanitarianism, and inclusive democratic values . . . Given this basic, but determined, foreign policy outlook, it would have been incongruous to exclude Turkey.[124]

There is little doubt that events in the Balkans, especially in Kosovo, have brought home to both political leaderships the danger of a spill-over effect, as well as the need for increased security cooperation. Indeed, both leaderships even contemplated "expanded war" scenarios, in which the Balkan wars extended to include a Greek-Turkish armed conflict. But the war also presented opportunities. The prewar social, political, and financial structures in the Balkans were at least partly destroyed and in dire need of reconstruction. This created wholesale structural collapse that Greece and Turkey could help ameliorate.

Papandreou also took note of the impact that the massive earthquakes had had in generating empathy, generosity, and kindness among the peoples of both countries towards one another, in what he termed "seismic diplomacy," or, as it has since become known in popular use, "earthquake diplomacy."[125] Indeed, there is little doubt that nature had lent a hand, although a cruel one, to the affairs of men; the unimagined scale of suffering must have dispelled some of the more atavistic Greek fears concerning its old archrival. Mutual suffering and mutual aid certainly brought the two nations closer together, reshaping popular as well as official attitudes.[126]

Commentators also noted the budding personal rapport between the respective leaders—Foreign Ministers Papandreou and Cem and Prime Ministers Costas Simitis and Bülent Ecevit—as another enabling factor. The two foreign ministers in particular were more moderate and forthcoming than their predecessors and possessed compatible personalities.[127] Observers also attributed importance to the Öcalan fiasco, which led to the resignation of Papandreou's predecessor, Theodoros Pangalos, who was one of the most vocal supporters of the policy of isolating Turkey.[128]

These dramatic changes never touched on the parties' fundamental positions on the core contested issues. Instead, as the Greek Ministry of Foreign Affairs explained,

> the common understanding was that through cooperation in sectors of a non-confrontational character a more positive and favourable climate could be created, through a step-by-step process, so that major issues could be approached in a friendlier atmosphere at a later stage.[129]

Cooperation over EU Accession

While for many years the European Union has been only another wrestling ring for the two parties, the Greek leadership decided, as part of the process of reconciliation, that the only way to resolve the long-lasting conflict was for Greece to "deal with Turkey as an equal partner in the Union."[130] In his testimony before the House Committee on International Relations–Europe Subcommittee, in June 2001, on the developments in Greece's foreign policy towards Turkey, John Sitilides of the Western Policy Center noted,

> The basis for Greek recalculation of foreign and security policies towards Turkey may be twofold. Greece recognizes the futility of "zero-sum" strategies, especially in an increasingly integrated region in an interdependent and globalized world. It has also decided that a genuinely Western and European Turkey offers the best prospect for lasting security, stability, and economic development in Greece, Cyprus, Turkey, and the entire region. These shifts have materialized along a sustained, though occasionally stalled, process over approximately the past half-decade.[131]

From then on, the effort was to build an island of agreement around Turkey's accession to the EU. Greece did not stop at lifting its veto. Instead, it offered—and extended—to Turkey close assistance and support in the long and arduous process of accession.[132] Intergovernmental cooperation, in turn, led to a series of contacts on subgovernmental levels. A first Turkey-Greece EU committee convened in February 2000, in Ankara, bringing together officials from both foreign ministries. Since then, Greek officials have offered training to their Turkish counterparts on issues of customs and finance, legal reform, agriculture, the environment, and law enforcement.[133]

In March 2002, Papandreou and Cem decided to launch exploratory talks with the purpose of finding a compromise formula for referring the controversy over the Aegean continental shelf to the ICJ. Papandreou, faithful to the Greek view of the Aegean dispute as limited to the continental shelf, made it clear that the talks would not include related territorial disputes over islets and waters. To date, and despite the deadline imposed by the EU, no formula has been agreed.

While Papandreou pledged to urge the EU to set a date for the launching of Turkey's accession negotiations, he also conditioned Greek support for Turkey's negotiations on Ankara's taking steps to resolve the outstanding disputes on Cyprus and the Aegean Sea.[134] The date for entry negotiations was finally set for October 2005.

Security Agreements

Following the March 1987 standoff in the Aegean, which brought the two countries to the brink of war, the Greek and Turkish prime ministers embarked on a bilateral dialogue. This led to the earlier mentioned "Davos process"; in fact a series of several agreements, including the Memorandum of Understanding on Confidence-Building Measures (the Athens Memorandum), signed in Athens in June 1988, and Guidelines for the Prevention of Incidents on the High Sea and International Airspace, signed in Istanbul in September 1988 (the Istanbul Guidelines).[135]

The Athens Memorandum included a statement of mutual respect for sovereignty, territorial integrity, and each party's rights to use the high seas and international airspace of the Aegean. It further outlined measures to reduce misunderstandings, accidents, or miscalculation during military exercises in the Aegean Sea. To that end, the parties undertook to avoid the isolation of certain areas, the blocking of exercise areas for long periods of time, and all exercises during the peak tourist period and national and religious holidays. The Athens Memorandum was a short document, consisting only of several concise and somewhat vague paragraphs.[136]

The Istanbul Guidelines required Greek and Turkish naval vessels to "refrain from acts of harassment of each other while operating in the high seas, in accordance with international law and customs." They further stipulated that naval units engaged in the surveillance of ships of the other party during military activities should not hamper the smooth conduct of those ships. With respect to military aircraft, the guidelines call on the pilots to "display the utmost caution when in proximity of aircraft of the other party" and refrain from any dangerous maneuver. These understandings too were brief, vague, and general.[137]

The compliance record with the 1988 agreements was poor. Ten years later, in June 1998, the two countries announced before NATO secretary general, Javier Solana, their intention to implement the 1988 memorandum and guidelines in full. This announcement came as a compromise outcome of months-long talks between Solana and the two countries' representatives to NATO. As commentators noted, "it took Turkey and Greece an entire decade to agree to implement what they had previously agreed upon."[138]

But even now, as was clear to the majority of observers, it was scarcely to be expected that the NATO-organized reaffirmation of commitments should bring about higher degrees of compliance. General skepticism attached not only to the intentions and motivations of both parties but also to the fact that the underlying disagreements in the Aegean were not addressed by the 1988 agreements nor readdressed in the latter's reaffirmation and that no mechanism was set up to monitor compliance or resolve disputes resulting from the agreements.

As the core disputes remained unsettled, the agreements' vague provisions were left exposed to unilateral interpretations, which each party based on its fundamental position in the Aegean dispute. Thus, it remained unclear whether, under the memorandum and guidelines, Greece had in fact acknowledged that the flights of Turkish military planes in the range of six to ten miles of territorial airspace would not be regarded as a violation or whether Turkey had initially agreed that its planes would not carry out exercises in this area. The one clear provision, which did not affect the parties' basic positions in the conflict, was the moratorium on military exercises in the Aegean during the tourism peak season and holidays, which was generally observed.[139]

In commenting on the Athens Memorandum and Istanbul Guidelines, Greek international relations scholar Athanassios Platias notes,

> As it turned out, the CSBMs agreed upon with Turkey for the Aegean were unsuccessful partly because the formal documents masked significant disagreements and differences in interpretation. If anything, the unrealistic expectations they aroused, the dispute over the interpretation of the documents, the consequent allegation of cheating and the ensuing distrust has actually made it more difficult now for Greece to discuss new CSBMs in the Aegean.[140]

In 1996, following the Imia/Kardak crisis, U.S. Secretary of State Madeleine Albright initiated a moratorium on military flights over Cyprus. This moratorium was never fully accepted or uniformly understood by all parties. Confusion over the details of the fuzzy agreement contributed to a subsequent incident mentioned earlier in this chapter, in which Turkish planes buzzed a military cargo plane carrying the Greek defense minister.[141]

The hesitation to move forward on the security front continued to inform the parties' relations well into the process of rapprochement. During Papandreou's visit to Ankara in January 2000, one of the initiatives considered by the two ministers was Cem's proposal to found a bilateral working group consisting of delegates of the respective defense and foreign ministries, to discuss security measures for reducing tensions in the Aegean Sea. The proposed measures included staging joint military maneuvers in the Aegean, downgrading unilateral military exercises, ensuring that military aircraft flying in the Aegean airspace were unarmed, and scheduling an exchange of port visits in the Aegean for Greek and Turkish naval vessels. Papandreou then referred the proposal to the Greek Ministry of National Defense, which turned it down, suggesting instead that the two countries first build on the 1988 bilateral memorandum.[142]

In December 2000, the NATO secretary general announced that Greece and Turkey agreed to inform each other in advance of national exercises. The first such notification took place at NATO's annual exercise conference, held in Italy that month.[143]

During the following two years, the two countries embarked on broader discussions of proposed security measures, some through NATO and some bilaterally. Among the proposed arrangements were a direct hotline between the two militaries' chiefs of general staff, exchanges of military observers for major military exercises, unarmed flights of warplanes, and mutual port visits by the respective navies.[144] In principle, these measures could all potentially form into effective means of enhancing transparency and bilateral ties, without affecting the underlying disputes in the Aegean or in Cyprus.

To observe the Olympic truce, declared in honor of the August 2004 Olympic Games of Athens, which was unanimously adopted by the United Nations General Assembly, Greece and Turkey agreed to cancel military exercises in the Aegean and not to participate in war games in Cyprus, which had been organized by their respective communities.[145]

In April 2005, the Greek foreign minister, Petros Molyviatis, and his Turkish counterpart, Abdullah Gül, agreed on three new confidence-building measures that would lead to increased cooperation and the development of new bilateral ties, including the development of direct communication between the Greek and Turkish national air communication centers to avoid misunderstandings that might lead to accusations of airspace violations.[146]

A few months later, in June 2005, the Turkish Land Forces commander met in Greece with the Greek defense minister and several Greek armed forces chiefs. The two sides discussed ways to enhance security cooperation between the two countries.

In April 2005, Turkish assembly speaker Bulent Arinc suggested that Turkey should lift its "casus belli" threat against Greece, in the case of a Greek extension of territorial waters to twelve nautical miles. Turkish Foreign Minister Abdullah Gül later commented that although there has been no change in Turkish policy in the Aegean, Arinc's suggestion was part of Ankara's policy for "resolution of all Greek-Turkish problems and the normalization of bilateral relations."[147]

ARMS CONTROL

In April 2001, Cem and Papandreou announced a joint commitment to the Ottawa Convention banning antipersonnel land mines.[148] They undertook to begin the procedures that would make both Greece and Turkey parties to the convention. They further agreed to deposit the instruments of ratification and accession with the UN simultaneously. To supplement this joint commitment, the two countries also agreed to cooperate in clearing land mines from along their borders.[149]

Interestingly, Turkey stood to gain much more than Greece from this joint undertaking, as it was Greece who had placed numerous land mines along the Greek-Turkish land boundary in the Evros region, while Turkey had not. In fact, Turkey had already instated a moratorium on the use, stockpile, or transfer of antipersonnel land mines as early as 1996.[150] According to reports, strong domestic pressure in Greece has been the most influential force in driving the reluctant Greek government to accede to the convention and begin demining operations along the Greek borders with Albania, Bulgaria, Yugoslavia, and Turkey.[151]

A similar demining agreement has been attained in Cyprus. On August 12, 2005, Turkey destroyed some of its land mines in the buffer zone to mark its participation in the demining campaign. Earlier, the Greek Cypriots began to clear thousands of their antipersonnel and antitank mines, having previously cleared thirteen minefields under the joint EU–United Nations Development Program (UNDP) "Partnership for the Future" demining program.[152]

CRIME, TERRORISM, AND LAW ENFORCEMENT

Of the nine agreements signed between Papandreou and Cem in their meeting in Ankara in January 2000 was the Agreement on Combating Crime, Especially Terrorism, Organized Crime, Illicit Drug Trafficking, and Illegal Immigration. In it, the two parties pledged to share information and experience on criminal technology, criminal investigations, scientific research, and other areas of common interest in combating terrorism, organized crime, transboundary crime, money laundering, and drug trafficking. The commitments undertaken also included cooperation in regional and international organizations. A coordination committee was set up to liaise among the various relevant security and law enforcement agencies in both countries.[153]

In January 2001, Greek and Turkish police authorities cooperated in a joint operation to arrest a gang attempting to smuggle heroin into Greece.[154]

In November 2001, Cem and Papandreou concluded an additional agreement on illegal immigration, an acute problem mainly for Greece, which has to cope with the entry of around 250,000 illegal immigrants into its territory annually, most of whom enter through Turkey. Under the terms of the agreement, Greece would be able to return illegal immigrants back to Turkey within fourteen days of their arrival. The two governments also pledged to share intelligence on immigrant-smuggling networks.[155]

Trade and Economic Cooperation

Following the establishment of the EU–Turkey Customs Union in 1996, all tariffs on Turkish-Greek trade were removed. With the Customs Union and improved relations between the commerce chambers of both countries, bilateral trade rocketed from a low of around $100 million a year, to around 1.9 billion in 2005.[156]

Earlier in the process, it was private actors who made serious efforts in advancing and promoting trade relations: in early 1997, the Greek-Turkish Business Cooperation Council instigated a quadripartite meeting in Istanbul of businesspeople from Greece, Turkey, Greek Cyprus, and Turkish Cyprus. This meeting sparked another initiative, led by the U.S. assistant secretary of state, Ambassador Holbrooke, and the former Norwegian foreign minister Jan Egeland to bring together members of the private sectors in Greece and Turkey. The group met three times during 1997–1998, positively advocating cooperative projects in various spheres, including trade, culture, environmental protection, and communications. However, these meetings produced no actual follow-up. The Greek business and industrial establishment was reluctant to move forward on cooperation without a clear green light from the government. The Turkish side, more forthcoming at first, also retracted as the political climate worsened throughout this period. As the Öcalan affair reached its climax in early 1999, the Turks announced an end to all cooperation with their Greek counterparts.[157]

But the January 2000 meeting between Papandreou and Cem marked a watershed in bilateral business too. The two ministers were hosted for lunch by the Turkish-Greek Business Cooperation Council in an effort to encourage joint ventures and mutual investment. Papandreou was accompanied by a delegation of Greek businesspeople, which included the president of the National Bank of Greece (NBG), who was reported as considering opening a branch in Turkey. By the end of the year, a branch of NBG opened in Istanbul.

The two ministers subsequently signed the Agreement on Economic Cooperation, which stipulated that cooperation shall henceforth be aimed at strengthening and diversifying the economic links between the parties and enhancing ties between their economic organizations and companies. The Turkish-Greek Joint Economic Commission was accordingly established to put forward recommendations for guidelines, to identify opportunities, and to serve as a consultation forum between the parties on economic matters.[158]

In February 2002, the first Greek-Turkish Economic Cooperation Ministerial Committee met in Athens.[159] The measures it explored followed the nine cooperation agreements concluded in early 2000, as well as the June 2000 Protocol on Technical, Scientific, and Economic Cooperation in the Field of Agriculture and two additional November 2001 agreements on veterinary protection and plant protection.[160]

Specific suggestions for bilateral work included construction projects in the Balkan countries, the participation of Turkish contractors in the projects planned for the 2004 Olympic Games in Athens, and a joint venture for the transportation of natural gas from Central Asia to western European countries.[161]

In September 2002, Greece submitted a request to open a fourth consulate in Turkey, in the city of Adana, specifically to promote bilateral economic activity.[162] The request has not yet been granted.

Alongside the governmental channels of cooperation, business people from both sides of the border now engage in cooperative economic endeavors. Accordingly, in June 2002, the commercial chambers of both countries hosted Greek and Turkish businesspeople for a Turkish-Greek coastal economic summit. The participants stressed that both countries needed each other on the international markets and that, regardless of the politicians, business enterprises can improve the relations between both countries.[163] The 2000 bilateral Agreement on Reciprocal Promotion and Protection of Investments and the 2003 Agreement on the Avoidance of Double Taxation have already spurred private investments in the respective countries. Around eighty Greek companies operate today in Turkey, mostly in the service sector, and Greek investments constitute more than 3 percent of all foreign investment in Turkey. Only ten Turkish companies, mainly in the tourism and logistics sectors, operate in Greece.[164]

Economic cooperation has thus increased on all levels, governmental and nongovernmental, despite the two countries' standing political disputes. Judging from the commercial chambers' meetings, businesspeople in both countries are determined no longer to let the broader political and territorial conflict of interests take their economic interests hostage.

Energy and Infrastructure

On March 30, 2002, Turkey and Greece signed a natural gas pipeline protocol, intended to carry Caspian gas to European markets, by extending an existing pipeline between Turkey and Iran. According to plan, the pipeline will begin in Ankara and end at Alexandroupolis, and will, during its first phase of its implementation, carry an annual 500 million cubic meters of gas to Greece through Turkey.[165]

In December 2003, the two countries signed an agreement on the extension of an Azerbaijan-Turkey natural gas pipeline into Greece. Reportedly, the 177-mile-long pipeline, which would cost around $250 million, would connect Ankara to Alexandroupolis in northern Greece and supply around 18 billion cubic feet of gas per year, starting in 2006.[166]

There are also initial plans for the integration of the natural gas and electricity systems of both countries. One project under examination concerns an agreement signed between a public Turkish electric company and the Greek Public Power Corporation to study the feasibility of constructing a high-voltage transmission line between the two countries, which would also serve Bulgaria.[167]

Such projects adjoining infrastructure greatly enhance the interdependence between the countries, making any escalation more costly to both.

Culture, Education, and Scientific Collaboration

Of the nine agreements signed in early 2000, two addressed culture, science, and technology. In November 2001, the two foreign ministers also agreed on additional protocols, setting up an exchange program between the two countries' diplomatic academies and outlining future cooperation in the education sector.

In their bilateral discussions, Cem and Papandreou addressed the possibility of Turkey's participation in cultural events planned for the 2004 Olympic Games in Athens. Three years later, when the Turkish Olympic team entered the stadium during the games' opening ceremony, it was greeted by a cheering Greek crowd. The possibility was even raised that the two neighbors should jointly host the 2008 European Cup soccer championship. Though a joint proposal for hosting the games was filed, Greece and Turkey lost to Austria and Switzerland. On the scientific front, the foreign ministers raised initiatives for cooperative scientific research on a number of diseases.[168]

Since 1999 the influence of the public media in both countries has turned from conservative suspicion towards a progressive, conflict-diminishing agenda, legitimizing and supporting the reconciliation process. There is also greater cross-cultural diffusion through music and films. All in all, according to some observers, "cooperation among local governments and municipalities, as well as higher educational institutions and voluntary organizations, has almost reached saturation point."[169]

Nonetheless, elementary and high school education still suffers, in both countries, from a strong ethnocentric bias. Although there have been efforts, both bilateral and regional, by Greek and Turkish historians to rid the schools' curricula of nationalistic and chauvinistic materials, and some unilateral steps have been made to introduce changes to curricula and textbooks by both countries' education authorities, by and large textbooks still portray the "other" as inferior, hostile, and threatening.[170]

Humanitarian Assistance

Following the devastating earthquakes of 1999, the two governments decided to join efforts in meeting natural disasters in the future. They informed the UN General Assembly of their decision to establish a joint standby disaster relief unit to reinforce and expand existing standby arrangements under the UN system. The General Assembly took note of this announcement and requested the secretary general to formulate the modalities for the utilization of such a unit by the relevant UN agencies.[171]

In accordance with their announcement before the General Assembly, on November 8, 2001, the two governments signed a Protocol establishing the Joint Hellenic Turkish Standby Disaster Response Unit (JHET-SDRU), with the aim of increasing the collective capacity of the two countries to provide prompt and effective humanitarian assistance to disaster-stricken populations.[172] The unit consists of around forty people from governmental and nongovernmental agencies in both countries, specializing in search-and-rescue missions, emergency medicine, engineering and geosciences.

The unit is managed by a coordinating committee comprised of equal membership and chaired by representatives of the parties on an annually rotating basis. Members of the unit remain at their permanent home-base locations and meet for exercises, training, or deployment. According to plan, the joint unit is to work closely with the UN and, in particular, with the UN Office for the Coordination of Humanitarian Affairs.

In addition to the bilateral protocol, a memorandum of understanding was signed between the two governments and the UN, with the purpose of developing cooperation arrangements and better coordinating and mobilizing humanitarian emergency assistance. The memorandum envisions deployment of the joint unit in three possible circumstances: under the authority of the UN, as part of an international response, or on a case-by-case basis, as required. It further provides that Greece, Turkey, and the UN will share information on emergencies and participate in international search-and-rescue exercises.[173]

People-to-People Initiatives

The growing rapprochement on the governmental level was accompanied by a host of subgovernmental initiatives. After the 1999 earthquakes, the mayors of Athens and Istanbul paid respective visits to each other's cities. In February 2000, the two mayors signed the Protocol of Friendship and Cooperation between Istanbul and Athens. The initiative expanded in April 2001 to include sixteen mayors of Greek towns and twenty-two mayors of Turkish towns situated along the common border, who concluded an agreement promoting cross-border cooperation in the diverse spheres of trade, tourism, education, agriculture, ecology, communications, and culture.[174]

Municipal cooperation has also been taking place in Cyprus. Launched in 1979, the Nicosia Master Plan is the oldest example of intercommunal ties in Cyprus. Under the auspices of the plan, and through meetings of experts, the municipalities of North and South Nicosia have worked together on water-supply and sewage issues. The plan is sponsored by the United Nations Organization for Project Services (UNOPS).

On the nongovernmental level, however, there are surprisingly few people-to-people initiatives between Greece and Turkey. One of the few in existence is WINPEACE—the Peace Initiative of Women from Turkey and Greece. Established in 1996, WINPEACE is a grassroots movement, which brings together women's organizations from the two countries under the flag of "social equality, equal opportunities and peaceful co-existence." Among other goals, WINPEACE has urged the Greek and Turkish governments to reduce their military budgets by 5 percent by 2003 and channel the resources saved towards women's needs, education, health, and the arts.[175]

Women's peace initiatives have also emerged in Cyprus, where the PeaceWomen Project, an offspring of the Women's International League for Peace and Freedom, has brought Turkish and Greek Cypriot women to march and demonstrate for peace.[176] Nevertheless, nongovernmental ties in Cyprus have been generally difficult to establish, because of the lack of mutual recognition on the leadership level. The TRNC community, especially, suffers from its government's lack of access to international funding. Consequently, the vast majority of bicommunal engagements have been informal and private. Until the opening of the checkpoints in 2003, the impediment to movement between the two parts of the island also impeded ongoing collaboration.

An exceptional initiative has been the Conflict Resolution Trainer Group, which, together with American partners, has sponsored a process of Greek-Turkish dialogue and cooperation over various issues. Still, the group's attempt to found a common, bicommunal NGO had failed, as the affiliation of an NGO with either of the two legal systems would imply governmental recognition. The problem of nonrecognition has also hampered another intercommunal initiative—the Initiative of Businessmen, founded in 1997, which prompted several economic agreements that could not be formalized due to their political implications.[177]

Regional Cooperation

Regional Security Cooperation

NATO

Both Greece and Turkey have been NATO allies since 1952. After the 1974 Turkish invasion of Cyprus, Greece departed from the alliance's military wing in protest. When it decided to resume its membership in 1980, reintegration proved difficult, not least because of Turkish-mounted obstacles. Thus, for several years, Turkey refused to agree to the implementation of NATO decisions on the establishment of two allied headquarters in Greece.

Until the rapprochement, NATO has largely proved incapable of bridging the differences between the two countries. Any unilateral intervention on its part in favor of one of the parties might have caused a rift within the already perilously structured organization. Worse yet, from a practical point of view, such intervention might well have proved unfeasible, as either country could have employed its veto power. NATO's impotence in this respect became most evident during the Imia/Kardak crisis of 1996, when it was the U.S. president, rather than NATO, who stepped in to avert war. However, in the years since the 1996 crisis, once the two countries had already been motivated to improve their relationship, NATO increasingly showed itself to be a positive platform for cooperation. Greek and Turkish military personnel have worked together in various NATO headquarters and participated in joint exercises. About two thousand Greeks and twenty-three thousand Turkish personnel took part in the alliance missions in Bosnia and Kosovo.

In October 1999, Turkey finally lifted its longstanding objection, and allowed NATO to establish the Joint Command Southcenter in Larissa, Greece, adding to three other subregional headquarters, one of which was the Joint Command Southeast in Izmir, Turkey. Greek and Turkish officers had been working side by side in both these headquarters. The chief of staff in Larissa was a Turkish major general, while his counterpart in Izmir was Greek. The Joint Command Southcenter was deactivated in 2004, as part of NATO's reorganization. The two countries now participate together in NATO exercises in the Aegean, making a crisis like the one in 1996 less probable. During NATO's Dynamic Mix exercise, which took place in Greece in May-June 2000, 150 Turkish marines landed on the beach at Kyparissia, Greece; a squadron of F-16 aircraft landed at the Anhialos base in central Greece. It was the first such event to take place after the Cyprus crisis of 1974.[178]

Observers, including former Turkish ambassador to NATO Osman Olcay, consequently expressed their beliefs that NATO may play a further positive role in the future, since reaching a compromise between the militaries may prove much easier than between politicians.[179]

But, as subsequent events have shown, any attempt at progress will always be conditioned on what remains unresolved. Thus, in a later NATO exercise, Destined Glory 2000, which took place only a few months after Dynamic Mix, Greece pulled out of the maneuvers because of a dispute with Turkey concerning overflights by Greek military jets above the Greek islands of Limnos and Ikaria in the eastern Aegean. Turkey insisted that these islands were in a demilitarized zone and refused to grant permission for the overflight.[180]

The dispute over the demilitarization of Aegean islands resurfaced in May 2001, when Turkish authorities rejected a flight plan submitted by Greece's navy commander, because the proposed route included a refueling stop on the island of Rhodes, which Turkey insisted must remain demilitarized. In response, the commander boycotted a NATO ceremony held at the Turkish Aksaz naval base.[181]

A year later, during NATO's Destined Glory 2002 exercise, Greece again cancelled a portion of the maneuvers, which were to take place in Greece, because of a dispute with Turkey, this time over the FIR regime. Turkey was scheduled to send eight aircraft to western Greece to take part in the flight exercises in the area. Greece demanded that the aircraft submit their flight plans to the Athens FIR, but Turkey refused, citing the practice whereby military planes were not bound to submit flight plans if they stayed within international airspace. Despite this, other parts of the exercises, held in the central Mediterranean Sea and in Italy were not cancelled.[182]

In February 2002, Papandreou himself intervened to make Athens take notice of the Turkish gesture of sending military flight information, through NATO, to the Greek FIR center. Athens, which had first ignored the gesture, has since come to treat the information sent by Turkey as "official NATO documents."[183] This is an example of how the NATO framework was instrumental in accommodating a compromise, albeit not a resolution, in the FIR controversy.

In July 2003, NATO's secretary general, Lord Robertson, facilitated talks between the Greek and Turkish permanent representatives to NATO, which resulted in two new agreements. These covered cooperation between the Greek and Turkish national defense colleges and exchange of personnel between Partnership of Peace training centers in the two countries. An earlier agreement had also been reached within the NATO context, which referred to "mutual notification of exercise schedules."[184]

THE EU RAPID-REACTION DEFENSE FORCE

The establishment of a new European Rapid Reaction Force (ERRF) was one of the plans agreed upon at the Helsinki European Council meeting in December 1999. The structure includes a military force of sixty thousand personnel, capable of operating independently of NATO to meet regional emergencies, such as the one presented by Kosovo in 1998 with the necessary promptness.

Since the end of 2000, Turkey has enhanced its military cooperation with the EU, offering military personnel and equipment to the ERRF. And although the ERRF was also designed with the expectation of substantial assistance from NATO, Turkey had conditioned any support to the ERRF—whether by itself or by NATO (in which it enjoys a member's veto power)—on its being allowed to play a central role in the force. But not being a member of the EU, its participation in the ERRF was blocked.[185]

In the December 2002 EU summit in Copenhagen, Turkey agreed to lift its NATO veto on allowing the EU access to NATO's military assets, in exchange for a promise that Cyprus would not take part in the ERRF.[186] Turkey's proposal was accepted, and the ERRF would in the future be able to serve as another regional platform for cooperation between the Greek and Turkish militaries, as NATO has done in recent years.

SEEBRIG

In September 1998, Greece and Turkey, along with Italy, established the Balkans rapid deployment task force known as the Southeast European Brigade (SEEBRIG), to be used for peacekeeping operations in the region, as well as for potential deployment in nearby areas such as the Black Sea, in the event of a crisis. The initiative is part of the Southeastern Europe Defense Ministerial (SEDM), an informal group of the defense ministers of southeast European countries.[187]

SEEBRIG consists of a force of three thousand, contributed by seven nations, including Greece and Turkey. As one analyst noted,

> although the Brigade is primarily designed to carry out short-term peace support missions, it will also promote better relations among the member nations in the Balkans. It has established several channels of communication among the countries, encourages military staffs to train together . . . serves as a point of Greek-Turkish teamwork, and can help make the Balkans an area of cooperation, not confrontation.[188]

Both Turkey and Greece have played a significant role in the establishment and operation of the brigade.

Regional Economic Cooperation

The collapse of the Soviet Union has made possible the formation of new market economies in the region, which have opened up limitless economic opportunities for Greek and Turkish entrepreneurs. While most of these opportunities are still pursued by independent businesspeople, recent years have seen important progress in broader regional cooperation. Another function of regional organizations has been to present interested private parties with a political platform on the basis of which they could urge their governments to enhance economic ties with other countries in the region.

One such organization has been the Black Sea Economic Cooperation (BSEC), whose Charter came into force in May 1999, setting up a regional structure for enhancing multilateral cooperation in the Black Sea area. Member states include Albania, Armenia, Azerbaijan, Bulgaria, Georgia, Greece, the Republic of Moldova, Romania, the Russian Federation, Turkey, and the Ukraine. The Council of Ministers, made up of the foreign ministers of the member states, meets biannually, and is the organization's highest decision-making body. Cooperation also takes place on the interparliamentary level.[189]

Under the auspices of BSEC, several working groups have been set up to address cooperation in energy, tourism, science and technology, health, transportation, electricity, investments, agriculture, finance and more. The BSEC has also formed the Business Council, which consists of private enterprise representatives of member states, acts as a center for the support of private-sector regional trade and business. The financial pillar of the organization is the Black Sea Trade and Development Bank, in which Greece, Turkey and Russia have the largest shareholding. The bank's headquarters is in Thessaloniki, Greece, and its president is Turkish.

Other initiatives contemplated by the BSEC are the establishment of a regional free trade zone, a regional stock market and future cooperation in the sphere of energy as well as with the World Trade Organization and the Organisation for Economic Cooperation and Development.

It is interesting to note that in a publication by the Turkish Ministry of Foreign Affairs, one of the achievements the BSEC is reported to have had is that it fosters economic cooperation even among member countries who are otherwise involved in ongoing political conflicts.

Another organization, the Southeast European Cooperation Process (SEECP) was launched in 1996, at Bulgaria's initiative. It consists of Albania, Bosnia and Herzegovina, Bulgaria, Croatia, Greece, Macedonia, Romania, Serbia, and Montenegro, as well as Turkey. SEECP defines itself as a program of cooperation in southeastern Europe, with the goals of consolidating security and political situations, intensifying economic relations and social cooperation, promoting democracy and justice, and combating crime.[190]

SEECP members have been gathering to discuss military conversion and reform issues, economic cooperation and the integration of regional electrical systems.

The Southeast European Cooperation Initiative (SECI) is a U.S. project, supporting business activity in the region. A mainstay of the initiative has been a center for the combating of cross-border crime, aimed at improving the business environment and making it more attractive to investments. Under the SECI's auspices, dedicated work groups address the issues of human trafficking, drugs trafficking, commercial fraud, stolen cars, financial crime, and customs evaluation.[191]

And Cyprus?

The islands of agreement between Greece and Turkey have hardly, as yet, been mirrored in Cyprus, except in the form of some unofficial non-governmental initiatives, mostly sponsored by third parties.

For a while, at the beginning of the process of reconciliation, the communities on the island seemed to follow the mainland countries' example and show a real interest in thawing their relationship. Bicommunal contacts between businesspeople, politicians, journalists, and environmentalists resumed. The UN secretary general reported a rise in the number of contacts between Greek and Turkish Cypriots and an easing of Turkish Cypriot regulations regarding visits of Greek Cypriots to the north. An unusual exercise of goodwill between the two communities occurred in March 2000, when Turkish Cypriots and Greek Cypriots united in search of bone marrow donors for two children, one from each community, who were suffering from leukemia.[192]

At the same time, however, tensions around the Green Line remained high. Turkish and Greek Cypriots frequently engaged in acts of mutual provocation, and soldiers on both sides kept on high alert, especially in Nicosia, where the Green Line is merely a fence. Since then, to reduce the risk of spiraling violence, the parties have voluntarily cut back on the number of troops along the line.[193]

Another proposed UN plan, which led to a further round of proximity talks in November 2000, envisioned the concept of two "component states" existing in tandem on the island. The plan was unique in its acquiescence to the ongoing presence in Cyprus of some Turkish troops. Despite this material breakthrough, Denktash was angered by the proposal's unevenness in containing provisions for the recovery of Greek Cypriot property lost in the 1974 campaign but remaining silent on the matter of Turkish Cypriot property. The talks subsequently failed.

The timing of the new proposals was also problematic; on the day they were announced, the EU, under Greek pressure, decided to make Turkish support for the UN's peace efforts in Cyprus a precondition for beginning accession talks with Turkey. On the Turkish side, this was interpreted as yet another example of the old UN-EU conspiracy favoring the Greek Cypriots. Denktash quit the proximity talks, declaring them "a waste of time."[194]

Negotiations were resumed only in December 2001, when Denktash and Clerides met face to face in Cyprus, for the first time since 1997, and agreed to hold direct talks with no preconditions. Many subsequent meetings failed to generate agreement.

In November 2002, as Cyprus's move towards EU accession grew imminent, the UN presented a new peace plan, described by observers as "the best chance in many years for a settlement to resolve the conflict."[195] The plan called for a devolution of power to two separate administrations within a one-state framework, drawing on the canton models of Belgium and Switzerland. It also recognized the right of Greek Cypriots to return to their homes in the north and the need for a recovery of some of the property lost in 1974. The Greek Cypriot leadership accepted the plan in principle. Denktash, however, claimed that the plan "failed to ease his concerns over the future status of his people."[196]

A month later, in the broadest enlargement step to date, the Copenhagen summit of the EU admitted Cyprus, along with nine other central and eastern European countries, as members. The accession of Cyprus was decided upon, even though no political settlement had been reached on the island. Although there were some suggestions to drop Cyprus from the current phase of enlargement and wait until a settlement had been reached, Greece quashed them by threatening to retaliate with a block on the accession of the other nine new members.[197]

In the meantime, western officials blamed Denktash personally for the failure of the Cyprus negotiations; one senior official was quoted as saying, "You can forget any politeness about Denktash: Either he is overridden by the new government in Ankara or there will be no settlement."[198] Officials in Ankara, concerned that Turkey's accession to the EU should still be held hostage by a political settlement in Cyprus, also suggested that a check should be put on Denktash to prevent him from using the opposition within some sections of the Turkish military to frustrate a deal. Most important, however, is what seemed to be a shift in the popular attitudes within the TRNC, as thousands took to the streets to urge Denktash to sign the peace deal and thus allow the participation of the TRNC in the EU. Polls showed a two-thirds majority in favor of a settlement, in defiance of Denktash's stance.[199]

In a gesture to quell international and domestic criticism, Denktash announced that he would open three checkpoints across the dividing line in Cyprus to enable the Greek Cypriots to visit their old homes. On April 23, 2003, the first time in twenty-nine years, Greek and Turkish Cypriots were allowed to cross the Green Line. Cypriots in their thousands took advantage of this offer, which also resulted in bringing the two communities closer together. When Denktash realized this, he tried to retract his gesture, since events on the ground were proving his long-standing position that the two communities could never coexist uncomfortably wrong. But by then, the momentum was already irresistible. One reporter noted that "the older generation feels an impulse of reconciliation. The young have satisfied their curiosity and learned, for example, that, as a Greek student put it, 'it's not Pakistan on the other side.'"[200]

Meanwhile, Denktash's demands for a lift of the economic embargo imposed on the TRNC since the 1974 invasion, as a reciprocal goodwill gesture, has remained unmet.[201]

In early 2004, the UN sponsored a new series of UN negotiations. Any agreement at that point would have allowed the Turkish Cypriots to enter the EU together with the Greek Cypriots on May 1. The target, as far as Europe was concerned, was to find a solution prior to this date and so to prevent Cyprus from bringing its problems with it into the EU.

The solution proposed was to form the basis for what became known as the "UN plan" or the "Annan plan." With over two hundred pages of text and nine thousand pages of appendices, it outlined a loose federation of two separate entities as well as the return of several but not all Greek Cypriot refugees to their homes in the north. A small number of Turkish troops and settlers would be allowed to remain in northern Cyprus. The plan also barred recourse to the European courts on all issues covered by it. The Greek Cypriot delegation rejected the proposed settlement, arguing that it should be given more land in exchange for allowing settlers and troops to stay. Papadopoulos also objected to the Turkish request for an extended transition period, during which wealthy Greek Cypriots would not be able to buy up land for development in the north, an objection in which he was backed by Greek Premier Kostas Karamanlis. Although it seemed that a settlement was likely this time round, and despite the strength of international pressure, Papadopoulos finally collapsed the talks with a last-minute veto.[202]

On April 23, 2004, the UN plan was put to two simultaneous referenda on the Greek and Turkish Cypriot sides of the Green Line. Both Papadolpoulos and Denktash advocated the communities to vote no. But Prime Minister Recep Tayyip Erdoğan, as well as Denktash's second in political command—Prime Minister Mehmet Ali Talat, who succeeded Denktash as president the following year—favored the plan's acceptance. Karamanlis remained neutral. In the final count of the vote, about 65 percent of Turkish Cypriots supported the plan, but 76 percent of Greek Cypriots voted to reject it, drawing much criticism from the international community. After the results became known, Papadopoulos said he was committed to a deal with the north.[203]

Though several "carrots" were associated with a positive result in the two referenda (mainly a pledge for significant international financial aid), it was the lack of relevant "sticks" for the Greek side that decided the Cyprus vote. The joint UN-EU effort was ill conceived: if Greek Cypriots voted in favor of the plan, they could join the EU together with the Turkish Cypriots; if they voted against it, they could join the EU alone.

Security seemed to be a primary Greek Cypriot concern. The overriding feeling was that the plan was pro-Turkish in that it allowed for Turkish settlers to remain in the north, while limiting the right of refugees to return from the south. It has also been suggested, however, that the dire economic situation in the TRNC, which Greek Cypriots have come to witness for themselves since the Green Line was opened by Denktash in 2003, has been a palpable deterrent for the Greek Cypriots. One analyst emphasized the fact that the costs of economic reunification, estimated at close to $20 billion, would have had to be borne by the Greek Cypriot community, with only a small portion covered by the international donor community and none by Turkey.[204]

In an attempt to compensate the TRNC for its affirmative vote on the Annan plan, and bypass the quagmire of legal difficulties that would be entailed by lifting the trade embargo, EU governments vowed in April 2004 to "put an end to the isolation of the Turkish Cypriot Community" and to help its economic development with an aid package of 259 million euros. The Cypriot government, however, blocked the aid delivery, claiming that if the north became more prosperous, the Turkish Cypriots would be less inclined to seek a peace settlement.[205] The only trade facilitation so far has been the Cypriot government's acceptance of the European Commission's Green Line Regulation, introduced in July 2004, which regiments some north-south trade on the island.

The Cypriot government has so far refrained, however, from using its veto power to delay the beginning of EU entry negotiations with Turkey, since such a step would only contribute to its isolation from its European partners, including Greece.[206]

The failure of the 2004 peace plan and referendum to bridge the Cyprus divide has been more than simply another failed attempt at resolution. Its impact is likely to be felt for some time to come. That it should have been rejected by the popular vote is likely to reverberate more strongly with the two communities than had it been rejected on the whim of hard-line leaders. It is now up to the next UN secretary general to be willing to invest quite so much as his predecessor in this issue.

Analysis

Geographically, culturally, and conceptually, Greece and Turkey straddle a junction of regions; formally, both are a part of an expanding Europe, but both (though only the European part of Turkey) are also Balkan states and Mediterranean states. Bounded by three seas on all sides, Turkey, in particular, is a crossroads country, a gateway from east to west and from north to south, over land and by water. Its northwest touches Bulgaria, its northeast the former Soviet Block, and to its south lies the Middle East. It is small wonder, then, that over the years there has been no shortage of external actors on the Greek-Turkish scene who have tried to influence the two countries' political interaction in the name of one or another alignment.

Where these actors have intervened to bring about peace, their vision has mostly proved premature, unripe as yet for the protagonists themselves. In the words of the former U.S. special Cyprus coordinator, M. James Wilkinson, reflecting on the international efforts in Cyprus,

> the persistence of Greek-Turkish confrontation, whatever its roots, runs counter to the common-sense conviction that, with reason and good will, civilized people in decent economic circumstances can settle their problems amicably. Greece and Turkey, for their part, are increasingly pluralistic and prosperous—qualities commonly supposed to be sure foundations of lasting peace and stability.

He then added,

> Western intermediaries approach the problems like sophisticated puzzles: one just has to keep resizing the parts and trading them back and forth until the two sides balance out. Sadly, however, whether because of process or content, it just has not worked that way. In the Aegean, Greeks and Turks do not even agree on a procedure to examine the pieces of the puzzle; in Cyprus, one or the other side has rejected comprehensive and balanced arrangements laboriously cobbled together over the years by UN, U.S., and European diplomats.[207]

Part of this comprehensive failure, no doubt, may be attributed to the deep, broad multidimensionality of the conflict, with its international as well as intranational challenges. The international aspects have been most evident in the territorial dispute over the Aegean Sea, in the ethnic frictions within both countries and in the proxy rivalry over the future of Cyprus. The conflict within Cyprus, between Greek and Turkish Cypriots, is an intranational conflict, being fueled and refueled through a continuous exchange with the mainland countries. Whenever points of friction arose over the treatment of minorities, the stationing of troops on the islands in the Aegean, and even the Imia/Kardak islets, the knot of tensions tightened closer.

Over the years, both the Greek and Turkish governments adopted shrill, often combative stands towards one another, rallying domestic constituents in support. As Haralambos Athanasopulos remarks,

> This resulted in the building of a psychological barrier of hatred between the peoples of Greece and Turkey, which prevented them from interacting with each other on a friendly and neighborly basis. The cultivation and exploitation of Greek and Turkish mutual suspicion and misperceptions as to their foreign policy objectives toward each other concerning their national security and territorial integrity have fueled a constant rivalry, antagonism and mutual distrust between the two countries.[208]

Inculcation with negative mutual perceptions was achieved through the education system, the media, and nation-building processes in both countries.

As long as the rivalry continued as conflict, therefore, violence was kept simmering on its several fronts, still contemplated or else shown to be contemplated as a very real option; this had been amply demonstrated by the several near-crisis events in the Aegean, and by the S-300 missiles showdown in Cyprus. One needs no further proof than to consider the readiness exhibited by both countries to engage in an armed conflict with each other over the sovereignty of the Imia/Kardak islets; that these miniscule bodies of land lacked any strategic, economic, or other material value was of no importance. It was enough that they had symbolic value as a territorial extension of the national identities inhabiting the Aegean space.

But over the past six years the Greek-Turkish conflict has suddenly run its course. From a defining factor of the two people's relationship, it has become only one component within a complete relationship. A congruence of human and natural events has dimmed the glory of strife. Cooperation and agreement reign.

As a result, the parties have been able to increase their bilateral trade volume exponentially, embark on bilateral scientific and cultural projects, join efforts in law enforcement and prepare together for the possibility of being struck by a natural disaster. Even before becoming Turkey's prime minister in 2003, Recep Tayyip Erdoğan had referred to Greece as "Turkey's closest neighbor and strategic partner."[209] His relationship with the newly elected Greek premier, Kostas Karamanlis, has grown so close that Erdoğan even invited Karamanlis to his daughter's wedding as an honorary guest and witness in July 2004.[210] A couple of months earlier, Erdoğan was the first Turkish prime minister to visit Greece since 1988. For two countries that had hardly any joint enterprise until 1999, this is all a remarkable achievement.

But even as they edge nearer each other than ever in modern history, Greece and Turkey continue to hold on to Cyprus and the Aegean Sea as bones of contention between them. The Cyprus dispute is substantially driven by religion, ethnicity, and historical animosity, heightened by the natural limitation of the island's geography. The Aegean contains all these components, in addition to questions of territory, security, and tangible benefits arising from control over the Aegean waters, seabed, and airspace.

In the case of Cyprus, the events leading to the division of the island in 1974 are recited by Turks and Greeks in squarely contradictory terms. The two sides of the Green Line in Nicosia are lined with memorials to past atrocities, with the identities of victims and perpetrators reversed. For the Greeks, Turkey forcibly invaded the island with the purpose of occupying it out of Greek hands—while for Turks, the invasion was an inevitable preemptive remedy against the ethnic cleansing that the Turkish population was certain to be subjected to following the Greek coup.

The Aegean territorial dispute is equally persistent. Both countries rely on legal documents that do little to resolve their differences, even in the matter of deciding the appropriate method of settling their conflict. Greece's stance has long been that there is only one open question in the Aegean—the continental shelf—which should be submitted to arbitration or adjudication. In general, Greece believes the letter of the existing agreement to be on its side and therefore favors acting through legal instruments and third-party arbitration and adjudication. Turkey, perceiving itself the weaker party, prefers bilateral negotiations on all issues and, as second best, submission of all disputes, en bloc, to adjudication without carving out single issues. This disparity of approach was what doomed the Berne Declaration of 1976 on the Aegean continental shelf.

So far, Greece has been at least nominally more successful in its method, having influenced the EU to force Turkey to submit the dispute to the ICJ by 2004 if resolution cannot be attained earlier. Bilateral negotiations are still ongoing, and the referral to the ICJ has been postponed in the hope that a solution might be found.[211]

Moreover, rather than acting to separate outstanding contested topics from one another, both countries have shown no scruples about entangling the issues of Cyprus, the Aegean, and EU membership as much as possible, so that any progress on one front was perpetually taken hostage by escalation on the others.

Until not long ago, international, especially European, involvement in the conflict has been largely noncommittal. The reasons are many, but perhaps the most fundamental is this: while Greece and Cyprus are already members of the European Union, and Turkey increasingly so, the conflict between Turkey and Greece sits at sharp odds with the West's notion of itself, of what it means to be Western and civilized. By protracting the dispute in terms of real or threatened violence, the two countries seemed to be continually reminding the community they wished to belong to that they were, in fact, not entirely of it. If, as Jacob M. Landau has put it, "there is a dialectical contradiction between modernism and patriotism," the Balkans' internal struggle between their own eastern and western identities is an uncomfortable reminder of this truth to a West that still likes to think of itself as both modern and patriotic at the same time.[212]

Nonetheless, the Balkan wriggling seems to come at the cost of much mental anguish for the wrigglers. Though a number of (mainly Greek) historians nowadays tend to date the conflict only to the time of the Turkish invasion of Cyprus in 1974, blaming on it the unnecessary rekindling of former tensions, A. J. R. Groom was surely right to observe that "Greece and Turkey . . . in various ways, deny their Ottoman past—a past that still lingers in the present. But to deny the past is to deny themselves—hence the identity problem which bedevils their relationship."[213]

Long fallen into the habit, so to speak, of displays of strength, the two countries continue to spend enormous sums on national defense. In April 2001, Papandreou offered a mutual arms reduction, but Turkey refused to commit itself, citing its special geostrategic situation and the potential threat from sources other than Greece as the reason.[214] Since then, both countries have on various occasions announced unilateral defense spending cuts—Greece to boost social spending and accelerate preparations for the 2004 Olympics, Turkey to meet recent financial crises and justify its appeal to foreign aid and under domestic pressure to have the military share some of the burden of cuts. In January 2004, the Turkish foreign minister, Abdullah Gül, accepted his Greek counterpart's proposal for a pledge for reciprocal reductions of military spending, a development seen as "one of the most significant steps toward reconciliation for years."[215] No action, however, has as yet been taken. And despite respective announcements on arms reductions, the volatile economic situation in both countries (especially Turkey), and the material incentives to cut back on the militaries' budget, the two governments' expenditure on defense in terms of their GDPs is still the highest in Europe.[216]

The EU entanglement continues to act simultaneously as an incentive for resolution and as an impediment to it. In December 2004, the EU announced that entry negotiations with Turkey would begin on October 3, 2005. When the day arrived, after an intense EU meeting that almost failed to approve the start of negotiations due to Austrian opposition to full membership for Turkey, a document stipulating the negotiation terms was finally drafted and subsequently approved. Cyprus, now a member, did not use its veto power to block these decisions.

While Turkey is now on course towards EU accession, that course is bound to be a long and bumpy one, as negotiations are expected to take at least four years to complete. Turkey has already carried out some legislative changes to fulfill the Copenhagen political criteria. Nevertheless, EU officials have criticized Turkey for the slow pace of reforms, predominantly in the area of human rights—freedom of expression, women's rights, religious freedoms, trade union rights, cultural rights, and critically, torture and ill-treatment towards which the EU maintains a zero-tolerance policy.[217] Turkey was recently granted the status of a functioning market economy by the EU, a fact that is expected to help with foreign investment. Political reforms, such as reducing the role of the military and furthering democratization, are another area in which more work is needed. For Turkey this would be a tricky undertaking, as the military is the strongest anti-Islamization force in the country.

Another point of friction for the Turks is that the failure to resolve the Cyprus conflict before Cyprus was admitted as a member in the EU in 2004 has left the TRNC with the short end of the stick. Turkey won EU kudos for its intense efforts to find a solution to the Cyprus issue prior to May 1, 2004. But commitment to and support of an eventual solution in Cyprus remain a deciding factor in the progress of Turkey's entry negotiations. The EU has not made it any easier for Turkey to put pressure on TRNC leaders—formerly Denktash and now Mehmet Ali Talat—to continue their efforts at reconciliation. The TRNC is still under a trade embargo, and EU efforts at economic assistance to the TRNC are constantly blocked by Cyprus.

In a show of support for the TRNC, Turkey extended its customs union agreement with the EU to the nine new members of 2004 but refused to include Cyprus in it.[218] This has already generated some threats within the EU to postpone Turkish accession negotiations.

The island of Cyprus has so far remained in the cold, outside the embrace of the newly reconciled mother countries. It is only in the past two years that some movement of people has been allowed across the Green Line and that any trade is taking place. There are, as yet, no formalized and institutionalized arrangements that involve ongoing and direct cooperation between the two sides. It would have been conceivable, for instance, that the Cyprus EU accession process might serve as a vehicle for some attempts at cooperation on the island. But instead, an "all or nothing" approach steadfastly remains the prevailing note.

The Workings of Islands of Agreement

Up until the past seven years, there were few formal islands of agreement between the parties. The few that did exist—namely, the Berne Declaration of 1976 or some security arrangements in the Aegean agreed on in 1988—were widely ignored. By contrast, the cluster of agreements signed in 2000 and since addressed a panoply of spheres of interaction, was generally complied with, and yielded substantial benefits for both sides.

The reconciliation process between Greece and Turkey can therefore be said to have metamorphosed a conflict with islands of agreement into a peaceful rivalry with some islands of disagreement. Although the issues at stake have not changed, the two sides no longer feel the threat of conflict looming whenever disagreement arises.

One may argue that, conceptually, the bulk of agreements attained by Greece and Turkey resemble more a phased peace agreement than the "independent" islands existing between India and Pakistan. To support this argument, one may refer to Papandreou's stated piecemeal approach, which sought to build upon the joint agreements to prepare the ground for "further steps along the way."[219] However, given the fact that the piecemeal method has been consciously designed to create a dynamic of cooperation by addressing low-politics issues first, while completely avoiding the red zones of the Aegean and Cyprus, I argue it should be understood precisely as a cluster of islands of agreement rather than as a phased peace process. As noted earlier, islands of agreement are recognizable by process, not by outcome.

In fact, Cem's first letter to Papandreou suggested that "*parallel to* the signing and implementation of such an agreement, we could also initiate a plan for reconciliation," implying that the proposed agreement was not such a comprehensive plan.[220] Indeed, in none of the ensuing accords was there any material reference to Cyprus or the Aegean Sea.

Cem's choice of the phrase "parallel to," in reference to the sequencing of agreements with Greece, exactly captures the propitious potential and flexibility we expect from islands of agreement: islands may lead to attempts to reach comprehensive agreement, but they may also cohabit with them independently. In the latter case, failure to achieve success does not necessitate a breakdown of issues across the board.

Building Islands of Agreement

All the issues chosen for the 2000 series of accords were extraneous to the core disputes. Either country could thus cooperate in the spheres of culture, education, agriculture, customs, and law enforcement without harming its basic position on either the Aegean or Cyprus. The guiding principle was therefore that of divisibility.

Where significant progress is yet to be made, not surprisingly, is in the highly sensitive security sphere. Earlier arrangements—the 1988 Athens Memorandum and Istanbul Guidelines on security arrangement in the Aegean—have time and time again failed to be fully implemented. Their reaffirmation in 1998 has therefore done little to improve their record. Though intended as limited-issue agreements, they were not, in fact, limited enough, thereby arousing unrealistic expectations. Most significantly, perhaps, the attempt to separate the issue of military encounters in the Aegean from the underlying territorial disputes has ultimately proved unfeasible. When such divisibility was observed—as with the full moratorium on military flights during the months of July and August—it was generally complied with.

While important security cooperation did occur within the framework of NATO operations, this again held only as long as it did not clash with the core disputes. When it did, as in the NATO exercises in 2000 and 2002, all goodwill and good intentions seemed to evaporate. As a result of these successive failures, the parties have since been hesitant to conclude further security arrangements.

In this context, the cooperation between the two countries over Turkey's accession to the EU is a remarkable example of half divisibility. Whereas formerly the EU was a compound battleground over Turkey's accession as well as Cyprus's, the battle—from a Greek perspective—has now been slimmed down to the future of the TRNC and Europe. On the other hand, when politics pulled towards issue entanglement, no islands could be created. In one such case, in the early 1990s, the Greek government proposed the withdrawal of all offensive weapons from the area adjacent to the Greek-Bulgarian-Turkish borders, with the purpose of enhancing stability by reducing the possibility of a surprise attack. Turkey rejected this proposal on the grounds that it failed to consider other areas of confrontation, such as the Aegean.[221]

On the whole, the Greek-Turkish process of rapprochement has been highly formal and institutionalized. Agreements were set in writing, with subsequent supplementary protocols. Joint committees were established under each agreement, alongside an overarching monitoring committee. The shortcomings of the former security arrangements—ambiguous wording and lack of any interpreting or monitoring mechanism—were thus corrected. Direct channels of communication between the foreign ministries and, perhaps more crucially, between the ministers themselves have proved invaluable in propelling the process forward and resolving occasional differences.

For a long time, the role played by regional frameworks—most notably, the EU and NATO—was that of a magnifying glass for the basic attitudes of the parties rather than that of a force for conceptual change. As long as Greece refused to agree to Turkey's accession to the EU, the union became a constant trigger for friction and frustration, powerless for decades to bring about any material transformation in the two countries' relationship. Similarly, despite high hopes to the contrary, NATO had for many decades been unable to intervene in the Aegean dispute or to diffuse tensions between the two militaries. Bilateral security arrangements advanced by NATO were either rejected or seemed to have little effect on the ground. Each side exercised its veto power—

Greece in the EU and Turkey in NATO—to perpetuate the balance of threat and block external initiatives.

It was only once bilateral relations had changed of the parties' own volition that both regional organizations began to materialize as fertile grounds for amity. The opportunities for cooperation created by a joint involvement with the organizations were vast, and so were the possibilities of realizing the benefits of cooperation within them, both at present and in the future. Turkey's accession process had become perhaps the most important sphere of cooperation between the two countries, enabling Greece to play a parental role, supporting, assisting, and training Turkey on its jagged road to the EU. With NATO having established a regional headquarters in Greece in 1999, Greek and Turkish officers also considerably enhanced their bilateral relations within the NATO framework. They now take part in joint exercises and operations and work together in the day-to-day routine of the alliance.

Interestingly, other regional organizations, such as SECI or BSEC, and even military cooperation through SEEBRIG have all served for some time as islands of agreement even before the eventual rapprochement between the two countries. As participation in these regional structures did not seem to threaten either party's bargaining position on their mutual core conflict and was independently considered important by each of them for other foreign policy considerations (mainly, regional positioning in the Balkans), joint membership and operation was feasible and practical.

The proven benefits of joint participation in regional structures were part of Papandreou's initial plan for the process of rapprochement. Papandreou envisioned the possibilities of enhanced collaboration in the framework of regional organizations when he concluded his June 1999 response letter to Cem, suggesting, "The South East European Cooperation, SECI and the Black Sea Economic Cooperation, where we have already achieved a good record of collaboration, can become important areas of successful work between us."[222]

Regional organizations now opened up invaluable avenues of communication and dialogue at both the political and, no less important, the bureaucratic level. Military professionals, as well as professionals in the spheres of economics, finance, agriculture, infrastructure, the environment, and so on, could now meet with their counterparts to design regional projects for the benefit of all countries. This ongoing involvement, particularly in recent years, has contributed to a culture of dialogue and cooperation in key sectors of government, the civil service, and the private sector.

So far, international law has not been instrumental in resolving the outstanding disputes between the rivals—not the general principles of international law, such as territorial sovereignty, right to self-determination, or the prohibition on the use of force; nor multilateral treaties, such as those pertaining to the law of the sea; nor still the more specific treaties, such as the Cyprus Treaty of Guarantee or the Treaty of Lausanne. All these merely armed the adversaries with opposing principles, clauses, and interpretations by which to reinforce their already chosen positions.

While it is true that the lack of enforcement mechanisms has made the working of these treaties less effective, it is nonetheless far from clear that the working of effective judicial mechanisms, such as the European Court of Human Rights or the European Court of Justice (ECJ) have had a positive effect. In 1996 the ECHR, in its first judgment on human rights violations in Northern Cyprus—*Loizidou v. Turkey*—found in favor of a Greek Cypriot woman who had owned property in the north and who claimed to have lost access to it since the Turkish invasion in 1974. The ECHR found Turkey to have effective control in the area and therefore to be responsible for human rights violations there. The ECHR also referred to the almost universal nonrecognition of the TRNC and considered that the member states of the Council of Europe were obliged under international law not to recognize acts of the TRNC.[223]

In May 2001, the ECHR, sitting as a grand chamber of seventeen judges, delivered its judgment in the first interstate case brought before it since its 1998 reform—*Cyprus v. Turkey*.[224] In the longest judgment in its history, the court ruled that Turkey was responsible for various breaches of the European Convention on Human Rights in the TRNC, referring specifically to missing Greek Cypriots and their relatives, to the homes and property of displaced persons, and to the living conditions of both communities in northern Cyprus. Following *Loizidou*, the ECHR refused to consider the TRNC as an independent sovereign unit and instead held that Turkey had effective control over the TRNC and was hence responsible for human rights violations there.

Commentators noted that the Annan plan was incompatible with some of the key components in the *Cyprus v. Turkey* ruling, especially with regard to the right of refugees to their property and the obligation for compensation in cases of expropriation.[225] Greek Cypriots, who objected to the plan, named its departure from this judicial ruling as another reason to reject it. At the same time, it has been clear for a while that no resolution would ever be found to the Cyprus conflict if the ECHR decision is to be fully and rigidly implemented.[226] The ECHR itself only asserted that "inter-communal talks cannot be invoked in order to legitimate a violation of the [European] Convention [on Human Rights]."[227]

As legal constraints are now cited by the EU as the obstacles barring the lift of the economic embargo on the TRNC, and as negotiated solutions might have to depart from the ECHR rulings, the case of Cyprus offers some food for thought on the eternal peace or justice debate.

The Way Ahead

According to 2004 research based on a public survey, Turks continue to have mixed feelings towards the newfound friendship with their neighbors. The survey found that "Turks perceive Greeks as unfriendly in comparison to other nationalities and ethnicities"—being less unfriendly than only the Armenians and ranking third among traditional foes, after the Armenians and the Russians.[228] Turks also consider Greece their worst friend in the international arena, but domestic problems and other regional and international entanglements are seen as bigger threats to Turkey's security than Greece. More than half the Turks who participated in the survey believe that Greeks and Turks could be friends. More than 60 percent are not disturbed by listening to Greek music on Turkish radio and television. However, friendship has its limits, as more than 70 percent of Turks would disapprove of their children marrying Greeks.

A public opinion polling Web site in Greece, which conducted a survey in the summer of 2004, asked its participants whether they would want Turkey to enter the European Union as a full member. Seventy-one point two percent of participants voted no, while only 22.4 percent voted in favor.[229]

But there is more than one way of gauging public opinion. In the summer of 2005, a new Turkish television series, *The Foreign Groom*, aired on Greek TV. Its subject was the forbidden romance of a young couple—Nazli, a Turkish woman, and Nikos, a Greek man. The two fall in love and plan to get married against their parents' wishes.[230] The Nikos-Nazli affair is symbolic of the Greek-Turkish rivalry, which often goes on—in popular opinion—because of the governments (represented by the older generations in the two families) and against the desires of the people (represented by the couple). In the end the two youths have their wish and marry, creating hope for peaceful coexistence: Nazli gives birth to a son who is named Aegean. The show received record ratings, proof, if proof were needed, that there was popular support for the Greek-Turkish "romance" and that both nations recognized familiar elements in each other's social and cultural life.

The process of reconciliation now appears to be irreversible. It is highly unlikely either Greece or Turkey will now resort to arms against one another. But until a final settlement of the core disputes is reached, the delicate balance struck by the two sides is at constant risk of being at least dramatically disturbed. The possibility that a Turkish vessel might be engaged in oil explorations in the Aegean continental shelf was sufficient to cause an upheaval in May 2001, well into the new "era of rapprochement."[231] A dogfight in the Aegean claimed the life of a Greek pilot in May 2006.[232]

And in the meantime, as Loucas Tsilas notes, "the capital of Cyprus, Nicosia, remains the only capital of a UN Member State that is divided by barbed wire and a Green Line of empty streets and phantom buildings."[233]

CHAPTER FOUR

Israel and Lebanon:
An Island of Agreement at Work

No one understands Lebanon. Not its supposed
owners or its makers; not its destroyers or its builders;
not its allies or its friends; and not those coming into it,
or those leaving it.

A. DARWISH, MAHMOUD. TRANSL. IBRAHIM MUHAWI, *MEMORY FOR
FORGETFULNESS: AUGUST, BEIRUT 1982*

My two former case studies were examples of how several islands of
agreement work in various spheres of multidimensional conflicts. Within
such conflicts they often appear as sequences or clusters, signaling varying degrees of conciliation, at times surprising even the most skeptical
observers by their sheer tenacity. In their plural form, they can interact
with one another, and at best form another, benign layer of multidimensionality over the original layer of conflict.

In this chapter I present a minimal-case scenario: a single, isolated island of agreement created and maintained within a raging military conflict, with no other fellow islands to bolster it or interact with it. The
setting is the protracted bloody feud between Israel and its northern
neighbors, in which the Israel-Lebanon Cease-fire Understanding of 1996
has, to date, stood as a solitary example of formal and direct sustainable agreement across the border since the collapse of the countries'
1949 armistice agreements in 1967. This island's singularity, along with
the wealth of available data on the varying stages of its existence right
down to the period following its termination, make it possible for us to
enter into the microlevel of the design and operation of such agreements, with the hope of drawing general insights as to their effects.[1]

I use the title "the Israeli-Lebanese conflict" as shorthand, for the
conflict is not a classic interstate dispute but rather a more complex political and military interaction between a state (Israel) and nonstate actors (Lebanese armed groups), in which the latter stand as proxies for

two other states—Syria and increasingly Iran too. In fact, the involvement of Lebanon—the state—itself in the conflict has been minimal. Repeatedly, it has been hijacked by the alliance among Lebanese armed groups and the governments of Syria and Iran, its territory subjected to use as a battleground for a fight in which Lebanon itself had the least interest. This was made possible as for most of its recent history, the state of Lebanon—as a single political unit that exercises a monopoly of power over its entire territory—has been largely nonexistent.

Though this decades-long conflict is multidimensional being only part of the broader Israeli-Arab conflict, it differs from the two former case studies in that, due to the political preferences of the protagonists, the relationship between the parties has been more or less exclusively limited to military exchanges, with repeated cycles of escalation and relative calm. Unlike the dyads in the previous two cases, there are no other governmental relations between Israel and Syria or Lebanon. Neither Arab country has ever maintained diplomatic relations, official trade, regulated movement of people or tourism, cultural or educational exchanges, or institutionalized bilateral cooperation of any sort with Israel. The two Arab countries do not even recognize the State of Israel. Outlawed on both sides (with some narrow exceptions for the Israeli Arab or Druze population), nongovernmental or private contacts are few and far between and are mostly conducted outside the region.

Since these spheres are politically, and therefore practically, nonexistent in the relationship, so, for the moment, is the possibility of cooperation within them. Here, conflict management and relationship management become one. Islands of agreement are reduced in their potential and limited to the security sphere. The 1996 understanding and its concomitant Israel-Lebanon Monitoring Group (ILMG)—the one formal and institutionalized island of agreement in the modern phase of this conflict—encapsulate this paradoxical situation, in which the only agreement is a four-provision "understanding" on how to fight and, more specifically, how to protect civilians from the scourge of war.

The Understanding and the group set up to monitor and regulate it faced many challenges during the course of their existence: fierce ongoing fighting; a lack of mutual diplomatic recognition; the complex relationship between Lebanese armed groups, the Lebanese government and the Syrian government; the varying and sometimes conflicting interests of Western powers in the region; and ongoing public scrutiny of, and at times dissatisfaction with, the regime's own operation by the local citizenries.

That such a fragile agreement regime should have survived against such odds for nearly four years is a tribute to its architects and participants alike. As a recent historical example, it affords us a unique opportunity to explore how islands of agreement may be established and sustained under the most adverse of circumstances.

The Historical Background

In the following historical account, I focus on the relationship between Israel and Lebanon as the two primary subjects of the 1996 Understanding, with only inevitable side glimpses at Syria and Iran. It must be borne in mind, however, that at least since the 1970s Lebanon did not exist as a fully independent state but was rather subjected to Syrian control. The fact that the Understanding featured Israel and Lebanon as the implementing parties and left only an "observer" role to Syria was merely a reflection of the Syrian practice of management behind the scenes, always effective and never fully acknowledged.

Although the roots of the Israeli-Lebanese conflict can be traced back to the period of the French mandate over Lebanon and the British mandate over Palestine, Lebanon has never posed a serious security threat to Israel, nor has its armed forces ever taken a significant part in the Arab-Israeli wars of 1948, 1967, or 1973, in all of which Syria was a principal party.[2]

The predominant effect of the 1948 war on Lebanon had been the sudden influx of Palestinian refugees who fled from Israel across the border and were forced by the local authorities into refugee camps.[3] A second wave of Palestinian flight into Lebanon took place in the aftermath of the 1970 Black September clashes between the Hashemite Kingdom and Palestinian nationalists within Jordan, which resulted in the killing of thirty-five hundred Jordanian and Palestinian militants and the expulsion by King Hussein of thousands of Palestinian Liberation Organization (PLO) members and supporters from Jordan. Palestinians in Lebanon now numbered around three hundred thousand, creating in effect an informal state-within-a-state known as the "Fatah Land" in south Lebanon. The Palestinian newcomers brought the intercommunal tensions already simmering among Christians and Muslims in Lebanon to boiling point. In April 1975, clashes between Christian Phalangist forces and Palestinian fighters enkindled a full-fledged civil war engulfing the entire Christian, Muslim, and Druze communities in the country: the Lebanese government collapsed; the army disintegrated. The internal fighting which was to last until 1990, and leave 100,000 people dead, also sucked Lebanon—much against its own interests—into the whorl of the Arab-Israeli conflict. The dissipation of the Lebanese state was the catalyst for both Israel and Syria in their future armed interventions in Lebanon.

The Fatah Land became the hub of PLO anti-Israeli activity, both inside Israel and around the world, marking the beginning of thirty-five years of fighting between Israel and Palestinian—later superseded by Islamic Shiite—armed groups in Lebanon: a period marked, alternately, by military operations and failed attempts at political settlements.

The Litani Operation

On March 14, 1978, Israel launched the first in a series of wide-scale military campaigns, naming it the Litani Operation, after the Litani River, which runs through southern Lebanon. It was Israel's first large military engagement since the end of the 1973 Yom Kippur War and the most comprehensive one up until the 1982 Lebanon War. The Litani Operation was essentially a fierce retaliation for repeated PLO attacks on civilians in Israel.[4] The final trigger was an attack on an Israeli passenger bus three days earlier, which left thirty-five civilians dead and nearly one hundred injured. The government was now convinced of the necessity of impairing the PLO's infrastructure and diminishing its ability to conduct future attacks. The response—an armed invasion by eight thousand Israeli soldiers intended to drive PLO forces north of the Litani River, which nonetheless left over a thousand Lebanese, most of whom were civilians, dead—received a spate of international condemnation. Even the United States, Israel's closest ally, termed it "an overreaction."[5] On March 19, five days into the operation, the United Nations Security Council adopted Resolution 425, which called for the immediate withdrawal of all Israeli forces from Lebanon, the restoration of international peace and security and the reestablishment of Lebanese governmental control over all Lebanese territory. Resolution 426, of the same day, established the United Nations Interim Force in Lebanon (UNIFIL), which still operates today, with the mandate of overseeing the implementation of Resolution 425.[6]

Israel withdrew its forces from Lebanon in June 1978, leaving behind it a Christian Maronite Lebanese militia, which later became known as the South Lebanese Army (SLA).[7] The Christian Maronites, by now deeply embroiled in intercommunal fighting with the Palestinians in south Lebanon, turned to Israel as a potential ally. Israel has already offered the Christians a hand early on in the civil war, by opening the "good fence"—passages in its northern border with Lebanon, through which for the years to come, and up until the Israeli withdrawal in 2000, Christian Lebanese from south Lebanon could enter into Israel for work, medical treatment, and commerce. UNIFIL, which found itself locked between Israelis, Palestinians, and Lebanese Christians, could not but fail in its mission, as the hostilities continued.

The 1982 Israel-Lebanon War and "The Security Zone"

In June 1982, Israel launched Operation Pines, which it later termed the Peace for the Galilee Operation, but which became known as the Lebanon War. The operation was described at first as a measured retaliation for the attempted assassination of the Israeli ambassador in London (even though the attempt was carried out by the Abu Nidal Palestinian faction, and not the PLO) and the firing of rockets into northern Israel by the PLO in the preceding weeks, though an extensive historical and academic debate surrounds the real or additional motivations driving the Israeli leadership.[8] Whatever its initial intent, most writers agree that as the operation progressed into war, inflicting thousands of casualties among civilians and combatants in Lebanon and hundreds among Israel Defense Forces (IDF) soldiers, Israel deserted its long-established national security strategy of conducting only defensive wars of necessity, and set out to attain wide-ranging political gains.[9] It was largely the then-Minister of Defense, Ariel Sharon, who shaped the three objectives of the Lebanon War: the creation of a forty-kilometer strip north of the Israeli border cleared of armed groups; the destruction or removal of all PLO forces, including in the Beirut headquarters; and the signing of a peace treaty with Bashir Gemayel, head of the Christian Phalange party, and help Gemayel to unite Lebanon under a Christian Maronite rule. This latter ambition was also intended to expedite the withdrawal of Syrian forces from Lebanon and bring Lebanon into the Israeli sphere of influence. Moreover, Sharon believed that if Israel were able to destroy the rapidly growing Syrian military forces in Lebanon, or at least strengthen its own deterrence vis-à-vis these forces, the blow to Syria might lead to the overthrow of the Syrian regime—a state of affairs which would leave Israel as the principal strategic power in the region. Israel did in fact attack Syrian forces in Lebanon during the war.[10]

In mid-June, 1982, Israeli troops advancing north reached Beirut and encircled it, in an attempt to drive out the 14,000 PLO operatives concentrated in the western part of the city or else to force them to surrender. Israel's cabinet and high military command preferred laying a siege to invading the city, due to an invasion campaign's prohibitive cost in terms of Israeli soldiers and Lebanese civilians' lives and in terms of the potentially thunderous political repercussions of storming an Arab capital.[11] On July 3, the Israelis gained control of the Green Line, which separated east from west Beirut, and began the siege. For seventy days, Israel attacked west Beirut with artillery almost daily, cutting off water and power for days on end. Blockades imposed by the Israeli forces created shortages of food, water, and fuel in the city.[12]

Through the intense mediation of U.S. envoy Philip Habib, a cease-fire agreement between Israel and the PLO was reached, whereby all PLO insurgents, headed by Yassir Arafat, were to leave Lebanon permanently. The Israelis gave final approval to a PLO withdrawal plan on August 19, and on August 21, American, French, Italian, and British forces (a total force of 2,130, named the Multinational Force (MNF)) arrived in Beirut to supervise the removal of the PLO to Tunisia (where the new PLO headquarters would later be established), Yemen, Jordan, and Syria.[13]

The continued use of force by Israel in what seemed to many in Israel and around the world a "war of choice," came to a catastrophic head in the massacre in the Sabra and Shatila refugee camps a month later. The massacre, carried out by Christian factions in an area under Israeli occupation, eroded the slim remainder of Israeli domestic consensus that surrounded all former Israeli-Arab wars, prompting the largest protest demonstration in Israel's history.

The death toll of the war was immense: over eighteen thousand Palestinians, Syrians, and Lebanese, at least a third of whom were Lebanese civilians, had died, as well as close to seven hundred IDF soldiers.[14]

U.S. President Ronald Reagan, prompted to action along with the leaders of France and Italy, put together a new multinational force, to help the Lebanese government restore order and stability. Though initially successful in its mission, the MNF came under increasing attacks from the various Lebanese factions. In April 1983 the U.S. embassy in west Beirut was bombed, killing 63 people. Six months later, in October, suicide bombers drove a car bomb into the American and French barracks in Beirut, killing 241 American and 58 French soldiers. The U.S. held

Iran and the rapidly growing Shiite Hezbollah group responsible. By early 1984, the MNF withdrew. Any future attempts by third parties to intervene in Lebanon would be cautioned by the dim fate of the MNF.

Meanwhile, the loss of popular support at home brought the Israeli government to seek a negotiated resolution.[15] Israeli leaders deemed the Christian factions, not the ineffectual Lebanese government, most attractive to play the role of principal partner in Israeli-Lebanese negotiations. The leaders of the Christian factions, however, were emphatic that to earn domestic support for the agreement, they could not sign a peace treaty with Israel, but at most a mutual security agreement, in which Israel would vouch to avoid further invasion of Lebanese territory, while the Lebanese government would promise to prevent hostile groups and organizations from threatening Israel's security.[16]

On May 17, 1983, after six months of negotiations mediated by the U.S., the two parties signed the Halde Agreement.[17] The architects of the agreement were careful not to give it the appearance of a formal peace treaty and so avoided the words "peace" or "recognition." However, they did include obligations with respect of sovereignty, independence, and borders, as well as a declaration ending the state of war, an obligation to outlaw and prevent terrorist activity, and preliminary arrangements for a normalization of relations between the two countries. The agreement also called for a guarantee of Lebanon's independence upon the withdrawal of Israeli and "other forces" (namely, but unnamedly—the Syrians). It was this final appeal that cause President Hafez al-Assad of Syria to press Prime Minister Amine Gemayel of Lebanon not to ratify the agreement.[18] Gemayel (who had taken took office following the assassination of his brother, Bashir, with whom Israel had originally planned to collaborate), succumbed. On March 5, 1984, ten months after the signing of the Halde Agreement, the Lebanese government unilaterally declared the agreement annulled.[19]

Israel was now forced to abandon its hopes for a political settlement. Instead, it was willing to settle for an Israeli-Lebanese agreement of a strictly military character. In November 1984, through the mediation of the UN, military talks began once more in the south Lebanese town of Naqura. The Lebanese, under Syrian encouragement, rejected Israeli demands for security limitations upon Lebanon as a threat to Lebanese sovereignty. It was clear to Israel that the weak and ineffectual Lebanese army would be unable to assume responsibility for keeping the peace in the area and armed groups at bay. It became gradually clear, too, that the Syrians would brook no agreement that would leave the Israeli army, the SLA, or UNIFIL with any stake in the areas to be vacated. At the end of two and a half months, the talks reached a cul-de-sac.[20]

Having failed to secure an agreement, on January 14, 1985, the Israeli government decided to unilaterally pull out most of its military from Lebanon and redeploy along the international Israeli-Lebanese border, while maintaining a "Security Zone" in southern Lebanon controlled by the SLA, with Israeli army (IDF) backing.[21] The government decision mentioned no further attempts to reach an agreement with Lebanon. Despite the cease-fire agreement to end the siege on Beirut calling for the withdrawal of *all* foreign forces from Lebanon, around 30,000 Syrian troops remained in Lebanon. The PLO was quickly resuming its anti-Israeli activities from its new refuges. Thus, in June 1985, Israel withdrew most of its forces from Lebanon, having achieved none of its goals.

The holding of the Security Zone became the basis of Israel's security policy in Lebanon up to the final withdrawal in May 2000. This gave birth to a host of problems: for one thing, Israel never officially laid out the principles of its security doctrine regarding the Security Zone, and the area's borders were never properly charted. For another, throughout its control of the Zone, Israel denied its status—and consequently, its responsibilities—as an occupying force, claiming that the presence of its military in southern Lebanon was for defensive purposes only. The Zone's northern limit—"the Red Line"—changed from time to time, according to the SLA's ability to control the area without massive IDF ground support. The prevailing wisdom was that a limited IDF deployment would continue until a political settlement of some kind was reached or until the SLA could hold the strip independently, without need of further IDF presence.[22] For Lebanese armed groups, the liberation of Lebanese territory from Israeli occupation became at once the justification and motivation for armed resistance.

Although the SLA played a crucial part in maintaining the Security Zone, and in many ways served as Israel's proxy, its interests not only diverged from those of Israel but also, at times, actually conflicted with them. This discrepancy not only made both the IDF's and the SLA's operation in the area harder all around, but also left Israel a frequent hostage to the SLA's interests. Over time, other points of friction occurred with the local population—of which Israel was part chaperon, part occupier, the SLA, and the international community.[23]

The 1990s Tests of Arms

In Lebanon, the Palestinians' loss of influence altered the balance of power between the sects. For the first time, the Shiites became a force to be reckoned with, in the shape of a powerful, armed group—Hezbollah—directly supported and funded by the Syrians, as well as by Iran.[24] This Iranian involvement began with the Islamic Revolution of 1979 and the rise to power of Ayatollah Khomeini, as the Iranian regime aspired to "export" the Islamic Revolution to the entire Muslim world. In 1982 Khomeini sent troops, known as the Islamic Revolutionary Guard Corps, to Lebanon, to help the Muslim Shiites fight against their Arab Christian neighbors. He also began training and sponsoring Hezbollah Shiite combatants. Hezbollah's warfare realized Syrian and Iranian aspirations to keep up the tension in Lebanon and put pressure on Israel.[25] The Israeli response to Hezbollah attacks consisted of limited military operations and the application of pressure on Syria through the United States, a method that did, at times, succeed in keeping Hezbollah's activities in check.

Under an international umbrella comprehensive Middle East peace talks were launched. In late 1991, in Madrid and lasted until the beginning of 1994. The talks included both bilateral and multilateral tracks. After two years of bilateral negotiations with both Syria and Lebanon it became clear that as long as Israel was unwilling to withdraw from the Golan Heights—Syrian territory occupied by Israel during the 1967 war and held thereafter—which was Syria's precondition for any peace treaty, there could be no progress regarding Lebanon either.

On July 25, 1993, following months of escalation in military activity in the area, Israel launched Operation Accountability, which aimed to damage the armed groups' infrastructure and exert pressure on the Lebanese government to restrain their activities and prevent them from firing into Israel. The operation ended on July 31, with an oral understanding between Israel and Lebanon, again reached through U.S. mediation. Its terms, which were never published and were thus subject to debate, seem to have included Syria's guarantee to influence the armed groups not to attack northern Israel, Lebanon's guarantee to deploy its army in southern Lebanon, and an Israeli commitment to refrain from injuring civilians in Lebanon. No monitoring of enforcement mechanisms were set. The understanding was short lived and warfare soon reverted to its former patterns.[26]

Israel met another failure to reach a decisive victory in its asymmetrical warfare against Lebanese armed groups when, on April 11, 1996, it launched Operation Grapes of Wrath. The operation followed a number of civilian casualties in Lebanon and the firing of Katyusha rockets into Israel throughout the preceding month. Peace talks with the Syrians, at Wye Plantation, Maryland, from mid-1995 until early 1996, had failed, and the Israeli prime minister, Shimon Peres, was facing difficult upcoming elections. The operation was intended to put pressure on Syria and Lebanon to restrain the armed groups and return to the negotiating table, while giving the Labor Party and its leader, Peres, an electoral edge over Israeli hard-liners. Though Israel enjoyed clear military supremacy, it failed to reach any of its goals, as 650 air raids and 24,000 artillery shells later, and a massive flow of civilians from south Lebanon to the north, Hezbollah was still able to fire Katyusha rockets into its northern territory.[27]

Israel was ready to continue the operation, but the tables turned when, on April 18, 1996, Israeli artillery shells were fired on a UNIFIL position in the village of Kafar-Qana. A hundred and two Lebanese civilians were killed, and approximately a hundred more, as well as four U.N. peacekeepers injured. Although Israel insisted that the shelling of the compound was a mistake, a UN report—vehemently rejected by Israel—did not dismiss the possibility that it was intentional.[28] The Kafar-Qana incident, however unintentional it may have been, caused massive damage to Israel's public image, as well as considerable internal pressure, especially from the domestic Arab sector, on the eve of the Israeli elections. It was clear that the operation could not continue, and a cease-fire was reached. Eight days later the United States, "after discussions with the governments of Israel and Lebanon, and in consultation with Syria," announced its "understanding," which was to set the formal basis for the rules of combat in Lebanon, up until Israel's final withdrawal in May 2000.[29] Meanwhile, Peres lost the elections and the Right regained power under the leadership of Benjamin Netanyahu.

To avoid repeating the mistakes of the 1993 Understanding, the April 1996 Understanding was both written and published, and an international monitoring group consisting of the United States, France, Syria, Lebanon, and Israel was established to supervise its implementation. As Secretary of State Warren Christopher noted, "as such, [the rules] should prove more enduring and less susceptible to misinterpretation."[30] The group met from August 1996 to February 2000, at which time the Israeli delegation left its 103rd meeting in protest. Despite the other members' efforts to reconvene the group, it never met again; but none of its participants has ever declared in public—even after the Israeli withdrawal from Lebanon three months later—that the Understanding or the ILMG were null and void.

The Final Israeli Withdrawal and Its Aftermath

The limited Israeli military operations in Lebanon brought no material change to the nature of the fighting on the Lebanese front. They were mainly retaliatory in nature and were aimed at stopping the firing into Israeli territory and at restraining, to some degree, the armed groups' operation within the Security Zone. The armed groups, encouraged by Syria, and supported by some parts of the Lebanese civilian population could not desist from their struggle against what they deemed to be the Israeli occupation of Lebanon. Thus, a kind of balance of terror was struck: when Israel inflicted injuries on civilians, its own civilians were targeted, and when Hezbollah stepped up its activity, Lebanon was punished. This cycle of retribution and retaliation continued to characterize the conflict between Israel and the Lebanese armed groups in the following years. Civilians, on both sides of the border, often paid heavily for this policy. The regime created by the Understanding and the ILMG, although at times successful in mitigating the clashes, did not alter—nor was it is intended to alter—the conflict's fundamental structure.

In his successful bid for the office of prime minister in 1999, new Labor leader Ehud Barak pledged to pull the IDF out of Lebanon. Putting the Israeli-Palestinian track on hold, Barak turned to Syria for a possible peace agreement, which, if successful, was to lead to a parallel agreement with Lebanon and allow for the orderly withdrawal of the IDF from Lebanon and the dismantling of the SLA. Syria barred any negotiation with Lebanon until progress in its own negotiation with Israel secured the Golan Heights.[31] Throughout the talks, Barak proclaimed his intention to pull out of Lebanon with or without a peace agreement by July 2000, partly to lean on Syria, which saw a unilateral Israeli withdrawal as a threat to its future capacity to conduct its proxy war in Lebanon. When the talks failed, Israel moved to execute its unilateral withdrawal plan. The withdrawal was ultimately carried out in a less-than-organized manner within a space of twenty-four hours, as the early dismantling of the SLA forced the IDF to pull out earlier than planned. On May 24, 2000, the last IDF soldier crossed the border from

Lebanon to Israel. A stream of SLA members and their families fled to Israel, seeking asylum from retribution by Hezbollah and the Lebanese government. Thereafter, the border passage was shut down.

In the weeks that followed, the UN conducted extensive negotiations with Syria, Lebanon, and Israel, to determine whether the line to which Israel had withdrawn met the requirements of Security Council Resolution 425. Throughout the process, there ws no direct contact between Israeli and Lebanese officials. On June 16, after Israel had performed all the amendments required by the UN, Secretary-General Kofi Annan announced that the line of withdrawal, demarcated by the UN and which had become known as the Blue Line, was in fact compatible with Resolution 425.[32]

With this affirmation by the UN of its compliance with Resolution 425, Israel secured the international community's disapproval of any subsequent attack by the Lebanese armed groups. But Lebanon and Syria both argued that the Israeli withdrawal was not complete, citing as their reason a twenty-five-square-kilometer area called the Shaba'a Farms. Israel claimed, and the UN affirmed, that this area was part of the Golan Heights, to be negotiated in future Israeli-Syrian talks. Lebanon, with Syrian support, argued that the Shaba'a farms belonged to Lebanon, and hence the Israeli withdrawal was, in fact, incomplete. UNIFIL, who remained in the area, has been unable to prevent still-recurring clashes, as Hezbollah continues to shell Israeli posts along the border, mainly (but not only) in the Shaba'a farms area, and as Israel continues its overflights in Lebanese airspace and retaliates with fire into Lebanon.

Hezbollah's continued struggle has by no means been motivated only by the Shaba'a farms controversy. Ever since its inception in the early 1980s, Hezbollah has declared itself at war with Zionism and the State of Israel. Even after Israel's retreat, Hezbollah leaders have repeatedly stated that their ultimate goal is to eradicate the state of Israel.[33] Nevertheless, if the organization's more-limited declared goal—liberating Lebanon from the "Zionist occupation"—accorded it international and domestic legitimacy, the Israeli withdrawal now denied Hezbollah the primary international justification for its military activities.

To preserve its relevance and continue to claim legitimacy, Hezbollah enhanced its ties with Palestinian armed groups, both in the refugee camps in Lebanon and in the West Bank and Gaza Strip.[34] It also formally dedicated a large number of its attacks to the Palestinian cause.

Syria's continued support for Hezbollah's activities served both as a constant reminder to Israel of the Golan Heights issue and as a tool for maintaining its influence in Lebanon.[35] After the death of the Syrian president, Hafez al-Assad, in June 2000 and the rise to power of his young son, Bashar, Iran's influence on Syria noticeably increased and, with it, the Iranian aid to Hezbollah in Lebanon. Israel attempted to re-design the rules of the game declaring it would retaliate for attacks into its territory by striking not only the Lebanese armed groups but Syrian targets in Lebanon as well—something it had largely refrained from do-ing in the past.[36] The threat was almost never executed.

In October 2002, tensions rose over a Lebanese pumping project in-tended to divert water from the Wazzani River to nearby hamlets in southern Lebanon. The Wazzani is a tributary of the Hatzbani River, which flows from Lebanon to Israel, where it joins the Jordan River—a prime source of water for both Israel and Jordan. As the region suffers from severe water shortage in general, any change in water supplies is critical. Israel, outraged by what it perceived to be a unilateral shift in the status quo, threatened to destroy the new pumping station. Hezbol-lah, in response, announced that the smallest move by Israel would trig-ger an unprecedented retaliation by the armed group. Efforts by the United States, the UN, and the EU to mediate the dispute all failed, and mutual deterrence still keeps an uneasy status quo.[37]

Up to December 2005, clashes following the Israeli withdrawal re-sulted in the killing of sixteen Israeli soldiers and six Israeli civilians by Hezbollah operations and of nine Lebanese combatants, two Lebanese civilians, and three Syrian soldiers in Lebanon by Israeli fire. Hezbollah also kidnapped and held hostage an Israeli civilian, whom it agreed to release, together with the bodies of three IDF soldiers it had killed in Is-rael, in exchange for Lebanese prisoners held in Israel. Israeli retaliation has been measured. Although significant, these clashes have altogether been less frequent than before, during the period of Israel's control of south Lebanon.

Dramatic political changes occurred in 2004–2005, as popular oppo-sition within Lebanon and fierce international condemnation colluded to undermine Syria's position in Lebanon. A combination of motives, ranging from Syria's support for insurgents in Iraq to the French presi-dent Jacque Chirac's close friendship with former Lebanese Prime Min-ister Rafik al-Hariri, whom Syria prevented from regaining power, led in September 2004 to the adoption of Security Council Resolution

1559, which called for a full Syrian withdrawal from Lebanon and the dismantling and disarming of all armed groups in Lebanon.

The assassination of al-Hariri by a car bomb on February 14, 2005, believed to have been carried out by Syrian agents, has not only inflamed international opinion but also sparked domestic Lebanese opposition to an unprecedented degree. Vast demonstrations and popular civic action against Syria began to organize in Lebanon, in what has since been termed the Cedar Revolution. These demonstrations were countered by pro-Syrian ones, organized by Hezbollah.[38] After protesting at first that Lebanon "had invited Syria to protect it" and that therefore Syria should not withdraw from Lebanon, the pro-Syrian Lebanese government soon resigned, and elections were set for the following May–June. Under growing pressure from the international community, including parts of the Arab world, Syria began its withdrawal from Lebanon in compliance with Resolution 1559, and on April 26, 2005, reported to the UN that its last remaining forces had departed from Lebanon (although observers seriously doubt whether Syria has truly ended its intelligence presence there).[39]

Hezbollah has not been dismantled or disarmed; instead, it grew substantially in political power in the national elections that were carried out in May–June 2005. For the first time, Hezbollah participated in the government, represented by two cabinet ministers. International actors were careful not to prod the Lebanese government, under Fouad Siniora, on Hezbollah's disarmament issue, so as not to destabilize it. They also continue to hope that ongoing political engagement may serve to shift the group's focus, in an evolutionary process, from an armed struggle to a political one.[40]

Whether or not this is the case, so far the intensity of cross-border clashes has waned dramatically, although they have not ceased entirely. In addition, the Israeli withdrawal has enabled Hezbollah to accumulate tens of thousands of various-range rockets, as well as other types of advanced weapons, supplied by Iran and Syria; it also allowed the armed group to deploy along the Israeli border in a complex system of aboveground and underground fortifications, without any intervention from the Lebanese government or UNIFIL. The future of Israeli-Lebanese relations and indeed, of Lebanon as a functioning independent state is unclear. But what is clear is that for as long as Israeli forces were deployed in Lebanon, a Syrian withdrawal would not have been possible, and no material change within Lebanese society and politics could be foreseen.

This realization is important for a correct assessment of the overall impact that the Israeli-Lebanon Understanding, in its time, had had on the rivalry—an assessment I shall return to later on.

An Isolated Island of Agreement

The April 26, 1996 Understanding has long stood as the sole formal and declared island of agreement in the dismal history of the Israel-Lebanese relationship, in which cross-border interaction has tended to mean the firing of projectiles from one side to the other. Confidence-building measures and people-to-people initiatives have likewise been nonexistent. On several occasions, the International Committee of the Red Cross (ICRC) and the German government brokered the exchange of bodies or the release of prisoners, but these exchanges were ad hoc with no lasting impact.

It is therefore almost ironic that the one agreement finally reached, the 1996 Understanding, was in some aspects the most ambitious island of agreement possible: a regulation of the ongoing fighting between the IDF and SLA on the one hand and the Lebanese armed groups on the other. Before exploring the provisions of the agreement and the motivations behind them, I will first look into the interests of the five members of the ILMG, all of whom had had a share in drafting and implementing the Understanding.

The Participants and Their Interests

> A Monitoring Group is established consisting of the United States, France, Syria, Lebanon and Israel. Its task will be to monitor the application of the Understanding stated above.
>
> FIRST NONNUMBERED PARAGRAPH OF THE ISRAEL-LEBANON CEASE-FIRE UNDERSTANDING.

THE UNITED STATES AND FRANCE

By 1996 both the United States and France had long-standing interests in the Middle East. The French influence on Lebanon and Syria originated with the French Mandate, which lasted from 1920 to 1943, at which time both Syria and Lebanon acquired their independence. The U.S. interest in Lebanon deepened during the 1950s, as the latter became a crossroads for the trade in oil, and grew stronger with the wish to limit Soviet influence in the Arab world.[41] President Dwight D. Eisenhower even sent several thousand American troops to aid Lebanese President Camille Chamoun in quelling an insurrection. The insurrection and ensuing clashes—the result of religious tensions within Lebanon encouraged by outside Arab actors—left around two thousand dead, and later became known as the "first Lebanese civil war."

Until 1967 France was Israel's closest ally in the West. After the Six-Day War, however, alliances shifted, and the role of principal ally was taken over by the United States, while France gravitated towards Lebanon and Syria. The American alliance with Israel, as well as the United States' wider interests in the Middle East, placed it in the position of broker in all political and military initiatives between Israel, Syria, and Lebanon since 1978.[42] With the gradual decrease in the power of the Soviet Union, American influence in the region grew, and the United States was able to intervene regularly to diffuse tensions.[43] The participation of the United States and France in the Monitoring Group was thus meant to serve a double purpose: first, to enable both countries to realize their vested interests in Middle East politics; and second, to balance out—both in practice and in appearance—each other's perceived support for one of the sides in the conflict.

SYRIA

Syrian political and territorial interests in today's Lebanon can be traced back as early as the seventh or eighth centuries, when early Syrian aspirations to control Lebanon were motivated by the concept of *Bilad al-Sham* (Land of the North), which envisioned all of the Levant as one nation. With the collapse of the Ottoman Empire after World War I, Syrian nationalists hoped to recover Syria's "natural borders," defined by the National Syrian Congress of 1919–1920 to include the territories of modern Syria, Lebanon, Jordan, and Israel, in what they termed "Greater Syria."[44] If the political arrangements in the Middle East in the wake of World War I curtailed this dream, they did not obliterate it; the idea of Lebanon as an integral part of Syria remained central to Syrian nationalists' perception even after both Lebanon and Syria gained their independence in the 1940s and was reinforced with the rise of the pan-Arabist Ba'ath Party in the 1960s. Publicly, it was most fully expressed by President Hafez al-Assad's speech on July 1976, intended to justify the Syrian invasion of Lebanon, in which he said, "In history Syria and Lebanon are one country and one people . . . That is why they have real and mutual interests and close relations."[45] To date, there is no international boundary or exchange of ambassadors between the two states.

Lebanon was never far from al-Assad's watchful eye; the eye of a regime determined to maintain power at any cost, and struggling with its own history of political instability.[46] Lebanon's geographic proximity, its tradition of granting freedom to political exiles, its historically free press (by regional standards) in combination with the weakness of its political structures and inter-communal strife, all gave rise to Syrian anxiety about pro-Western and anti-Syrian activity in and from Lebanon. Likewise, Syria had an interest in maintaining peace among the religious and ethnic factions in Lebanon's complex political environment, out of concern that civil war in Lebanon might also lead to instability within Syria. Later, the armed conflict between Israel and Lebanon became a further threat to the stability the Syrians were so keen on preserving and increased their fear of an Israeli maneuver through a weak Lebanon towards their own border. To overcome this danger, Syria strove to effectively integrate Lebanon into one Arab front, stretching from Ras Naqura in the west of Lebanon to the Aqaba port in Jordan.

On the night of May 31, 1976, as civil war broke out—a war which was to last until 1990 and leave 100,000 dead—in Lebanon, Syrian military forces, encouraged by Lebanese Christian factions, invaded the country. The invasion was subsequently given a stamp of legitimacy by two Arab summits, convened in October.[47]

Soon thereafter, and for years to follow, Israel and Syria were to reach tacit understandings (never negotiated or formalized, except by mutual signaling) on the "red lines" of military presence and activity in Lebanon that both sides would be willing to tolerate from each other, including size of troops, geographical areas of operation, and the type of weapons deployed.[48] Implicitly acknowledging each other's presence in Lebanon, Israel and Syria refrained from bilateral military clashes in Lebanon, but for the notable exception of the 1982 war.

The Arab legitimization of the Syrian military's hold on Lebanon was reinforced in the 1989 Tai'f agreement, drafted by representatives of Saudi Arabia, Morocco, and Algeria, and ratified thereafter by the Lebanese parliament. The agreement declared that "in view of the fraternal relations binding Syria to Lebanon, the Syrian forces shall thankfully assist the forces of the legitimate Lebanese government to spread the authority of the State of Lebanon within a set period of no more than two years." It further detailed the areas of Syrian military deployment in Lebanon and founded a joint Syrian-Lebanese committee to decide on the extent of these forces and the duration of their deployment.[49]

Two subsequent treaties—the Brotherhood, Cooperation, and Coordination Treaty of May 1991 and the Lebanon-Syria Defense and Security Agreement of July 1991—reaffirmed the principles of cooperation and alliance between the two countries, granted Syria the role of protecting Lebanese independence and sovereignty, and, in effect, entrenched the Syrian military hold on Lebanon—thereby completing the process begun in 1976.[50]

Subsequent agreements and arrangements between Syria and Lebanon, ostensibly intended to regulate the movement of people and goods, in effect opened the floodgates for Syrian workers to enter into the new territory.[51] By 2005 there were approximately one million Syrian workers earning their living in Lebanon and, until the Syrian withdrawal from Lebanon, about forty thousand soldiers and several thousand undercover intelligence agents deployed there.[52]

The Syrian interests in Lebanon, alongside its powerful military hold over the country, made Syria the de facto ruler of Lebanon, with little to no international protest up until 2004. Despite international calls for the withdrawal of "all foreign forces" from Lebanon during the Lebanon War, most international observers saw the Syrian presence in Lebanon as fulfilling an important, stabilizing role, keeping a check on intercommunal tensions from reerupting into another civil war.[53] Furthermore, so long as Israel was occupying Lebanon, Syria could appear to better advantage as Lebanon's welcomed defender against Israeli aggression.

If maintaining control of Lebanon was Syria's primary interest, another was to use the active conflict between the Lebanese armed groups and Israel, not to achieve an Israeli withdrawal from Lebanon, but rather an Israeli withdrawal from the Golan Heights: to remind Israel that until it returned it to Syria, there would be no peace on the Israeli northern border.[54] Syria's primary interest in the conflict was thus to ensure the armed struggle was perpetuated, without risking its own forces or territory, and to portray the violence as the result of popular resistance to foreign occupation, with itself as liberator. To this end throughout the 1990s, Syria enhanced its ties with Hezbollah to include financial and material support, as well as political alliance.

As the Understanding was being contemplated, it was clear that Syria would not let Lebanon and Israel engage in any kind of dialogue, even a purely military one, without its close supervision. It was likewise evident that no agreement could hold without Syrian support. It was widely recognized that the armed groups answered to Syria much more than to the Lebanese government, who was also largely subject to Syrian rule. In fact, the main efforts of mediating the Understanding were centered in Jerusalem and Damascus, not Beirut.

For the United States and France, and Israel too, the interest in Syrian involvement in the Monitoring Group derived also from the prospect of some direct communication, however nebulous, between Israel and Syria, which did not exist in any other forum or channel. Though formally these contacts were limited by the scope of the Understanding, the hope was that in maintaining this open and direct avenue of communication, contact might diffuse into broader political dialogue in the future.

To allow for Syria's participation in the regime, while enabling it to keep its preferred backstage attitude, Syria was accorded the role of a mere "observer" in the Monitoring Group, leaving Israel and Lebanon as the two formal implementing parties.

LEBANON

For many years, Lebanese nationalists had their own aspirations for a Greater Lebanon, which were, to some degree, fulfilled during the French Mandate years, when the territories of both modern Syria and Lebanon were under French rule.[55] As the time of partition drew near, however, it became clear that Syria would receive the lion's share of the *Bilad al-Sham*. In time, ravaged by civil wars and factious struggle, Lebanon lost all independent power and largely became a pawn on an international chessboard played by the Syrians, the Israelis, the Iranians, and the Palestinians. In many ways, over its short national history Lebanon's fate has been to become its stronger neighbors' battleground.

Lebanon's consuming alliance—willing or otherwise—with Syria, especially after the 1970's civil war and the Syrian invasion into Lebanon, prevented it from making any separate deal with Israel, while at the same time forcing it to allow the Lebanese armed groups to play the part they were encouraged to play by Syria.

Both the Hezbollah and Amal (another Shiite political and armed group) movements, apart from their military branches, have been legitimate parties in the Lebanese parliament since the early 1990s. Both are engaged in extensive social, cultural, and educational activities, separate from their military functions. The Lebanese government has never formally withdrawn its support for the military operations of the Lebanese armed groups in and from its territory. This support gradually increased as Salim al-Huss, who was known to be a stronger affiliate of Syria, replaced Rafik al-Hariri as prime minister in early 1999. But Lebanon has also paid a heavy price for the ongoing fighting with Israel: the enormous reconstruction efforts that followed the Israel-Lebanon war and the civil war have been constantly frustrated by cross-shelling on both sides and ensuing Israeli bombardments that have gravely affected towns and villages throughout Lebanon, especially in the south.

The Understanding, then, was an obvious boon to this long-suffering country. The new rules of engagement, along with the international monitoring, were to help the Lebanese government protect its citizens' lives and property. On the political level, too, the Understanding would be perceived as an unprecedented achievement for Lebanon, in that it brought with it both international and more crucially—albeit implied— Israeli recognition of the Lebanese armed groups' struggle against Israeli occupation of southern Lebanon. Moreover, the Lebanese government wanted to avoid an escalation that might extend the armed conflict into northern Lebanon and threaten the stability of the government, as happened in 1982.

The Lebanese government also strove to maintain what little hold it had on the Lebanese armed groups and preserve some kind of central government, or at least the appearance of one, in order to restrain them. For this reason, it joined Israel in preferring itself as the formal party to the Understanding, rather than Hezbollah or any of the other Lebanese armed groups.

ISRAEL

After the bitter, incessant fighting in the eleven years following Israel's incomplete withdrawal from Lebanon in 1985 and the failure of the preceding operation "Accountability" to bring any real change to the situation, Israel was interested in a formula that would ensure the safety of the inhabitants of its northern border, without fundamentally altering the balance of power in the area. As both Syria and Israel were entrenched in their positions regarding the Golan Heights, a comprehensive peace settlement was unattainable for the foreseeable future. A decisive military resolution of the conflict across the Lebanese border was also impossible to achieve despite clear Israeli military superiority. Israel's hope was that, through the Understanding, it would be able to maintain its presence in Lebanon while minimizing the risk to its northern inhabitants. Implicitly, there was hope that Israeli soldiers would be less vulnerable too.

Objecting at that time to the Resolution 425 formula, in the face of mounting public pressure with every Israeli casualty in Lebanon, Israel was further hoping to maintain the armed conflict in southern Lebanon at the lowest possible level of intensity. Establishing "rules of engagement" that would exclude Israel completely from the sphere of combat and contain the conflict on Lebanese soil alone was also consistent with Israel's security doctrine. Furthermore, Israel found value in the ILMG as a forum that would open up a standing bilateral channel of communication, however limited, with Syrian and Lebanese officials.

However, the political price to be paid was by no means negligible. By becoming a party to the Understanding, Israel in effect consented to a recognition of sorts of the legitimacy of the Lebanese armed groups' struggle against its own forces in Lebanon.[56] At a time when the Israeli government and military officials, as well as the media and the general population, were habitually using the term "terrorists" in reference to the Hezbollah or Amal armed groups, such recognition was not to be taken lightly. In the words of Israeli journalist Zvi Barel, "the Hezbollah now became a full partner in the peace process, enjoying complete support and legitimacy throughout Lebanon."[57] Other commentators further criticized the legitimization of, or at least the acquiescence to, Syria's hold on Lebanon, implicit in the Understanding.[58]

The Understanding

> It is recognized that the understanding to bring the current crisis between Lebanon and Israel to an end cannot substitute for a permanent solution. The United States understands the importance of achieving a comprehensive peace in the region. Towards this end, the United States proposes the resumption of negotiations between Syria and Israel and between Lebanon and Israel at a time to be agreed upon, with the objective of reaching comprehensive peace. The United States understands that it is desirable that these negotiations be conducted in a climate of stability and tranquility.
>
> THIRD NONNUMBERED PARAGRAPH OF THE ISRAEL-LEBANON CEASE-FIRE UNDERSTANDING, APRIL 26, 1996.

The Israel-Lebanon Cease-fire Understanding and the ILMG were an unprecedented attempt to establish and set to work a conflict management agreement and enforcement mechanism within an ongoing armed conflict. The Understanding was meant to achieve neither peace nor a halt in the military confrontation; on the contrary, it was established under the assumption that the fighting in Lebanon would continue. Although not a formal treaty, the Understanding was nevertheless a binding agreement on rules of engagement, the sole purpose of which was to exclude civilians from the sphere of combat. Its title, Israel-Lebanon Cease-fire Understanding, was thus misleading, for it was never intended as a real cease-fire. Grimly, the assumption shared by all parties involved was that no comprehensive settlement of the Israeli-Syrian-Lebanese conflict was in sight. In awareness of this position, but without wishing to relinquish the peace process entirely, the announcement on the Understanding, cited above, provided that it did not exclude the need to reach a final and permanent solution to the conflict and that the United States would continue its efforts towards the conclusion of such an end.

The Understanding differed from the general conventions on the laws of war, not only substantively but also conceptually. It was an ad hoc agreement, between countries already at arms with each other, and was meant to fashion agreed-upon rules to the particular circumstances of their conflict. The formation of a special monitoring body was designed to ensure greater enforcement than was possible under the general laws of armed conflict.

The agreement's first goal was to safeguard, as much as possible, the lives and property of civilians on both sides of the border. A more implicit goal was to set such ground rules for the armed conflict between Israel and Lebanon as would confine it within manageable limits and prevent a wide-scale escalation of violence in the region. The protection of civilians was one way of preventing such escalation, but if this protection were to be achieved, there had to be a substantial mitigating change in the conflict as a whole. Such a change, so it was hoped, would help build a climate of stability and tranquility, more conducive to future peace negotiations. These further expectations from the Understanding were to remain unfulfilled.

The Understanding as eventually concluded was not what American and French mediators' had hoped for. Initial American proposals, supported by Israel, included the disarmament of Hezbollah and an end to its operations against Israeli troops in the Security Zone. Provided there were no attacks for three months, so the plan went, talks would then begin on an Israeli withdrawal from Lebanon. These proposals were automatically rejected by both Syria and Lebanon, who considered them to be a realization of Israel's goals. The mediators—Warren Christopher and French foreign minister Hervé de Charrette—were thus left with less room to work in.[59]

On April 24, 1996, Secretary Christopher, standing alongside Prime Minister Peres in Jerusalem, announced the conclusion of the Understanding, as his French counterpart, Minister Charrette, made the same announcement in Beirut, accompanied by Prime Minister al-Hariri.

The core of the Understanding itself consisted of only four provisions. Short and concise, they left ample room for debate, interpretation, and elaboration of more specific rules. However, the fact that, to be binding, the interpretation and subrules had to be accepted by all parties restricted the ability of the parties to create too detailed a subcodex.

The following elaboration of the articles and the debates surrounding them is helpful to a fuller appreciation of the conflict, the parties' concerns, and the challenges faced by the ILMG.

ARTICLE I

> Armed groups in Lebanon will not carry out attacks by
> Katyusha rockets or by any kind of weapon into Israel.

This first provision reflected Israel's most fundamental interest—preventing any attack, as well as the threat of an attack, on the inhabitants of northern Israel. The specific mention of Katyusha rockets was a reference to Hezbollah's trademark weapon. Israel's goal was twofold: first, to neutralize Hezbollah's potential pressure in the form of attacks on Israeli towns and villages; second, true to classic Israeli security doctrine, to shift the fighting into enemy territory.[60] This second purpose was served by the comprehensive prohibition on *any* form of attack against Israeli territory, including military targets in Israel. Indeed, the Lebanese delegation to the group often protested that Article I created a gross asymmetry in the rules of engagement, granting Israel complete immunity while singling out Lebanon as the legitimate battlefield as long as no civilians were hurt. This was the case even though much of

Israeli attacks on Lebanese armed groups were launched or emanated from within Israel.

Crucially, the obligation to refrain from any attack into Israel was not placed directly on Lebanon, as the sovereign state, but rather on the armed groups operating within it, as neither Israel nor Lebanon was interested, from a political standpoint, in defining the situation as an international armed conflict between Israel and Lebanon. Despite repeated Israeli rhetorical insistence on Lebanon's responsibility for the activities of the armed groups within its territory, Israeli officials were always careful not to claim that Israel was at war with Lebanon. Lebanon, too, found it more convenient to present the struggle as a popular resistance movement fighting against the Israeli occupation of Lebanon rather than as an international armed conflict between two independent states. The Lebanese Armed Forces themselves never took any real part in the armed conflict, and apart from occasionally firing antiaircraft rounds at Israeli warplanes flying in Lebanese airspace, largely refrained from attacking IDF or SLA positions.

But although the obligation rested with the armed groups, representation and participation in the Monitoring Group were limited to officials of the Lebanese army and foreign office. For Israel, it was politically impossible and contrary to its long-lasting position on the matter to deal directly with the Lebanese armed groups, whom it referred to as "terrorists."

In Israel, therefore, strong political opposition revolved around the possibility that by agreeing to the Understanding, Israel had essentially recognized the legitimacy of the armed groups' activities against IDF and SLA targets in Lebanon, in stark denial of its official policy. For now, as long as the Lebanese armed groups operated in a manner consistent with the Understanding, not only were they not "terrorists," but their operations were recognized as legitimate by official ILMG reports, which often noted that a "Lebanese armed group conducted a legitimate military attack against a legitimate military target."[61] Worse still from an Israeli perspective, Israeli spokespersons now had to acknowledge the killing of Israeli soldiers as being "within the rules."[62] In practice, most of the violations of Article I committed by the Lebanese armed groups occurred due to the unintentional impact of rounds directed at IDF positions along the border. At times, rounds struck the southern side of the Israeli-built fence, which did not always follow the international boundary but in some parts invaded Lebanese territory, a discrepancy noted by ILMG statements. On eight separate occasions, however, Hezbollah did intentionally fire Katyusha rockets and other projectiles into populated towns and villages in northern Israel. These escalated attacks were mostly conducted in retaliation for the killing of Lebanese civilians by SLA or IDF fire.

Throughout most of these exchanges, the parties submitted complaints to the ILMG, halted their operations, and further escalation was prevented. Submission of complaints began to be perceived as an acceptable substitute for violent retaliation. In June 1999, however, following a round of severe clashes, including a wide-scale attack on northern Israel and a counter Israeli air raid on infrastructure in Lebanon, twelve Lebanese civilians were killed and sixty-two were injured; in Israel, two civilians were killed, and ten were injured.[63]

Israel's minister of defense at the time, Moshe Arens, announced that Israel was withdrawing from the ILMG, arguing that the Understanding was violated whenever it suited Hezbollah to do so.[64] But Arens's government had only a week or so more in power; and to no one's surprise, when the new prime minister, Ehud Barak, took office, he immediately resumed Israel's participation in the Group.

ARTICLE II

> Israel and those cooperating with it will not fire any
> kind of weapon at civilians or civilian targets in
> Lebanon.

This provision articulated the most fundamental Lebanese interest, which was to protect Lebanese civilians and civilian property from Israeli fire, especially in the areas adjacent to the Security Zone.

"Those cooperating with" Israel were the SLA forces. In this context, Israel and Lebanon faced a similar problem—that of being formally accountable for forces they could not fully control. Though Israel had considerable sway over the SLA it was hardly absolute.[65]

Although Israel attempted on several occasions to disassociate itself from the actions of SLA soldiers, the other parties to the ILMG fiercely objected. Regardless of the precise international legal standard by which states are responsible for forces operating on their behalf, the Understanding placed full responsibility on Israel for any SLA action.[66] This was crucial if any system of accountability was to exist.

In monitoring the implementation of Article II, the ILMG was further faced with the difficult task of determining who and what could be defined as "a civilian" or "a civilian target." The international laws of war rely on the basic, status-based distinction between combatants and civilians and between military and civilian targets.[67] However, the definitions of these concepts in international conventions leave ample space for debate over the legitimacy of specific targets. This space increases the more the armed conflict moves away from the traditional war to involve nonstate actors and guerilla tactics. Whereas the IDF and SLA positions were distinct military facilities, and easily identifiable as such, the Lebanese armed groups, by nature, were operating from within villages, civilian buildings, cars, and infrastructure for their purposes. Both sides employed Lebanese civilians in some military and paramilitary functions. This situation generated extensive debates over the status of targeted people and structures.

But the most fundamental and recurrent controversy with regard to the interpretation of Article II had risen with regard to the use of the verb "target." The Israeli position, which relied on principles of the general laws of war, was that the verb meant an act carried out intentionally; therefore, in order for an attack to be considered a violation of the Understanding, it had to be deliberately directed against civilians or civilian targets or else conducted in a manner which affected civilians in an excessive, disproportionate, and unreasonable way.

To support its position, Israel pointed to the generally accepted interpretation of the laws of armed conflict, which are essentially based on a balance and compromise between military necessities on the one hand and humanitarian considerations on the other.[68] The basic principle, which was first set in the 1868 St. Petersburg Declaration, is that the "only legitimate object which States should endeavour to accomplish during war is to weaken the military forces of the enemy."[69] Attacks may thus be directed only against military forces and objects and must be carried out in a way that would minimize harm to civilians or civilian objects.[70]

At the same time, however, the protection given to civilians and civilian targets by the laws of war is by no means absolute. When an attack is directed against a military target and meets the conditions of military necessity, proportionality, and reasonableness, it is legitimate even if civilians suffer collateral injury or damage.[71] International law scholar Yoram Dinstein emphasizes that the key words in the international conventions' provisions on the protection of civilians are "intentional targeting." Dinstein adds that

> if one is shelling from afar a legitimate target, there may be people present within that target who belong to categories that are not to be intentionally targeted, but this does not taint the shelling with illegitimacy. On the contrary, a belligerent who wishes to avoid excessive casualties has to evacuate these people from the target which is within its control and is likely to be targeted.[72]

The Lebanese position, on the other hand, was that, given the object and purpose of the Understanding, an attack should be judged by its outcome and not by the intentions of the attacker. The Lebanese position relied, among other things, on the wording of the following article, which provided that "*under no circumstances* shall civilians be the target of attack" (emphasis mine). It is also true that the trend in international humanitarian law—even if not implemented in practice—is to enhance protection for civilians, regardless of the conduct of the adversary; as Dieter Fleck notes, "[Article 51 of Additional Protocol I] now expressly confirms that the violation of international legal obligations by the adversary does not exempt the attacker from his legal obligations with regard to the civilian populations."[73]

The Lebanese argument was based, among other things, on the status of the Understanding vis-à-vis the international laws of war, a debated question in itself: Israel claimed that the interpretation of the Understanding should be guided by the accepted norms of international law, while Lebanon saw the Understanding as sui generis, a unique and independent agreement that set stricter rules for the protection of civilians.[74]

Although some of Israel's violations were doubtlessly the result of direct and intentional counterfire by the SLA at civilian populated areas, for the most part, high levels of noncompliance were the result of the unfeasibility of the idea of absolute protection for civilians, especially in such a densely populated theater of war. Settling the controversy over Articles II and III was therefore pivotal for the acknowledgement of violations on both sides and the justifications that could be made with regard to specific belligerent actions. It would also determine whether more burden of care for civilian protection was to be placed on the forces initiating and conducting an attack or on those responding to it.

After extensive deliberations within the ILMG, the Lebanese position won out. In addition, despite early disagreements, it became routine that every damage or injury reported to the ILMG, even the most minor one, was acknowledged thereafter as violative of the Understanding.[75]

The positive aspect of this process was the very broad legal defense henceforward accorded the civilians in Lebanon, who were suffering from the impact of attacks and counter-attacks on an almost daily basis. The negative one was that, as the sole focus of the Group turned to the outcome of attacks in terms of their eventual impact on civilians, discussions became routine and predictable, affording little opportunity for attention to the different conditions of each and every incident. Specifically, the perspective of the attacker was deliberately ignored for the sake of the victim. This, in turn, prevented the Group from developing a meaningful sub-codex of more specific rules of engagement to be implemented in different circumstances. As I will argue later on, it is possible that this attempt to accord absolute protection to civilians and their property had, in the end, proved counter-productive.

ARTICLE III

> Beyond this, the two parties commit to ensuring that under no circumstances will civilians be the target of attack and that civilian populated areas and industrial and electrical installations will not be used as launching grounds for attacks.

This article contained, in fact, two operative parts. On the basis of the first part, Israel had on several occasions filed violation reports to the ILMG over injuries or damages suffered by Lebanese inhabitants of the Security Zone in the course of attacks carried out by Lebanese armed groups. This practice was accepted despite early objections on the part of the Lebanese delegation, which claimed that Lebanon alone had the power or legitimacy to protect Lebanese civilians.[76]

The second part of the article, which prohibited the launching of attacks from within populated areas, represented one of Israel's central interests and was also the most difficult one for Lebanon to meet. One of Israel's greatest difficulties in its operations in Lebanon was the armed groups' assimilation within the civilian population, which imposed heavy constraints on the Israeli army's ability to target or counterfire at the armed groups, and often caused civilian casualties and further cycles of escalation.

The armed groups' practices were a combination of a deliberate tactic of using civilians as human shields, in violation of international humanitarian law, as well as an inevitable reliance on the civilian population, as in any guerilla warfare.[77] Members of the armed groups lived and operated—as they still do—inside the Lebanese villages and were dependent upon their fellow villagers for supplies and support. Most of the armaments of these groups were stored within the villages, which were used in effect as exit and return bases. This, in itself, was already a violation of the Understanding in the eyes of the Israelis and Americans, but for obvious reasons was never accepted as such by the ILMG.[78] Indeed, to a large extent, repeated Israeli outcries that "the terrorists must be taken out of the villages" were meaningless, for the armed groups were themselves part of the villages, and the villages part of the armed groups. Once out of the village and without protection of fortifications, the armed groups were exposed to every form of attack or counterfire by the IDF or SLA forces.

On the Lebanese armed groups' part, therefore, the prohibition on shielding, despite its firm anchoring in international laws of war, was impractical and unfeasible. As international scholar Edward Kwakwa has noted,

> guerilla warfare normally forces a status of quasi-belligerency on the civilian populace of the country or territory in which the conflict is taking place. It is used as a means of redressing the unequal correlation of forces between a governing administration or armed forces with extensive resources, on the one hand, and insurgents, on the other . . . [The guerillas] hide among the civilian populace or in remote areas and conduct hit-and-run attacks . . . [Their] strategy of melting away into the countryside and towns also makes them difficult targets and enhances their advantages in military terms.[79]

The ILMG, which needed to apply the provision in a practical manner, was thus faced with the difficult task of interpreting its exact scope. To do this, it had to define what a "civilian populated area" was and what actions amounted to "launching an attack." Both questions required the articulation of still-more-specific rules, which in turn had to balance between the desire to protect civilians and the freedom of the Lebanese armed groups, already in gross military inferiority, to fight the Israeli forces. They also captured an underlying debate regarding who should bear the brunt of responsibility—those who initiate the attack or those who respond to it.

Finally, the group was able to articulate a rule according to which a parameter of one hundred meters around any house was considered a "civilian populated area." Any attack from within this parameter was a violation of the Understanding, whereas any action taken outside the parameter was a legitimate one. Although at first the armed groups moved away from inhabited areas, in respect of the one-hundred-meter rule, as the IDF increased its reliance on air force in the spring of 1999, the armed groups retreated to launching attacks from closer proximity to houses. Full adherence to the one-hundred-meter rule would have exposed the armed groups to easy targeting by the Israeli air force. The Understanding would have thus become tantamount to a prohibition on guerilla warfare; a prohibition which neither Lebanon nor the armed groups have never agreed to.

An inevitable spiral of violence ensued: in December–January 2000, seven IDF soldiers were killed by Hezbollah attacks launched from populated areas.[80] The IDF responded by a third escalated attack on Lebanese infrastructure.[81] The monitoring group reconvened in February 2000 to discuss a bevy of violation reports from both sides. While the group was in session, another IDF soldier was killed by Hezbollah fire originating from within a village. The Israeli delegation then walked out of the meeting, and the group's operation never resumed.

ARTICLE IV

> Without violating this Understanding, nothing herein
> shall preclude any party from exercising the right of
> self-defense.

Beyond simply repeating the internationally recognized right to use force in self-defense, anchored in the UN charter, Article IV essentially validated the continuation of belligerence between the two parties, as both sides justified their actions by claiming self-defense: Israel protecting itself against the armed groups' attacks on Israeli citizens, and the Lebanese armed groups fighting against Israeli occupation of southern Lebanon.[82] By acknowledging each party's right to self-defense, the Understanding in effect acknowledged the continuation of fighting.

However, the Israeli position sought to broaden the implication of the article to mean an acknowledgement of the right to self-defense as pertaining not only to the right to carry out military activities in Lebanon but also to specific exchanges of fire; in other words, to endow Article IV with an operative meaning, which would allow the use of military power, especially in situations of clear self-defense, even where its exercise caused reasonable and proportionate collateral damage to civilians. Israel was armed with an American side letter, signed by Secretary Christopher, recognizing Israel's right to exercise self-defense in Lebanon, although not explicit as to the relation between this right and the Understanding.[83]

The Lebanese delegation, conversely, focused on the first four words of the article, together with the beginning words of Article III: "under no circumstances." According to this interpretation, the right to self-defense only meant that one may lawfully return fire but that counterfire, like direct fire, must not violate the Understanding. This approach was also consistent with the Lebanese interpretation of Article II, which focused on the outcome rather than on the intentions or circumstances of the actions taken.

Even had the other parties to the ILMG accepted the Israeli position, two main problems would have remained: The first would have been to prove that a situation was one of a clear and imminent danger, thus justifying a reasonable and proportionate defensive reaction, even at the price of injuring nearby civilians. The other, a more institutional one, would have been for the ILMG, as an international forum established to enhance the protection of civilians, to conclude what a "reasonable price" might be for civilians to pay for the belligerent actions of combatants. None of these were possible. The Lebanese interpretation thus prevailed over the applicable principles of international law, and any component of mens rea as a requirement of culpability, as well as any justification of self-defense, was rejected if an action resulted in injury or harm to civilians.[84]

The Format and Mechanism of the Israel-Lebanon Monitoring Group

> Complaints will be submitted to the Monitoring
> Group. In the event of a claimed violation of the
> Understanding, the party submitting the complaint will
> do so within 24 hours. Procedures for dealing with the
> complaints will be set by the Monitoring Group.
>
> FIRST NONNUMBERED PARAGRAPH OF THE ISRAEL-LEBANON CEASE-
> FIRE UNDERSTANDING, APRIL 26, 1996.

The Understanding itself provided no guidance on how the MG was to operate. Rules of operation for the Group were concluded by the participants themselves in an Agreed Protocol.[85]

The most distinct feature of the Understanding regime was the requirement of unanimity in each and every decision, procedural or substantive, taken by the ILMG. While the demand for unanimity often raised obstacles in reaching agreements, it was nonetheless vital to the working of the Group. For one thing, it protected each party's sense of sovereignty, freeing it from a threat of coercion. For another, it forced each side to accept responsibility for actions carried out by the forces it was accountable for. Instead of being "found guilty" by a third party, the responsible party thus had to assume, as well as accept, blame. This latter principle made the work of the Group a "partnership," however qualified, rather than another battlefield. The sense of a cooperative enterprise was important to the participants themselves as well as to their spectators, as it broadcast a message of unity behind a common goal.

The Protocol provided that in cases where unanimity could not be reached, the matter would be referred to the respective foreign ministers for a follow-up. This option was rarely invoked, and the general rule was that the Group would continue its deliberation, sometimes for days on end, "until white smoke appeared."[86]

The ILMG would convene at the invitation of the American or French chair, whenever a violation report was submitted to him by Israel or Lebanon.[87] This gave both countries, as the direct parties to the conflict, control over the level of intervention by the ILMG, as the Group could not convene unless requested to by either party. Meetings were conducted in the UNIFIL compound in Naqura, south Lebanon. UNIFIL's role was limited to hosting the discussions, and its officers did not take part in the Group's substantive work. This was to keep the Group's distinctiveness and protect its delicate political balance.

As the Understanding itself provided, violation reports had to be submitted in an agreed-upon format within twenty-four hours of any alleged violation. The limited time frame was set to allow the Group to act quickly and preempt escalation. A similar motivation marked the Protocol's provision that a final report must be issued by the ILMG within seventy-two hours of the submission of a violation report, during which time each side was supposed to hold its fire and refrain from retaliation for violations.[88] In practice, the seventy-two-hour limit turned out to be unfeasible, for various practical and logistical reasons. Nevertheless, occasional Israeli suggestions to set designated dates for meetings were rejected by the other members of the Group, in part because of the reluctance to give the ILMG a character of regularity (which might imply consent for a regular dialogue) and in part because the immediate convention of the Group to account for each and every incident, trivial as it may seem, was perceived as a valuable show of special effort by all parties to provide protection for civilians and adhere to the agreed regime.

The Syrian, Israeli, and Lebanese delegations were each headed by a high-ranking military officer, in line with the Syrian preference for maintaining a purely apolitical, military character for the ILMG. The American and French delegations were each headed by a professional designated diplomat, aided by military experts to advise him on technical military issues. The group itself did not operate as either a "truth commission" or a fact-finding mechanism. The Protocol did provide that, upon agreement, the Group could hold verification missions in Israel or Lebanon to determine the actual facts of an incident.[89] In practice, however, only two such missions were ever carried out. Discussions often relied on the evidence presented by the delegations themselves.

The tone of the exchanges within the ILMG evolved significantly over the course of the group's operation: while at the early stages nearly all discussions were arguments and tended to be aggressive, quarrelsome, and inflammatory, as the group matured, its tone mellowed and became more explanatory and polite. In many cases there was a genuine attempt to convince the other parties to see one's own concerns and grievances. Naturally, the nature—and pitch—of the debates would alter in response to the gravity of the incidents under discussion as well as to the general atmosphere.

A similar positive development was evident in the parties' willingness to acknowledge their responsibility for actions carried out by those they represented. At the earlier periods, consensus could only be reached in a "he said, she said" formula, stating the parties' competing recounts of events. Later, as parties became more willing to assume responsibility, this format was no longer necessary, for the parties felt more confident in assigning and accepting responsibility in definite terms.

With the change in atmosphere and the building of mutual trust over time, more frank and effective discussion on matters not formally within the purview of the Understanding also became possible. Both sides grew more willing to address other problems raised by their opponents, mainly on a humanitarian basis, though most such issues were raised outside the formal discussions. One such case, for example, concerned a ship carrying foreign workers, which was abandoned off Lebanon's shores by its crew, who stole the passengers' money and passports. The Israeli navy towed the ship from the sea to the Naqura port. The resettlement of the workers, who remained in Naqura for several weeks, was discussed by the heads of the Israeli and Lebanese delegations, though eventually was dealt with by the International Committee of the Red Cross. Another issue was a seventy-two-hour cease-fire reached between the parties to enable the recovery of bodies of Hezbollah members by the ICRC.[90]

Purely military issues were also brought up outside the framework of formal discussions.[91] The evolution of the dynamic among the parties allowed the ILMG to become a more-effective channel that frequently acted as a crisis prevention mechanism. Delegates from both sides had, on various occasions, requested the chairman to pass conciliatory messages to their counterparts following exceptionally harsh events that held the potential for escalation. One such incident occurred in December 1999, when a mortar round fired by the SLA struck the village of Arab Salim, injuring fifteen schoolchildren, four of them seriously. The Israeli delegate to the ILMG asked the chairman to pass a conciliatory message to the Lebanese delegate and to urge restraint. After several messages were conveyed back and forth by the chairman, Prime Minister Barak issued an apologetic statement, and retaliation was avoided.[92]

The outcome of each meeting was a final report and a concluding, consensual press statement. The report included the internal discussion held in the Group, but, unlike the conclusions, was kept discreet and unpublished, in order to facilitate a frank and open exchange to the greatest possible extent.[93] The main product of the ILMG was thus the published press statement, which would describe the course of the meeting, its factual findings with regard to each violation report, whether or not a violation had been committed, a naming of the responsible party, and the group's recommendations. The report's significance derived from the fact that it was the only formal sanction at the group's disposal. The publication of the ILMG's conclusions, as well as their unanimity, gave them an added value of accountability and assumption of responsibility. Since the ILMG could not impose on the parties an obligation to pay compensation, take specific actions against individuals responsible for committing violations, or force them to take any other concrete steps (in terms of the use of certain weapons, locations, or means), its only power lay in the public shame it could attach to the violating party. The shame sanction operated as a kind of peer pressure not only between the participants of the ILMG but also among all the potential readers of the press statements.[94] The necessity to obtain the violating party's consent to the conclusions, in turn, gave the press statements additional force in national and international public opinion.[95]

Another more covert but still influential means at the chairman's disposal was political pressure. In difficult cases, when it was apparent that agreement could not be reached, the chairman would attempt to lean on the delegations in Naqura via their political superiors.[96] This kind of move would usually be coordinated between the chair and cochair, and it was common for high-ranking officials in Washington and Paris to contact the parties' ambassadors to the capitals or else the parties' officials in Damascus, Beirut, or Jerusalem.

Perhaps the most important function of the Group was to provide its members with an alternative to retaliation. While the seventy-two-hour rule had mostly proved ineffectual, and the parties often retaliated by force to violations, still, especially in the earlier period of the Group, the parties did at times resort to submitting violation reports instead of counterattacks. As to this, the Israeli head of delegation remarked,

> The Monitoring Group's effectiveness lies in its role as a tensions-curbing mechanism. In a number of instances, had the specific problem arisen before Operation Grapes of Wrath, it would have provoked an escalation . . . Thanks to the Understandings achieved after Operation Grapes of Wrath, problems are discussed by the ILMG, which . . . makes its own decisions, and that's all there is to it.[97]

A Lebanese commentator also explained that "the complaints lodged by Lebanon or even those specifically made by Israel constitute a commitment not to bring about a large scale military escalation, even nominally."[98]

After a period of about two years, however, the Group's effect—in terms of preventing violations or military escalation—began to wane. Its operation became routine, with every player knowing what role to play and how the game would turn out. Very few discussions of principle now took place, and the positions of each side were known in advance. There was a significant increase in the number of violation reports, and a corresponding decrease in the duration of each meeting. The ILMG began to decline in public opinion. And yet the participants themselves still appreciated the group's value, not so much for its actual effectiveness but rather for its very existence. Both sides acknowledged the importance of a regulatory body, even if a nominal one, that managed the conflict, as well as the opportunity to communicate directly with the opposing side and learn its concerns and positions without mediatory intervention. It was for this primary reason that the Group survived for nearly four years.

Analysis

The Israeli-Lebanese conflict has continued for decades with poor prospects for resolution. Its interrelatedness with the Israeli-Syrian and even the Israeli-Palestinian conflicts has made it impossible to resolve in isolation. All efforts to reach a peace agreement or even a more-limited cease-fire arrangement have failed. The ongoing fighting over the years has claimed a death toll of many thousands in Lebanon and over a thousand in Israel. It has also inflicted extensive damage on property and made life for the inhabitants of the area generally unbearable.

The 1996 Israeli-Lebanon Cease-fire Agreement formed a conflict management regime within one dimension of the rivalry only, namely, the actual belligerence on the ground. On many counts, the Understanding offered its parties an unstable, easily disturbed equilibrium. But despite its frequent violations, all parties were always highly conscious of its existence and the obligations it imposed and, at least in part, adjusted their conduct to conform to its provisions. One Israeli artillery commander in Lebanon told reporters that he had "clear instructions not to fire within 500 meters of any settlement" and added that, given these new safety rules, "There are very few places where I can fire freely."[99]

It may be said, therefore, that the Understanding is both a natural and a unique example of an island of agreement within the context of an enduring rivalry: natural, because it was an attempt to manage an armed rivalry that is still enduring today; unique, because the endeavor to regulate a conflict through an agreement on particular rules of engagement was altogether novel. Having expired, the Understanding regime provides us with a body of statistical and historical data by which to compare events before, during, and after the operation of a particular island of agreement and from which to contemplate the success or failure of its various components.

The regime created by the Understanding was designed to achieve three interrelated goals. The first and most obvious was to protect civilians on both sides of the border by excluding them from the sphere of combat. The second, and more implicit, was to prevent further escalation of belligerent actions by reducing the overall military activity in the area. This goal, it was hoped, would in turn advance a third—the creation of a more tranquil political atmosphere and possibly a subsequent resumption of peace talks between Israel and Syria and, thereafter, between Israel and Lebanon.

In terms of its first and primary goal, the Understanding proved partly effective. The first year and a half registered a sharp decrease in civilian casualties on both sides of the border. Later, numbers gradually rose, but casualty numbers were still smaller on average than in years preceding the Understanding. Civilian property was increasingly impacted by military operations, although less from intentional targeting and more as the inadvertent result of regular exchanges of fire. The designers of the Understanding had hoped that the fewer civilian casualties there were, the less incentive there would be to carry out wide-scale retaliations and counterattacks, and hence escalation might be prevented. This expectation was not fulfilled. In fact, the effectiveness of the agreement in providing protection for civilians was undermined by its failure to reduce the general level of belligerency in the area. It may even be that the experience of the Understanding proves the possible danger of the "pressed balloon effect," by which those operations and actions not explicitly prohibited under an island of agreement are actually exacerbated. In this light, it is perhaps the more remarkable that the total number of civilian injuries throughout the years of the Understanding remained lower than in former years.

As for the third goal, despite early expectations that the peace process should be contingent upon de-escalation, peace talks between Israel and Syria, which after several failed attempts in the past resumed in the late fall of 1999, ended at the end of January 2000 in a stalemate. They were precipitated by no significant reduction in the level of belligerency on the ground.[100] In fact, if there was any connection between peace negotiations and violence, it went the other way: once talks were under way, the parties showed greater restraint. The peace talks also had a real effect on the nature of the dialogue within the group, which grew more open and amicable at that time.

A statistical analysis of the history of the ILMG shows significant levels of noncompliance on both sides.[101] More specifically, Lebanon was mostly "found guilty" for violating the prohibition of Article III in launching attacks from within populated areas, while Israel was at fault mainly for hurting civilians or civilian targets in Lebanon, in violation of Article II.

It would be grossly mistaken to assume that the lack of political (or politico-military) will was the sole or even primary cause of noncompliance. Rather, I would argue, it was the design of the Understanding and the nature of its provisions—most notably, the overambitious and impractical granting of complete immunity to civilians—that brought on the bulk of violations.

The Design of the Regime: Analysis of Components

There was something paradoxical in the way in which the Understanding sought to isolate and regulate the actual belligerency by a formal agreement. If the underlying assumption was that the conflict would continue, then the limitations which the Understanding endeavored to impose on it were ultimately impossible: if the parties were to comply in full, they would hardly fight; if they chose to fight, it was necessarily at the price of violating the agreement.

In attempting to form an insulated haven for civilians and their property from the hazards of conflict, the Understanding was doomed to fail. Wars are not intended to be sterile operations and cannot operatively be conducted as such. This is especially true when they are conducted within or around populated areas and when the population itself participates in them. The degree of harm to civilians can be regulated up to a point; the overriding fact that harm will ensue while hostilities persist cannot. Military necessity may call for a certain operation despite its foreseen collateral impact on civilians. Furthermore, spillover effects, unforeseen enemy reactions, the unexpected movement of civilians, a sudden change in weather conditions, or a chance failure of ammunition all threaten to do damage even when none is intended.

The Understanding also failed in its attempts to induce the Lebanese armed groups to conduct their attacks from open areas only. Given the asymmetry in technology and warfare capabilities, in order to adhere to the prohibition on shielding, the armed groups would have had to paralyze a large portion of their combat capabilities. Similarly, in view of the armed groups' dependence on the Lebanese villages, to isolate the villages from the sphere of combat would have meant, in effect, to surrender guerilla warfare, something that the armed groups had no intention of doing and that the Understanding was not meant to achieve.

More successful was the attempt to isolate Israeli territory from the sphere of battle. Putting aside the deliberate retaliations against Israeli territory, there were, in all, fewer unintentional violations of Article I than of Articles II or III. Considering the effects of interdependence, this is not a surprising observation, for theoretically as well as practically, belligerence could continue almost uninterrupted without affecting Israeli territory. Unintentional violations were the result of misfire or large impact radius of rounds fired against IDF positions along the Lebanese side of the border.

Separation of segments was also successful when the isolation was based on a temporal criterion. Thus, on one occasion in which the parties agreed on a seventy-two-hour cease-fire, for the purpose of recovering Hezbollah members' bodies, the agreement was observed. Obviously, there was a strong interest on all sides to comply. But this limited temporal segmentation also gave little incentive to defect, as it did not interfere with the overall continuation of the conflict.

In general, therefore, the more commonplace isolation of geographic or temporal dimensions seemed likely to prove more successful than the attempt to regulate codes of combat in a manner that permeated the entire belligerent activity.

Attempts at segmentation of the conflict itself, mainly the Israeli-Syrian part of it, had mixed results at best. From its inception, the understanding's regime was clearly limited to the armed conflict in Lebanon. There was never any aspiration to address the long-standing Israeli-Syrian conflict, at least directly. There was also significant reluctance on the part of Syria to assume formal responsibility for the armed groups' activities. At the same time, given its control over the Lebanese government and even more so over the Lebanese armed groups, Syrian involvement in the regime was inevitable. This complicated state of affairs led, from the very beginning, to an ambiguity with regard to the role of Syria in the regime. Syria's phantomlike position of "observer" was unlikely to sit well in a regime founded on the idea of public responsibility and accountability. Indeed, the wink-in-the-eye approach to Syria's role in the conflict may have been detrimental to the regime's success.

Whether the regime managed to create an equal cost-benefit calculus for both sides is another key question in judging its success or failure.

Prior to the Understanding, the parties were trapped in cycles of action, reaction, and escalation. In accepting the Understanding, both agreed to refrain from certain practices that were otherwise part of their available arsenal, while still engaging each other by other means. Thus, the accord aimed to establish a shift in focal point, an uneasy equilibrium that, in theory, should have diverted the parties from perpetual escalation to cadences of partial escalation and partial restraint. But the decision to assume limitations on operations could work only so long as both parties felt these limitations did not place them at a disadvantage.

For a while, it seemed as if the Understanding was successful in charting new ground for the old rivals. A year on, however, it became clear that the new equilibrium was unstable, as the parties frequently violated and, in the last few months of the Group's life, widely ignored their obligations. Each party felt the other was breaking its restraints—that the outcome was asymmetrical and the obligations largely unfeasible.

Lebanon bore the brunt of most of the civilian casualties and had to accept the designation of its territory as the only legitimate battlefield. Israel faced the continuous attacks launched at its forces from within villages and repeated Katyusha launches into its territory, aimed at its civilian population. While civilian casualties on both sides of the border were, on average, lower than before the Understanding, casualty figures among combatants were persistently high; and while the Understanding was established to protect civilians, not combatants, the heavy death toll among combatants on both sides gave the parties the sense that they were selling themselves short and that in adhering to the Understanding, they were allowing their costs possibly to exceed their benefits. These perceptions would drive them back to cycles of escalation and restraint, with Katyusha rockets and air strikes marking the widest swings of the pendulum.

In demanding compliance from the enemy, as well as ensuring compliance by their own forces, the parties engaged in prolonged deliberations about what constituted noncompliance. The four concise provisions of the Understanding were intentionally and realistically formulated to leave room for questions and debate: attacks were not to be launched into Israel, but it was not made clear whether Israeli territory was bound by the international boundary or by the existing border fence, which did not always follow the boundary. Civilians and civilian targets in Lebanon were not to be targeted, but the civilian nature of people or structures was frequently debated. The verb "targeted" itself left sufficient room for actions against civilians or their property that could not be narrowly defined as "targeting." Similarly, civilian populated areas were not to be used as launching grounds for attacks, but the precise boundaries of these areas remained undefined. Early on, it was decided that the Understanding formed *lex specialis* and that if interpretation conflicted, the Understanding and not international humanitarian law should govern the parties' conduct.

This terminological flexibility, not to say vagueness, left room for the parties to engage in "borderline" activities, which, while running counter to the spirit of the Understanding, could not be clearly deemed violations of it. Such were the supersonic Israeli air force flights over Beirut, the expulsion of civilians from south Lebanon by the SLA, or the killing by the Hezbollah of Lebanese civilians who cooperated with the IDF or the SLA.[102] The ILMG's requirement of consensus decisions made it impossible to deal with such cases within the terms of the agreement, as no consensus could be reached on whether such actions were in fact violations. Clarity and, it might be claimed, the proper assignation of moral responsibility were thus frequently exchanged for a wider agreement base.

To the ambiguity of the Understanding's provisions on some points was added the uncertainty factor. As the obligations imposed by the agreement were largely unsuccessful in isolating the regulated segments from the nonregulated ones, the element of uncertainty became an especially powerful enabler of noncompliance. Lebanese armed groups launching attacks against IDF border positions could not be certain that their shells would not impact on the Israeli side or that the detonation of road-side bombs against SLA soldiers would not injure family members or innocent bystanders. IDF and SLA forces returning fire could likewise not be certain that they were not impacting on civilians or that land mines they had placed in open areas would not be activated by innocent shepherds. Even the most "surgical" air strikes or the use of relatively accurate antitank missiles could cause collateral damage or injury to civilians. While some collateral impact could be foreseen, much could not.

Some degree of uncertainty might have been removed, and indeed was removed in the course of time, by employing more precautions or refraining from certain types of action altogether. Thus, in the last two years of the Group's operation, there were fewer civilian casualties resulting from Lebanese armed groups' road-side bomb attacks or from

Israeli land mines left in open fields. Still, some operations could not be rescinded altogether and were inevitably followed by a large number of unintentional violations.

Here we come to the absolute necessity of management regimes, properly designed. There can be no doubt that the Understanding would not have survived, even to the limited extent it had, without the operation of the Monitoring Group. This is perhaps best demonstrated by the rapid dissolution of an earlier attempt to establish a conflict management regime, following Operation Accountability in 1993. The Understanding formed in the wake of that operation, as one legal scholar noted, was not worth the paper it was not written on; and, in any case, the absence of any written agreement entailed the absence of a monitoring body.[103] Without such a mechanism, the inherently unstable equilibrium established by the 1993 Understanding stood no chance of being maintained.

While the mise-en-scène set by the Grapes of Wrath Understanding was equally unstable, the monitoring group it established acted as an underpinning of the worded agreement: a stabilizing, normalizing force. Participation in the group became a show of each party's degree of commitment to the regime, as well as a sort of insurance against its provisions being exploited by the other side. Through its regular operation and derivative benefits, the mechanism bestowed a mantle of authority on the agreement, turning it, in effect, into an institution in its fuller sense.

The design of the mechanism has proved critical to the regime. One element was the Group's composition: the participation of the American and French delegations endowed the Group with the aura of an objective and authoritative international tribunal.[104] The Group's structure was narrow enough to prevent overpoliticization and, at the same time, broad enough to encompass a diverse range of influences on the implementing parties. It also bound the regional participants in ties of international obligation and decorum, making defection harder. Even a fierce critic of the Understanding, like the Israeli defense minister, Moshe Arens, admitted, "Abandoning the Understandings, which constitute an agreement with international connotations, is not a simple step."[105] The multinational consensus behind each press statement added to the shame associated with condemnation of violations, both domestically and internationally.

No less important was that participation in the mechanism was limited to the governments involved, thereby excluding the direct involvement of more marginal and extreme interest groups. This allowed the central participants—Israel, Syria, and Lebanon—to take a broader view of their interests. While in operations on the ground the interests of the governments were often hijacked by the diverse interests of the Hezbollah (as the loudspeaker of Syria) or the SLA, the discreet nature of the ILMG discussions gave the official representatives the opportunity to take a more moderate, long-term approach.

Direct contact between officials from countries who had no other direct channel of communication was another clear benefit for all. As one unnamed Israeli official explained in the aftermath of another round of clashes, "Israel has no intention of leaving the five-nation monitoring group, since it gives Israel contact with Syrians and others that it would otherwise not be able to have."[106]

According to its guidelines, the Group had to convene with every violation report submitted. This lent its discussions an air of relevance and practical meaning. To the national and international spectators, it gave a sense that something was being done. To the participants, it was a reminder that the other members were keeping a watchful eye upon their every move. Through repeated discourse and practice, and the fear of public shaming, the ongoing operation of the regulating mechanism was internalized into the decision-making process of its participants, enhancing the regime's effectiveness.

The group's monitoring function did not in itself enhance transparency, as it was vested with very few investigative powers of its own. Instead, the Group acted as a forum for the parties' presentation of their independent findings, through means and sources of their own. Discussion of violation reports were important for keeping a balanced and comprehensive record of both parties' behavior under the regime. They also helped the parties to form a continuous assessment of the costs and benefits they—and their opponents—accrued by remaining bound by the agreement. Most important, the discussions required the parties to account for their actions, or the actions of those represented by them, before the American and French representatives, who had little independent knowledge of actual occurrences on the ground.

Thus, transparency did increase not through the ILMG's formal operation as a monitoring body but rather through the forum it provided for the parties to engage in direct communication, something unavailable to them since the dissolution of the armistice commissions in 1967.

And, however limited in their subject matter, there could be no gainsaying the value of these direct exchanges, which allowed the rival parties to meet on common human ground and feel, as it were, the pulse of the conflict. For the first time in a long time, the warring sides could be made to take in the volume of the conflict on the "blind" side of the border. Accounts of individual grievances and injuries were sounded out, albeit indirectly, and listened to, and most importantly—responded to and accounted for in a way that was both confidential and public at the same time. Responsibility, in the joint public statements, was assumed consensually. In a way, it may be hazarded, the dignity of the process often shifted the focus away from political mudslinging and back to the human proportion of suffering endured.

No less noteworthy were the informal discussions that the forum sometimes enabled; the direct and relatively discreet channel of the Group made it possible to convey messages—ranging from the purely military to the more political—across the table. It also facilitated mutual gathering and sharing of information on such matters as humanitarian issues, which the parties did not want put on the official record of the Group so as not to broaden its official scope. Such informal exchanges often allowed the parties to signal to each other future actions or reactions under different scenarios. Altogether, these regular, direct, yet quiet communications helped to develop some degree of trust and understanding among the participants, which in turn, strengthened the personal commitment of the individuals participating in the Group to its workings and preservation.

With these options on offer, the Israel-Lebanon Monitoring Group thus became an available alternative to the all too known pattern of escalation and moderation. The submission of a violation report to the Group often allowed the parties to refrain from further violent retribution without loss of face vis-à-vis their rivals or domestic constituencies. Discussion sometimes superseded fire, encouraging each side to strive for a more restrained posture. Up to a degree—and more so at the earlier stages of the regime—all parties learned to refrain from knee-jerk retaliation after suffering each other's blows, stating they would rather allow the Monitoring Group to play out its role.

But any tacit hopes that the Group, once operational, would broaden its mandate beyond the limits of the Understanding were left ungratified. Even in the security sphere, the Group had only limited success in facilitating agreement on nonregulated segments of the conflict and adding them to the regulated ones. One possible reason for this failure was the degree of instability which the understanding attempted to bring under its fold. If even the initial undertakings could not be entirely sustained, it was only natural that there should be reluctance, on all parts, to add new commitments and obligations.

But the more profound reason for the monitoring group's limited success was grounded in the power relations within it, the differing interests of Syria and Lebanon, and the opposing interests of Syria and Israel. The clear Syrian interest in the continuation of the conflict rendered Syria—and consequently, the Lebanese armed groups—an impossible partner for any additional agreement or understandings. The solution, from the Syrian perspective, always lay and indeed still lies in the Golan Heights and nowhere else. To follow this logic, any agreement that would have further reduced the costs of the conflict would have been an undue concession to Israel. Even though such an agreement (especially one that would arrange for a secure Israeli withdrawal from Lebanon with the necessary guarantees) would have made a huge difference to Lebanon, it would have been of no use to Syria. These linkage politics of tying the Golan Heights to the conflict in Lebanon thus made it impossible to further mitigate the conflict by agreement.

Could a More Effective Regime Have Been Designed?

The problem of noncompliance in the case of the Understanding can probably best be described as reflecting a tension between the ideal and the achievable: realpolitik dictates that the ideal of protecting civilians must be limited by what is achievable in practice if it is to have any impact. The case of the Understanding shows that insisting on compliance with an ideal can be counterproductive. In reaching for the ideal, the Understanding extended itself to a gesture that could never be sustained in equilibrium, one both too modest on some counts and too ambitious on others.

In the absence of material enforcement mechanisms, each party ended up relying on its own unilateral actions to maintain deterrence against gross defections from the regime by the other. These deterrent actions were successful only in part, as their repetition further undermined the stability of the regime. Was there any other option available to the architects of the Understanding?

We could, for instance, imagine a regime that might limit the sphere of combat to certain geographical parts, prescribe practical limitations on the use of certain types of weapons, impose mutual limitations on certain types of warfare, acknowledge the right to act in self-defense, entrust the Monitoring Group with stronger investigative powers, require the parties to demonstrate positive actions taken to ensure future compliance, acknowledge the role of Syria as an accountable participant, etc. Such an "ideal" regime would strive to isolate more separable segments of the conflict, incorporate all the relevant actors, and impose more practical limitations on the parties. Perhaps it would even be accompanied by enforcement mechanisms, such as a duty to pay compensation for violations.

However, while more practical and elaborate provisions might have been easier to apply and perhaps, in the long run, been even more effective in their result, it is unlikely that they could have been agreed upon: Lebanon would have found it impossible to agree to acknowledge that its citizens were killed in "Israeli self-defense"; Israel would have refused to equate the status of Israeli territory with that of Lebanese territory and thus acknowledge the right of the Lebanese armed groups to attack the former; Lebanese armed groups would not have complied with the prohibition on shielding as long as they were subject to Israeli air force attacks; and Israel would never have agreed to relinquish its air strikes in Lebanon, as these dramatically reduced the number of casualties suffered by its ground troops. And, whatever the terms finally struck, both parties would still have had to face the problem of controlling the semi-independent forces they represented—a near-impossible task.

Moreover, even if different provisions could have generated a more stable regime, it is likely that the latter would have been truncated anyway, due to the Syrian interest in the continuation of the conflict. It is also clear that any attempt to establish a regime under which Syria would have been held as an equally responsible party to the conflict and subsequently to the rules of the regime would never have been accepted by Syria. Syria had nothing to gain from an official public discussion of its behind-the-scenes actions in Lebanon and everything to lose. So as long as its role in the regime was kept secondary, and primary outside it, no more-stable regime could arise.

Proof of these claims may be found in events following the breakup of the Monitoring Group. In February 2000, when Israel suspended its participation in the Group after several IDF soldiers were killed by Hezbollah fire from inhabited areas, in violation of Article III, extensive diplomatic negotiations took place on its return to the discussion table.

Israeli officials named a series of requirements, the fulfillment of which would be a necessary condition to the resumption of the discussions. Among these requirements were a continuous period of at least two weeks in which the armed groups would refrain from any belligerent activity, and a broadening of the prohibition on launching attacks from inhabited areas.[107] These requirements were never met, and discussions were never resumed. The attempt to shift the footing of the Understanding to a different equilibrium, whether in the form of a partial cease-fire or in a general tightening of the regime, thus failed.

Protecting Lives or Protracting Conflict?

From the time of its conception, the idea of creating a joint conflict management mechanism by which to regulate the effects of an already decades-old conflict evoked wide-ranging skepticism and not a little opposition. During the three and a half years of the monitoring group's operation, it was constantly overshadowed by doubts of its success or proper function. Even with hindsight, it is uncertain whether a clear test of success can be applied to either the agreement or the monitoring mechanism, in part because a direct causal connection between the workings of diplomacy and events on the ground is difficult to establish and in part because any attempt to assess the feasibility and success of alternatives must remain theoretical. No one, furthermore, could say with certainty what would have come to pass had the Understanding not been reached nor the Group formed.

One thing, however, is beyond dispute: the Israel-Lebanon Monitoring Group outlived all expectations. When it was first agreed that the positions of chair and cochair should rotate between the American and French delegates, it was decided that the American chair would begin the first tour and that rotation would take place every five months. The story goes that no one on either side believed the group would survive its first three months, and therefore the Israelis should not worry about the French ever taking the chair. That the group eventually survived for nearly four years undoubtedly exceeded the wildest hopes of its own architects, not to mention those of its participants and spectators.[108] Given the high levels of noncompliance with the Understanding exhibited on both sides during those three and a half years, it must be concluded that the parties found substantial benefits in the monitoring mechanism itself—benefits which made sticking to the Group worthwhile, regardless of, or apart from, the value of the agreement.

The story of the Understanding is thus instructive not only with regard to questions of compliance with and effectiveness of an international conflict management regime but also with regard to the wider risks and benefits such regimes are likely to entail for the future relationship between the rivals. Unlike the experience of islands of agreement in the India-Pakistan or the Greece-Turkey contexts, the long-term effects of which are still partly unknown, the Understanding is firmly and finally placed within a concrete time frame in the past; a much fuller body of evidence is therefore available from which to study not only the effects of the regime while it was still in place but also the events following its cessation.

As the history of the Israeli-Lebanese conflict shows, the more drastic moves have always been carried out by Israel. The invasion of Lebanon in 1978, the withdrawal three months later, the second invasion in 1982, the incomplete withdrawal in 1985, and the final complete withdrawal to the Blue Line in May 2000 were each large-scale unilateral Israeli moves that sought, however unsuccessfully, to redefine the terms of the conflict and its arena. As long as there was no change in the Syrian-Lebanese ties, and as long as Israel kept its control over the Golan Heights, the key to any break from the violent status quo lay, in practical terms, with Israel.

No doubt, many catalysts played a part in the final Israeli decision to withdraw from Lebanon. The predominant one was Israeli public opinion, which, like that of other western countries embroiled in protracted guerilla warfare, grew more and more intolerant of the increasing number of casualties. For a long time, voices were raised in both official and unofficial public circles expressing a growing opposition to the IDF's continued presence in Lebanon. The shift in public opinion also changed the confrontation's definition from "ongoing security operations" to "war" and finally repositioned it in the center of the public agenda. A similar shift took place regarding the consideration of international opinion and the lawfulness of the acts of war performed in Lebanon, with wide-reaching effects on both the activities of the IDF and the way in which they were presented and justified.[109]

The question of the role played by the Understanding regime in the process leading up to the Israeli decision to withdraw is impossible to answer decisively, for the regime made only one factor of many. It is possible but unlikely that it had no real influence. Since the Understanding was the first sustainable agreement, however limited, to be reached between the rivals since the Lebanon War and since it laid down the formal basis for the Israeli operation in Lebanon for several years, it is hard to imagine that its existence had no effect whatsoever on the Israeli decision-making process.

While assuming the risk of not being able to meet the burden of proof, I will argue that the Understanding was in fact a delaying factor in Israel's ultimate decision to withdraw from Lebanon on the basis of Security Council Resolution 425.

For fifteen years, from January 1985 until May 2000, the Israeli security doctrine in Lebanon relied on two integrated notions: the indispensability of the Security Zone and the necessity of bilateral agreements—first with Syria and then with Lebanon—as a preliminary condition for withdrawal. The debate over the logic and effectiveness of this doctrine has been extensive, but for a long time the doctrine was not seriously challenged. Only in 1997, following a sharp increase in IDF casualties (including the collision of two helicopters that resulted in the death of all seventy-three soldiers on board), did Israeli politicians and mainstream public opinion begin questioning the efficacy of the Security Zone and the possibility of unilateral withdrawal.[110]

The Understanding both suited and reaffirmed the Israeli doctrine. While the document itself did call for broader peace efforts, this was only on the implied premise that the prevailing situation between Israel and Lebanon would continue until such efforts were successful. In return for what many had seen as the implicit acknowledgement of the legitimacy of the armed groups' attacks on IDF and SLA soldiers in Lebanon, Israel—also implicitly—gained the formal recognition of its own presence there. Moreover, as the agreement and its monitoring mechanism were endorsed by both the United States and France, the Israeli policy was ostensibly confirmed and accepted by these two international patrons.

Even when Israeli leaders began openly contemplating a withdrawal, a formal agreement was still posited as a condition. Thus, on April 1, 1998, in response to mounting domestic pressure, the Israeli government under Prime Minister Netanyahu first endorsed Security Council Resolution 425, calling for "security arrangements" that would ensure Israel's safety following a withdrawal. The Syrian and Lebanese governments rejected the decision, claiming that Resolution 425 left no room for negotiating arrangements and that Israel must withdraw immediately, without preconditions. In 1999 Prime Minister Barak of Israel again tied a withdrawal from Lebanon to a peace agreement with Syria. As mentioned above, it was only when the negotiations with Syria collapsed that Barak decided to pull out from Lebanon without any assurances from either Syria or Lebanon, but solely on the basis of Resolution 425.

Seen from this perspective, it is clear that the Understanding's regime, formation, and regular operation were founded on the Israeli establishment's view of the continued Israeli presence in Lebanon as a necessary evil, which could only be rectified or changed by formal agreement—first with Syria and then with Lebanon. Moreover, from the establishment's angle, if rules of engagement could be agreed upon, there was hope that arrangements for a future withdrawal could be too. The Understanding's continued operation may thus have been an obstacle for anyone wishing to question the ethics or efficacy of the reigning policy or suggest an alternative: *that* was made possible only with the final pullout in May 2000.

All this is not to say that nothing would have been better than something and that the Understanding should never have been concluded. As one Israeli reporter remarked of the diplomatic discussions following operation "Grapes of Wrath," "the political officials were concerned with the policy of 'the possible,' meaning, what could be achieved, and not necessarily with what we want or need to achieve."[111] Early negotiations over a "cease-fire" indicated that Lebanon would not be prepared to take any action against Hezbollah as long as Israeli troops still occupied South Lebanon; Israel would not pull out before there were strong guarantees for a cessation of all belligerent threats from the north; and Syria would on no account give up its trump card in any future negotiation over the Golan Heights.[112] In this brittle situation, managing the conflict might well have been the only way to prevent further escalation.

If there is any negative speculation to be entertained regarding the Understanding, it is only that—alongside its management function—it may have also, over its existence, served to numb both sides into acting by habit under the old order, rather than encouraging them to question the assumptions on which the order was founded. Whether or not more civilians would have been killed—or spared—in the absence of the Understanding regime, we can only surmise. But statistics show the agreement did have a positive effect in reducing the number of civilian casualties in comparison with earlier times.

For Lebanon, the Israeli withdrawal has brought about the long-coveted hope for change. Over the past six years, economic conditions have been steadily improving and construction projects are mushrooming throughout the country. Intercommunal tensions, which harbored the most serious threat to internal stability following the Syrian withdrawal, have so far been kept at bay. The government, however, has been unwilling and unable to disarm or disband Hezbollah, who de facto controls the southern part of the country, replacing the 1970s Palestinian 'Fatah Land' with a new Shiite 'Hezbollah Land.'

For Syria, the outcome has so far been much less favorable: with the international affirmation of the Israeli withdrawal, Syria lost what was probably its most highly prized bargaining chip vis-à-vis Israel—the legitimacy of the Lebanese armed groups' operations from Lebanon. The retraction of international legitimacy coupled with the explicit Israeli threat of a harsh reaction to any attack—this time against Syrian rather than Lebanese, targets—shackled Syria's maneuvering power in its support for the armed groups. And while, to date, these armed groups continue in their belligerent operations, they are subject to much more international criticism.[113] Moreover, without the Israeli withdrawal, Security Council Resolution 1559 and the ensuing Syrian withdrawal from Lebanon in 2005 could not have taken place. Now, for the first time in Lebanon's modern history, there is a chance to cut the seemingly Gordian Syrian-Lebanese knot.

Whether or not the withdrawal was a wise strategic move on the part of Israel is still widely debated. In the six years following the pullout, the number of Israeli military and civilian casualties greatly diminished. Nevertheless, tensions along the border are still extreme, and the heavy Hezbollah armaments, supplied by Iran and Syria,[114] are a cause for great concern on the Israeli side. Hezbollah is also very much involved in providing support, training, and assistance to Palestinian armed groups, whether independently or as a vehicle for Iran. Iran is alleged to be directly financing some of the terrorist attacks on Israeli citizens in recent years and to be sheltering in Theran—as Syria does in Damascus—some of the Palestinian terrorist groups.

It should also be noted that the withdrawal from Lebanon may have had negative repercussions elsewhere. Many Israeli officials, some of whom claim to have had it from the horse's mouth, i.e. Arafat himself, have argued that the unilateral withdrawal, widely portrayed in Arab media as Hezbollah's victory, was what inspired the Palestinian armed groups to launch a second *Intifada* only a few months later. Interestingly, in the summer of 2001, as Israeli-Palestinian violence reached new peaks, American diplomats contemplated the possibility of using the Understanding and the ILMG as potential models for a management mechanism for the Israeli-Palestinian conflict.[115] However, this never came to pass.

The clouds have hardly lifted from the Israeli-Lebanese border. For Lebanon, the problem is not just a redefinition of its relationship with Syria, on the one hand, and Israel, on the other. It is also the need to redefine itself: not only its destroyers or its builders, its allies or its friends, need to understand Lebanon. Lebanon, too, has to reach a new idea of itself as a single, independent, sovereign state with a unified national identity and concomitant responsibilities. But for as long as Israel and Syria are stalling a solution of their own conflict over the Golan Heights, they are also making it that much harder for Lebanon to reinvent itself.

CHAPTER FIVE

Testing Theory in Practice

Only the dead have seen the end of war.

(ATTRIBUTED TO PLATO)

Parties to an enduring rivalry often perceive it to be cyclical. The seeming inevitability of their situation, its aforeknown cadences, its predictable routines of eruptions and responses pose a strong temptation to conceive action on either side not so much as a matter of choice but as a spectacle of history repeating itself. In the words of King Solomon, "What has been is what will be, and what has been done is what will be done; and there is nothing new under the sun."[1] The question therefore arises whether by championing management, we are in fact catering to this passive, fatalistic psychological setup, or whether we are instead proposing to erode it, little by little, by running rings around the conflict until the space it takes up is narrowed somewhat, and other parts of the relationship can breathe?

Adopting Barbara Tuchman's yardstick for determining an enduring political attitude (in her case, political folly), I have deliberately selected conflicts whose endurance cannot be attributed to miscommunication, misperceptions, or the irrational stubbornness of a certain leader at a certain point in time, though all of these components do figure in all three histories.[2] Rather, each of the conflicts treated here stems from issues fundamental to the governments and societies involved and has, with time, grown more and more ingrained in their politics as well as in their consciousnesses.

Costs run high: they range from the daily noticeable to the unbearable in terms of human suffering, physical and economic damage, continuing psychological strain, and the cumulative effects which violence as a habit must have on self-perception, and common values; not to mention the enormous portions of yearly budgets and resources spent by the adversaries as a matter of course on security, defense and armaments, while pressing domestic needs go unattended.

In all three cases, frustration from failed attempts at either peaceful resolution or a definite military victory, alongside the realization of benefits entailed in possible containment or cooperation, have driven the parties to explore ways in which the scope of the conflict may be narrowed or forms of cooperation outside its confines may be established.

India and Pakistan have been able to form islands of agreement throughout the history and breadth of their relationship in such diverse spheres as trade and culture, telecommunications and postal services, civil aviation, and sports. The Indus Waters Treaty has enabled millions of people in both countries to benefit from the unobstructed flow of fresh water. The two countries have also been successful, to some degree, in isolating their islands from the scope of the conflict: water installations have never been targeted, cross-border telecommunications and postal services have continued uninterrupted since their establishment in 1974, and the limited scope of their cross-border trade is growing, however slowly.

Greece and Turkey, who have experimented with agreements in previous decades, have now made collaboration the rule over the exception. The recent rush of agreements between them has undoubtedly yielded palpable rewards in every sphere of state life, including European integration, tourism, environmental protection, trade, investment, law enforcement, culture, agriculture, and infrastructure, and more. As a fatal dogfight over the Aegean Sea has demonstrated as recently as May 2006, the core conflict is still alive, so that the islands cannot yet fully amalgamate to form a secure stretch of land. At the same time, the measured response of the politicians on both sides to the incident, in which a Greek pilot lost his life, proved that the islands are now nonetheless stable enough to resist crisis.

Although Israel, Lebanon, and Syria have so far limited their relationship to the battlefield, they have also for a stretch of time found a way to confine the destructive effects of their conflict through conscious and deliberate decision. And even within this narrow setting, the parties saw the open communication channel established through the Israel-Lebanon Monitoring Group (ILMG) as being of value in its own right, quite apart from its monitoring function.

These different histories contain vital insights into the possible uses and misuses of islands of agreement in the context of enduring inter-state rivalries. The lessons they teach us may be put to use in future attempts to design such islands, either in relation to themselves or, indeed, in the context of other conflicts around the world.

Characteristics of Islands of Agreement

I wish, now, to return to the theoretical framework outlined in the first chapter and test it through the different particular experiences we have encountered. To do this, we must first explore how each component I have listed as necessary to the building and sustainment of islands has (or has not) been implemented. The conclusions we draw from each particular experience should, in turn, contribute towards a justifiable generic prescriptive model for the future design and operation of islands of agreement.

Divisibility

The divisibility component stems from the principle by which islands of agreement can better succeed if they are designed to keep relatively "dry," safe from constant overflooding by the conflict. To stand better chances of sustainment, therefore, islands of agreement should address those spheres, or issues within spheres, that can to some degree be severed from the core dispute. In other words, they must pertain to issues with high prospects of "dryness."

The importance of the divisibility factor has been amply demonstrated in all three cases. The bulk of islands concluded between Greece and Turkey in 2000 and since skirted the issue of Cyprus or the allocation of rights in the Aegean Sea, and were thus generally successful. Agreements between India and Pakistan regulated civil aviation, infrastructure, movement of people, cultural cooperation, maritime shipping, and other matters not directly pertaining to the territorial dispute over Kashmir. And although, of these, most if not all were occasionally put in jeopardy or actually violated, on the whole they managed to survive over long periods. Thus, though military communications were damaged in times of increased tension, and interstate civil aviation was halted after the bombing of the Indian parliament in 2001, interaction in both cases resumed after the crises had abated.

In contrast, efforts to reach agreement on issues that were indivisible from the core dispute have shown themselves to be unsustainable. The 1976 Berne Declaration, which attempted to set out some ground rules for the future negotiations on the delimitation of the continental shelf—one of the most hotly contested issues between the two countries—proved useless in the long run. The two 1988 Greco-Turk security agreements pertaining to the Aegean also failed, as their provisions were too interrelated with the parties' fundamental disagreements on their respective rights in the Aegean. Provisions that affected these disagreements to a lesser degree, such as the prohibition on carrying out military exercises during the peak of the tourist season, were better complied with.

Correspondingly, India and Pakistan have successively failed to reach accord on the Siachen Glacier, Sir Creek, or their maritime boundary, as all three were perceived by either one rival or both as too closely bound with the Kashmir quarrel. Unsurprisingly, the most susceptible to violations in the Kashmir region were the various security agreements signed. Border arrangements between troops on both sides generally did not cover the Line of Control in Kashmir and so were mostly complied with.

The Israel-Lebanon Understanding's bold attempt to regulate the ongoing belligerence between Israel and the Lebanese armed groups relocated the principle of divisibility within the conflict itself, so that Lebanese territory was distinguished from Israeli territory as a war zone, while civilians were singled out from combatants for protection. This was a bold attempt, since this ambitious types of divisibility, already attempted by the general laws of war, is becoming increasingly difficult to sustain under modern conditions of armed conflict.

In principle, temporal or geographical limitations have proved easier to comply with than those pertaining to modes of operation. Temporary cease-fires or moratoria on exercises were generally complied with. Israel and the Lebanese armed groups observed the twenty-four-hour cease-fire undertaken to allow Hezbollah to collect the bodies of its fallen combatants; Greece and Turkey refrained from military maneuvers in the Aegean Sea during the holidays; Indian and Pakistani military forces observed their pledge not to engage in hostilities during the harvest season. Parties were also successful in confining conflict to certain areas. Israeli territory was generally safe from deliberate attack during the years of the Understanding, and border arrangements that do not include the Line of Control (LoC) in Kashmir are still a common occurrence.

Somewhat exceptional within the context of the divisibility principle is the Indus Waters Treaty, which, despite containing a substantial territorial component tied to Kashmir, has so far been kept successfully out of conflict's range. This may be accounted for in two ways. For one thing, the access to fresh water is a matter of survival—this is what makes joint water resources a particularly agreement-prone matter.[3] For another, the substantial involvement of third parties in designing and maintaining the regime has contributed materially to its ongoing stability. Despite a number of still-outstanding disputes over water (Tulbul, Baglihar, and others) the Indus Waters Treaty promises to endure.

Divisibility is not a neutral attribute; issues are intertwined and indivisible not only when objective characteristics—such as geography—make them so but also when a political strategy dictates that they should be. Hence, even when issues seem divisible at first glance, a political decision to link them may well come to override this divisibility. One example is the Turkish and Greek governments' decision to link the question of Cyprus's accession to the EU with that of Turkey's. It was only after the linkage was severed, at least to some degree, that Greek-Turkish cooperation over the latter's accession became possible. Similarly, a cooperation agreement between Israel and Lebanon over the Wazzani waters was prevented for political considerations, even though it could have easily been separated from the main festering disputes in the area. And while, during their 1998 bilateral talks, India had proposed to Pakistan a safety package to prevent unauthorized nuclear war, according to reports, no progress could be made, as Pakistan linked any such progress to progress over Kashmir.[4] Indivisibility can therefore be said to be a tool for propelling a conflict, just as divisibility is a prerequisite for limiting it.

A Symmetry of Costs and Benefits

Another necessary characteristic of islands presented in Chapter 1 is a right balance of the costs and benefits which must be entailed by any such agreement for both parties. This, I have argued, was a derivative of the parties' concern about relative gains that would in all likelihood cause them to abstain from entering into any regime in which they might be exploited by an advantageous rival.

The case studies, however, reveal that of much greater importance to the parties than *real* relative gains are *perceived* relative gains. The majority of the islands of agreements examined in the previous chapters imposed *identical* obligations or prohibitions upon the two rivals. But an agreement that imposes identical provisions on two rivals who differ greatly in power, wealth, military capabilities, and general circumstances does not result in identical costs and benefits for both sides. That is, an identical bilateral commitment, which makes for formal equality, may all too easily result in material inequality (this is why, increasingly, multilateral trade and environmental regimes tend to take into account gaps in development among various parties).[5] Thus, the open-skies policy of India and Pakistan benefited the former much more than the latter, and the agreement between Greece and Turkey by which both had undertaken to clear land mines imposed cumbersome obligations on Greece, whereas Turkey had placed no land mines along its Greek border.

On the strength of this phenomenon, and judging by the sheer volume of agreements in which it occurs, it would seem that parties in general are more concerned with the *appearance* of a balanced regime than with a substantively balanced one. Note also that for the stronger party, devising an actually balanced agreement would mean giving explicitly preferred conditions to the weaker party, thereby exposing the agreement to wide criticism from domestic constituents.

Greater caution with respect to relative costs and benefits is exercised in security or security-affecting regimes (such as water or trade) than in seemingly more benign spheres (such as education or postal services). Accordingly, in the rare instances in which a nonidentical agreement has been devised so as to take into account special differences—geographical, military, or other—it was usually in the spheres of water management, trade, or security. The Indus Waters Treaty required Pakistan to make the necessary adjustments to render the regime more effective and balanced. To ensure an equal share of the burdens and benefits, the treaty scheme provided Pakistan with international—and Indian—monetary compensation for its efforts. The Israel-Lebanon Understanding imposed nonidentical obligations on its signatories, partly due to the very different nature of the fighting forces on each side (a standing army against a guerilla force), and partly because Israel was able to leverage its clear power superiority to win a blanket prohibition on any attack into its territory.

Concerns about relative gains in more sensitive spheres has at times hindered cooperation: Pakistan has refrained from reciprocating India with a most favored nation status, and Turkey has rejected the Greek proposal for the withdrawal of all offensive weapons from the area adjacent to the Greek-Bulgarian-Turkish borders, as it considered such an agreement would benefit Greece substantially more than itself.

The concern about asymmetry in costs and benefits seems to account for the lack of islands of agreement in which the parties trade off across differing spheres (for example, granting water rights in return for movement of people). Despite the attractive theoretical possibility of designing such regimes, islands of agreement in all three case studies have tended to stick to trade-offs within single issues only. One unusual attempt made by the United States in 1997 to mediate an agreement by which Greece would release funds from the EU to Turkey in exchange for Turkey's agreement to third-party mediation on the Imia/Kardak dispute fell through. A likely explanation for this general finding lies in the difficulty of comparing surplus from different spheres, which is essential to ensure that an agreement is well and truly balanced.

At the same time, in some cases, such as the 1972 Simla agreements between India and Pakistan or the 2000–2001 agreements between Greece and Turkey, a cluster of single-issue agreements was concluded in a way that allowed at least for the implicit possibility of cross-issue exchanges.

Practicality

Islands of agreement are more sustainable when their provisions impose practical limitations and obligations. Practicality, in all three case studies, has shown itself to be a function of several variables, including divisibility, clarity of provisions, the level of certainty of the probable results of actions, and the strength of the parties' political will. Thus, in the Israel-Lebanon Understanding, excluding Israeli territory from the sphere of combat proved a practical limitation. It was fairly easy for the Lebanese armed groups to comply without giving too much ground militarily or politically, since, after all, their justification was that they were a resistance to the Israeli occupation of Lebanese ground. In comparison, according absolute immunity to civilians was an impractical, indeed, a utopian provision, which could not be sustained, given the inhabited terrain in which the fighting took place.

Another way to examine the practicality consideration is to borrow the term "depth of cooperation" introduced by George Downs, David Rocke, and Peter Barsoom from the political economy school of international regimes. "Depth of cooperation" is defined by them as "the extent to which it requires states to depart from what they would have done in its absence."[6] They argue that more-ambitious regimes usually entail deeper obligations with higher costs, which must turn cooperation into an even more mixed-motive game than usual, with strong incentives for players to defect. Such regimes, they find, induce high levels of noncompliance, so that efforts to develop sanctions or other means of enforcement must be increased. The conclusion of Downs and his colleagues is that since enforcement is a necessary—even if an insufficient—element in deep-cooperation regimes, states will refrain from designing or entering such regimes if they are unable to employ enforcement mechanisms.[7]

Conceptually, therefore, depth of cooperation is intertwined with both effectiveness and compliance: deeper cooperation is supposedly more effective in generating the desired result but is also more likely to be defected from due to the high costs it entails for the parties. Any cooperative regime, therefore, must strike a sensitive balance among the depth of obligations it requires, anticipated levels of compliance, and the consequential effectiveness of that compliance in promoting the desired outcome. Once this balance is disturbed, the result is an ineffective regime.

Calculating the right balance in terms of islands of agreement must take into account the special context of an enduring rivalry, in which levels of suspicion and distrust, as well as an interest in weakening the rival, increase the perceived costs of cooperation. Governments wishing to create an island thus walk a political tightrope in seeking the support of their constituencies for both the perpetuation of the conflict and the cooperative endeavor with the rival at the same time.

Formality

The vast majority of the islands of agreement discussed in the previous chapters have been formal, assuming the guise of treaties, agreements, memoranda, joint declarations, or even understandings written and publicized by a third party outlining what the rivals have committed to. Some can be characterized as bilateral treaties, in their legal sense, while others might be defined as "soft law" instruments.

This is no doubt a somewhat selection-biased, penny-under-the-lamppost finding, since it is by nature easier to track formal agreements than informal ones. Nevertheless, there is enough evidence to suggest that formal arrangements have on the whole been more sustainable than informal ones. One example is the 1993 Accountability Understanding between Israel and Lebanon, which was deemed by Israeli jurists "not worth the paper it was not written on," and indeed was not.[8] Another is the agreement on disengagement in the Siachen Glacier, which was never detailed in writing and, for this among other reasons, was never complied with thereafter.

More often than not, formality is a necessity, especially where the gravity of the issue or the complexity of the arrangements require clear, written articulation. No less often, it is also a political tool for publicizing the good intentions of both governments and expressing greater commitment to the arrangements involved. These considerations were evident in agreements such as the 1992 India-Pakistan Code of Conduct for Treatment of Diplomatic/Consular Personnel (which only repeated obligations already undertaken by the parties in multilateral contexts), or the February 2000 Protocol of Friendship and Cooperation between the mayors of Istanbul and Athens. A similar perception of formality as reinforcing and stabilizing existing mutual commitments drove the leaders of India and Pakistan to incorporate a previous mutual verbal commitment to refrain from targeting each other's nuclear installations into a formal agreement later on.

In the three cases I examined, formality also seemed to increase the reputation costs of defection, since when an agreement was written and publicized, there could have been little dispute over its actual existence (notwithstanding controversies over interpretation). In general, verbal arrangements are perceived as weaker or at least as less significant than written agreements, hence easier to disown later on.

Reputation concerns meant that little significance, if any, was accorded to the title or general form of the agreement: as long as there was a commitment, whether stipulated in a declaration or a treaty, the assumption was that it was meant to be binding, and violations were judged with severity regardless of the type of agreement breached. In other words, for parties in conflict, there seems to be no soft law, only hard law.[9]

Reputation, of course, matters not only vis-à-vis the rival but, perhaps no less importantly, vis-à-vis third parties. Thus, in expressing apprehension concerning Indian officials' threats to defect from the Indus Waters Treaty, Indian constitutional law scholar, A. G. Noorani, commented,

No words need be wasted on the international repercussions of India's denunciation of the Treaty . . . What message will this send, moreover, to

Nepal with which India concluded the Mahakali Treaty on February 12, 1996, or to Bangladesh with which it concluded the agreement on the waters of the Ganga on December 12, 1996?[10]

Altogether, informal arrangements are more prevalent in the framework of nongovernmental cooperation and people-to-people initiatives, where the goodwill and common interest of the participants make formality less necessary. Naturally, looser contracts are also a function of the generally lower stakes involved in nongovernmental agreements. Informality has been the prevailing mode, too, when agreement was reached between low-ranking officials on a local and limited basis, as was the case in local border agreements between regional commanders along the LoC in Kashmir.

In some cases, such as the India-Pakistan moratorium on nuclear tests, the formality of arrangements evolved with time, as political realities, which had earlier prohibited the conclusion of more formal undertakings, later enabled them. India was the first to declare such moratorium in 1998, and Pakistan followed suit with a moratorium of its own. Later on, the memorandum of understanding which accompanied the Lahore Declaration incorporated and thus upgraded these respective unilateral moratoria into a formal mutual commitment. This is an instance of tacit (or quasi-tacit) bargaining, which yielded at first an informal agreement and later, through corresponding unilateral undertakings, a formal strengthened one.

While we tend to hold formality as a positive indication of the seriousness which parties assign to their commitments, formality can often turn into a double-edged blade: when violated, formal agreements are more easily given over as munitions in the rhetorical war between the adversaries, as was the case with the Indian-Pakistani agreements on military exercises or air violations. At the same time, if either the Greek Cypriot or Turkish Republic of Northern Cyprus (TRNC) governments were to increase troops along the Green Line in Nicosia, the other party would not be able to point to any formal agreement of which this was a violation. It was perhaps to retain this room for maneuver that the mutual voluntary decision in recent years to reduce the number of troops along the line was never accredited a formal signature.

This ambivalence attendant on formality also means that sometimes formality and documentation can become an obstructing factor in negotiations towards islands of agreement. In 1997 the Dutch president of the EU Council of Ministers suggested that Greece and Turkey establish a so-called "committee of wise men," in an effort to promote direct dialogue. Both countries appointed two members each to the group, but reports they later submitted to the EU showed little progress. In part, this was because the Greeks insisted that every exchange be made in writing. Formalizing the process in such a way would have added legal and political weight to any understanding reached but at the same time would have inhibited a more open and candid discussion.[11] In comparison, the success since 1991 of the Neemrana Track II initiative in bringing Indians and Pakistanis to discuss the most contentious issues of their conflict has been attributed, at least in some degree, to the informality of the discussions.

Clarity and Ambiguity

Every legal text exists in the fraught space between clarity and ambiguity—saying more or saying less—and the articulation of an agreement's provisions is no exception; where an island of agreement is concerned, much depends on the possibility of bypassing thorny issues through some rhetorical compromise. Such compromises often allow the conclusion of the agreement in the first place but run the risk of simply deferring disputes from the negotiation to the implementation phase of the regime.

When agreement drafters attempt to bypass profound underlying differences by concluding a sufficiently vague arrangement, which would allow both sides to read it according to their respective conflicting interpretations, the outcome generally proves less sustainable. This is especially true when the obligations imposed by the agreement are deeper and more closely connected to the core disputes. Thus, on the one hand, if the 1988 military arrangements in the Aegean Sea were concluded in the first place, this was owing in part to a sufficient ambiguity of wording which allowed them to avoid allocation of the contested rights in the Aegean. On the other hand, the same ambiguity deferred decision and left room for competing claims on the requirements of the regime, a fact which could not but bring, eventually, to its ineffectual operation. Avoidance of core disputes does not make them go away.

This is, of course, not to say that clear provisions are not violated, only that in a more explicit, elaborate, and determinate agreement there is less excuse for violations.

Some ambiguity, however, may at times be resolved, or at least sustained, through a process of negotiations and renegotiations of an incomplete arrangement. Differences in interpretation of the terms "inhabited areas," "civilians," and "civilian targets" were obstinate bones of contention for the Israeli and Lebanese delegations to the ILMG. India and Pakistan utilized the offices of their two water commissioners to sound out their conflicting positions on the Tulbul water project or the Baglihar Dam as relating to navigation or to water storage, before going on to discuss them through political channels or refer them to third-party arbitration.

The option of renegotiation, however, highlights the need for consultation mechanisms (such as the ILMG or the Indus Waters Commissioners), through which the parties may have an opportunity to fix the prevailing interpretation of a certain treaty article and develop a subcodex of rules for their agreement. In fact, when such mechanisms are installed, a reasonable level of ambiguity can frequently become fruitful ground for positive exchanges and deliberations, reinforcing both mechanism and regime together. This is how Israeli and Lebanese delegates managed to agree, in the course of time and many repeated discussions, that "an inhabited area" meant anything in the radius of one hundred meters from a house—a unique agreement, as although the prohibition on conducting attacks from inhabited areas is stipulated in the international laws of armed conflict, its exact scope is nowhere defined.

Monitoring and Enforcement Mechanisms

In none of the cases I examined did the parties agree in advance to subject themselves to material enforcement mechanisms, such as military or economic sanctions, or to mandatory dispute resolution in general. Whenever rivals attempted to force each other into court—more specifically the International Court of Justice (ICJ)—to reach a judicial settlement of their dispute, as Greece did with Turkey in 1976 in the matter of the Aegean Sea, or Pakistan with India in 1999 over the Atlantique incident—the attempt failed. In both cases the would-be respondent objected to jurisdiction, and the ICJ, which requires for its adjudication the consent of both parties, was left powerless.

On some, rare, occasions the rivals did agree to submit portions of their disputes to third-party arbitration, as occurred in 1965 over the Indian-Pakistani dispute in the Rann of Kutch or, more recently, over the Baglihar Dam. Although Turkey consented, as part of its EU accession process and under considerable EU pressure, to submit the Aegean matter to the ICJ if no negotiated agreement was attained by 2004, the procedure was deferred and its fate still hangs in the balance.

Exceptional in this context was India and Pakistan's agreement, within the Indus Waters Treaty regime, to provide for the submission of disputes arising under the treaty to a decision by a neutral expert or to third-party arbitration. Possibly the two consented to this formula under pressure from third parties who, in the figures of the World Bank and a conglomerate of states, had been heavily involved in the conclusion of the treaty. These third parties insisted on incorporating into the treaty structure a dispute settlement mechanism that would not leave the complexity and delicacy of the treaty framework to the mercy of its two primary parties. The 2005 decision to refer the matter of the Baglihar Dam to a neutral expert was the first time in the treaty's forty-five years of existence that such a course was taken. The outcome is still pending.

In exploring why states do not generally agree to subject themselves to mandatory dispute resolution clauses in international agreements they conclude, Andrew Guzman argues that, "dispute resolution clauses are more likely in low-stakes than high-stakes agreements, in multilateral rather than bilateral agreements, and when tribunals are more accurate."[12] As Guzman has found, out of a hundred international agreements registered with the UN, only twenty contained mandatory dispute resolution clauses. The fact that in the context of enduring rivalries parties are even more reluctant to subject themselves to such clauses is hardly surprising.

While material enforcement mechanisms are generally absent from the parties' bilateral agreements, "social enforcement strategy," which "leverages an international actor's standing and reputation for good faith throughout the international community," can be found in many of them.[13] Reporting, monitoring, and verification measures were included in mechanisms such as the ILMG's procedures of violation reports and press statements, the bilateral Indian-Pakistani Water Commissioners Committee, or the Greek-Turkish Coordination Committee, set up to facilitate and supervise cooperation among the various relevant security and law enforcement agencies. Notably, most of these mechanisms relied for their function on reporting or monitoring by the rival's own means or by those third parties; when a party was obligated to report its own actions or data, compliance was problematic, as in the case of the India-Pakistan Agreement on the Prohibition of Attacks on Nuclear Facilities, in which both parties failed to provide an update on their nuclear facilities.

Institutionalism

In the cases explored, when islands of agreement not only allocated rights and obligations but also included an ongoing mechanism of dialogue, communication, and consultation, the benefits entailed by the regime invariably increased. A positive experience within existing institutions encouraged greater cooperation and allowed the parties to broaden the scope of their exchanges. The fruitful Greek-Turkish collaboration within NATO since late 1999 encouraged further joint effort in exercises, peacekeeping operations, and ongoing NATO-related activities. The ILMG gave the parties a platform for deliberation on issues falling outside the purview of the Understanding and channels of communication by which to diffuse tensions and convey political messages. Meetings between Greek and Turkish trade representatives paved the way for more bilateral initiatives in the spheres of business and finance. These meetings also made it possible to harness and incorporate domestic actors (private investors and businesspeople) into the governmental cooperative endeavor. Consequently, Greek-Turkish trade volume has doubled between 2000 and 2005, and Greek and Turkish businesses are increasingly engaged in joint-venture investments in third countries.

At least in some instances, it was evident that the monitoring institution had gained a status of its own, exceeding the original framework within which it was established—so much so, that even when the regime itself was perceived to have failed to fulfill its original goal, the parties were still hesitant to dissolve the institutional mechanism set to implement it. Thus, the ILMG was viewed by many as an important asset quite independent of the Understanding it was established to monitor; and the channels of communication created through the hotlines between India and Pakistan were preserved despite their disappointing performance during the 1990 crisis in Kashmir or the Kargil War, and there have even been many suggestions to upgrade and multiply them.

A word of caution, however, is warranted here. It is normally taken for granted that interpersonal ties between communities are beneficial, since they bring people together, enhance dialogue and communication, help to change negative perceptions and stigmas, and increase the general interdependence between the rival societies. As one commentator noted regarding the India-Pakistan conflict, "people who have never visited each other's country perceive situations and develop preconceived notions about the other as portrayed by the elite or media. In this context, to dispel myths about each other, there should be mechanisms to facilitate visits of people across the border."[14]

Yet communication is not a guarantee for reconciliation; in fact, at times it can do quite the opposite. As much as direct contacts can bring people together, they can also reinforce suspicion, breed disappointment, and widen psychological and cultural divides. Greek Cypriots who crossed the Green Line to Northern Cyprus for the first time discovered that a reunification of the island would mean incorporating an ailing economy into their own. Later, a majority of Greek Cypriots voted no on the UN peace plan. When the hotlines between Indian and Pakistani directors of general military operations were exploited to convey disinformation, they deteriorated relationships more than if the hotlines had not been there in the first place. Similarly, false statements made in the early stages of the Monitoring Group's operation only contributed to the already high levels of mutual distrust. Both mechanisms ultimately survived these abuses; but their negative experiences remain a good reminder that direct communications are not risk free.

When monitoring institutions are established by third parties without the active, ongoing support of the parties themselves, their status vis-à-vis the parties and their ability to influence them are significantly hampered. India has consistently ignored the UNMOGIP operations along the LoC, refusing even to file complaints with the force. Similarly, Turkey and the TRNC view UNFICYP with lingering suspicion, as they feel that in deploying it, the UN had disregarded the unconstitutional manner in which the Greek-Cypriot government had been installed. Cooperation between Israel and UNIFIL, prior to the Israeli withdrawal from Lebanon, was even less to be expected, given that UNIFIL's mandate was to ensure the Israeli withdrawal at a time when Israel had no such intention.

Representation and Accountability

Islands of agreement must be concluded between parties that are capable and willing to represent and account for forces or elements whose actions the agreement addresses. This means they must also take into account the interests or actions of third parties, who, despite not being official parties to the agreement, may nevertheless affect its operation and sustainability.

The clearest example of the importance of representation and accountability is found in the Israeli-Lebanese dilemma. By ordering Israel to account for the South Lebanese Army operations and Lebanon to account for Hezbollah, Amal, and all the other Lebanese armed groups, the Understanding aimed to balance between the need to account for all relevant nonstate actors and the equally strong interest not to allow these actors to hijack the intergovernmental discussions. The interests of Syria, whose hold on the Lebanese government could not be ignored, were also wisely incorporated into the framework of the ILMG, while carefully taking into consideration the necessary political limitations of its participation.

Pakistan's reluctance to formally account for the operations of Muslim insurgents in Kashmir has made it well-nigh impossible to conclude and sustain islands of agreement to regulate the security sphere in general and to combat terrorism specifically. Much the same situation occurred when India refused, in some periods, to include representatives of the All Party Hurriyat Conference (APHC) in its political dealings over Kashmir; although at the present moment some APHC involvement in the process is emerging, it is questionable to what extent the organization is accountable for—or representative of—all the insurgent groups operating in Kashmir.

By the same token, although there is little challenging by official mediators (such as the UN) of the legitimacy of the leadership on both parts of the island of Cyprus as representing their constituencies in any future agreement, it is also clear that any agreement between the Turkish and Greek Cypriots would depend upon its endorsement by the mother countries (even if such endorsement would not in itself be sufficient to force the island parties into an accord).

Intergovernmental, Subgovernmental, and Nongovernmental Cooperation
Both the Indo-Pak and Greco-Turk rivalries exhibit the potential of forming islands of agreement in multinational settings, as well as on various strata of bilateral relationships between governments, bureaucracies, NGOs or private actors.

Cooperation between Greece and Turkey in the framework of regional organizations has taken place within NATO, the EU's Southeast European Brigade (SEEBRIG), the Black Sea Economic Cooperation (BSEC), the Southeast European Cooperation Process (SEECP), and the Southeast European Cooperation Initiative (SECI). India and Pakistan have come together under the auspices of South Asia Association for Regional Cooperation (SAARC) and the South Asia Cooperative Environment Programme (SACEP).

For the most part, multinational regional organizations were unable to accommodate multilateral agreements whenever the latter touched on contentious issues between the rivals. For example, SAARC's convention on combating terrorism could have little effect on Indian-Pakistani relations, which ordinarily rose and fell to the ebb and flow of Kashmiri insurgency. NATO standard operating procedures on military exercises likewise ran aground on the disputed rocks of the Aegean. SAARC's latest initiatives, including the agreement on double taxation and, even more notably, the South Asia Free Trade Area (SAFTA), are ambitious attempts to shift gears and regulate relations on a regional basis even when the attempt to do so bilaterally has failed.

Otherwise, the function of regional frameworks has been limited to hosting high-level meetings or providing a public setting for goodwill gestures, as when Pakistani President Musharraf's crossed over the SAARC summit stage to shake the hand of Indian Prime Minister Vajpayee.

On the subgovernmental level, Greek and Turkish municipalities have struck independent protocols on cooperation, as did the municipalities of Nicosia on both sides of the Green Line, while the Indian Border Security Forces and Pakistan Rangers concluded their own local border understandings. In both cases, islands of agreement launched ongoing bilateral ties between respective ministries and agencies, ranging from commerce, environment, and agriculture to narcotics control.

Perhaps an unsurprising finding is that the militaries in all three cases have tended to support, if not drive, harder-line policies. The Greek Ministry of Defense had recommended to the Greek foreign minister, Papandreou, to decline a Turkish offer for enhanced security cooperation. The Turkish military was reported to have seconded Denktash's objections to a peace deal with his Greek Cypriot counterparts (first Clerides, then Papadopoulos). In Pakistan, the military chiefs, headed by General Musharraf, are believed to have contrived the Kargil War. And in Israel it was the military that consistently argued against the unilateral withdrawal from Lebanon, even when Prime Minister Barak had already announced the date by which withdrawal would take place. Paradoxically, during his prior career, as the chief of the general staff of the Israeli Defense Forces (IDF), Barak himself forcefully advocated the wisdom of maintaining the Security Zone.

There are, however, a few examples to the contrary, such as the Indian naval commanders who kept pressing towards rapprochement, continually suggesting joint exercises and other forms of cooperation with their Pakistani counterparts, but with little backing from the politicians.[15]

On the nongovernmental level, trade associations and research centers in Greece and Turkey have established their own bilateral ties; peace movements in India and Pakistan have initiated conferences and activities, as Indian and Pakistani musicians produced joint albums and performed together in concerts; and human rights activists in both dyads have met to pursue their agendas collectively. Between Greece and Turkey these nongovernmental and private contacts were scarce before the governmental process of rapprochement but grew apace when it began. In both rivalries, private contacts were conducted under the auspices of the governments (as, for example, with Greek-Turkish cooperation in preparing for the 2004 Olympic Games), encouraged by the governments (as in the sphere of bilateral and regional trade), or else conducted with the governments' acquiescence. Thus, the Greek Ministry of Development and the Scientific and Technical Research Council of Turkey (TÜBITAK), in the framework of their bilateral science and technology cooperation program, now fund Greek-Turkish research initiatives in research and technology.

In the Middle East dispute, cross-border exchange remains minimal. Despite a few occasional visits by Arab members of Knesset to Syria and Lebanon and movement of Druze villagers between the Golan Heights and Syria, there are no reciprocal ongoing ties between the Israeli community and the Lebanese or Syrian populations.[16] In fact, legislation on both sides prohibits such ties. And while there is some ongoing concomitant participation of the three countries in regional organizations (such as the EU–Mediterranean Pact or the United Nations Environment Programme's Mediterranean Action Plan), there is no actual bilateral cooperation between them within these frameworks. This is mainly due to the reluctance of the Lebanese and Syrian governments to officially recognize the State of Israel—a recognition they would be willing to grant only under a future comprehensive peace treaty. Lack of official recognition on the governmental level precludes the possibilities of cooperation in multilateral and nongovernmental settings. This has also been largely the case in nongovernmental intervention in Cyprus.

The Role of Third Parties

The manifold ways in which third parties are involved in the conclusion and sustainment of islands of agreements is amply manifested in all three case studies.

At times, third-party mediation efforts proved crucial to the conclusion of an island of agreement: Britain mediated the cease-fire following the 1965 war between India and Pakistan; the Soviet Union made strenuous mediation efforts to secure the 1966 Tashkent Declaration; the United States brokered the 1974 cease-fire in Cyprus and, with the help of France, proposed and mediated the 1996 Understanding between Israel and Lebanon. The NATO secretary general secured the reaffirmation in 1998 by Greece and Turkey of their security commitments made ten years earlier.

Third parties have also been supportive of Track II and people-to-people initiatives, such as the American sponsorship of the India-Pakistan Neemrana process or international NGOs' projects relating to business and economic ties in Cyprus.

Especially effective third-party involvement was exhibited by the World Bank, which, through the political commitment of its leaders and the power of its purse, has played an indispensable role in the negotiation of the 1960 Indus Waters Treaty. Without its assurances, guarantees, and side payments, as well as its ongoing activity as the Treaty's guarantor, it is doubtful whether such a delicate yet intense framework of interdependence could have been contrived, let alone maintained. The Bank's efforts were complemented by side payments to Pakistan from Australia, Britain, Canada, Germany, New Zealand, the United States—and India itself—with the purpose of developing better allocation of water and correcting any possible imbalance of costs and benefits that might have been created under the Treaty.

When successful, the involvement of third parties in the establishment and operation of islands of agreement confirms itself an important stabilizing and sustainment factor, adding to the regime's "compliance-pull"; even such a hawkish figure as Israeli Minister of Defense Moshe Arens, who had personally objected to the Understanding regime, nonetheless later acknowledged the difficulty Israel would have in walking out on it.[17] Despite the failed attempts to mediate an agreement on the Wazzani River, international involvement in the dispute was instrumental in preventing an outbreak of violence over this issue. In Pakistan, diplomats dismissed Indian officials' threats to retreat from the Indus Waters Treaty, saying "it is not easy for a country to unilaterally withdraw from an international treaty for which the World Bank stands as a guarantor."[18] The potential role of third parties as a safeguard was also acknowledged by the Pakistani prime minister, who, to alleviate Indian security concerns, proposed to bring in international companies to participate in a planned Iranian project to lay down a gas pipeline from Iran, through Pakistan, to India.

But there are also plenty of examples of less successful third-party interventions. The UN has brokered almost all the Cyprus peace talks, including those aimed at partial settlements, without success; the failure of the Annan plan to win a majority vote among Greek Cypriots was a particularly scathing defeat; India has consistently refused to allow the UN to mediate in the Kashmir dispute; international efforts to stop the Kargil War in its earlier phases yielded no result; the United States failed in its own attempt to secure an agreement on Cyprus, as well as on the Imia/Kardak feud; NATO's repeated efforts to mediate in the Aegean conflict were shattered; and ventures by the UN, the United States, and the EU to obtain an agreement on the Wazzani waters all met a dead end. Moreover, UN peacekeeping forces in all three theaters of war, and especially in Kashmir and south Lebanon, have shown a poor record of effectiveness.

The question why and under what conditions some third-party efforts prove successful, while others fail, warrants a separate analysis, which exceeds the scope of this book. It appears that although the causes of successful intervention may be isolated with hindsight (and even then run the risk of seeming tautological—since nothing succeeds like success), the cases explored here show that preconditions for successful third-party intervention are hard to generalize in advance.

The Role of International Law

The attempt by the international community to engineer global rules that would regulate relationships among countries is currently on the increase and penetrates almost every sphere of state life. Indeed, modern international law addresses, simultaneously, everything from modes and means of warfare to environmental protection and free trade. Interstate disputes are in many ways a moment of truth for international law—the time when it is most required, its very raison d'être. But at the same time it is the moment when states' primal instinct to resist international law as curbing their sovereignty is most fiercely awakened.

The experience of the conflicts studied here has been that, by and large, general international law has had little impact on the settlement of core bilateral disputes. The protagonists in the disputes over Kashmir or Cyprus have all argued and reargued the principles of state sovereignty, territorial integrity, the right to self-determination, human rights, and the prohibition on the use of force in support of their directly conflicting stances. Israel and Lebanon have both claimed their right to self-defense, as well as the prohibition on aggression by the other side, to legitimize their ongoing belligerence. And there can be little doubt that the lack of effective adjudication mechanisms has prevented observers in all three cases from testing the relative force of these competing legal claims. But even when such enforcement mechanisms did operate, as in the case of the European Court of Human Rights decision in *Cyprus v. Turkey* (which ruled that Turkey was responsible for various breaches of the European Convention on Human Rights in the TRNC), the practical—as well as normative—effects of this mechanism of intervention are questionable.

But while largely ineffective vis-à-vis core disputes, international law has been instrumental in various ways in the establishment of islands of agreement. A mixture of influences informs the exchange between islands and general international law, including incorporation and departure, choice and creation, trailing and development.

At times, islands of agreements fully correspond to international legal rules, as in the 1992 India-Pakistan Declaration on the Complete Prohibition of Chemical Weapons, the two countries' Code of Conduct for Treatment of Diplomatic/Consular personnel, or the 2001 joint statement by Papandreou and Cem on their commitment to the anti–land mines Ottawa convention. The fact that there was an internationally recognized rule already in place presumably made the island of agreement, which incorporated this rule, easier to conclude. In the case of the Ottawa convention, it was strong domestic pressure in Greece that drove the reluctant Greek government to accede to the convention and begin demining operations along the Greek borders. The existence of a multilateral convention, widely accepted, had no doubt helped to mobilize Greek civil society and aided it in promoting its cause.

The reaffirmation of internationally recognized rules and standards in a bilateral undertaking does not alter the legal status of the rule or standard. Rather, it is intended to bolster the mutual relationship by acknowledging, as it were more intimately, what is already an accepted norm.

It is also possible that the international rule, with its body of accepted practical application and interpretation, then operates to stabilize and reinforce the island of agreement. This is not to say, of course, that an agreement would not be violated if it coincided with an already accepted international rule. For example, the 1992 Code of Conduct in Diplomatic and Consular Affairs was occasionally violated by both India and Pakistan. However, when alleging violations, commentators emphasized that the violating actions ran counter both to the 1992 code and the 1961 and 1963 International Conventions on Diplomatic and Consular Relations, to reiterate the gravity of the protested actions. But in the case of the 1992 Indo-Paki declaration on chemical weapons, India admitted to having chemical weapon stockpiles only when the chemical weapons convention came into force in 1992. Thus, India in effect complied with the multilateral convention, rather than with the bilateral island of agreement.

Nevertheless, while the designers of global legal mechanisms hope to produce arrangements that would ultimately govern any interstate relationship, incorporating international law into islands of agreement is not always possible or, indeed, desired, for a variety of reasons. At times, the existing legal arrangements do not address the specific situation at hand. Thus, the 1961 agreement between India and Pakistan on the transference of bank accounts was conceived to meet a specific need, which arose out of the 1947 partition at a time when there was no relevant treaty to rely on. The parties then had to create their own international law.

At other times, the existing legal arrangements tend to be heterogeneous, offering several competing rules and principles, and forcing the designers of the agreement to choose one over the others. Thus, at the time of the conclusion of the 1960 Indus Waters Treaty, there were four different customary rules on the sharing of transboundary watercourses—absolute territorial sovereignty, absolute territorial integrity (riparian rights), equitable utilization, and community of interest (joint management)—a fact which forced the parties to choose and follow one, namely the last.[19] It was some years before the international community came to address the issue of water allocation through international conferences and treaties, with the intention to devise generally applicable international rules,[20] so far with little success.

In yet other instances, the existing legal arrangements did purport to cover the specific situation but were too vague or too broad, leaving room for competing claims. One such case is the controversy between Greece and Turkey over the division of the Aegean continental shelf, in which both countries rely on different provisions of the international law of the sea to sustain their contradictory stances. While the 1976 Berne Declaration ordered the parties to "study state practice and international rules on this subject with a view to educing certain principles and practical criteria which could be of use in the delimitation of the Continental shelf between the two countries," this instruction was of little practical use.[21] The problem of conflicting interpretation was, of course, not unique to multilateral arrangements. Neither the 1960 Cyprus Treaty of Guarantee nor the 1960 Indus Waters Treaty, both specific to their signatories and circumstances, was able to provide a satisfactory answer to controversies over their applications.

There may also be cases, in which the parties choose to depart from the formula designed by an international treaty and tailor an ad hoc arrangement that in their opinion better suits their own specific situation. One such example may be found in the Israel-Lebanon Understanding's intention to accord absolute protection to civilians during belligerence, in departure from the customary laws of war, which acknowledge the principles of military necessity and proportionality, and the collateral effects of "lawful" warfare on civilians. This departure was welcomed, at the time, by the international community as a "race to the top"—an accordance of greater protection to civilians than the minimal standard stipulated by the laws of war. And it is quite certain neither the United States nor France would have sponsored an agreement purporting to grant any less protection to noncombatants than that offered by international norms. It is also unlikely such an agreement would have been deemed lawful under international law. Nevertheless, this may not always be the case; if and when an agreement is reached in Cyprus, it is highly probable that its designers too would have to depart from the strict application of the European Convention on Human Rights, as interpreted by the European Court of Human Rights (ECHR), with regard, for instance, to the rights of Greek Cypriots to property in northern Cyprus.

The 1997 UN Convention on International Watercourses, in an uncommon gesture of acknowledgment of the difficulties inherent in a one-size-fits-all regime, recognized that its provisions could not create effective and appropriate arrangements for all international watercourses and ordered riparians to "consult with a view to negotiating in good faith for the purpose of concluding a watercourse agreement or agreements," if and when either of them "considers that adjustment and application of the provisions of the present Convention is required because of the characteristics and uses of a particular international watercourse."[22] This provision is essentially an invitation to riparians to negotiate ad hoc agreements on water sharing instead of strictly adhering to universal allocation rules. Interestingly, even this general invitation has been rejected by the majority of the international community, which prefers bilateral water commitments to the general, multilateral undertaking under the Watercourses Convention. To date, the convention failed to attract a sufficient number of ratifications necessary for it to enter into force.

In another case of deliberate departure from a multilateral rule— GATT Article XXIV(11)—the parties to the treaty, bearing in mind the unique circumstances of the two countries, granted India and Pakistan an exemption from the treaty provisions in their dealings with one another.

All these cases exemplify the top-down influence of international law over the development of islands of agreement. No less interesting, however, is the countermovement by which islands of agreement themselves come, in time, to form a source of international law. These specifically tailored agreements serve as important precedents and proof of state practice, which, if motivated by a sense of legal obligation *(opinio juris)*, may in time crystallize into customary international law and be implemented in similar future cases.

Some acknowledgement of this complementary exchange between ad hoc agreements and international law may be found in the words of two members of the World Bank's legal department, in their discussion of the desired relationship between international legal rules governing the allocation of international watercourses and bilateral or multilateral specific arrangements of such allocations:

> because water is an inter-disciplinary resource, international legal norms cannot by themselves provide resolution to disputes over international watercourses. Equally important is the fact that there can be no resolution of water disputes without international legal norms on international watercourses. As a matter of historical fact, the conclusion of bilateral and multilateral agreements has always been instrumental in reducing conflict among different riparians. Arrangements providing for cooperative management schemes have shown their virtue for enhancing cooperation as well as for managing conflict, especially when all the riparians of an international watercourse are parties to such arrangements.[23]

And although the Indus Waters Treaty itself was careful to provide that "nothing in this Treaty shall be construed by the Parties as in any way establishing any general principle of law or any precedent," this provision was apparently intended more to allay the concerns of the parties themselves and less for the appeasement of third-party observers.[24] The fact remains that bilateral agreements can transcend the circumstances of their genesis to establish general principles of law. As scholars note, the principles governing the modern law of international watercourses have developed from a series of international and domestic treaties, rulings, and interpretations, later codified in the governing multilateral treaties.[25]

Conversely, specifically devised provisions might come, in time, to be regarded as a travesty. As the moral and ethical norms of the international community change, older rules and norms are discarded. The international community in 1923 gave its blessing to the mandatory population exchange between Greece and Turkey under the Treaty of Lausanne. There is little doubt that today's international community would have had more qualms about concluding such a treaty.

It is impossible to state in advance what the desired relationship between international law and islands of agreement should be in every particular case. The proper development of international law depends on a proper tension being maintained between regimentation and flexibility. Indeed, international law recognizes the equal legal force of multilateral and bilateral treaties. When we consider the current trend for increased universal regimentation of international relations in the form of ever-broadening legalization, multilateralism, and stronger dispute-resolution and enforcement mechanisms, against the fluidity of circumstances and conditions to which international law applies, we must question whether the resolution of complex disputes can safely rely on universally articulated principles. In a world in which scientific and medical knowledge, environmental and political conditions, and technological capabilities change by the hour, we need to weigh more carefully whether, especially for parties in conflict, more universal regimentation is better than creative license for bilateral arrangements.

The Normative Dilemma

There is no moral or logical edict telling us every enmity is total: human instinct may be to mythicize and dramatize enmity, so that over the generations it begins to appear to us to correspond with such natural oppositions as fire and water or magnetic poles. But as shown by the three histories above, the definition of someone as an enemy is not necessarily a given natural phenomenon. Nor is it always clear just when a party turns from a rival or a nonrival into an "enemy," although it is clear that the turning point does not necessarily involve a declaration of war. Most often, the decision to regard someone as an enemy rests with politicians.

But even when there is a clear-cut case for enmity, this does not inevitably mean the end of all ties and relationships. As at least two of my case studies make abundantly clear, even in conflict there is life beyond conflict. The potential for broad multiple ties is present in most rivalries that extend over time. It is up to governments and populations to conceptualize this potential and to activate it.

Once they choose to do so, however, they must also be alive to the risks involved. The aim of my narrative has been to articulate the rich, often untapped potential of interstate relationships, both within and outside conflict, by taking a wide-zoom view of each rivalry as a complex and detailed interaction. But as I have also been careful to show, for all their undoubted advantages, islands of agreement may be a two-pronged tool, harboring danger as well as promise, in particular, in the danger of anchoring—by normalizing—perceptions of the conflict and its durability. Other hazards include the "pressed balloon effect," which means that the mitigation of conflict in one sphere may exacerbate it in another; the apprehension of present islands as a litmus test for the rival's trustworthiness in future, a test which is often disappointing; and the possible postponement of the comprehensive resolution of the core disputes as a result of the earlier removal of bargaining chips from the negotiation table.

Alongside evident benefits, the case studies explored here have also exhibited at least some of these disadvantageous outcomes. In none of the rivalries treated here have islands germinated a fundamental change of position on the core disputes. Violations of agreement by parties, such as the violation of the declaration on chemical weapons by India, have been viewed as the ultimate proof of the violating party's untrustworthiness. The Israeli-Lebanese Understanding may well have caused a pressed balloon effect, in the guise of increased attacks that were allowed under the regime. Worse still, the Israeli-Lebanese regime may have worked to defer a fundamental change in the status quo, by affixing the parties' perceptions of the conflict and the necessary terms for its transformation. When the hoped for shift in attitude did occur with the Israeli withdrawal from Lebanon four years after the conclusion of the Understanding, the change it brought about was far more dramatic than anything the Understanding could have generated, bringing to a significant reduction in the level and frequency of hostilities for several years and, perhaps more meaningfully still, opening the door for international pressure on Syria to also withdraw from Lebanon, as it finally did in 2005. Agreement on Cyprus and the Aegean has been elusive for many years. With most of the bargaining chips now off the table, it is doubtful there remain sufficient incentives to promote a resolution of these disputes in the near future.

As all three rivalries continue, to various degrees, we are faced with the challenge of assessing what islands of agreement have meant in each.

The islands between India and Pakistan do not seem as yet to have wielded any dramatic change over the core conflict. Despite the islands' standing of sixty years, a comprehensive peace process is still very much out of sight. In my account in Chapter 2, I have raised the troubling possibilities that, however indispensable, the islands of agreement existing between the two nations have also made the situation between them more bearable; that access to fresh water, some trade and cross-border services all make resolution less urgent; and that in providing these advantages, islands allow reluctant leaders to convince their constituencies of the inevitability of enmity and of the worthwhile effort of pursuing it.

The Israeli-Lebanese Understanding has contributed to the protection of civilians but by doing so, possibly decreased the political pressure on the relevant parties to mitigate the conflict any further; and while fewer civilians were killed, combatants were increasingly affected. As earlier noted, the material change, in the guise of the Israeli withdrawal—whether or not wise in itself—may have been deferred. Perhaps most important, the interests then at play in prolonging the conflict still perpetuate it today, even after the withdrawal.

In contrast, Greece and Turkey's experience with islands of agreement is clearly a positive one. The political process of rapprochement has advanced step by step with the conclusion of each island until a more peaceful, well-rounded relationship was formed, even as the tensions over Cyprus and the Aegean Sea persisted. Turkey's accession to the EU is on course, even if the course is to be a long one, and notably, it is advancing with Greek assistance. Even the calamitous failure of the

UN peace plan for Cyprus in 2004 has not rocked the foundations of the new-found amity between the motherlands.

One might argue that there is no necessary causal connection between islands and the ensuing improvement of the relationship in the Greek-Turkish case but that, on the contrary, the leaders' initial desire to attain peace is what led them to turn to the islands method in the first place. By the logic of this argument, the islands are merely symptoms rather than primary causes. In fact, they are not islands of agreement but an incremental peace process.

In truth, however, the process of island making is always intended to be cyclical, whatever its cause or mode of generation: even though islands are often created without a broader peace effort in mind, the hope is that their continued operation, the fact that they are being observed and kept to, and their magnetic pull towards cooperation in spheres around and outside themselves would render them catalysts, whose influence exceeds their original design. One might equally imagine how a negative experience with islands of agreement may obstruct the progress of reconciliation.

As to the relation between islands of agreement and broader peace efforts, it is noteworthy that the concluders of islands in all three case studies seem almost embarrassed by the narrowness of their ambition, so that with the conclusion of every agreement—usually in the preamble—they reaffirm their commitment to peace as well as to the agreement's more immediate goal. In both the India-Pakistan and Greece-Turkey cases, the formula often bears some reference to broader peace efforts, mostly noting that the agreement at hand was designed to improve the overall relationship and contribute to a more peaceful atmosphere. In the case of Israel and Lebanon, while the Understanding declared explicitly that it was not a peace agreement—a unique declaration, not to be found in any of the other islands of agreement examined here—its possible contribution to broader peace efforts was still noted in the document.

Naturally, if and when a comprehensive agreement is found to all outstanding disputes in any of these rivalries, the retrospective analysis of the role and impact of islands on the process would require revision. For one thing, the negotiation process of these ultimate agreements might offer new insights into the niggling question of whether, by removing bargaining chips from the process, they have rendered the conclusion of a more comprehensive agreement more difficult—for instance, by limiting the scope of the discussions to the most disputed issues, as other spheres were already regulated under existing islands. This speculation is especially pertinent to the Aegean and Cyprus disputes.

To return to the normative question of whether islands of agreement are a recommended tool, a number of methodological qualifications moat off our vision: Given what we know and what we may only come to know in time, or indeed never, any prediction necessitates numerous counterfactual exercises. In addition, benefits in the form of containment or material gains from cooperation are much more immediately apparent than possible long-term harm. The dim prospect that limited agreement processes may in fact delay a grander peace is difficult to weigh against the lure of direct tangible rewards, such as spared lives and saved resources.

Perhaps more fundamentally still, islands of agreement challenge us to decide whether we believe in changes that develop through incremental steps or only in those that are brought about by revolution. The latter approach represents an ethical and moral skepticism towards management, in its definition as any amelioration effort that does not strive to alter the fundamental rivalry but only perpetuates the existing status quo, fastens power relations and preexisting notions and thus inhibits any material change.

Writing about the work of the International Committee of the Red Cross to help victims of war, Michael Ignatieff has given us some words of caution: "But lurking in the back of every delegate's mind is the possibility that in patching up the wounded, housing the homeless, and comforting the widows and orphans, they are simply prolonging the conflict, giving a society the capacity to keep on destroying itself."[26] And in a reference to ethnic conflict, he futher suggests that "sometimes, hard as it is, the best thing to do is to do nothing: To let a victor emerge and then to assist him to establish and sustain the monopoly on violence upon which order depends."[27] The crucial dilemma, in other words, is this: is it preferable to make the conflict more bearable and thus run the risk of outstretching it for a longer period, or is it better to let it run its natural course—which would presumably be shorter, if bloodier?

In his article "Stopping Wars and Making Peace," Michael Reisman argues that pauses in the conflict (including those imposed by third parties) may actually extend or exacerbate it, "as they allow the party that is beleaguered to regroup, rearm, and resupply, while snatching from the party that is prevailing the consummation of the victory." It then follows, argues Reisman, that "because victory ends conflict, pauses may actually extend or exacerbate the conflict."[28] Edward Luttwak has sounded similar arguments.[29]

When we consider protracting a conflict, even for the purpose of mitigating it, we must also remember that time is not a neutral factor in ongoing disputes. Physical changes on the ground, political or military occurrences, local, regional or international developments—all affect the rivals' situation. When it works to congeal the status quo over time, therefore, management may well affect long-term options, far beyond its proclaimed ambition. Thus, demographic changes on the ground that occur in the shadow of the status quo may substantially influence the outcome of any potential territorial settlements that would be essential for the resolution of the conflict.

Conversely, we are faced with the grim prospect that the revolution—the breakthrough to resolution—might come too late; that until it comes, the conflict, grinding on, would erode all hope of change, inflicting ever-increasing damage, destruction, and death; that refraining from management efforts because of the potential risks involved is an immoral tradeoff—to be made by those who are willing to tolerate an intolerable present for the benefit of an uncertain positive future. The obvious argument here is that the victim cannot wait to be less victimized while he or she gambles on an abstract future victory.

While I myself lean towards the latter opinion, there is clearly no way of settling this debate by empirical means—that is, by proving through some scientific calculation what would cause less damage or bring most good in the long run. One is invariably left to guess what history would have looked like had a different path been taken.

However, I would like to suggest that this entire polemic may be rooted in the limited view of management I brought under observation in Chapter 1, as an activity predominantly related to the military aspects of the conflict. Considered more broadly, so as to include relationship spheres outside military engagement, management takes on a somewhat different aspiration, which we can articulate in the form of an eternal question: Is it right, in a situation of an ongoing conflict, to try to develop an out-of-conflict relationship, or not? So that when we ask if it is right that the International Committee of the Red Cross should care for orphans or that there should be a cease-fire, we may also ask whether it is right that there should be trade, tourism, environmental cooperation, etc. Under the assumption that we can have no accurate projection for the consequences of management for the conflict in the long run, I believe there is a strong case for management to be made.

While there is no saying for certain that islands bring us closer to peace, there is enough evidence to suggest that in their full form of relationship management (as found, for example, in the cases of Greece and Turkey or India and Pakistan) they do lessen the likelihood of wholesale cataclysm. And, by creating more spheres of interaction between the parties, they also generate greater interdependence and therefore more stakeholders in the momentum towards peace. The continuation of stability promises there will be ever more people who rely on free movement, free trade, and so on. Since escalation normally closes off spheres and damages whatever remains, the expectation is that a growing number of actors on both sides would oppose it when islands are strongly present. All these benefits are absent from the Israeli-Lebanese conflict, where the one institutionalized island of agreement regulated the conflict itself, not touching on other areas of potential interstate relationships.

Would these stakeholders be more numerous, or would their opposition to escalation or, indeed, to the continuation of the conflict as it stands be any greater if there were no islands of agreement? Would business people, for example, make stronger advocates for reconciliation if there were no opportunities of trading with the enemy whatsoever than if trade were allowed alongside the conflict? Probably not. If anything, having been given the taste of the benefits of cooperation, stakeholders, one would imagine, would only crave more. And while their interests may be insufficient to overcome the profound, underlying interests that perpetuate the conflict, these interests may nevertheless suffice at the very least to prevent things from getting out of hand.

Finally, thinking about conflict management in its broader sense of relationship management rather than in the narrow sense of conflict regulation makes it apparent that management is not necessarily a tool for resolution or a freezer for a status quo or yet a stalling tactic until resolution dawns. Instead, it is there to chaperon the mutual relationship throughout its various stages and gradations and is never ousted, even by a resolution.

This means that resolution and management are anything but mutually exclusive. The two can exist side by side, ideally with close monitoring of their reciprocal effects on each other. In other words, management does not replace the need for resolution; first, since as long as there are disputes that perpetuate the instability of the system, management will never suffice to prevent violent outbursts. But more important, because every ongoing relationship requires management.

The double burden of guilt and false modesty is thus lifted from the shoulders of those who engage in managerial efforts. That we acquiesce to the establishment of islands of agreement does not necessarily mean that we have made our peace with conflict—only that we have made sure that no opportunity for lessening pain and suffering on the one hand and for enhancing positive interaction on the other has been neglected.

We use islands of agreement as instinctive tools in our everyday relationships with parents, children, spouses, and colleagues. So ingrained have they become in our behavior that we use them at times without knowing that we are doing so. But when it comes to the international arena, we have somehow let this instinctual knowledge slide. When presented by an international conflict of any form, we tend to be drawn to it and forget everything else the parties may ever have had in common. Of course this is because international conflict ups the stakes for all concerned. But it is nonetheless regrettable.

My proposition—that in order to attain a rounded view of conflict, we need to see it as part of a rich and continuing relationship—is not a hierarchic one. It does not mean the relinquishment of prevention or resolution efforts, nor is it intended as a realist countermeasure to idealist aspirations to revive Isaiah's vision. It is simply a claim about missed opportunities.

Epilogue

As this book was ready to go to press, fighting erupted between Israel and the Hezbollah Lebanese armed group on the largest scale since the end of the 1982 Lebanon War. It began on July 12, 2006 with the firing of Katysuha rockets and mortar rounds into Israel, and the kidnapping of two Israeli soldiers and the killing of three others on the Israeli side of the border. Hezbollah named the attack "Operation Truthful Promise" after its leader Hassan Nasrallah's public pledges to capture Israeli soldiers and exchange them for several convicted Lebanese prisoners in Israel.

Israeli Prime Minister Ehud Olmert termed the attack an "act of war," and held the government of Lebanon responsible, among other things for its failure to fully implement UN Security Council Resolution 1559 of 2004, which called for the complete disarming and disbanding of Hezbollah. Despite Lebanese Prime Minister Fouad Siniora's denial of any foreknowledge of Hezbollah's attack and his denunciation of it, Olmert vowed a "very painful and far-reaching response."[1]

Israel indeed retaliated with a widescale operation, code-named "Change of Direction," which included massive air-strikes on Hezbollah and Lebanese infrastructure, and the placing of an air and naval blockade on Lebanon. For Israel, this was a second front, in addition to the reignited Palestinian one in the Gaza Strip. For the following month, Hezbollah, reinforced by munitions and weapons shipments from Iran and Syria, launched thousands of rockets deeper into Israel than ever before. For the first time since its withdrawal in the summer of 2000, Israel invaded south Lebanon with 30,000 ground troops. IDF soldiers and Hezbollah forces engaged in fierce guerilla warfare in the midst of populated villages in southern Lebanon. When a UN-brokered cease-fire came into effect on August 14, 2006, over 1,400 Lebanese and 163 Israelis were already dead; infrastructure on both sides of the border was decimated; the Lebanese coastline was covered with an oil spill from a power station struck by Israel and Israeli forests were lost in fires sparked by Hezbollah rocket-fire; hundreds of thousands of Lebanese and Israelis were displaced from their homes. The financial damage to Israel has been estimated at US$1.6–US$3 billion, and for Lebanon—five times as much. Both sides have been accused by the UN and international human rights organizations for violating the laws of war.

The cease-fire stipulated by UN Security Council Resolution 1701, approved by the governments of both Israel and Lebanon, also called for the Israeli withdrawal from Lebanon, the disarming of Hezbollah, and the deployment of the Lebanese armed forces—as well as of an enlarged and reinforced UNIFIL force—in southern Lebanon. Israel completed its withdrawal on October 1, 2006 (leaving a small force in the area of Ghajar, a village split in two by the border). For the first time since before 1970, thousands of Lebanese soldiers deployed in south Lebanon, in an attempt to regain control of the area from Hezbollah. The two kidnapped Israeli soldiers are still being held by Hezbollah, and indirect negotiations for a prisoner exchange are under way.

The "Second Lebanon War," as it has become known in Israel, or the "July War," as it is commonly referred to in Lebanon, has brought the challenges of the Lebanese-Israeli relationship to the extreme point of sufferance. The Lebanese government has been struggling to be effective, sovereign, and independent, while being careful—some would say, too careful—not to disturb the delicate sectarian fabric within the country. As the war progressed, Prime Minister Siniora found himself between a rock and a hard place on the international political scene: though it was obvious he was both surprised and dismayed by Hezbollah's attack on July 12, he still made every effort to prevent an internal national rift with the organization. Exacerbating this tension was the involvement of the rest of the Arab world in the conflict: Iran and Syria aiding Hezbollah, while Egypt, Jordan, Saudi Arabia and even the Palestinian National Authority, while condemning Israel's retaliation, also criticizing Hezbollah's actions as "irresponsible." If this was unprecedented it was also an expression of the growing Sunni-Shiite divide within the Arab world. Siniora had to be careful this divide, already cataclysmic in Iraq, does not swallow up Lebanon too. It was partly this concern that brought him to thank Hezbollah for its "sacrifices for the independence and sovereignty of Lebanon,"[2] and to declare that "Lebanon would be the last country to sign a peace treaty with Israel."[3]

Israel, too, suffered from a lack of vision and direction. From the start, the Israeli government oscillated between the need to hold a universally recognized national entity, i.e. Lebanon and its democratically elected government responsible for attacks emanating from within Lebanese territory, and the equal need to make clear that its conflict was with Hezbollah, not the Lebanese people. Its tactical fumbling throughout the war was in part the result of a schizoid strategy—one that sought national retribution and deterrence but was also hesitant to destabilize the secular Siniora government. It was partly this indecision that brought the Israeli government to term the conflict "a campaign" rather than "a war." Though Israel initially stated that the military operation was designed to bring to the defeat of Hezbollah, as the war progressed, Israel was forced to realize that the elimination of the military wing of Hezbollah and the transformation of the group into a solely political and social movement, if it were ever to occur, would only come about through a political and social process within Lebanon. Having enjoyed unprecedented support at the beginning of the war, the Israeli government is now facing vast domestic criticism for failing to attain its stated war goals. The war has also intensified tensions between the Jewish and Arab populations in Israel, as some Arab Israeli leaders have expressed support for Hezbollah.

An equally powerful influence on the Israeli-Lebanese relationship has been Syria's vacillation between overtures of peace with Israel and outright threats of war. Throughout the recent war, tensions between Israel and Syria escalated, with both countries mobilizing forces along the border. Israeli officials have taken care to pronounce that Israel had no intentions of spreading the conflict to Syria, and that the mobilization of forces was defensive only. President Bashar al-Assad of Syria, concerned that the conflict in Lebanon would destabilize his own regime, reiterated his preparedness for war. Moreover, as Nasrallah and Hezbollah were increasingly heralded as heroes across the Arab world as a David who is bringing down the Israeli Goliath, al-Assad was encouraged to state that force seems the only way to get the Golan Heights back from Israel. Commentators in Israel now fear that al-Assad may seek to replicate the Hezbollah guerilla model of fighting to get the Golan Heights back. Israel, for its part, has shown little interest in entering into peace negotiations with al-Assad, claiming he is an untrustworthy and too-weak a partner.

At this time, it seems unlikely that the Lebanese army or indeed the reinforced UNIFIL would attempt to disarm Hezbollah by force. At most, they may succeed in keeping the armed group away from the Israeli border and prevent it from launching attacks into Israel from southern Lebanon. Whether the war will prove a jumpstart for the much hoped-for political and social process of the disarmament of Hezbollah is yet to be seen, although chances of that seem low.

Without a peace deal with Syria, it is highly unlikely that a fundamental positive shift in Israeli-Lebanese relationship is imminent. Nevertheless, with the intervention of the United States, Europe, or parts of the Arab World, it might be possible to conceive of security arrangements—perhaps resemgling the 1949 armistice regime—ensuring non-aggression, release of prisoners, and perhaps some territorial arrangements in the Shabaa Farms area. Such arrangements, already suggested by Siniora during the war, might set off a direct dialogue between the two countries. At least initially, if any island of agreement is in sight, it is much likelier to happen in the security sphere than in any other, once again, leaving the potential of broader management unrealized.

Israel–Lebanon Monitoring Group Statistics

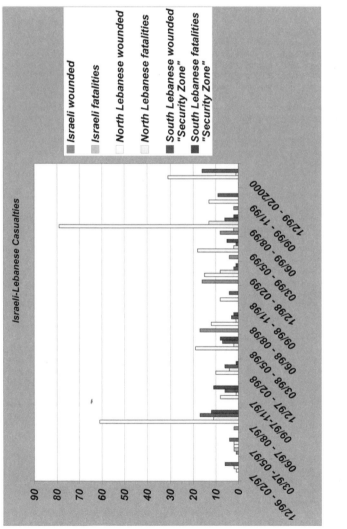

Figure 1. Israel-Lebanon Monitoring Group: Statistics on Civilian Casualties. *Source:* ILMG Press Statements.

Maps

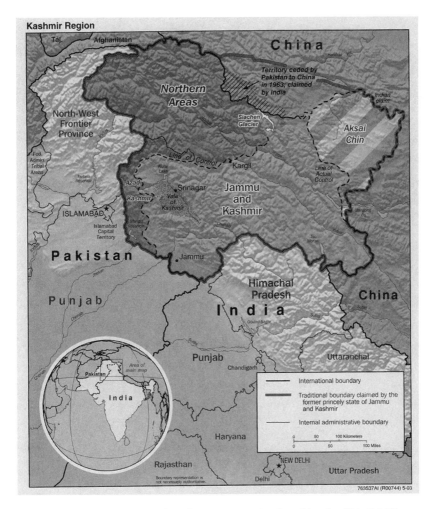

Map 1. The Disputed Area of Kashmir. *Source:* Produced by the CIA (2002); available on the Perry-Castañeda Library Map Collection database, University of Texas at Austin.

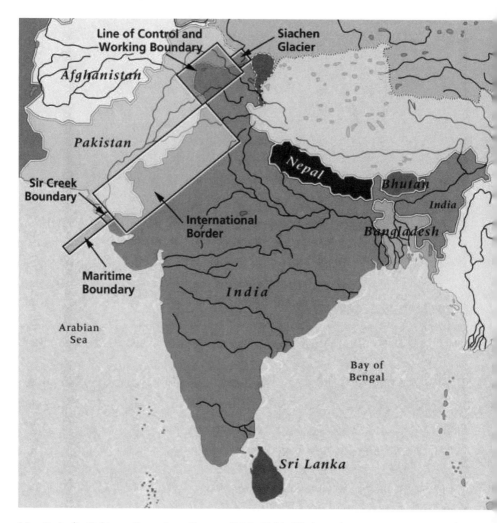

Map 2. India-Pakistan Boundary. *Source:* Shirin Tahir Khely and Kent L. Biringer, "Reducing Risk in South Asia: Managing India-Pakistan Tensions," Sandia National Laboratories, SAND 98–0505–20, Albuquerque, N.Mex., March 2001.

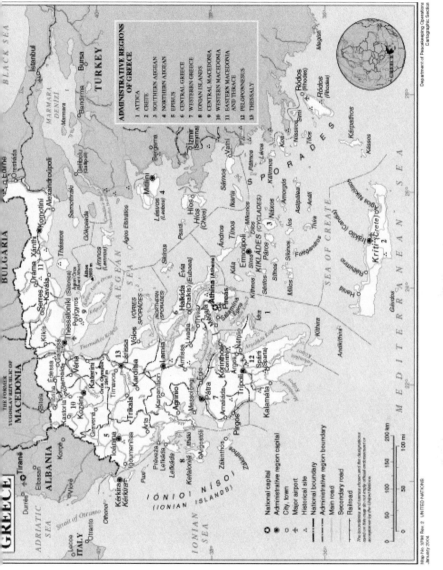

Map 3. Greece, Turkey, and the Aegean Sea. *Source:* United Nations Cartographic Section, map no. 3798, rev. January 2, 2004.

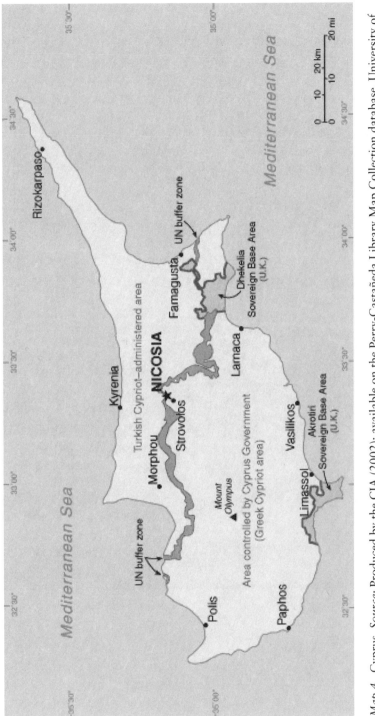

Map 4. Cyprus. *Source:* Produced by the CIA (2002); available on the Perry-Castañeda Library Map Collection database, University of Texas at Austin. www.lib.utexas.edu/maps/map_sites

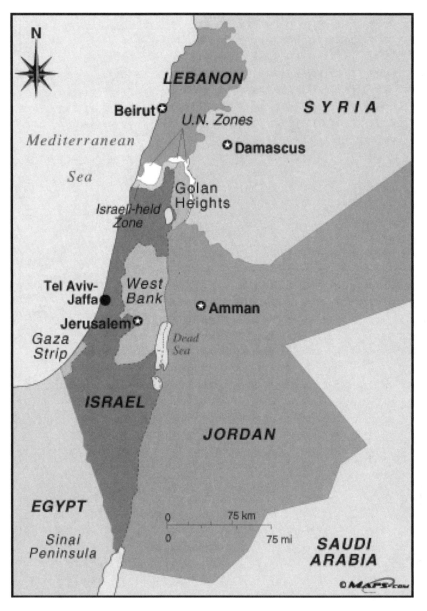

Map 5. Israel, Lebanon, and Syria. *Source:* Magellan Geographix,
www.maps.com.

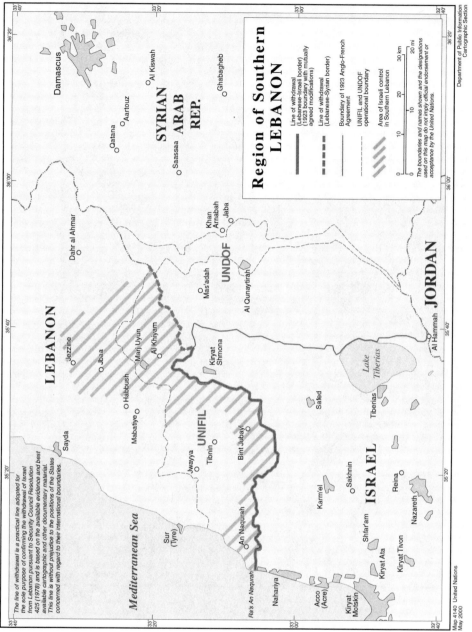

Map 6. Region of Southern Lebanon. *Source:* United Nations, Department of Public Information, Cartographic Section,

Notes

Introduction

1. Albert Einstein, *Why War? A Correspondence Between Albert Einstein and Sigmund Freud,* trans. Stewart Gilbert (Redding, Calif., 1991), pp. 3, 5.
2. Primo Levi, *The Drowned and the Saved,* trans. Raymond Rosenthal (New York, 1988), p. 200.

1. Islands of Agreement

1. Guinness World Records Web site, *www.guinnessworldrecords.com* (accessed 12/10/05); Glenn Frankel, "Sneers from across the Atlantic; Anti-Americanism Moves to W. Europe's Political Mainstream, *Washington Post,* February 11, 2003, A1; David Usborne, "Canada Makes Show of Force over Disputed Arctic Territory," *The Independent,* August 25, 2005, 24.
2. Giles Tremlett, "Spain Lashes Out as Gibraltar Celebrates Anniversary," *Guardian,* August 4, 2004, 10.
3. See opposite briefs submitted to the Israeli High Court of Justice in a case concerning the legality of Israel's policy of targeted killings of Palestinian terrorists: *The Public Committee Against Torture in Israel v. Government of Israel,* HCJ 796/02, unpublished (2002–2004).
4. Sigmund Freud, in Albert Einstein, *Why War? A Correspondence between Albert Einstein and Sigmund Freud,* trans. Stuart Gilbert (Redding, Calif., 1991), p. 10. 1st edition is from 1933.
5. Ibid., pp. 15–16.
6. Quincy Wright, *A Study of War* (Chicago, 1942); Lionel Curtis, *World War, Its Cause and Cure,* London, Oxford University Press, 1945; Kenneth D. Bolding, "War as a Public Health Problem: Conflict Management as a Key to Survival," in M. Schwebel, ed., *Behavioral Science and Human Survival*

(Palo Alto, Calif., 1965); Norman Z. Alcock, *The War Disease* (Oakville, Ontario, 1972); Leonard Berkowits, "Studies of the Contagion of Violence," in Herbert Hirsch and David C. Perry, eds., *Studies on the Contagion of Violence* (New York, 1973), pp. 41–51; Frances Beer, "The Epidemiology of Peace and War," *International Studies Quarterly* 23 (1979): 45–86. See also Hank W. Houweling and Jan G. Siccama, "The Epidemiology of War, 1816–1980," *Journal of Conflict Resolution* 29 (1985): 641–663.

7. Antione de Saint-Exupéry, *Flight to Arras,* trans. Lewis Galantiere (New York, 1965), p. 46.

8. For a survey of sociological, psychological, and social-psychology theories of conflict, see Allan C. Tidwell, *Conflict Resolved? A Critical Assessment of Conflict Resolution* (London, 1998), pp. 30–85.

9. J. K. Holsti holds the Napoleonic wars responsible for the advent of this conceptual revolution. See J. K. Holsti, "Paths to Peace? Theories of Conflict Resolution and Realities of International Politics," in Ramesh Thakur, ed., *International Conflict Resolution* (Boulder, Colo., 1988), pp. 105–131.

10. Bernard Brodie, *War and Politics* (New York, 1973), p. 274.

11. Holsti, "Paths to Peace," p. 109.

12. Freud, in Einstein, *Why War?* p. 20.

13. Brodie, *War and Politics,* p. 274.

14. See John Mueller, "The Obsolescence of Major War," in Robert J. Art and Kenneth N. Waltz, eds., *The Use of Force: Military Power and International Politics* (Lanham, MD, 1999), pp. 427–440, 427, and compare Carl Kaysen, who claims that it is not moral attitudes towards war that had changed, but rather the cost-benefit calculus of war, which had begun yielding negative outcomes, stripping war from its romantic aura; see Carl Kaysen, "Is War Obsolete?" *International Security* 14, no. 4 (1990): 42–64.

15. For a more skeptical view of the motivations behind intergovernmental bodies and civil society's "fight for peace," see W. Michael Reisman, "Stopping War and Making Peace: Reflections on the Ideology and Practice of Conflict Termination in Contemporary World Politics," 6 *Tulane Journal of International and Comparative Law* 5, 8–11 (1998).

16. Brodie, *World Politics,* p. 274.

17. See Monty G. Marshall and Ted Robert Gurr, *Peace and Conflict 2005: A Global Survey of Armed Conflicts, Self-Determination Movements, and Democracy,* Center for International Development and Conflict Management, University of Maryland, June 1, 2005.

18. Project Ploughshares, Armed Conflicts Report (2005), *www.ploughshares.ca* (accessed 12/30/05); Kosimo Project, Heidelberg Institute on Conflict Research, University of Heidelberg, *www.hiik.de/en/index_e.htm* (accessed 12/30/05); Uppsala Conflict Dataset, Uppsala University, Department of Peace and Conflict Research, *www.pcr.uu.se/database/index.php* (accessed 12/30/05).

19. Uppsala Conflict Dataset; see also Lotta Harbom and Peter Wallensteen, "Armed Conflict and Its International Dimensions, 1946–2004," *Journal of Peace Research* 42, no. 5 (2005): 623–635.

20. On bargaining theory, see Kenneth Arrow, "Information Acquisition and

the Resolution of Conflict," Stanford Center on Conflict and Negotiation, Working Paper 41 (1993); Clifton Morgan, *Untying the Knot of War: A Bargaining Theory of International Crises* (Michigan, 1994). On social psychology, see, for instance, Herbert Kelman's models of facilitation, building on theories of social psychology—Herbert Kelman, "Interactive Problem Solving: An Approach to Conflict Resolution and its Application in the Middle East," *Political Science and Politics* 31, no. 2 (1998): 190–198; Herbert Kelman and Stephen P. Cohen, "The Problem-Solving Workshop: A Social-Psychology Contribution to the Resolution of International Conflict," *Journal of Peace Research* 13, no. 2 (1967): 79–90. On the "problem-solving" approach to conflict resolution, see also Edward E. Azar, *The Management of Protracted Social Conflict: Theory and Cases* (Brookfield, Vt., 1990). On the integration of several approaches, see Kenneth Arrow et al., eds., *Barriers to Conflict Resolution* (Stanford, 1995), compiling contributions by scholars from the fields of psychology, economics, law, political science, business management, and even urban planning.

21. See Joe Vellacott, "Dynamic Peace and the Practicality of Pacifism," in Larry J. Fisk and John L. Schellenberg, eds., *Patterns of Conflict, Paths to Peace* (N.Y., 2000), pp. 202–205, 202.

22. For a sample of practical negotiation guides, see Roger Fisher and William Ury, *Getting to Yes: Negotiating Agreement without Giving In* (New York, 1981; repr., 1991); William Ury, *Getting Past No: Negotiating Your Way from Confrontation to Cooperation* (New York, 1991); Charles B. Craver, *The Intelligent Negotiator: What to Say, What to Do, And How to Get What You Want Every Time* (New York, 2002); Russel Korobkin, *Negotiation Theory and Strategy* (New York, 2002); Stuart S. Nagel, *Handbook of Win-Win Policy Analysis* (London, 2001); Robert H. Mnookin, *Beyond Winning: Negotiating to Create Value in Deals and Disputes* (Cambridge, 2000).

23. Two recent edited volumes published by the Washington Institute of Peace dedicated to intractable conflicts and their mediation mark a welcome shift towards an emphasis on management. The very acceptance that some conflicts may indeed be intractable is laudable in itself. See Chester A. Crocker, Fen Osler Hampson, and Pamela AAll, eds., *Grasping the Nettle: Analyzing Cases of Intractable Conflict* (Washington, D.C., 2005), and in particular Jacob Bercovitch's chapter, pp. 104–120; Chester A. Crocker, Fen Osler Hampson, and Pamela AAll, eds., *Taming Intractable Conflicts: Mediation in the Hardest Cases* (Washington, D.C., 2004).

24. See, for instance, William I. Zartman, ed., *Preventive Negotiation: Avoiding Conflict Escalation* (New York, 2001); Bernard Mayer, *The Dynamics of Conflict Resolution: A Practitioner's Guide* (San Francisco, 2000); Barbara A. Nagle-Lechman, *Conflict and Resolution* (New York, 1997); Christopher Mitchell and Michael Banks, *Handbook of Conflict Resolution: The Analytical Problem-Solving Approach* (London, 1996). One interesting work, sponsored by the Carnegie Commission on Preventing Deadly Conflict, set out to compare the costs of prevention to the costs of conflict, in support of preventive intervention efforts by world powers and international organizations—see Michael E. Brown and Richard N. Rosen-

crance, eds., *The Costs of Conflict: Prevention and Cure in the Global Arena* (Carnegie Commission on Preventing Deadly Conflicts, Carnegie Corp. of NY, 1999).

25. Elise Boulding, foreword, in Louis Kriesberg, Terrell A. Northrup and Stuart J. Thorson, eds., *Intractable Conflicts and Their Transformation* (Syracuse, N.Y., 1989), pp. ix–x.

26. See Kriesberg, Northrup, and Thorson, "Conclusion," in *Intractable Conflicts*.

27. John C. Campbell, ed., *Successful Negotiation: Trieste, 1954* (New Haven, Conn., 1976), p. 105, quoted by William Zartman and Maureen R. Berman, *The Practical Negotiator* (New Haven, 1982), p. 45.

28. Michael Ignatieff, *The Noble Warrior* (New York, 1998), p. 119.

29. Holsti, "Paths to Peace," pp. 111–113.

30. Michael Ignatieff, *Virtual War: Kosovo and Beyond* (New York, 2000), p. 212.

31. Holsti refers to the "significant portion . . . of the wars of the last three hundred years [that] have involved issues of fundamental importance to dynasts, governments, and societies as a whole," in Holsti, "Paths to Peace," p. 112.

32. Goertz and Diehl define enduring rivalries as "repeated conflict among the same set of states," in Gary Goertz and Paul F. Diehl, "Enduring Rivalries: Theoretical Constructs and Empirical Patterns," *International Studies Quarterly* 37 (1995): 147–171; Bennett offers "dyads with a long history of repeated conflict, within which conflicts are connected over time," in D. Scott Bennett, "Integrating and Testing Models of Rivalry Duration," *American Journal of Political Science* 42 (1998): 1200–1232, and also examples in which "one or both states occasionally use military force or the threat of it in an attempt to shift the resolution of the issues at stake in their favor," in D. Scott Bennett, "Security, Bargaining, and the End of Interstate Rivalry," *International Studies Quarterly* 40 (1996): 157–184, 160; and Thompson prefers the term "principal rivalries" to highlight the conceptualization of the rivalry's severity, rather than its endurance, in William R. Thompson, "Principal Rivalries," *Journal of Conflict Resolution* 39 (1995): 195–223, 200. Others suggest the term "protracted conflicts" to mean "hostile interactions which extend over long periods of time with sporadic outbreaks of open warfare fluctuating in frequency and intensity"; see Edward E. Azar, Paul Jureidini, and Ronald McLaurin, "Protracted Social Conflict: Theory and Practice in the Middle East," *Journal of Palestine Studies* 8, no. 1 (1978): 41–60, 55, quoted by Bennett, "Security, Bargaining," p. 160. The editors of the 2004 United States Institute of Peace volume *Taming Intractable Conflicts* explain that in their view, "intractable conflicts" are "conflicts [that] are stubborn or difficult but not impossible to manage." See Crocker, Hampson, and AAll, *Taming Intractable Conflicts*, p. 7. Thompson, "Principal Rivalries"; see also Goertz and Diehl, who capture the skepticism with which one should view the various "scientific" definitions offered by different scholars: "Another, often unstated,

basis for judging any definition of enduring rivalries is that it matches our intuition about what cases qualify as enduring rivalries and exclude those from historical knowledge that we think deserve to be excluded" (Goertz and Diehl, "Enduring Rivalries," p. 164).

33. "Report of the Independent Inquiry into the Actions of the United Nations during the 1994 Genocide in Rwanda," Annex to Letter Dated December 15, 1999 from the Secretary-General Addressed to the President of the Security Council, UN Doc. S/1999/1257 (1999).

34. "A Policy Action Plan," Africa Briefing No. 34, International Crisis Group, Nairobi/Brussels, October 19, 2005.

35. See Bennett: "Rivalries are expected to end when conditions (and in turn, offers) are such that the net utility associated with accepting a given settlement offer and ending a rivalry becomes greater than the utility of continuing it" (Bennett, "Integrating and Testing," p. 1204).

36. Gary Goertz and Paul F. Diehl, "The Initiation and Termination of Enduring Rivalries: The Impact of Political Shocks," *American Journal of Political Science* 39 (1995): 30–52, 30.

37. See I. William Zartman, in Crocker, Hampson, and AAll, *Grasping the Nettle*, p. 62.

38. For instance, in Adekeye Adebajo and Elizabeth M. Cousens, eds., *Managing Armed Conflicts in the 21st Century* (Portland, Oregon, 2001), the majority of works deal with the transition to peace (whether by UN nation-building efforts or through the operation of truth commissions), UN and NATO peacekeeping and intervention efforts, or modern warfare in general (civilian-military relations, mercenaries, and private security organs); see also the way John Darby uses the term "management," in John Darby, "The Management and Resolution of Ethnic Conflicts," in Adel Safty, ed., *Leadership and Conflict Resolution: The Middle East, Greece-Turkey, Caucasus, Post-Soviet Russia, Rwanda, Northern Ireland, Latin America* (Famagusta, Cyprus, 1999), pp. 27–36; and Antonia Handler Chayes and Abram Chayes, *Planning for Intervention: International Cooperation in Conflict Management* (The Hague, Netherlands, 1999). See also David Carment and Patrick James, eds., *Peace in the Midst of Wars: Preventing and Managing International Ethnic Conflicts* (New York, 1998).

39. See Osgood, who suggested a reciprocal concession technique for preventing further escalation of the international arms races, in Charles Egerton Osgood, *An Alternative to War or Surrender* (Urbana, 1962); Etzioni developed the concept of "encapsulation," in which the superpowers agree to exclude some of the more extreme conflict forms—see Amitai Etzioni, "On Self-Encapsulating Conflict," *Journal of Conflict Resolution* 3 (1964): 8; Dahrendorf introduced a process similar to encapsulation in the context of social struggles among groups competing on access to authority, in Ralf Dahrendorf, *Class and Class Conflict in Industrial Society* (Stanford, 1959). Others have used the term "conflict regulation" in a much broader way, to include third-party intervention, legal regulation, bargaining, etc.—see Paul Wehr, *Conflict Regulation* (Boulder, Colo., 1979).

40. Crocker, Hampson, and AAll, *Grasping the Nettle*, p. 376.
41. William Zartman, "Alternative Attempts at Crisis Management: Concepts and Processes," in Gilbert R. Winham, ed., *New Issues in International Crisis Management* (Boulder, Colo., 1988), p. 199–223, 222; Peter Wallensteen, *Understanding Conflict Resolution: War, Peace and the Global System* (Thousand Oaks, Calif., 2002), p. 53. One interesting exception may be found in social process theories, particularly the study of protracted social conflict (PSCs), as developed by Edward Azar, John Bourton, Gil Friedman, Louis Kriesberg, Harvey Starr, and others. PSCs are defined in the literature as "a conflict in which the issue(s) under contention are perceived by *both* adversaries to be *significantly linked to existential* group needs." See Gil Friedman, "Conceptualizing Protracted Conflict and Protracted Conflict Management," in Harvey Starr, ed., *The Understanding and Management of Global Violence: New Approaches to Theory and Research on Protracted Conflict* (New York, 1999), pp. 35–67, 36. Crucially, the focus of PSC research is not on the nation state as the unit of analysis, but rather on the "identity group—racial, religious, ethnic, cultural and other." See Edward E. Azar, "Protracted International Conflict: Ten Propositions," *International Interactions* 12, no. 1 (1995): 59–70, reprinted in Starr, *The Understanding and Management of Global Violence*, pp. 23–33, 25. PSC scholars, uniquely among their colleagues, acknowledge that "the intractability of protracted conflicts places the entire enterprise of explaining protracted conflict *resolution* on shaky ground. Rather, the intractable nature of protracted conflicts entails that conflict management rather than conflict resolution becomes paramount." See Friedman, "Conceptualizing Protracted Conflict," p. 47.
42. Oddly, though the worlds of law and business have welcomed this idea, it has been absent from the conflict studies literature. See Max Bazerman, ed., *Negotiation, Decision-Making and Conflict Management* (Cheltenham, U.K., 2005); Robert H. Mnookin, *Beyond Winning* (Cambridge, Mass., 2000).
43. On how framing affects negotiators' perceptions, expectations, and strategies, see Amos Tversky and Daniel Kahneman, "The Framing of Decisions and The Psychology of Choice," *Science* 40 (1981): 453–463; Max H. Bazerman and Margaret A. Neale, *Negotiating Rationally* (New York, 1992), pp. 31–41; Margaret A. Neale and Max H. Bazerman, "The Effects of Framing and Negotiator Overconfidence on Bargaining Behavior," *Academy of Management Journal* 24 (1985): 34–49.
44. Article XXII of the Treaty of Guadalupe Hidalgo, February 2, 1848, U.S.-Mexico, 9 Stat. 922.
45. Article XXIII of the Treaty of Amity and Commerce between the United States and Prussia, July 9 and September 10, 1785, 8 Stat. 84, TS No. 292, 8 Bevans 78, pp. 85–86.
46. *Paquete Habana*, 175 U.S. 677; 20 S. Ct. 290; 44 L. Ed. 320; 1900, p. 700.
47. Roger Fisher mentions the possibility for countries "to agree on issues on which they have common interests, limiting disagreement on those issues on which they truly disagree." See Roger Fisher, *International Conflict for Beginners* (New York, 1969), pp. 94–95.
48. On the aftermath of the fall of the UN-protected city of Srebrenica in 1995, see

Bosnia-Herzegovina, Amnesty International Report 2002, *www.amnesty.org* (accessed 12/6/05); see also Amin Saikal's criticism of the United States' failure to protect the "safe haven" of the Kurdish population in Northern Iraq against the Turkish invasion in March 1995, in Amin Saikal, "The Role of the United Nations in the Middle East," in Tom Woodhouse, Robert Bruce, and Malcolm Dando, eds., *Peacekeeping and Peacemaking: Towards Effective Intervention in Post–Cold War Conflicts* (London, 1998), pp. 133–144, 142–143. See Treaty on the Limitation of Anti-Ballistic Missile Systems, May 26, 1972, U.S.-USSR, 23 UST 3435, 944 UNTS 13.

49. See Azar, "Protracted International Conflict," p. 30. Elsewhere he argues (with others) that "animosity causes the conflict to spill over a broad spectrum of issues and in and of itself push the rivalry outside the inter-state framework." See Azar, Jureidini, and McLaurin, "Protracted Social Conflict," p. 55, quoted by Friedman, "Conceptualizing Protracted Conflict," p. 40.

50. Goertz and Diehl, "The Initiation and Termination," p. 34.

51. On the complexities of multidimensional conflicts, see L. N. Rangarajan, *The Limitation of Conflict: A Theory of Bargaining and Negotiation* (London, 1985), pp. 119–138.

52. James D. Morrow, "The Strategic Setting of Choices: Signaling, Commitment, and Negotiation," in David A. Lake and Robert Powell, eds., *Strategic Choice and International Relations* (Princeton, N.J. 1999), pp. 77–114, 101.

53. "Eritrea Says it has Released 71 Soldiers," *Reuters*, August 28, 1998; see Christopher Bowe, "US go-ahead for Governor's Cuban Visit," *Financial Times* (London), October 20, 1999, 17; Azar, *The Management of Protracted Social Conflict*, p. 94.

54. Elizabeth A. Neuffer, "Koreans Risk Heartbreak in Reunion of Families," *Boston Globe*, April 27, 2002, A8.

55. Declaration of Principles on Interim Self-Government Agreements, September 13, 1993, Isr.-PLO, 32 ILM 1525 (1993); Interim Agreement on the West Bank and the Gaza Strip, September 28, 1995, Article X, Isr.-PLO, 36 ILM 551 (1997).

56. General Framework Agreement for Peace in Bosnia and Herzegovina, December 14, 1995, Bosn. & Herz.-Croat.-Fed. R. Yugo., 35 ILM 75 (1996).

57. Report of the Sharm el-Sheikh Fact-Finding Committee ("Mitchell Report"), April 30, 2001; Palestinian-Israeli Security Implementation Work Plan ("Tenet Cease-Fire Plan") June 13, 2001; and Work Plan for Implementation of the Cease-Fire ("The Zinni Cease-Fire Plan") September 26, 2001—all available on the Israeli Ministry of Foreign Affairs Web site, *www.mfa.gov.il* (accessed 11/30/05).

58. See Thomas Schelling, *The Strategy of Conflict* (1960; repr. Cambridge, Mass., 1980), pp. 53–80, 257–266, defining the non-use of nuclear weapons or chemical weapons as resulting in a "limited war."

59. Robert Keohane, *After Hegemony: Cooperation and Discord in the World Political Economy* (Princeton, N.J., 1984), pp. 12, 50–53. Harrison Wagner claims that when one observes a conflict, one must assume that there is no mutual interest to resolve it before wondering why a mutual interest was not realized. Similarly, when one observes cooperation, the assumption must be that

there is harmony—a situation in which neither party gains from defection. See Harrison Wagner, "The Theory of Games and the Problem of International Cooperation," *American Political Science Review* 70 (1983): 330–346.

60. See Keohane, *After Hegemony*, pp. 12, 50–53.

61. Treaty Banning Intermediate-range Nuclear Force Missiles, INF Treaty, January 25, 1988, United States-USSR, 27 ILM 90 (1988).

62. Memorandum of Understanding Between USA and USSR Regarding the Establishment of a Direct Communications Link, June 20, 1963, U.S.-USSR, 14 UST 825; Agreement on Measures to Improve the Direct Communications Link, September 30, 1971, U.S.-USSR, 22 UST 1598; USSR-USA: Memorandum of Understanding on the Direct Communications Link, July 17, 1984, 23 ILM 1393.

63. On the importance of regime design on its effectiveness and sustainability, see Stephen Krasner, ed., *International Regimes* (Ithaca, N.Y., 1983); Ronald B. Mitchell and Patricia M. Keilbach, "Situation Structure and Regime Implementation Mechanisms: Reciprocity, Coercion, and Exchange," *International Organizations* 55, no. 4 (2001): 891–917; Ronald B. Mitchell, "Regime Design Matters: International Oil Pollution and Treaty Compliance," *International Organizations* 48, no. 3 (1994): 425–458; Kenneth Oye ed., *Cooperation Under Anarchy* (Princeton, N.J., 1986).

64. Schelling, *The Strategy of Conflict*, p. 261.

65. Charles de Montesquieu, *De L'esprit des Lois, Oeuvres Complètes* (Éditions du Seuil, Paris, 1964), pp. 527, 531; translation of this citation appears in Mark W. Janis, *An Introduction to International Law* (Boston, 1988), p. 51.

66. Hans Vogel, "Arms Production and Exports in the Dutch Republic," in Marco Van Der Hoeven, ed., *Exercise of Arms: Warfare in the Netherlands, 1568–1648* (Leiden, 1997), pp. 197–210, 207.

67. Alfred Thayer Mahan, *The Influence of Sea Power Upon History* (Gertna, La., 2003), p. 41.

68. I acknowledge the fact that there may be instances in which leaders have a vested interest in keeping the rival alive, for political motivations, so that the interest in harming the rival is curtailed by the need to keep the rival fit for fighting. In the present context I proceed with the assumption that in most cases of enduring rivalries, overall, the need to harm the rival triumphs most of the time.

69. See also Robert Jervis, "Security Regimes," in Krasner, *International Regimes*, pp. 173–194, 177.

70. Compare John J. Mearsheimer, "A Realist Reply," *International Security* 20, no. 1 (1995): 82–93, with Robert O. Keohane and Lisa L. Martin, "The Promise of Institutionalist Theory," *International Security* 20, no. 1 (1995): 39–51.

71. Duncan Snidal, "Relative Gains and the Pattern of International Cooperation," *American Political Science Review,* 85, no. 3 (1991): 701–726; Keohane and Martin, "The Promise of Institutionalist Theory"; James D. Morrow, "Modeling the Forms of International Cooperation: Distribution Versus Information," *International Organization* 48, no. 3 (1994): 387–423.

72. See Koehane, *After Hegemony,* pp. 91–92.
73. Donald J. Puchala and Raymond F. Hopkins, "International Regimes: Lessons From Inductive Analysis," in Krasner, *International Regimes,* pp. 61–92, 88.
74. On the role of the ongoing dialogue among bureaucrats in securing compliance with international treaties, see Abram Chayes and Antonia H. Chayes, "Adjustment and Compliance Processes in International Regulatory Regimes," in Jessica T. Mathews, ed., *Preserving the Global Environment: The Challenge of Shared Leadership* (New York, 1991), p. 280; Abram Chayes and Antonia Handler Chayes, *The New Sovereignty* (Cambridge, Mass., 1995).
75. Andrew Hurrell claims that the traditional institutionalist scholarship focuses on self-interest and the exchange of commitments, while it "downplays the traditional emphasis on the role of community and a sense of justice" and the enhancement of cooperation through a *perception* of common interests. See Andrew Hurrell, "International Society and the Study of Regimes: A Reflective Approach," in Robert J. Beck, Anthony Clark Arend, and Robert D. Vander Lugt, eds., *International Rules: Approaches From International Law and International Relations* (New York, 1999), pp. 206–224, 210.
76. See Koehane, *After Hegemony,* pp. 51–55; Kenneth A. Oye, "Explaining Cooperation Under Anarchy: Hypotheses and Strategies," in Oye, *Cooperation Under Anarchy,* pp. 6–7.
77. Joint Declaration for Keeping the Water Infrastructure out of the Cycle of Violence, February 1, 2001, available on the Israeli Ministry of Foreign Affairs Web site, *www.mfa.gov.il* (accessed 11/30/05).
78. David Rudge, "Agricultural Water Cut; Israel, PA Sign Water Declaration," *Jerusalem Post,* February 2, 2001, 8A.
79. See Schelling, *The Strategy of Conflict,* pp. 53–67.
80. Karin Landgren, "Safety Zones and International Protection: A Dark Grey Area," 7 *International Journal of Refugee Law* 436–458 (1995).
81. Sophie Haspeslagh, "Safe Havens," in *Beyond Intractability Project,* November 2003, *www.beyondintractability.org* (accessed 11/30/05).
82. See Reisman, "Stopping War," p. 40; see also Abram Chayes and Antonia Handler Chayes, "On Compliance," *International Organizations* 47, no. 2 (1993): 175–205, 188.
83. Chayes and Chayes, "On Compliance," 189.
84. Ibid., 190. See also Chayes and Chayes, *The New Sovereignty,* pp. 24–25.
85. On various models of how cooperation in the international arena can be maintained in the absence of enforcement mechanisms, see Oye, *Cooperation Under Anarchy.*
86. See Chayes and Chayes on the importance of monitoring and verification measures in international regimes, in Chayes and Chayes, *The New Sovereignty,* pp. 174–196; and on reporting and data collection, pp. 154–173. On the importance of assurance and verification provisions in international regimes, see Kenneth W. Abbott, "Trust But Verify: The Production of In-

formation in Arms Control Treaties and Other International Agreements," *Cornell International Law Journal* 26 (1993): 1–58; Kenneth W. Abbott and Duncan Snidal, "Why States Act Through Formal International Organizations," *Journal of Conflict Resolution* 42 (1998): 3–32.

87. See Landgrin, "Safety Zones," p. 452.

88. Keohane, *After Hegemony*, p. 8. The most widely recognized definition of a regime was offered by Stephen Krasner: "Implicit or explicit principles, norms, rules, and decision-making procedures around which actors' expectations converge in a given area of international relations. Principles are beliefs of fact, causation, and rectitude. Norms are standards of behavior defined in terms of rights and obligations. Rules are specific prescriptions or proscriptions for action. Decision-making procedures are prevailing practices for making and implementing collective choice." See Stephen D. Krasner, "Structural Causes and Regime Consequences: Regimes as Intervening Variables," in Krasner, *International Regimes*, pp. 1–2.

89. See Maurice Schiff and L. Alan Winters, "Regional Cooperation, and the Role of International Organizations and Regional Integration," World Bank Policy Research Working Paper 2872 (July 2002).

90. On the role of institutions in dispersing information and reducing uncertainty, see Keohane, *After Hegemony*, pp. 92–95; Keohane and Martin, "The Promise of Institutionalist Theory"; Lisa L. Martin and Beth Simmons, "Theories and Empirical Studies of International Institutions," *International Organizations* 52 (1998): 729–757.

91. See Kenneth A. Oye, "Explaining Cooperation Under Anarchy: Hypotheses and Strategies," *World Politics* 38, no. 1 (1985): 1–24; Keohane, *After Hegemony*.

92. Chayes and Chayes, *The New Sovereignty*, pp. 207, 213.

93. Robert O. Keohane and Joseph S. Nye, "Transgovernmental Relations and International Organizations," *World Politics* 27, no. 1 (1974): 39–62, 45–46. Nye and Keohane did not address bilateral ties between rivals; nevertheless, their observation is not wholly irrelevant to such settings too.

94. Conference on Security and Cooperation in Europe: Final Act, August 1, 1975, 14 ILM. 1292; Document of the Stockholm Conference on Confidence- and Security-Building Measures and Disarmament in Europe, September 19, 1986, reprinted in *SIPRI Yearbook 1987: World Armaments and Disarmaments* (New York, 1987) (entered into force January 1, 1987), p. 355; Charter of Paris for a New Europe, November 21, 1990, 30 ILM 190, 207; Supplementary Document to Give Effect to Certain Provisions Contained in the Charter of Paris for a New Europe, 30 ILM 209; Vienna Document 1990 of the Negotiations on CSBMs Convened in Accordance with the Relevant Provisions of the Concluding Document of the Vienna Meeting of the CSCE, November 17, 1990, reprinted in *SIPRI Yearbook 1991: World Armaments and Disarmaments* (New York, 1991), p. 475.

95. Martha Finnemore and Kathryn Sikkink, "International Norm Dynamics and Political Change," *International Organizations* 52 (1998): 887–917.

96. James Risen, "U.S. Seeks Means to Bring Suspect From Afghanistan," *New York Times*, August 20, 1998, A1.

97. George Mitchell, *Making Peace* (New York, 1999), p. 25.

98. James Risen, "U.S. Seeks Means to Bring Suspect From Afghanistan."

99. See ASEAN Web site, *www.aseansec.org* (accessed 11/30/05).

100. Andrew Hurrell, "Security in Latin America," *International Affairs* 74, no. 3 (July 1998): 529–546.

101. Anne-Marie Slaughter, *A New World Order* (Princeton, N.J., 2004); for more on the role of NGOs in the international community, see P. J. Simmons, "Learning to Live with NGOs," *Foreign Policy* 112 (1998): 82–96; Christoph Schreuer, "The Waning of the Sovereign State: Towards a New Paradigm for International Law?" 4 *European Journal of International Law* (1993): 447. On the role of state actors in establishing "epistemic communities," see Richard M. Haas, "Introduction: Epistemic Communities and International Policy Coordination," *International Organizations* 46, no. 1 (1992): 1–35; Richard M. Haas, "Epistemic Communities, World Order, and the Creation of A Reflective Research Program," *International Organizations* 46, no. 1 (1992): 367–390.

102. Anne-Marie Slaughter, "Hague Lectures: International Law and International Relations," 285 *Recueil des Cours* 8 (2000); see also Connie Peck, "Sustainable Peace: The Role of the UN and Regional Organizations in Preventing Conflict," in *Carnegie Commission on Preventing Deadly Conflict Series* (Washington, D.C., 1998), pp. 185–202.

103. Yerevan Press Club project, *www.mediadialogue.org* (accessed 12/24/05).

104. The Eurasia Foundation, *www.eurasia.org* (accessed 12/23/05).

105. On the possible roles of mediators in overcoming barriers to negotiated agreements, see, for instance, Robert H. Mnookin and Lee Ross, introduction, in Kenneth Arrow et al., eds., *Barriers to Conflict Resolution*, pp. 3–24; Saadia Touval and I. William Zartman, *International Mediation in Theory and Practice* (Boulder, Colo., 1985); I. William Zartman and Saadia Touval, "International Mediation: Conflict Resolution and Power Politics," *Journal of Social Issues* 41 (1985): 27–46; Kenneth Cloke, *Mediating Dangerously: The Frontiers of Conflict Resolution* (San Francisco, 2001).

106. See Cloke, who argues that "what is most useful to mediators in the concept of neutrality is not its emphasis on formality, perspective, objectivity, logic, or dispassionate judgment, but its concern for fairness and lack of selective bias. Parties most often want mediators to be honest, empathic, and 'omnipartial,' meaning on both parties' sides at the same time" (Cloke, *Mediating Dangerously*, p. 13). But compare to Morgan, who argues that under certain conditions, biased mediators can act more effectively than unbiased mediators, namely, when they have greater resources or due to their motivations in acting as mediators (Morgan, *Untying the Knot,* pp. 134–138).

107. James Fearon notes that domestic actors may want to punish a leader who loses a crisis or war, and terms such punishment "audience costs." See James D. Fearon, "Domestic Political Audiences and the Escalation of International Disputes," *Am. Pol. Sci. Rev.* 88 (1994): 577–592. The same costs can apply when the leader averts a crisis or war through the establishment of an island of agreement. A third party may have to cover these audience costs, in one way or another.

108. Robert D. Putnam, "Diplomacy and Domestic Politics: The Logic of Two-Level Games," *Int. Org.* 42, no. 3 (1988): 44. In addition, as some studies have demonstrated, domestic political divisions may actually promote cooperation rather than inhibit it—see Richard C. Eichenberg, "Dual Track and Double Trouble: The Two-Level Politics of INF," in Peter B. Evans, Harold K. Jacobson, and Robert D. Putnam, eds., *Double-Edged Diplomacy: International Bargaining and Domestic Politics* (Berkeley, Calif., 1993), pp. 45–76.

109. On side payments in instituting international regimes, see Mitchell and Keilbach, "Situation Structure and Regime Implementation," in Koehane, *After Hegemony,* pp. 89–92.

110. John D. Ciorciari, "Prospective Enlargement of the Roles of the Bretton Woods Financial Institutions in International Peace Operations," 22 *Fordham Int'l L. J.* 292 (1998): G. T. Keith Pitman, "The Role of the World Bank in Enhancing Cooperation and Resolving Conflict on International Watercourses: The Case of the Indus Basin," in M. A. Salman and Laurence Boisson de Chazournes, eds., *International Watercourses: Enhancing Cooperation and Managing Conflict: Proceedings of a World Bank Seminar,* Salman (Washington, D.C., 1998), pp. 155–166.

111. On reputation costs, see also Barry Nalebuff, "Rational Deterrence in an Imperfect World," *World Pol.* 43 (1991): 313–335; Christopher Gelpi, "Crime and Punishment: The Role of Norms in Crisis Bargaining," *Am. Pol. Sci. Rev.* 91 (1997): 339.

112. For the failure of international law to resolve international disputes over water resources, see Joseph W. Dellapenna, "Treaties as Instruments for Managing Internationally-Shared Water Resources: Restricted Sovereignty vs. Community of Property," 26 *Case W. Res. J. Int'l L.* 27 (1994).

113. Notification by the depositary addressed to the ICRC on March 11, 1983, available on the ICRC Web site, *www.icrc.org* (accessed 12/30/05).

114. United Kingdom Reservations to the Six Core United Nations Human Rights Instruments, available on the House of Commons Web site, *www.parliament.the-stationery-office.co.uk* (accessed 11/30/05).

115. Consent can be granted in either general or ad hoc in a specific matter—see Statute of the International Court of Justice, June 26, 1945, art. 36, 59 Stat. 1055, 1060.

116. Chayes and Chayes, *The New Sovereignty,* pp. 112–134.

117. Robert H. Mnookin and Lewis Kornhauser, "Bargaining in the Shadow of the Law: The Case of Divorce," 88 *Yale L.J.* 950 (1979).

118. Vienna Convention on Consular Relations, April 24, 1963, 21 UST 77, 596 UNTS 261; Vienna Convention on Diplomatic Relations, April 18, 1961, 23 UST 3227, 500 UNTS 95.

119. See Jonathan I. Charney, "International Agreements and the Development of Customary International Law," 61 *Wash. L.Rev.* 971 (1986).

120. Statute of the International Court of Justice, see note 115 above, art. 38 (1) (b).

121. *The Paquete Habana.*

122. As Chayes and Chayes note, "treaties implicating national security would

demand strict compliance because the stakes are so high, and to some extent that prediction is borne out by experience." Chayes and Chayes, "On Compliance," p. 198.

123. In the context of failed negotiations, Rangarajan emphasizes that "the failure of a negotiation not only leaves the original complainant uncompensated but his bitterness is increased by failure" (Rangarajan, see note 51 above, p. 283). The same logic applies here.

124. Mnookin, *Beyond Winning,* pp. 1–43; David A. Lax and James K. Sebenius, *The Manager as a Negotiator: Bargaining for Cooperation and Competitive Gain* (New York, 1986), pp. 88–116; Howard Raiffa, *The Art and Science of Negotiation* (Cambridge, 1982), pp. 131, 144; Dean G. Pruitt, *Negotiation Behavior* (New York, 1981), 137–162.

125. See, for instance, Kal Raustiala and Anne-Marie Slaughter, "International Law, International Relations, and Compliance," in Walter Carlsnaes et al., eds., *Handbook of International Relations* (Thousand Oaks, 2002), pp. 538, 539–45.

126. James D. Fearon, "Counterfactuals and Hypothesis Testing in Political Science," *World Politics* 43 (1991): 169–195, 170.

2. India and Pakistan

1. Sharif al-Mujahid, "India-Pakistan Relations: An Analysis," *Foreign Policy of Pakistan—An Analysis,* Department of International Relations, University of Karachi, 1964, p. 43. Quoted by Khan Zaman Mirza, "Pakistan's Foreign Policy in the 1990s with Reference to Kashmir Dispute," in Verinder Grover and Ranjana Arora, eds., *50 Years of Indo-Pak Relations,* vol. 1 (New Delhi, 1998), pp. 118–134.

2. Manorama Kohli, "Pakistan's Quest for Security: An Overview," in Grover and Arora, *50 Years,* vol. 1, p. 191.

3. Communist and humanist activist M. N. Roy, in an editorial in *Independent India,* September 19, 1948, quoted by R. M. Pal, "What Led to the Two-Nation Theory and Partition," in Grover and Arora, *50 Years,* vol. 1, p. 9.

4. Kohli, "Pakistan's Quest," p. 191.

5. Ravi Nanda, *Kashmir and Indo-Pak Relations* (New Delhi, 2001), p. 31. See also Victoria Schofield, *Kashmir in Conflict: India, Pakistan and the Unfinished War* (London, 2000), pp. 27–28.

6. Estimations vary. These numbers appear in Joseph B. Schechtman, "Evacuee Property in India and Pakistan," in Grover and Arora, *50 Years,* vol. 1, p. 31; Ian Talbot, *Freedom's Cry: The Popular Dimension in the Pakistan Movement* (Karachi, 1996).

7. Quoted by Schechtman, "Evacuee Property," p. 30.

8. Sumit Ganguly, *Conflict Unending: India-Pakistan Tensions Since 1947* (New Delhi, 2001), pp. 18–19.

9. Lars Blinkenberg, *India—Pakistan: The History of Unsolved Conflicts,* vol. 1: *The Historical Part* (Odense, 1998), pp. 91–96.

10. International Crisis Group Report, "Kashmir: Learning From the Past," ICG Asia Report No. 70, Islamabad/New Delhi/Brussels, December 4, 2003, pp. 1, 6.

11. See Text of India's Complaint to the UN Security Council, January 1, 1948 (S/628), reprinted in Ganguly, *Conflict Unending*, pp. 152–157.

12. Resolution 39 (1948), Adopted by the Security Council at its 230th Meeting, held on January 20, 1948, UN Doc. S/654 (January 20, 1948).

13. Resolution 47 (1948), On the India-Pakistan Question, Adopted by the Security Council at its 286th Meeting, held on April 21, 1948, UN Doc. S/726 (April 21, 1948).

14. Resolution Adopted by the United Nations Commission for India and Pakistan August 13, 1948 UN Doc. S/1100, para. 75. The decision on a plebiscite was already introduced in an earlier UN resolution, from April 21, 1948.

15. Resolution Adopted at the meeting of the United Nations Commission for India and Pakistan on UN Doc. S/1196, para. 15 (January 10, 1949).

16. Agreement Regarding the Establishment of Cease-fire Line in the State of Jammu and Kashmir. Signed at Karachi, on July 27, 1949, came into force on 30 July 1949, 81 UNTS 273.

17. Kashmir Papers, Reports of the United Nations Commission for India and Pakistan, June 1948–December 1949, Government of India, New Delhi, 1952; cited in Schofield, *Kashmir in Conflict*, p. 70.

18. Resolution 91 (1951), Concerning the India-Pakistan Question, Adopted by the Security Council on March 30, 1951, UN Doc. S/201/Rev. 1 (March 30, 1951).

19. Nehru-Liaquat Pact—Agreement Regarding Treatment of Minorities, April 8, 1950, 131 UNTS 4.

20. Sisir Gupta, *Kashmir: A Study in Indo-Pakistan Relations* (Bombay, 1966), p. 353.

21. Quoted by Blinkenberg, *India-Pakistan*, p. 164.

22. Agreement Relating to a Cease-fire and the Restoration of the Status Quo as at January 1, 1965 in the Area of Gujarat/West Pakistan Border and Concerning the Arrangements for the Determination of the Border in That Area, June 30, 1965, 548 UNTS 277.

23. Tashkent Declaration, signed at Tashkent, on January 10, 1966, came into force on 10 January 1966, 560 UNTS 39; the Tashkent Declaration was accompanied by the Indo-Pakistan Agreement on Withdrawal of Troops, January 22, 1966, available on *www.southasiafoundation.org* (accessed 12/28/05).

24. Ganguly, *Conflict Unending*, pp. 51–70; Nanda, *Kashmir and Indo-Pak Relations*, pp. 79–81; Sumit Ganguly, *The Origins of War in South Asia: The Indo-Pakistani Conflicts Since 1947*, 2nd ed. (Boulder, Colo., 1994).

25. Nanda, *Kashmir and Indo-Pak Relations*, pp. 51–70.

26. Agreement on Bilateral Relations, signed at Simla on 2 July 1972, came into force on 4 August 1972, 858 UNTS 71.

27. Schofield, *Kashmir in Conflict*, pp. 119–120.

28. Indo-Pak Agreement Regarding Delineation of the Line of Control, August 29, 1972, available on South Asia Foundation Web site, *www.southasia foundation,org* (accessed 12/28/05).

29. Tripartite Agreement between India, Bangladesh, and Pakistan for the Normalisation of Relations in the Subcontinent, April 9, 1974, available on South Asia Foundation Web site, *www.southasiafoundation.org* (accessed 12/28/05). The India-Pakistan Agreement on Repatriation of Prisoners of War and Civilian Internees, August 28, 1973, 12 ILM 1080 (1973).

30. Kashmir Accord, November 13, 1974, available on *www.jammu-kashmir .com* (accessed 12/28/05).

31. Schofield, *Kashmir in Conflict,* pp. 143–145; Ganguly, *Conflict Unending,* pp. 93–94.

32. "Kashmir: Learning from the Past," cited in n. 10, pp. 13–14.

33. Ibid., pp. 15–16.

34. Ibid.

35. "Best Overall Performance Award to Punjab," *Press Trust of India,* August 5, 2005.

36. Agreements were reached with the Mizo, Tipura, and Gurkha rebels, but not with Nagaland and Manipur, where only cease-fires have been effected.

37. Ganguly, *Conflict Unending,* p. 85.

38. Kanti Bajpai et al., eds., *Brasstacks and Beyond: Perception and Management of Crisis in South Asia* (New Delhi, 1995), pp. 52–53.

39. Ganguly, *Conflict Unending,* pp. 86–87.

40. Also disputed are two hundred kilometers beyond the LoC, dividing the old states of Jammu and Kashmir and Pakistan's Punjab, which India considers to be part of the international boundary but which Pakistan refers to as the "Working Boundary" because of the dispute over Kashmir. For a detailed description of the different parts of the boundary, see Shirin Tahir-Kheli and Kent L. Biringer, "Preventing Another India-Pakistan War: Enhancing Stability Along the Border," SAND 98–0505–17, Cooperative Monitoring Center Occasional Paper, Sandia National Laboratories, Albuquerque, N.Mex., October 2000.

41. Raspal S. Khosa, "The Siachen Glacier Dispute: Imbroglio on the Roof of the World," *Contemporary South Asia* 8 (1999): 187–210.

42. Ashutosh Misra, "Beyond Kashmir: The Siachen, Sir Creek, and Tulbul/ Water Disputes," in Kanti Bajpai et al. eds., *Kargil and After: Challenges for Indian Policy* (New Delhi, 2001), pp. 196–241, 200–203.

43. Samina Ahmed and Varun Sahni, "Freezing the Fighting: Military Disengagement on the Siachen Glacier," SAND 98–0505–1, Cooperative Monitoring Center Occasional Paper, Sandia National Laboratories, Albuquerque, N. Mex., 1998.

44. Misra, "Beyond Kashmir," p. 204, 208; Khosa, "The Siachen Glacier Dispute," p. 199; Ahmed and Sahni, "Freezing the Fighting."

45. C. Rajan Mohan, "Olive Branches Flutters on Siachen," *Indian Express,* May 17, 2005.

46. Smruti S. Pattanaik, "Indo-Pak Relations: Need for a Pragmatic Approach," *Strategic Analysis* 23, no. 1 (April 1999), pp. 85–110.

47. B. Muralidhar Reddy, "India Pakistan Take a Step Forward on Siachen," *Hindu,* October 5, 2005, p. 1.

48. Indo-Pakistani Western Boundary Case Tribunal, February 19, 1968, cited in A. G. Noorani, "Easing the Indo-Pakistani Dialogue on Kashmir: Confidence Building Measures for the Siachen Glacier, Sir Creek, and the Wular Barrage Disputes," Occasional Papers 16, Henry L. Stimson Center, Washington D.C. (April, 1994), p. 100.

49. Pattanaik, "Indo-Pak Relations."

50. Ayesha Siddiqa-Agha, "Maritime Cooperation between India and Pakistan: Building Confidence at Sea," SAND 98–0505–15, Cooperative Monitoring Center Occasional Paper, Sandia National Laboratories, Albuquerque, N. Mex., November 2000.

51. Joint Statement, India—Pakistan in Islamabad, October 4, 2005, available on the Ministry of External Affairs, India, Web site, *www.meaindia.nic.in* (accessed 12/28/05).

52. Siddiqa-Agha, "Maritime Cooperation."

53. Indus Waters Treaty, September 19, 1960, India-Pak., 419 UNTS 125, United Nations, Legislative Texts and Treaty Provisions Concerning the Utilization of International Rivers for Other Purposes than Navigation 300, UN Doc. st/leg/ser.b/12 (1960) (hereafter, Indus Waters Treaty).

54. Mir Abdul Aziz, "Wular and the Proposed Barrage," *Muslim,* October 24, 1986, cited by Misra, "Beyond Kashmir," p. 225.

55. Misra, "Beyond Kashmir," pp. 224–229.

56. Khalid Mustafa, "Pakistan will Discuss Wullar Barrage on Basis of Historical Stance," *Daily Times,* July 15, 2004.

57. "Pakistani Minister Says War with India Only Option to Resolve Dam Issue," *BBC Worldwide Monitoring,* February 16, 2005.

58. For a detailed description of the Indian and Pakistani nuclear programs, see Sumit Ganguly, "Nuclear Proliferation in South Asia: Origins, Consequences and Prospects," in Shalendra Sharma, ed., *The Asia-Pacific in the New Millennium* (Berkeley, Calif. 2000); Itty Abraham, *The Making of India's Atomic Bomb* (New Delhi, 1998); George Perkovich, *India's Nuclear Bomb* (New Delhi, 1999); Ziba Moshaver, *Nuclear Weapons Proliferation in the Indian Subcontinent* (New York, 1991); Samina Ahmed, "Pakistan's Nuclear Weapons Program: Turning Points and Nuclear Choices," *International Security* 23 (1999): 178–204.

59. Sridhar Krishnaswami, "U.S. Lifts Sanctions Against India, Pak," *Hindu,* September 24, 2001, p. 1.

60. Comprehensive Test Ban Treaty, 35 ILM 1439 (1996).

61. Proceedings of the 2000 Carnegie International Non-Proliferation Conference, March 16–17, Washington, D.C., 2000.

62. See Jasjit Singh, ed., *Nuclear India* (New Delhi, 1998); Amitabh Mattoo, ed., *India's Nuclear Deterrent: Pokharn II and Beyond* (New Delhi, 1999); Raj Chengappa, *Weapons of Peace* (New Delhi, 2000); Ashley J. Tellis, "The Changing Political-Military Environment in South Asia," Rand Corporation Papers (RP-947), 2001.

63. The Lahore Declaration, February 21, 1999, Peace Agreements Digital Collection: India-Pakistan, United States Institute of Peace, *www.usip.org* (accessed 12/28/05).

64. Joint Statement, February 21, 1999, Memorandum of Understanding, February 21, 1999, Peace Agreements Digital Collection: India-Pakistan, United States Institute of Peace, *www.usip.org* (accessed 12/28/05).

65. See Kanti Bajpai, "Bomb, Wars, Coups, and Hijacks: Making South Asia Into a Flashpoint," in Kanti Bajpai et al., eds., *Kargil and After: Challenges for Indian Policy* (New Delhi, 2001), pp. 15–31.

66. For a full chronology of the Kargil crisis see Ayesha Ray, "Kargil and India-Pakistan Relations," in Kanti Bajpai et al., eds., *The Kargil War*, pp. 443–458; on the war itself and its political implications, see also Praveen Swami, *The Kargil War* (New Delhi, 1999).

67. "Pakistani Action in Kargil Came as A Shock to Indian Leadership," SAPRA India Foundation Research Bureau, New Delhi, May 27, 1999.

68. B. Muralidhar Reddy, "Sharif Knew About Kargil, Alleges Musharraf," *Hindu*, August 8, 2004, p. 9.

69. Shaukat Qadir, "An Analysis of the Kargil Conflict 1999," *Royal United Services Institute for Defence and Security Studies Journal* (April 2002): 24–30, 30.

70. Narendra Gupta, "Air Operations in Kargil," *Hindu*, June 19, 1999, p. 10.

71. Ganguly, *Conflict Unending*, pp. 118–119.

72. "India Shoots Down a Pakistani Jet," *New York Times*, August 15, 1999, section 4, p. 2.

73. Sumita Kumar, "Trends in Indo-Pakistan Relations," *Strategic Analysis* 24, no. 2 (May, 2000), p. 25.

74. "Delhi Rules Out Role for APHC," *Agence-France Presse*, June 29, 2001.

75. Arpit Rajanm, "Bargaining in Crisis," IPCS Article No. 695, Institute of Peace and Conflict Studies, New Delhi, February 7, 2002.

76. "Kashmir: Learning from the Past," p. 18.

77. Michael Sullivan, "Militants Attack Indian Army Base in Kashmir," NPR, May 14, 2002.

78. On the mass movement of people across borders, see Inter-Dominion Agreement for Preventing Mass Exodus of Minorities, December 14, 1948, available on the South Asia Foundation Web site, *www.southasiafoundation.org* (accessed 12/28/05). On the protection of minorities, see Nehru-Liaquat Pact. On the protection of places of worship, see Indo Pakistan Agreement on Maintenance of Places of Religious Worship, August 4, 1953; see also the Pant Mirza Agreement to Prevent Border Incidents and Protect Places of Worship, May 17, 1955. A later agreement, concluded in 1961, addressed the transfer of bank accounts of displaced persons—Agreement On Transfer of Bank Accounts and Sage Deposits, July 10, 1961; all available on South Asia Foundation Web site *www.southasiafoundation.org* (accessed 12/28/05). On water allocation, see Inter-Dominion Agreement Between India and Pakistan on the Canal Water Dispute Between East and West Punjab, signed May 4, 1948, 54 UNTS 45.

79. Inter-Dominion Agreement for Preventing Mass Exodus of Minorities.

80. Jawaharlal Nehru, "We Cannot be Enemies Forever," in Grover and Arora, *50 Years,* vol. 2, pp. 237–244, 241–243.

81. Agreement on Border Disputes (with Joint Communiqué), New Delhi, September 10, 1958, 369 UNTS 81; Agreement (with Appendices) on East Pakistan Border Disputes, New Delhi, October 23, 1959, 362 UNTS 3; Agreement (with Annexes) on West Pakistan-India Border Disputes, New Delhi, January 11, 1960, 375 UNTS 119.

82. Indo Pak Agreement on Joint Commission, December 24, 1982, available on the South Asia Foundation Web site, *www.southasiafoundation.org* (accessed 12/28/05).

83. Hasan Askari Rivzi, "Pakistan-India Relations in the Eighties," in Grover and Arora, *50 Years,* vol. 2, pp. 385–407, 394–395.

84. Rivzi, "Pakistani-India Relations," p. 395.

85. Pattanaik, "Indo-Pak Relations."

86. See Nazir Kamal and Amit Gupta, "Prospects of Conventional Arms Control in South Asia," SAND 98–0505–5, Cooperative Monitoring Center, Sandia National Laboratories, Albuquerque, N. Mex., June 1999.

87. Sam Bateman, "Asia-Pacific Maritime Confidence Building," in J. R. Junnola ed., *Maritime Confidence Building in Regions of Tension,* Report No. 21. Henry L. Stimson Center, Washington, D.C. (2001), pp. 33–36.

88. Kanti Bajpai, "Bombs, Wars," p. 28.

89. "India, Pakistan Agree to Carry Forward Peace Process," BBC Worldwide Monitoring, September 15, 2005.

90. Harinder Baweja, "The Logic of Third Party Mediation over Kashmir," in Michael Krepon and Chris Gagne, eds., *The Stability-Instability Paradox: Nuclear Weapons and Brinkmanship in South Asia,* Henry L. Stimson Report No. 38, Washington, D.C. (June 2001).

91. Swati Pandey and Teresita C. Schaffer, "Building Confidence in India and Pakistan," *South Asia Monitor* 49, August 1, 2002.

92. "Confidence Building Measures and Kashmir," and "Confidence Building Measures in South Asia," Henry L. Stimson Center, Washington, D.C., available on *www.stimson.org* (accessed 12/29/05).

93. "Army Ready for War, Chief Says," *Statesman,* January 12, 2002.

94. "Army Chief's Statement a Reflection of Ground Reality," *Hindu,* January 13, 2002, p. 9.

95. "Confidence-Building Measures in South Asia."

96. The Agreement between India and Pakistan on the Advance Notice on Military Exercises, Maneuvers, and Troop Movements, April 6, 1991, 1843 UNTS 71.

97. See Articles 1, 4–6, 10–11 of the Agreement on Military Exercises.

98. "Confidence Building Measures and Kashmir."

99. Agreement between Pakistan and India on Prevention of Air Space Violations and for Permitting Over Flights and Landing by Military Aircraft, signed April 6, 1991, 1843 UNTS 59 (hereafter, Agreement on Air Space Violations).

100. See Articles 1–7 of the Agreement on Air Space Violations.

101. Pandey and Schaffer, "Building Confidence in India and Pakistan."
102. Aerial Incident of August 10, 1999 *(Pakistan v. India)*, Judgment (Jurisdiction), International Court of Justice, June 21, 2000, available on *www.icj-cij.org* (accessed September 21, 2006).
103. Paragraph 5 to the memorandum of understanding attached to the Lahore Declaration.
104. Atul Aneja, "India, Pak. Naval Hotline?" *Hindu,* July 15, 2001, p. 8.
105. "LOC Access Talks on Saturday," *Statesman* (India), October 26, 2005.
106. The Agreement on the Prohibition of Attack against Nuclear Installations and Facilities, signed December 31, 1988; instruments of ratification exchanged December 1990, available on the Indian Embassy in Washington Web site, *www.indianembassy.org* (accessed 12/28/05).
107. See Hasan Askari Rizvi, "Pakistan-India Relations in the Eighties," in Grover and Arora, *50 Years,* vol 2. pp. 384–407, 407 n. 80.
108. Pandey and Schaffer, "Building Confidence in India and Pakistan."
109. India-Pakistan Joint Declaration on the Complete Prohibition of Chemical Weapons, August 19, 1992, available on the Indian Embassy in Washington Web site, *www.indianembassy.org* (accessed 12/28/05).
110. Thalif Deen, "Disarmament: Pakistan Insists on Defense Against Chemical Weapons," *Inter-Press Service,* October 22, 1997.
111. Nuclear Threat Initiative Web site, *www.nti.org* (accessed on 12/15/05).
112. Mahendra Ved, "PM Meets Cong. Team Over Signing of CTBT," *Times of India,* December 18, 1999, p. 1.
113. Paragraph 4 of the Memorandum of Understanding attached to the Lahore Declaration.
114. The Lahore Declaration.
115. Articles 2–3 of the Memorandum of Understanding attached to the Lahore Declaration.
116. Jyoti Malhotra, "N-Capabilities Factor for Regional Stability: India Pak." *Indian Express,* June 21, 2004, p. 1. A follow-up joint statement dated December 15, 2004, is listed as Joint Statement, Second Round of India-Pakistan Expert Level Talks on Nuclear CBMs, available on the Indian Ministry of External Affairs Web site, *www.mea.gov.in* (accessed 12/27/05).
117. Qudssia Akhlaque, "India Pakistan Sign Two Agreements," *Dawn,* October 4, 2005.
118. Kamal and Gupta, "Prospects of Conventional Arms Control in South Asia," p. 6.
119. P. R. Chari, "Indo-Soviet Military Co-operation: A Review," in *Asian Survey* 19, no. 3 (March 1979): 243, quoted by Kohli, "Pakistan's Quest," pp. 192, 193.
120. Moonis Ahmar, "War Avoidance between India and Pakistan: A Model of Conflict Resolution and Confidence-Building in the Post–Cold War Era," in Grover and Arora, *50 Years,* vol. 2, pp. 413–433, 415.
121. See Ground Rules Annexed to the 1959 Agreement on Border Disputes, available on Indian Ministry of External Affairs Web site, *www.mea.gov.in* (accessed 12/27/05).

122. See also "Confidence Building Measures and Kashmir."

123. "India, Pak. Agree on Truce in Harvest Season," *Hindu,* May 7, 2000, p. 11; this time it was reported that no agreement could be reached on the erection of structures along the boundary, as India accused the Pakistani side of violating the understandings time and again.

124. Luv Puri, "LoC opened as India Sends Relief to Pakistan Occupied Kashmir," *Hindu,* November 8, 2005, p. 12.

125. Rajiv Chandrasekaran, "India Demands Pakistan Convert Words into Deeds: Officials Await Action on Militants," *Washington Post,* January 14, 2002, A11.

126. Pattanaik, "Indo-Pak Relations."

127. B. Muralidhar Reddy, "India, Pakistan to Share Intelligence on Narcotics Trafficking," *Hindu,* 17 June, 2004, p. 11.

128. G. T. Keith Pitman, "The Role of the World Bank in Enhancing Cooperation and Resolving Conflict on International Watercourses: The Case of the Indus Basin," in Salman M. A. Salman and Laurence Boisson de Chazournes, eds., *International Watercourses: Enhancing Cooperation and Managing Conflict,* World Bank Technical Paper No. 414 (1998), p. 155.

129. Hafez-ur-Rahman Khan, "Indo-Pakistan Waters Dispute," in Grover and Arora, *50 Years,* vol. 1, pp. 19–29, 19.

130. M. R. Hafezneia, "Geopolitical Analysis of the Kashmir Crisis," in Grover and Arora, *50 Years,* vol. 1, pp. 108–112, 111.

131. For a detailed report of the negotiations over the Indus Waters Treaty, see Asit K. Biswas, "Indus Waters Treaty: The Negotiating Process," *Water International* 17 (1992): 201.

132. See Biswas, "Indus Water Treaty," 201; Pitman, "The Role of the World Bank."

133. For a detailed analysis of the Indus Waters Treaty provisions, see Niranjan D. Gulhati, *Indus Water Treaty: An Exercise in International Mediation* (Bombay, 1973).

134. Indus Waters Treaty, Articles II–III.

135. Indus Basin Development Fund Agreement, Australia, Canada, Germany, New Zealand, Pakistan, the United Kingdom, the United States and the World Bank, signed at Karachi, September 19, 1960, 12 UST 19, 444 UNTS 259. See also Tufail Jawed, "The World Bank and the Indus Basin Dispute: Indus Waters Treaty III," *Pakistan Horizon,* 19, no. 2 (second quarter, 1966): 139. Gulhati, *Indus Waters Treaty,* 105.

136. Indus Waters Treaty, Article VIII.

137. Provisions regarding the referral to a neutral expert are covered by Appendix E to the treaty; provisions governing the establishment of a court of arbitration are covered by Appendix G to the treaty.

138. Article XII of the Indus Waters Treaty.

139. See Patricia Wouters, foreword, in *International Water Law: Selected Writings of Professor Charles B. Bourne* (Boston, 1997).

140. Quoted by A. G. Noorani, "A Treaty to Keep," *Frontline* 19, no. 8 (April 13–26, 2002): see also Qudssia Akhlaque, "India Cannot Scrap Indus Treaty," *Dawn,* May 26, 2002.

141. Praveen Swami, "A Treaty Questioned," *Frontline* 19, no. 9, (April 27–May 10, 2002), p. 34.

142. See Surya P. Subedi, "Current Development: Hydro-Diplomacy in South Asia: The Conclusion of the Mahakali and Ganges River Treaties," 93 *American Journal of International Law* 953 (1999).

143. See Joseph W. Dellapenna, who observes that "the most cordial and cooperative of neighbouring states have found it difficult to achieve mutually acceptable arrangements to govern their transboundary surface waters even in relatively humid regions where fresh water is usually found in sufficient supply to satisfy most or all needs." Joseph W. Dellapenna, "Foreword: Bringing the Customary International Law of Transboundary Waters Into the Era of Ecology," *International Journal of Global Environmental Issues* 1 (2001): 243.

144. India-Pakistan Agreement Regarding the Design of the Salal Hydro Electric Plant of River Chenab, April 14, 1978, available on the South Asia Foundation Web site, *www.southasiafoundation.org* (accessed 12/28/05).

145. "India, Pak. to Continue Talks on Tulbul Project," *Hindu*, November 6, 1998; cited by Misra, "Beyond Kashmir," p. 236.

146. For a review of conflicts and agreements over international watercourses, see Wouters, forward.

147. Pitman, "The Role of the World Bank," p. 155; also Jagat S. Mehta, "The Indus Water Treaty: A Case Study in the Resolution of an International River Basin Conflict," *Natural Resources Forum* 69 (1988).

148. Douglas Brown, "India and Pakistan: A More Harmonious Phase," *Daily Telegraph*, August 15, 1949, quoted by Rashid Ahmad Khan, "Indo-Pakistan Trade: Prospects and Constraints," in Grover and Arora, *50 Years*, vol. 2, pp. 192–204, 193. Sreedhar, *India Pakistan Trade: Problems and Prospects*, in Grover and Arora, *50 Years*, vol. 2, pp. 207–214, 207.

149. Kahn, "Indo-Pakistan Trade," p. 194.

150. General Agreement on Tariffs and Trade, Geneva, October 30, 1947, 55 UNTS 194, Article XXIV(5); GATT 1994 Article XXIV (11).

151. On "economic warfare," see Naema Sultan Begum, "Indo-Pakistan Trade Relations," Grover and Arora, *50 Years*, vol. 2, pp. 157–166, 165. Also Kahn, "Indo-Pakistan Trade." On the new trade agreements, see Trade Agreement between India and Pakistan, January 22, 1957; Trade Agreement between the Government of India and the Government of Pakistan, March 21, 1960; Trade Agreement between the Government of India and The Government of Pakistan, September 1, 1963; all available on the Ministry of External Affairs Web site, *www.mea.gov.in* (accessed 12/28/05).

152. Protocol between the Government of India and the Government of the Islamic Republic of Pakistan Regarding Shipping Services, January 15, 1975, available on the Ministry of External Affairs Web site, *www.mea.gov.in* (accessed 12/28/05). Agreement between India and Pakistan for Avoidance of Double Taxation of Income Derived from International Air Transport, December 31, 1988, available on the South Asia Foundation Web site, *www.southasiafoundation.org* (accessed 12/28/05). A general double taxation avoidance agreement is only being negotiated as yet. A 1947 treaty on

the avoidance of double taxation of income was deemed inoperative by India after the 1971 war.

153. Quoted in Pattanaik, "Indo-Pak Relations."

154. Kahn, "Indo-Pakistan Trade," p. 195.

155. Bidana M. Chengappa, "India-Pakistan Trade Relations," *Columbia International Affairs Online* 23, no. 3, June 1999; *www.ciaonet.org* (accessed September 21, 2006); Shirin Tahir Kehli, "India and Pakistan: Opportunities in Economic Growth, Technology and Security," A Report of the Balusa/Princeton Group, May 2–4, 1997.

156. *Pakistan Times* (Lahore), November, 20, 1977, quoted by Kahn, "Indo-Pakistan Trade," p. 197.

157. Saqlain Imam, "India and Pakistan Must Come Together to Restore their Economic Sovereignty," in Grover and Arora, *50 Years,* vol. 2, pp. 222–226, 222.

158. Bidana M. Chengappa, "India-Pakistan Trade Relations," *Columbia International Affairs Online* 23, no. 3, June 1999. www.ciaonet.org (accessed September 21, 2006).

159. Bajpai, "Bombs, Wars," p. 23.

160. Moonis Ahmar, *Chronology of Conflict and Cooperation in South Asia 1947–2001* (Karachi, 2001).

161. "Of Peace and Progress," *Financial Express,* September 20, 2005.

162. Vijay Sakhuja, "From Bus Service to Shipping: Agenda for India Pakistan Maritime Cooperation," *Observer Research Foundation: Strategic Trends* Vol. 3, issue. 19 (May 16, 2005).

163. Kahn, "Indo-Pakistan Trade," p. 202.

164. S. Mitra Kalita, "Firms Plan Landmark India-Pakistan Business Deal," *Washington Post,* July 28, 2005, D01; "India Pakistan Agree to Open Bank Branches," *Hindu Business Line,* November 7, 2005.

165. Suba Chandran, "Indo-Pak Summit—CBMs in the Economic Field," IPCS Article No. 513, Institute of Peace and Conflict Studies, New Delhi, June 27, 2001.

166. For a detailed analysis of the pipeline project, its potential benefits, and the obstacles it faces, see "India-Pakistan—Peace Pipe," Oxford Analytica Weekly Column, *Columbia International Affairs Online,* July 18, 2001.

167. Reported in the media; see, for instance, Jawed Naqvi, "India Accuses Pakistan of Harassing Its Diplomats," *Dawn,* November 10, 2001.

168. Vienna Convention on Diplomatic Relations, April 18, 1961, 500 UNTS 95; Vienna Convention on Consular Relations, April 24, 1963, 596 UNTS 261. See Naqvi, "India Accuses Pakistan"; "Pakistan Condemns India Over Illegal Diplomat Detention," *People's Daily,* December 21, 2001.

169. Ray, "Kargil and After," p. 440.

170. Michael Sullivan, "India Expels Pakistani Ambassador as Tensions Mount over Kashmir," "All Things Considered," NPR, May 18, 2002.

171. Agreement between the Government of India and the Government of the Islamic Republic of Pakistan Regarding Visa, September 14, 1974, available on Ministry of External Affairs Web site, *www.mea.gov.in* (accessed 12/28/05).

172. Lahore Joint Statement, Article 3(d).

173. B. Muralidhar Reddy, "Pak. Unimpressed with CBMs," *Hindu*, July 11, 2001, p. 1.

174. Pranab Dhal Samantha, "From April, Srinagar Can Take Bus to Muzaffarabad," *Indian Express*, February 17, 2005.

175. Sirah Ishrad Kahn, "Interview with Sudhir Vyas, Deputy High Commissioner, Islamabad," *Newsline*, July 2002.

176. Agreement between the Government of India and the Government of the Islamic Republic of Pakistan on Telecommunication, September 19, 1974, available on the Indian Ministry of External Affairs Web site, *www.mea .gov.in* (accessed 12/28/05).

177. Article VII of the Agreement on Telecommunication.

178. Agreement between the Government of India and the Government of the Islamic Republic of Pakistan Relating to the Exchange of Postal Articles, September 14, 1974, Article X, available on the Indian Ministry of External Affairs Web site, *www.mea.gov.in* (accessed 12/28/05).

179. Cultural Cooperation Agreement between the Government of the Republic of India and the Government of the Islamic Republic of Pakistan, December 31, 1988, available on the South Asia Foundation Web site, *www.south asiafoundation.org* (accessed 12/28/05).

180. Articles III and IV of the Cultural Cooperation Agreement.

181. Articles V, VII, and X of the Cultural Cooperation Agreement.

182. Pattanaik, "Indo-Pak Relations."

183. Ahmar, *Chronology of Conflict and Cooperation.*

184. See Pakistan-India Peoples' Forum for Peace and Democracy Web site, *www.pipfpd.org* (accessed 9/21/06).

185. K. K. Katyal, "The Tragedy of Track II," *Hindu*, February 19, 2001, p. 12.

186. C. Raja Mohan, "Diplomatic Notebook—In Defence of Track II Diplomacy," *Hindu*, June 4, 2001, p. 13.

187. See "History and Evolution of SAARC," SAARC Secretariat Home Page, *www.saarc-sec.org* (accessed 12/24/05).

188. For a full text of the agreement, see the SAARC Web site, *www.saarc-sec.org* (accessed 9/21/06).

189. Article 3 of SAPTA.

190. Rizvi, "Pakistan-India Relations," p. 385.

191. B. Muralidhar Reddy, "Foreign Secretaries Could Meet at *SAARC* Forum," *Hindu*, July 23, 2001, p. 13.

192. These include the United Nations Convention on the Law of the Sea, opened for signature December 10, 1982, UN Doc. A/CONF.62/122 (1982), 21 ILM 1261 (1982); the Convention on Biological Diversity, June 5, 1992, 31 ILM 818; the Convention on Wetlands of International Importance Especially as Waterfowl Habitat, opened for signature February 2, 1971 (1975), ATS No. 48 (entered into force December 21, 1975); the Convention on International Trade in Endangered Species of Wild Fauna and Flora, March 3, 1973, 27 UST 1087, 993 UNTS 243; the UN Convention to Combat Desertification in Countries Experiencing Serious

Drought and/or Desertification, June 17, 1994, 33 ILM 1328 (1994) (entered into force December 26, 1996).

193. Gaurav Rajen, "Cooperative Environmental Monitoring in the Coastal Regions of India and Pakistan," SAND 98–0505/11, Cooperative Monitoring Center, Sandia National Laboratories, Albuquerque, N.Mex., June 1999, p. 10.

194. See United Nations Environment Programme Web site, *www.unep.org* (accessed 12/23/05).

195. Rajen, "Cooperative Environmental Monitoring," p. 24.

196. "Three Day Meet of COSCAP-SA Inaugurated Today," Government of India Press Information Bureau, November 29, 2004, available on *www.pib.nic.in* (accessed 12/28/05).

197. South Asians for Human Rights Web site, *www.hurights.or.jp* (accessed 12/23/05).

198. Renuka Senananyake, "A New Dawn for Human Rights," *Financial Express*, August 27, 2000.

199. Kumar, "Trends in Indo-Pak Relations."

200. Bajpai, "Bombs, Wars," p. 17.

201. J. N. Dixit, introduction, in Rajeev Sharma, ed., *The Pakistan Trap* (New Delhi, 2001), pp. 1–12, 4.

202. Khan Zaman Mirza, "Pakistan's Foreign Policy in the 1990s with Reference to Kashmir Dispute," in Grover and Arora, *50 Years*, vol. 1, p. 120.

203. Kohli, "Pakistan's Quest," p. 192, quoting the leader of Pakistan's military coup, Ayub Khan.

204. See Smruti S. Pattanaik, "Pakistan's Kashmir Policy: Objectives and Approaches," *Strategic Analysis* 26, no. 2 (April–June 2002).

205. International Crisis Group Report, "India/Pakistan Relations and Kashmir: Steps toward Peace," ICG Asia Report No. 79, Islamabad/New Delhi/Brussels, June 24, 2004, p. 3.

206. International Crisis Group Report, "Kashmir: The View From New Delhi," ICG Asia Report No. 69, New Delhi/Brussles, December 4, 2003, pp. 18–20.

207. Tipu Salman Makhdoom, "Historical Perspective on the Kashmir Crisis," *Jurist*, June 7, 2002.

208. Pervaiz Iqbal Cheema, "CBMS and South Asia," *Regional Center for Strategic Studies Newsletters* 5, no. 4 (July 1999).

209. Text of Prime Minister Vajpayee's extempore speech to Indian-American audience, Washington, D.C., September 2000; quoted in Baweja, "The Logic of Third Party Mediation."

210. Musharraf himself stated that there could be no military solution to the dispute over Kashmir: see Farhan Bokhari, "No Military Solution in Kashmir, Says Musharraf," *Financial Times*, July 21, 2001, 1. In a similar vein, Vajpayee declared, "In our search for a lasting solution to the Kashmir problem, both in its external and internal dimensions, we shall not traverse solely on the beaten track of the past. Rather, we shall be bold and innovative designers of a future of peace and prosperity for the entire South Asian

region." See Ranjit Devraj, "South Asia: Vajpayee Offers Kashmir Peace Pledge," *Inter Press Service*, January 2, 2001.

211. Ahmar, "War Avoidance between India and Pakistan."

212. For a detailed analysis of the defense expenditure in India and Pakistan, see P. R. Chari and Ayesha Siddiqa-Agha, "Defence Expenditure in South Asia: India and Pakistan," Regional Centre for Strategic Studies Policy Paper No. 12, Colombo, Sri Lanka, June 2000.

213. *CIA World Factbook 2005, www.cia.gov* (accessed 12/23/05).

214. Ashutosh Misra, "Siachen Glacier Flashpoint: A Study of Indian Pakistani Relations," *Durham Middle East Papers*, no. 65 (June, 2000): 38–39.

215. "Pakistani Minister Says War with India 'Only Option.'"

216. Dellapenna, "Foreword," p. 244.

217. Pandey and Schaffer, "Building Confidence in India and Pakistan."

218. Ibid.

219. Kanti Bajpai, "CBMs: Context, Achievements, Functions," in Dipanker Banerjee, ed., *Confidence Building Measures in South Asia* (Colombo, Sri Lanka, 1999), pp. 26–27.

220. Baweja, "The Logic of Third Party Mediation," p. 89.

221. Pandey and Schaffer, "Building Confidence in India and Pakistan."

222. Kahn, "Interview with Sudhir Vyas, Deputy High Commissioner."

223. Ibid.

224. Pattanaik, "Pakistan's Kashmir Policy"; elsewhere, Pattanaik notes the importance of such increasing ties in bringing the parties closer together: Pattanaik, "Indo-Pak Relations."

225. Tim McGirk, "A Whole New Line: Pakistan's President Pervez Musharraf Takes a New Approach to the Age-old Kashmir Dispute," *Time Magazine, Asia*, November 8, 2004, p. 10.

226. Siddharth Varadarajan, "Looking Beyond Musharraf's Proposals," *Hindu*, November 1, 2004, p. 10.

227. B. Muralidhar Reddy, "The Musharraf's Formula," *Frontline* 21, no. 23 (November 6–November 19, 2004), p. 25.

3. Greece and Turkey

1. Bahar Rumelili, "Civil Society and the Europeanization of Greek-Turkish Cooperation," in *South European Society and Politics* 10, no. 1 (March 2005): 45–46, 47.

2. Dimitris Avramopoulus, Excerpts from Conference Held on March 29, 2000, hosted by the Western Policy Center, Washington, D.C.

3. Quoted by George McGhee in *The US-Turkish-NATO Middle-East Connection* (New York, 1990), p. 89.

4. Richard Clogg, "The Troubled Alliance: Greece and Turkey," in Richard Clogg, ed., *Greece in the 1980s* (London, 1980), pp. 123–149. Richard Clogg, *A Concise History of Greece* (Cambridge, 2002), pp. 91–97.

5. Sükrü S. Gürel, "Turkey and Greece," in Canan Balkir and Allan M. Williams, eds., *Turkey and Europe* (London, 1993), pp. 161–190, quote on p. 162.

6. Turkey's territory stands at 780,580 square kilometers compared with Greece's 131,940; Turkish population numbers 70 million to 10.7 million in Greece. See *CIA World Factbook, www.cia.gov* (accessed 12/21/05).

7. Quoted by Hosein Isiksal, "An Analysis of the Turkish-Greek Relations from Greek 'Self' and Turkish 'Other' Perspective: Causes of Antagonism and Preconditions for Better Relationships," *Alternatives: Turkish Journal of International Affairs* 1, no. 3 (Fall 2002): 116–135.

8. Ibid.

9. *CIA World Factbook 2005.*

10. Helen Chapin Metz, ed., *Turkey: A Country Study,* 5th ed. (Washington, D.C., 1996), p. 33.

11. Ibid., p. 34. Greek policy of territorial gains from the Ottoman Empire dated back almost to Greek independence, during which period Thessaly (1881), Macedonia, southern Epirus, several Aegean islands and Crete (1912–1913) were taken. See Gürel, "Turkey and Greece," p. 162.

12. Metz, *Turkey,* p. 35.

13. Erik J. Zürcher, *Turkey: A Modern History* (London, 1993), p. 168.

14. Treaty of Peace with Turkey, July 24, 1923, 28 LNTS 12.

15. See Convention Concerning the Exchange of Greek and Turkish Populations, signed at Lausanne, January 30, 1923, 32 LNTS 16; the mandatory exchange did not include some Greeks in Istanbul and Turks in Western Thrace and the Dodecanese Islands.

16. Thomas W. Gallant, *Modern Greece* (New York, 2001), p. 153.

17. Treaty of Friendship and Collaboration between the Turkish Republic, the Kingdom of Greece, and the Federal People's Republic of Yugoslavia, signed February 28, 1953; entered into force May 29, 1953, 167 UNTS 21.

18. Vamik D. Volkan and Norman Itzkowitz, *Turks and Greeks* (Cambridgeshire, 1994), p. 137; Nicole Pope and Hugh Pope, *Turkey Unveiled: Atatürk and After* (London, 1997), pp. 97, 115–118; Douglas A. Howard, *The History of Turkey* (Westport, Conn., 2001), p. 121.

19. Bahar Rumelili, "The European Union and Cultural Change in Greek-Turkish Relations," Working Paper Series in EU Border Conflicts Series, No. 17, University of Birmingham, Birmingham, UK, April 2005, p. 16.

20. See Articles 37–45 to the Treaty of Lausanne.

21. "Country Reports on Human Rights Practices—Greece," Bureau of Democracy, Human Rights, and Labor, U.S. State Department, March 4, 2002, p. 13. Loucas Tsilas, "Greek-Turkish Relations in the Post–Cold War Era," 20 *Fordham International Law Journal* 1589 (1997).

22. "Report to the OSCE—Implementation Meeting on Human Dimension Issues—Greece," International Helsinki Federation of Human Rights (IHF), Greek Helsinki Monitor (GHM) and Minority Rights Group—Greece (MRG-G), Warsaw, October 17–27, 2000 (hereafter, the Helsinki Report), p. 1.

23. See the Helsinki Report; "Second Report on Greece," *The European Commission Against Racism and Intolerance (ECRI),* June 27, 2000; "Third

Report on Greece," *The European Commission Against Racism and Intolerance (ECRI)*, June 8, 2004.

24. Greek Helsinki Monitor Press Release, January 19, 2005, available on *www.florina.org* (accessed 12/28/05).

25. Helsinki Report; U.S. State Department Country Reports on Human Rights Practices, Report on Greece for 2004, released February 28, 2005; Michael Stephen, "The Human Rights of the Turkish Minority in Western Thrace," Republic of Turkey, transcript of speech made at the symposium on human rights in Greece, November 12, 1998, in Bonn, Germany, and posted on the Web by the Republic of Turkey, Ministry of Foreign Affairs, now available on the Middle East Information Web site, *www.middleeat info.org* (accessed 12/27/05). See also Rumelili, "The European Union and Cultural Change," pp. 16–20.

26. Daphne Papahadjopoulos, "Greek Foreign Policy in the Post–Cold War Era: Implications for the European Union," Centre for European Policy Studies (CEPS) Papers Series, No. 72, Brussels, 1998, p. 28.

27. The Helsinki Report; U.S. State Department Report on Greece.

28. Papahadjopoulos, "Greek Foreign Policy," p. 27.

29. Metz, *Turkey,* p. 103.

30. Vincent Boland, "Faith, Hope and Parity," *Financial Times*, London, August 27, 2005, 16.

31. See "Background Information on Terrorist Groups, Patterns of Global Terrorism," Office of the Coordinator for Counterterrorism, U.S. Department of State, Appendix B, April 30, 2003, *www.state.gov* (accessed 12/23/05).

32. In Turkish eyes, "Greece has acted with impunity, disregarding the fact that Öcalan was a criminal sought by Interpol, lying about its actions to Turkey and its partners and deceiving the Kenyan authorities." See "Greece and the PKK Terrorism II," Foreign Ministry Publications, Republic of Turkey Ministry of Foreign Affairs, *www.mfa.gov.tr* (accessed 11/10/04).

33. For a detailed history of the island of Cyprus, see Sir George Hill, *A History of Cyprus* (Cambridge, 1949); Doros Alastos, *Cyprus In History* (London, 1955); H. D. Purcell, *Cyprus* (London, 1969); Thomas Ehrlich, "Cyprus: The 'Warlike Isle': Origins and Elements of the Current Crisis," 18 *Stanford Law Review* 1021 (1966); Zaim M. Nectaigil, *The Cyprus Question and the Turkish Position in International Law,* 2nd ed. (New York, 1993); Joseph S. Joseph, *Cyprus: Ethnic Conflict and International Politics,* 2nd ed. (Basingstoke, UK, 1997); Partick R. Hugg, "Cyprus in Europe: Seizing the Momentum of Nice," 34 *Vanderbilt Journal of Transnational Law* 1293, 1301 (2001).

34. Clement H. Dodd, "A Historical Overview," in Clement H. Dodd ed., *Cyprus: The Need for New Perspectives* (Huntingdon, UK, 1999), pp. 1–15, 2–3; Joseph, *Cyprus,* p. 16.

35. Purcell, *Cyprus,* pp. 192–194.

36. Ioannis D. Stefandis, *Isle of Discord: Nationalism, Imperialism and the Making of the Cyprus Problem,* vol. 1 (London, 1999). See also "The Convention of Defensive Alliance Between Great Britain and Turkey with Re-

spect to the Asiatic Provinces of Turkey," June 4, 1878, art. I, 153 Consol. T. S. 68–73.

37. Dodd, "A Historical Overview," p. 3.

38. Ibid., pp. 3–4; Ehrlich, "Cyprus: The 'Warlike Isle,'" p. 1026.

39. M. James Wilkinson, "Moving Beyond Conflict Prevention to Reconciliation: Tackling Greek-Turkish Hostility," in Adel Safty, ed., *Leadership and Conflict Resolution: The Middle-East, Greece-Turkey, the Caucasus, Post Soviet Russia, Rwanda, Northern Ireland, Latin America* (Famagusta, Cyprus, 1999), pp. 135–177, 138; Michael Schmidt, "Aegean Angst: A Historical and Legal Analysis of the Greek-Turkish Dispute," 2 *Roger Williams U. L. Rev.* 15, 22 (1996); Dodd, "A Historical Overview," 6.

40. Hugg, "Cyprus in Europe," 1310; Dodd, "A Historical Overview," 5; Volkan and Itzkowitz, *Turks and Greeks,* p. 137.

41. Basic Structure of the Republic of Cyprus, February 11, 1959, reprinted in Abram Chayes et al., *International Legal Process: Materials for an Introductory Course* (Boston, 1969), p. 559; Treaty of Guarantee Between the Republic of Cyprus, the Kingdom of Greece, the United Kingdom, and the Republic of Turkey, August 16, 1960, 382 UNTS 3; Treaty of Alliance between the Kingdom of Greece, the Republic of Turkey and the Republic of Cyprus, August 16, 1960, 397 UNTS 289.

42. Hugg, "Cyprus in Europe," pp. 1311–1312.

43. Necatigil, *The Cyprus Question and the Turkish Position in International Law,* pp. 32–33; Volkan and Itzkowitz estimate that the Turkish Cypriots, consisting of 18 percent of the population on the island, were forced to live in territory comprising only 3 percent of the island (*Turks and Greece,* p. 140).

44. See Report of the Secretary General of the United Nations to the Security Council on the United Nations Operations in Cyprus, UN Doc. S/5950 (September 10, 1964).

45. Security Council Resolution on the Creation of the United Nations Peacekeeping Force in Cyprus (UNFICYP), March 4, 1964., S. C. Res. 186 UN SCOR, 19th Sess., Supp. for Jan.–Mar. 1964, pp. 102–103, UN Doc. S/4474 (1964).

46. United Nations Force in Cyprus, *www.unficyp.org* (accessed 12/22/05).

47. "Cypriots Turks Suffered Because They Were, to a High Degree, Dehumanized in the Eyes of Greek Cypriots;" see Volkan and Itzkowitz, *Turks and Greeks,* p. 141.

48. Hugg, "Cyprus in Europe," p. 1315.

49. General Assembly Resolution on the Withdrawal of Foreign Armed Forces from Cyprus, United Nations Resolution No. 3212 (XXIX), November 1, 1974.

50. See Press and Information Office, Republic of Cyprus, *About Cyprus* (Cyprus, 2001), p. 23.

51. See UN SCOR, 30th Sess., Supp. for July-September 1975, pp. 39–40, UN Doc S/11789. Annex to Interim Report of the Secretary General Pursuant to Security Council Resolution 370 (1975).

52. The unilateral declaration was condemned by the UN in Security Council Resolutions 541 (18 Nov. 1983), 37th Sess., 2500th mtg., S/RES/541 (1983)

and 550 U.N. SCOR, 39th Sess., 2539th mtg. (1984), deeming the declaration both unlawful and invalid and calling for its immediate revocation.

53. Security Council Resolution 541, November 18, 1983. 37th Sess., 2500th meeting, S/Res/541 (1983).

54. "Cyprus to Protest to UN Against Turkish Troops' Weapon Upgrade," *BBC Worldwide Monitoring*, June 3, 2005.

55. Both quotes appear in Press and Information Office, Republic of Cyprus, *About Cyprus*, p. 25.

56. Glenn E. Curtis, ed., *Greece: A Country Study*, Federal Research Division, Library of Congress (Washington, D.C., 1994), p. 28.

57. The Four Guidelines, 75 Reports SG S/12323 of April 30, 1977, pp. 2–3, paragraph 1 (for the resumption of inter-communal talks).

58. Eric Solsten, ed., *Cyprus: A Country Study*, Federal Research Division, Library of Congress (Washington, D.C., 1993), pp. 43–45.

59. UN Doc., The Ten Point Agreement, S/13369 (May 31, 1979).

60. Wilkinson, "Moving Beyond," p. 149.

61. Suzanne Palmer, "The Republic of Northern Cyprus: Should the United States Recognize it as an Independent State," 4 *Boston University Law Review*, 423 450 (1986).

62. Set of Ideas, Annexed to United Nations, Security Council, Report of the Secretary General to his Mission of Good Offices in Cyprus, UN Doc. S/24473, New York (August 21, 1992). The Security Council subsequently adopted the Secretary General's report—see Security Council Resolution 774 UN SCOR, 47th Sess., 309th meeting, p. 94, UN Doc. S/Res/774 (1992).

63. Dodd, "A Historical Overview," p. 12.

64. See United Nations Security Council Resolution 789 (1992), S/Res/789 (1992), November 25, 1992.

65. Clement H. Dodd, *The Cyprus Imbroglio* (Huntington, UK, 1998), p. 54.

66. Ibid., pp. 54–55. In practical terms, the reopening of the airport would have meant increased trade, tourism, and a de facto lifting of the economic embargo off the Turkish Cypriots. Varosha was to become a free trade zone and a prosperous tourism center. Additional measures included reducing the size of the Turkish contingency on the island, extending the UN buffer zone around the Green Line to include Varosha, and some people-to-people initiatives—see Necatigil, *The Cyprus Question*, p. 397. The Greek Cypriots expressed concern over the implied recognition in the TRNC, if the proposed CBMs were to be implemented.

67. Haralambos Athanasopulos, *Greece, Turkey and the Aegean Sea: A Case Study in International Law* (Jefferson, N.C., 2001), p. 46; Lt. Col. Michael N. Schmitt, "Aegean Angst: A Historical and Legal Analysis of the Greek-Turkish Dispute," 2 *Roger Williams University Law Review* 15, 20–24 (1996).

68. Convention Relating to the Regimes of the Straits (Straits of the Dardenelles Convention), July 24, 1923, appendix, Art. 4(3), 28 LNTS 115, 129.

69. Convention Relating to the Regimes of the Straits (Montreux Convention), July 20, 1936, 173 LNTS 213.

70. Treaty of Paris, February 10, 1947, 61 Stat. 1245, 49 UNTS 3.

71. Papahadjopoulos, "Greek Foreign Policy," p. 34.
72. United Nations Convention of the Law of the Sea, opened for signature December 10, 1982 (hereafter UNCLOS), Art. 2–3, 18–19, 121(2) reprinted in 21 ILM 1261, 1263–1267, 1273–1277, 1291.
73. The current six miles of territorial sea leave 43.6 percent of the Aegean under Greek control, 7.4 percent under Turkish control, and the remaining 48.8 percent as high seas. Extending the six miles to twelve would grant Greece control over 71.5 percent of the Aegean and Turkey 8.8 percent, and the high seas would be left at only 19.7 percent. See Ali Karaosmanoglu, "Las Disputal Greco-Turcas Sobre el Mar Egeo y Chipre," *Meridiano*, Centro Espagnol de Relacione Internacionales (CERI), No. 13, February, 1997, p. 23; quoted by Papahadjopoulos, "Greek Foreign Policy," p. 35. See also Schmitt, "Aegean Angst," p. 25.
74. See Schmitt, "Aegean Angst," p. 28, referring also to Malcolm D. Evans, *Relevant Circumstances and Maritime Delimitation* (New York, 1989). Turkey did extend its own territorial waters in the Mediterranean Sea and the Black Sea to twelve nautical miles; see Athanasopulos, *Greece, Turkey and the Aegean Sea,* p. 71.
75. Athanasopulos, *Greece, Turkey and the Aegean Sea,* pp. 137–138.
76. Papahadjopoulos, "Greek Foreign Policy," p. 36.
77. For an analysis of the legality of the Greek decree on airspace, see George Assonitis, "The Greek Airspace: The Legality of a 'Paradox,'" 8 *United States Air Force Academy Journal of Legal Studies* 159 (1997–1998); but compare Schmitt, "Aegean Angst," pp. 45–46.
78. Andrew Wilson, *The Aegean Dispute* (London, 1979), p. 24.
79. According to the Greek Ministry of Foreign Affairs, the Athens FIR was agreed upon at the Regional Air-Traffic Conferences in 1950, 1952, and 1958, in all of which Turkey participated and fully accepted the boundaries of Greece's FIR. See The Athens Flight Information Region (FIR Athens), Hellenic Republic, Ministry of Foreign Affairs, 2002, *www.mfa.gr* (accessed 12/22/05).
80. See UNCLOS, Art. 76(1) and 121(2), reprinted in ILM 1261, 1285, 1291; Convention on the Continental Shelf, April 29, 1958, Art. 1, 15 UST 471, TIAS No. 5578, 499 UNTS 312.
81. Papahadjopoulos, "Greek Foreign Policy," p. 34.
82. UNCLOS, Art. 83(1), reprinted in 21 ILM 1261, 1286.
83. United Nations Security Council Resolution 395, 31 UN SCOR (1953rd meeting), p. 15, UN Doc. S/INF/32 (1976).
84. See Aegean Sea Continental Shelf *(Greece v. Turk.),* Interim Protection, 1976 ICJ REP. 3 (Order of September 11); and 1978 ICJ REP. 3 (Judgment of December 19).
85. The Berne Declaration on the Procedure to be Followed for the Delimitation of the Continental Shelf by Greece and Turkey, Signed in Berne, November 11, 1976, available on *www.turkishgreek.org/Bern.htm* (accessed 9/22/06). Athanasopulos, *Greece, Turkey and the Aegean Sea,* p. 48.
86. Schmitt, "Aegean Angst," pp. 41–42.

87. Athanasopulos, *Greece, Turkey and the Aegean Sea*, p. 10.
88. Turkish Embassy in Washington, D.C., Aegean Disputes, available on *www.turkishembassy.org* (accessed 12/21/05).
89. Wilkinson, "Moving Beyond," p. 144.
90. See Canan Balkir and Allan M. Williams, introduction, in Canan Balkir and Allan M. Williams, eds., *Turkey and Europe* (London, 1993), 1–23. See also Patrick Hugg, who notes, "Turkey's general Muslim Character itself may generate the most pervasive European bias against Turkey. From general uneasiness over cultural differences, to overt xenophobia and religious discrimination, the Muslim and Christian worlds often distrust one another. This broad tension—easier to recognize than to measure or justify—unavoidably instills a heavy inertia against integration between the two spheres. The general European uneasiness about Islam will inevitably generate resistance to the acceptance of Turkey." Patrick R. Hugg, "The Republic of Turkey in Europe: Reconsidering the Luxemburg Exclusion," 23 *Fordham Int'l L. J.* 606 (2000), p. 627.
91. Agreement Creating an Association between the Republic of Turkey and the European Economic Community (The Ankara Agreement), September 12, 1963, entered into force December 1, 1964. 3 I.L.M. 65 Papahadjopoulos, "Greek Foreign Policy," p. 51. An association agreement between the EEC and Cyprus had been signed as long ago as 1972, but its implementation was suspended following the 1974 Turkish invasion. In 1987 Cyprus and the EC agreed on the gradual implementation of a customs union, and in 1990 the Cypriot government applied for a full membership in the EU.
92. Declaration Adopted by the 15 Ministers of Foreign Affairs of the EU at the Last General Affairs Council on July 15, 1996, SN 3543/96.
93. Agenda 2000, Communication of the European Commission, DOC 97/6, Strasbourg, July 15, 1997.
94. Luxembourg European Council, December 12 and 13, 1997, Presidency Conclusions, Luxembourg, December 13, 1997, European Council, DOC/ 97/24.
95. Lee Hockstader and Kelly Couturier, "Ankara Ready to Sever European Ties," *Washington Post*, December 15, 1997, A22; Hugg, "The Republic of Turkey in Europe," pp. 651–652.
96. See Statement by the Ministry of Foreign Affairs of the Republic of Turkey, Concerning the EU Luxemburg Summit Conclusions on Cyprus, December 14, 1997, *www.mfa.gov.gr* (accessed 12/22/05).
97. Agreement between the Government of the Republic of Turkey and the Government of the Turkish Republic of Northern Cyprus on the Establishment of an Association Council, August 6, 1997, *www.mfa.gov.tr* (accessed 12/22/05).
98. For a criticism of the Luxemburg conclusions, see Hugg, "The Republic of Turkey in Europe."
99. Presidency Conclusions at the Helsinki European Council, December 10–11, 1999. Available on www.europa.eu.int/council (accessed 9/21/06).

100. See the Presidency Conclusions at the Nice European Council Meeting, December 7–9, 2000, pp. 1–2. Available on *www.europa.eu/european-council* (accessed 9/23/06). For a detailed analysis of the Nice summit and its implications for the Cyprus conflict, see Hugg, "Cyprus in Europe."

101. Kenneth B. Moss, "Untying the Aegean Knot: Options for Washington," *Western Policy Center Paper,* August/September 2001, p. 1.

102. Mehmet Ali Birand, "Turkey and the 'Davos Process,' " in Dimitri Constas, ed., *The Greek-Turkish Conflict in the 1990s* (New York, 1991), pp. 27–39, 30–31.

103. Ibid., p. 36.

104. Wilkinson, "Moving Beyond," p. 141.

105. Papahadjopoulos, "Greek Foreign Policy," p. 25.

106. Tasos Kokkinides, "Fuelling Balkan Fires: The West's Arming of Greece and Turkey," *British American Security Information Council (BASIC),* Report No. 93 (London, 1993).

107. Gürel, "Turkey and Greece," p. 164.

108. McGhee, *The US-Turkish-NATO Middle East Connection,* p. 178.

109. "Cyprus Conflict Comes to a Boil, U.N., U.S. Fault Turkey for Greek Cypriot Deaths," *CNN World News,* August 15, 1996, available on *www.cnn.com* (accessed 9/23/06); "Greek Cypriot Shot Dead After Crossing into Turkish Part of Island," *Deutsche Presse-Agentur,* October 13, 1996. UN reports condemned the "deteriorating situation" in Cyprus, noting that the two incidents in which the casualties were suffered were the worst since 1974; see Press Release, United Nations Security Council, "Security Council Extend Mandate of UNFICYP Until 30 June 1997," UN Doc. SC/6307 (December 23, 1994).

110. An Initiative for Peace, in the Turkish Embassy in Washington, D.C., Background Note on Aegean Dispute, now available on the Australian-Turkish Media Group Web site, *www.atmg.org* (accessed 12/25/05); "Statement by Prime Minister Yilmaz on the Aegean Questions," March 24, 1996, Republic of Turkey, Turkish Ministry of Foreign Affairs, *www.mfa.gov.tr* (no longer available).

111. Helena Smith, "Peace Hope in Aegean," *Guardian,* July 16, 1997, 14.

112. Wilkinson, "Moving Beyond," pp. 159–160.

113. Hugg, "Cyprus in Europe," p. 1323; Dodd, *The Cyprus Imbroglio,* p. 102.

114. "Cyprus Missile Deal Heightens Tensions," *Guardian,* January 6, 1997, 10; Reuters, "Cyprus Greeks in Missile Deal with Russians," *New York Times,* January 6, 1997, A6; on the strategic implications of the S-300 deployment, see Dan Lindley, "The Military Factor in the Eastern Mediterranean," in Dodd, *Cyprus: The Need for New Perspectives,* pp. 195–230, 207–211.

115. The declaration noted that "any attack against the Turkish Republic of Northern Cyprus will be considered as an attack against the Republic of Turkey" and promised that "in the event that the joint Greek-Greek Cypriot front continues its endeavors to alter the balance between Turkey and Greece . . . and to endanger the security of the Turkish Cypriot people, reciprocal military and political measures will continue to be put into effect

without hesitation." See Joint Declaration, January 20, 1997, *www.mfa .gov.gr* (accessed 12/22/05).

116. Carol Migdalovitz, *Cyprus: Status of U.N. Negotiations*, Congressional Research Service (CRS) Issue Brief for Congress, updated March 19, 2002, p. 5.

117. Stephen Kinzer, "Politically Weak at Home, Turks Flex Muscles Abroad," *New York Times*, June 20, 1998, A5.

118. Letter from Mr. Ismail Cem, Foreign Minister of the Republic of Turkey, to Mr. George Papandreou, Foreign Minister of the Republic of Greece, May 24, 1999, available on *www.turkishgreek.org* (accessed 9/25/06).

119. Letter from Mr. George Papandreou, Foreign Minister of the Republic of Greece, to Mr. Ismail Cem, Foreign Minister of the Republic of Turkey, June 25, 1999, available on *www.turkishgreek.org* accessed 9/25/06.

120. "Continued Progress on Turkey Relations," Woodrow Wilson International Center for Scholars, Washington, D.C. (December 1999), *www.wilson center.org* (accessed 12/25/05).

121. "Expanded Cooperation with Turkey Across Bilateral Spectrum," Woodrow Wilson International Center for Scholars, Washington, D.C. (January 2000), *www.wilsoncenter.org* (accessed 12/25/05). Planes leaving the Larnaca airport in Cyprus are still not permitted to fly in Turkish airspace, so there are no direct flights from Cyprus to Turkey.

122. Stephen Kinzer, "Greeks, Turks OK Cooperative 'New Era,' " *New York Times*, January 21, 2000, p. 18.

123. Leyla Boulton, "Greek Bank in Turkish Investment Plan: Unusual Partnership Aims to Cross Political and Cultural Divide to Tap Attractive Market in Unlisted Companies," *Financial Times*, September 13, 2000, 37.

124. George Papandreou, "Revision in Greek Foreign Policy," Western Policy Center Paper, Washington, D.C. (January 2000), p. 1.

125. Ibid; see also Stephen Kinzer, "Natural Disaster Helps Draw Two Enemies Closer," *New York Times*, August 22, 1999, Sec. 4 3.

126. See "U.S. Policy in the Eastern Mediterranean: Managing The Greece, Turkey, Cyprus Triangle," Testimony of John Sitilides, Executive Director, Western Policy Center, before the House Committee on International Relations–Europe Subcommittee, June 13, 2001. Available on *www.comm docs.house.gov* (accessed 09/26/06).

127. Hugg, "Cyprus in Europe," p. 1327; a *New York Times* correspondent described Cem as "a thoughtful former journalist who disdains rabble-rousing statements" and Papandreou as "equally earnest and soft-spoken." See Stephen Kinzer, "Natural Disaster Helps Draw Greece, Turkey Closer."

128. F. Stephen Larrabee, "Greek-Turkish Rapprochement: Is It Durable?" Western Policy Center Paper (May/June 2000), p. 2.

129. Hellenic Republic Ministry of Foreign Affairs Official Web site, *www.mfa.gov .gr* (accessed 10/18/05).

130. Dick Leonard, "Finnish Presidency Ends in Success," *Europe*, February 2000, 4, quoted by Hugg, "Cyprus in Europe," p. 1328.

131. "U.S. Policy in the Eastern Mediterranean."

132. Joint Declaration on Turkey-Greece Cooperation in EU Matters, Ankara,

April 6, 2001, Republic of Turkey, Ministry of Foreign Affairs, *www.mfa .gov.tr* (accessed 12/22/05).

133. "U.S. Policy in the Eastern Mediterranean."

134. "Support for Turkey's EU Accession Talks in Return for Progress on Cyprus and Aegean Issues," Woodrow Wilson International Center for Scholars, Washington, D.C. (August 30, 2002), *www.wilsoncenter.org* (accessed 12/25/05).

135. "Memorandum of Understanding on Confidence-Building Measures," Athens, May 17, 1988; reprinted in Athanasios Platias, *Greek Deterrence Strategy,* Institute of International Relations, Appendix 2, *www.idis.gr* (accessed 12/22/05). This is another example of an agreement titled "Confidence-Building Measures," which is, in fact, an island of agreement. Guidelines for the Prevention of Accidents and Incidents on the High Seas and in International Airspace, Istanbul, September 8, 1988; reprinted in Platias, *Greek Deterrence Strategy,* Appendix 3 (hereafter, The Istanbul Guidelines).

136. The Athens Memorandum, paragraphs 1–3.

137. The Istanbul Guidelines, paragraphs A–B.

138. "To date the agreements have constantly been breached by both sides, and the violations opened the way to a multitude of dangerous accidents in the Aegean, prompting international anxiety over a heated confrontation between the two NATO allies," Sibel Utku, "Turkey and Greece Take a Small Step Forward," *Turkish Daily News,* June 14, 1998.

139. Maj. Kevin Dougherty and Maj. Aric Whateley, "A Summary of the Longstanding Disputes Between Greece and Turkey," *Foreign Area Officers Association Journal,* January 21, 2000, *www.faoa.org/journal* (accessed 9/26/ 06); Utku, "Turkey and Greece Take a Small Step."

140. Platias, *Greek Deterrence Strategy,* Chapter 2 (5).

141. Rupert Cornwell, "Greece Claims Turkey Buzzed Minister's Jet," *Independent,* October 17, 1997, 12.

142. "Political, Military Confidence Building in the Works," Woodrow Wilson International Center for Scholars, Washington, D.C. (December 2000), *www.wilsoncenter.org* (accessed 12/25/05).

143. "Confidence-Building Between Greece and Turkey," *NATO Update,* December 6–12, 2000, *www.nato.int/docu* (accessed 9/26/06).

144. "Turkey, Greece Discuss Aegean Confidence Measures," *Reuters,* December 5, 2002.

145. George A. Papandreou, "An Olympic Truce for the Athens Games: Passing the Torch," *International Herald Tribune,* June 4, 2004, 8.

146. Mandy Kirby, "Turkey, Greece Claim Commitment to Reducing Tensions over Territorial Violations," *World Markets Analysis,* April 13, 2005.

147. "Ankara Denies Pledge to Revise Aegean Policy," *Turkish Daily News,* April 13, 2005.

148. Joint Statement by Mr. Ismail Cem, the Minister of Foreign Affairs of the Republic of Turkey, and Mr. George Papandreou, the Minister of Foreign Affairs of the Hellenic Republic on Anti-Personnel Land Mines, Ankara, April 6, 2001, *www.mfa.gov.tr* (accessed 12/22/05). Convention on the Prohi-

bition of the Use, Stockpiling, Production and Transfer of Anti-Personnel Mines and Their Destruction, Ottawa, September 18, 1997, 36 ILM 1507.

149. Elif Unal, "Turkey and Greece Agree to Clear Landmines," *Reuters,* April 6, 2001.

150. "Turkey Decides to Accept the Ottawa Convention on Land Mines," *Turkish Daily News,* March 16, 2002.

151. Kathy Tzilivakis, "Greece to Scrap Evros Landmines Ahead of Turkey," *Athens News,* March 30, 2002.

152. "Landmine Monitor Report 2005: Cyprus," International Campaign to Ban Landmines, *www.icbl.org* (accessed 12/25/05).

153. Agreement between the Republic of Turkey and the Hellenic Republic on Cooperation of the Ministry of Internal Affairs of the Republic of Turkey and the Ministry of Public Order of the Hellenic Republic on Combating Crime, Especially Terrorism, Organized Crime, Illicit Drug Trafficking and Illegal Immigration, Ankara, January 20, 2000 (came into force on July 17, 2001) available on *www.mfa.gov.gr.*

154. "1,129 Pound of Heroin Seized From Buses," *Chicago Tribune,* January 1, 2001, 9.

155. Helena Smith, "Ankara and Athens Agree on Migrants," *Guardian,* November 9, 2001, 15.

156. "Greece Minister Considers Turkey 'Strategic Economic Partner,'" *BBC Worldwide Monitoring,* June 30, 2005.   .

157. Wilkinson, "Moving Beyond," pp. 161–162.

158. Agreement between the Republic of Turkey and the Hellenic Republic on Economic Cooperation, Athens, February 4, 2000 (came into force November 24, 2001) available on *www.mfa.gov.gr.*

159. "Greek-Turkish Economic Cooperation Interministerial Talks Commence," *Embassy of Greece News Flash,* Washington, D.C., February 13, 2002, *www.greekembassy.org* (accessed 12/25/05).

160. "Bilateral Relations (The Rapprochement Process)," Hellenic Republic, Ministry of Foreign Affairs (updated to December 16, 2002), *www.mfa .gov.gr* (accessed 12/22/05).

161. "Economic Cooperation with Turkey Furthered through Interministerial Talks," Woodrow Wilson International Center for Scholars, Washington, D.C. (March 2002), *www.wilsoncenter.org* (accessed 12/25/05).

162. "New Consulate Sought in Turkey to Promote Economic Relations," Woodrow Wilson International Center for Scholars," Washington D.C. (September 13, 2002), *www.wilsoncenter.org* (accessed 12/25/05).

163. "Turkish-Greek Economic Summit Ends with More Cooperation," *Turkish Daily News,* June 14, 2002.

164. Rumelili, "The European Union and Cultural Change," p. 24.

165. "Turkey and Greece Sign Gas Pipeline Protocol," *Turkish Daily News,* March 29, 2002.

166. "Turkey Country Analysis Brief," Energy Information Administration, Department of Energy, U.S. Government, Washington, D.C., *www.eia.doe .gov* (accessed 12/27/05).

167. "Joint Ventures with Turkey in Energy Market," Woodrow Wilson International Center for Scholars," Washington, D.C. (February 2000), *www .wilsoncenter.org* (accessed 12/25/05).

168. "Step-By-Step Progress in Turkey Rapprochement," Woodrow Wilson International Center for Scholars," Washington, D.C. (July 2001), *www.wilson center.org* (accessed 12/25/05).

169. "Education for the Muslim Minority Children," Institute of Language and Speech Processing, Athens, *www.ilsp.gr* (accessed 10/19/05). Ahmet O. Evin, "Changing Greek Perspectives on Turkey: An Assessment of the Post-earthquake Rapprochement," *Turkish Studies,* 5, iss. 1 (Spring 2004): 4–20.

170. Rumelili, "The European Union and Cultural Change," pp. 5–9.

171. "Emergency Response to Disasters," General Assembly Resolution 54/30 of November 22, 1999.

172. "Emergency Response to Disasters," Report of the Secretary General, UN General Assembly, 57th Sess., August 16, 2002.

173. Memorandum of Understanding between the United Nations, the Government of the Hellenic Republic, and the Government of the Republic of Turkey on Cooperation in the Field of Humanitarian Assistance Response, September, 16, 2002). Available on *www.reliefweb.int* (accessed 09/26/06).

174. "Broad Cross-Border Cooperation with Turkish Cities, Towns," Woodrow Wilson International Center for Scholars, Washington, D.C. (April 2001), *www.wilsoncenter.org* (accessed 12/25/05).

175. WINPEACE—Peace Initiative of Women From Turkey and Greece, *www .winpeace.net* (accessed 12/25/05).

176. See PeaceWomen Project, *www.peacewomen.org* (accessed 12/23/05).

177. Oliver Wolleh, "Cyprus: A Civil Society Caught Up in the Question of Recognition," in Paul von Tongeren, ed., *Searching for Peace in Europe and Eurasia: An Overview of Conflict Prevention and Peacebuilding Activities* (Boulder, Colo., 2002), pp. 156–168.

178. NATO Allied Forces in Southern Europe, "Exercise Dynamic Mix 2000," *www.afsouth.nato.int* (accessed 12/23/05).

179. Utku, "Turkey and Greece Take a Small Step Forward."

180. John Ward Anderson, "Greece, Turkey Dash Latest Hopes for Thaw; Sudden End to NATO Drill Spells Uncertain Future," *Washington Post,* October 26, 2000, A28.

181. "Aegean Islands 'Demilitarization' Issue Resurfaces," Woodrow Wilson International Center for Scholars, Washington, D.C. (May–June 2001), *www.wilsoncenter.org* (accessed 12/25/05).

182. "Airspace Dispute with Turkey Leads to Cancellation of Part of NATO Exercise," Woodrow Wilson International Center for Scholars, Washington, D.C. (September 20, 2002), *www.wilsoncenter.org* (accessed 12/25/05).

183. Mete Belavocikli, "Turkey Begins Informing Greece of Its Military Flights over the Aegean Sea: Papandreau Facilitates Turkish Flight Information Gesture," *Turkish Daily News,* February 8, 2002.

184. Statement by the Secretary General of NATO, Press Release 087, 23 July 2003, official Web site of NATO, *www.nato.int,* (accessed 10/19/05).

185. Michael R. Gordon, "Turkey Offers Troops for New European Force, with a Proviso," *New York Times*, November 22, 2000, A9; John Hulsman, "Strengthening Alliances: Resolving the EU-Turkey Impasse on European Security," Woodrow Wilson International Center for Scholars, Washington, D.C. (April 2001), *www.wilsoncenter.org* (accessed 12/25/05).

186. Ian Black, "Turkey Relents to Pave Way for EU Force," *Guardian*, December 16, 2002, 10.

187. Elizabeth G. Book, "Multi-National Brigade Set to Deploy in Balkans," *National Defense* 87, no. 589 (December 1, 2002): 36.

188. Adm. T. Joseph Lopez, "A Politico-Military Success in the Balkans," Woodrow Wilson International Center for Scholars, Washington D.C. (December 16, 1998), *www.wilsoncenter.org* (accessed 12/25/05).

189. The origin of the BSEC is the 1992 Istanbul Declaration, which first set out the initiative of a regional economic cooperation structure. The BSEC charter was later concluded in Yalta, in June 1998, and was ratified by the member states' parliament on May 1, 1999. See "The Work Programme of Turkey During Its Chairmanship of the Black Sea Economic Cooperation Organization" (BSEC), May–November 1, 2001, Press Statement, Republic of Turkey, Ministry of Foreign Affairs, April 2, 2001, *www.photius.com* (accessed 12/22/05).

190. Charter on Good-Neighbourly Relations, Stability, Security, and Cooperation in Southeastern Europe, Bucharest, February 12, 2000, available on *www.mfa.gov.gr.*

191. Southeast European Cooperation Initiative, *www.secinet.org* (accessed 12/22/05).

192. Chris Drake, "Dying Boy Helps Heal Island's Wounds; Turkish and Greek Cypriots Put Aside Years of Enmity in the Desperate Hunt for a Bone Marrow Donor," *Guardian*, March 29, 2000, 19.

193. "Turk, Greek Cypriots Increase Insults, Obscenities," *Deutsche Presse-Agentur*, June 11, 1999; Douglas Frantz, "Cyprus Still Split by a Zone Where Time Stands Still," *New York Times*, January 22, 2002, A10.

194. Chris Morris, "Turks Dismiss Cyprus Talks," *Guardian*, November 25, 2000, 18; Leyla Boulton, "Turk Cypriot Leader May Quit U.N. Talks," *Financial Times*, November 28, 2000, 2; Leyla Boulton, "Turks Feel Growing Sense of Betrayal over EU Demands," *Financial Times*, November 29, 2000, 2.

195. Andreas Hadjipapas, Carola Hoyos, and Quentin Peel, "U.N. Sets Out a New Peace Plan for Cyprus," *Financial Times*, November 12, 2002, 1.

196. See Philip H. Gordon and Henri J. Barkey, "Two Countries and One Continent's Future," *New York Times*, December 2, 2002, A21; Michael Theodoulou, "Cypriot Leader to Miss EU Summit," *Times*, December 11, 2002, 17.

197. Gordon and Barkey, "Two Countries and One Continent's Future."

198. Leyla Boulton, "Turkish Cypriots May Pose Threat to EU Talks," *Financial Times*, December 16, 2002, 6; Leyla Boulton, "Denktash Line on Peace Plan Rouses Turkish Cypriots Ire," *Financial Times*, December 17, 2002, 6.

199. Helena Smith, "Turkish Cypriots Turn on Denktash," *Guardian*, December 16, 2002, 10.

200. Martin Woollacott, "Comment and Analysis: Free Movement May Still Heal the Division of Cyprus: Greek and Turkish Cypriots Are Acting as If They Already Had a Deal," *Guardian*, May 9, 2003, 24.

201. Angelique Chrisafis, "Dazzled Cyprus Fears a False Dawn," *Guardian*, May 3, 2003, 22.

202. "Unity?" *Economist*, April 3, 2004.

203. "Cyprus 'Spurns Historic Chance,'" *BBC News*, April 25, 2004.

204. Van Coufoudakis, "A Briefing on Cyprus: A Year After the Referendum— A Year After EU Accession," *American Hellenic Institute—Washington D.C.*, April 13, 2004.

205. "Northern Cyprus Aid Put on Shelf," *Financial Times*, December 27, 2005, 5; "Red Tape Snarls Bid to End Turkish Cypriot Isolation," *Financial Times*, December 15, 2004, 8.

206. Quentin Peel, "How Cyprus's Wounds Are Hurting Europe," *Financial Times*, December 23, 2004, 21.

207. M. James Wilkinson, "Moving Beyond," p. 136.

208. Athanasopulos, *Greece, Turkey and the Aegean Sea*, p. 131.

209. "Erdogan, Seeking Support for Turkey's EU Accession, Meets with Simitis in Athens," Woodrow Wilson International Center for Scholars, Washington, D.C. (November 22, 2002), *www.wilsoncenter.org* (accessed 12/25/05).

210. Media Info 2004—Media Services for the Olympics, *www.mediainfo 2004.gr* (accessed 10/19/05).

211. "Since 2002, over 30 rounds of secret negotiations have taken place at the technical level on the Aegean border disputes between the two foreign ministries. Reportedly, however, the two sides are very close to an agreement" (Bahar Rumelili, "Civil Society," pp. 45–56, quote on p. 50); see also Tarik Oguzlu, "The Latest Turkish-Greek Détente: Instrumentalist Play for EU Membership, or Long-Term Institutionalist Cooperation?" *Cambridge Review of International Affairs*, 17, iss. 2 (July 2004): 337–354.

212. Jacob M. Landau, ed., *Ataturk and the Modernization of Turkey* (Boulder, Colo., 1984), xiii.

213. A. J. R. Groom, "Cyprus: Back in the Doldrums," in *300 The Round Table: A Quarterly Review of the Politics of the British Empire*, issue no. 300, London (1986), pp. 362–383, quoted by Gürel, "Turkey and Greece," p. 162.

214. "Mutual Landmine Clearance Along Turkish Border," Woodrow Wilson International Center for Scholars, Washington, D.C. (April 2001), *www .wilsoncenter.org* (accessed 12/25/05).

215. Robin Gedye, "Turkey and Greece in Defence Pact," *Daily Telegraph*, January 21, 2004, 14.

216. For Greece, the estimate is that 4.3 percent of its GDP is spent on military expenditure; for Turkey, the estimate is 5.1 percent. See the Central Intelligence Agency, *The World Factbook 2005, www.cia.gov* (accessed 12/22/05).

217. Olli Rehn, Member of the European Commission, Commissioner for Enlargement, "Accession Negotiations with Turkey: Fulfilling the Criteria," to the European Economic and Social Committee EU-Turkey JCC in Brussels on November 28, 2005, official site of the European Commission, Press Room, Press Releases, Speech/05/733, *www.europa.eu.int* (accessed 12/22/05).

218. Stephen Castle, "Turkey Agrees to EU Customs Union," *Independent*, July 30, 2005, 27.
219. Letter from Minister Papandreou to Minister Cem.
220. Letter from Minister Cem to Minister Papandreou.
221. Platias, *Greek Deterrence Strategy*, chapter 2(5).
222. Letter from Minister Papandreou to Minister Cem.
223. *Loizidou v. Turkey*, 23 Eur. Ct. HR 513 (1996).
224. *Cyprus v. Turkey*, App. No. 25781/94, 35 Eur. Ct. HR 967 (2001).
225. Frank Hoffmeister, "*Cyprus v. Turkey*. App. No. 25781/94," 96(2) *American Journal of International Law* 445–452 (2002).
226. Coufoudakis, "A Year After."
227. *Cyprus v. Turkey*, para. 174.
228. Ali Carkoglu and Kemal Kirisci, "The View from Turkey: Perceptions of Greeks and Greek-Turkish Rapprochement by the Turkish Public," *Turkish Studies 5*, no. 1 (Spring 2004): 117–153, 122–124.
229. See public opinion polling Web site *www.dimoskopisi.gr* (accessed 12/04/05).
230. Penelope Papailias, "TV across the Aegean: The Greek Love Affair with a Turkish Serial," C. P. Cavafy Professorship in Modern Greek, University of Michigan, available on *www.lsa.umich.edu* (accessed on 12/27/05).
231. The incident concerned a Turkish oceanographic vessel, the *Piri Reis*, that was conducting scientific research in the Aegean. Rumors that the *Piri Reis* might be engaged in oil explorations had to be officially refuted by Athens; see "Government Denies Crisis Over 'Piri Reis' Survey in Aegean," Embassy of Greece—Press Office, Washington, D.C., May 31, 2001, *www.greekembassy.org* (accessed 12/23/05). Only the personal involvement of the two foreign ministers averted collision.
232. Papailias, "TV across the Aegean."
233. Tsilas, "Greek-Turkish Relations in the Post–Cold War Era."

4. Israel and Lebanon

1. For a lengthier discussion of the 1966 Israel-Lebanon Cease-fire Understanding and the Israel-Lebanon Monitoring Group, see Adir Waldman, *Arbitrating Armed Conflict: Decisions of the Israel-Lebanon Monitoring Group* (Huntington, N.Y., 2003).
2. Following the 1948 Israeli War of Independence and pursuant to the United Nations Security Council Resolution of November 16, 1948, the two countries signed the Israeli-Lebanese General Armistice Agreement, March 23, 1949, which governed their relationship until the 1967 Six Day War. Asserting that the war constituted a material breach of the armistice agreement, Israel unilaterally annulled its 1949 armistice agreements with Lebanon as well as its three other agreements with Syria, Egypt, and Jordan. Lebanon, on the other hand, continues to assert that the armistice agreement is still valid. See Security Council Official Records, Third Year, No. 126 (381st meeting), (1949) p. 53; UNTS, vol. 42, No. 655, pp. 288–298.
3. According to the United Nations Relief and Work Agency (UNRWA), over

370,000 are registered as refugees in Lebanon. See *www.un.org/unrwa* (accessed 11/25/05).

4. See Shai Feldman, "Israel in Lebanon," in Ariel E. Levite, Bruce W. Jentleson, Larry Berman, eds., *Foreign Military Intervention: The Dynamics of a Protracted Conflict* (New York, 1992), pp. 129–161, 132–133. For an elaborate study of the Litani Operation, see Yair Evron, *War and Intervention in Lebanon: The Israeli-Syrian Deterrence Dialogue* (London, 1987), pp. 71–83.

5. Twenty Israelis were killed in the operation. See Robert Fisk, *Pity the Nation: The Abduction of Lebanon* (Berkeley, Calif., 2002), p. 124.

6. S.C. Res. 33/425, UN SCOR, 33d Sess., 2074th meeting, para. 2–3, UN Doc. S/pv/2074 (1978).

7. The origins of the SLA were in the early alliance that Israel struck with the Christian factions in Lebanon, beginning with the "Good Fence" policy in the mid-1970s, during the civil war in Lebanon. See Naomi Joy Weinberger, *Syrian Intervention in Lebanon: The 1975–1976 Civil War* (New York, 1986), pp. 284–288.

8. See Ze'ev Schiff and Ehud Ya'ari, *Israel's Lebanon War,* Ina Friedman, ed. and trans. (London, 1986), pp. 97–100. On the motivations driving the Israeli leadership, see Evron, *War and Intervention in Lebanon;* Feldman, "Israel in Lebanon," Gad Barzilai, *Democracy in Wars: Dispute and Consensus in Israel* (Tel-Aviv, 1992) (in Hebrew, translation mine); Avner Yaniv, *National Security and Democracy in Israel* (Boulder, Colo., 1993); *A War of Choice,* Yaffe Center for Strategic Studies, Tel-Aviv University (Tel-Aviv, 1985) (in Hebrew, translation mine); Schiff and Ya'ari, *Israel's Lebanon War.*

9. See Yaniv, *National Security and Democracy in Israel;* Feldman, *Israel in Lebanon;* Avner Yaniv, *Dilemmas of Security: Politics Strategy and the Israeli Experience in Lebanon* (New York, 1987), pp. 22–23.

10. Evron, *War and Intervention in Lebanon,* p. 117; see also Dilip Hiro, *Lebanon: Fire and Embers: A History of the Lebanese Civil War* (New York, 1993), pp. 81–85.

11. Itmar Rabinovich, *The War for Lebanon, 1970–1985,* (Ithaca, N.Y., 1985), p. 139.

12. M. Thomas Davis, *40 km into Lebanon* (Washington, D.C., 1987), p. 99; Richard Gabriel, *Operation Peace for Galilee: The Israel-PLO War in Lebanon* (New York, 1984), p. 145.

13. Davis, *40 km,* pp. 100–101. See also Loren Jenkins, "Palestinian Convoy Travels to Syria; Overland Evacuation Underway," *Washington Post,* August 27, 1982, A1.

14. Casualties estimates vary to a great degree. For one estimate, see Gabriel, *Operation Peace for Galilee,* pp. 164–176.

15. Israeli Cabinet Decision of June 5, 1982. *www.mfa.gov.il* (Israeli Ministry of Foreign Affairs Web Site) (accessed 9/21/06). See Shai Feldman and Heda Rechnitz-Kizner, *Deception, Consensus and War: Israel in Lebanon,* Jaffe Center for Strategic Studies (Boulder, Colo., 1984); Barzili, *Democracy in War,* p. 190.

16. On the Israeli-Maronite relations, see Reuven Erlich, "The Concept of the Security Zone and its Reality Test," in Yaacov Bar-Siman-Tov, ed., *The Security Zone in Lebanon—Rethinking,* Leonard Davis Institute for International Relations (Jerusalem, 1997), pp. 9–28 (in Hebrew, translation mine); Kenneth J. Alnwick and Thomas Fabyanic, *Warfare in Lebanon* (Washington, D.C., 1988), pp. 15–16; Yair Evron, *War and Intervention in Lebanon,* pp. 25–28, 42–45, 71–82.

17. [Draft] Agreement Between the Government of the State of Israel and the Government of the Republic of Lebanon, May 17, 1983; reproduced in Ruth Lapidoth and Moshe Hirsch, *The Arab-Israeli Conflict and Its Resolution: Selected Documents* (Dordrecht, 1992), p. 299.

18. See Neil Quilliam, *Syria and the New World Order* (Reading, UK, 1999), pp. 142–143; Moshe Ma'oz, *Syria and Israel: From War to Peacemaking* (New York, 1995), p. 179.

19. See Erlich, "The Concept of the Security Zone." The head of the Israeli delegation to the Halde talks, Ambassador David Kimchi concludes his article on the agreement with the following words: "The May 17th agreement with Israel was a dream, but a dream late in coming. Its main supporters— The United States and Israel—had lost the sense of need to help the Lebanese reach a peaceful coexistence. Since the tragic murder of Bashir Gemayel by the Syrians in September 1982, the leaders of Lebanon have shown that they have no interest whatsoever in achieving a real settlement." See David Kimchi, "The Israeli-Lebanese Agreement, 1983–1984," in *Lebanon—Collection of Essays,* IDF Field Intelligence Publications (Tel-Aviv, 1995) (in Hebrew, translation mine).

20. See Zeev Shiff, "The Withdrawal from Lebanon is Linked to an Agreement with Syria," in Bar-Siman-Tov, *The Security Zone in Lebanon,* pp. 53–57 (in Hebrew, translation mine).

21. "Cabinet Communique on the Withdrawal from Lebanon." Israeli Cabinet Resolution 291 of January 14, 1985. *www.mfa.gov.il* (accessed 9/21/06).

22. Erlich, "The Concept of the Security Zone," p. 29; and compare Avraham Sela, "The Security Zone—Lebanese and Regional Perspectives," in Bar-Siman-Tov, *The Security Zone in Lebanon,* p. 36 (in Hebrew, translation mine).

23. For a historical survey of the Israel-SLA relationship, see Aharon Amir, *The Black Book: South Lebanon—The Betrayal, the Escape, the Disgrace* (Jerusalem, 2001) (in Hebrew, translation mine).

24. See Magnus Ranstop, *Hizb'allah in Lebanon* (London, 1997), pp. 30–33; for criticism of the Israeli shortsightedness of this development, see William Harris, *Faces of Lebanon* (Princeton, N.J., 1997), p. 176.

25. H. Agha and A. Khalidi, *Syria and Iran: Rivalry and Cooperation* (London, 1995), pp. 15–20; A. Ehteshami and R. Hinnebusch, *Syria and Iran: Middle Powers in a Penetrated Regional System* (London, 1997), pp. 120–122.

26. For the debate over the exact content of the 1993 Understanding, see Waldman, *Arbitrating Armed Conflict,* p. 20.

27. Hala Jaber, *Hezbollah: Born with a Vengeance* (New York, 1997), p. 202.

28. Report dated May 1, 1996 of the Secretary-General's Military Adviser Concerning the Shelling of the United Nations Compound at Qana on April 18, 1996, UN Doc. S/1996/337 (May 7, 1996).

29. "Israel-Lebanon Cease-fire Understanding, April 26, 1996," available on the U.S. Embassy in Tel-Aviv Web site, *www.usembassy-israel.org.il,* (accessed 12/23/05).

30. "Cease-fire Understanding in Lebanon and Remarks by Prime Minister Peres and Secretary of State Christopher," available on the Israeli Ministry of Foreign Affairs Web site, *www.mfa.gov.il* (accessed 12/13/05).

31. "Old Games, New Rules: Conflict on the Israel-Lebanon Border," International Crisis Group, Middle East Report No. 7, Beirut/Brussels, November 18, 2002, p. 1.

32. See Report of the Secretary-General on the Implementation of Security Council Resolutions 425 (1978), and 426 (1978), UN Doc. S/2000/590, (June 16, 2000).

33. Deputy Secretary General of Hezbollah, Sheik Na'im Qasem quoted Imam Khomeini in a speech on June 6, 2002: "I ask the Muslims, why are you fighting over the Jordan River when all of Palestine is plundered? Muslims Should Annihilate Israel." See "Jubilant Jihad Warriors," *Jerusalem Post,* June 19, 2002, 7. Hezbollah never refers to Israel as such, but only as "the Zionist entity."

34. On the "Palestinianisation" of Hezbollah, see "Old Games, New Rules," pp. 13–15.

35. Daniel Byman, "Should Hezbollah be Next?" *Foreign Affairs,* November/ December 2003, 54.

36. Editorial, "Insecurity in Lebanon," *Boston Globe,* August 26, 2001, D6.

37. Gareth Smyth, "Lebanon Braced for Running Battle over Its Troubled Waters," *Financial Times,* London, October 12, 2002, 11.

38. Andrew Lee Butters, "The Cedar Siding," *New Republic,* March 21, 2005, 18.

39. See, e.g., Robin Wright, "Syrian Intelligence Still in Lebanon: Operatives Remain as Troops Leave, Say U.S. and U.N. Officials," *Washington Post,* April 27, 2005, A18.

40. Missy Ryan, "Cedar Revolution Shows its Splinters," *National Journal,* October 8, 2005, 41.

41. See Robert W. Stookey, "The United States," in *Lebanon in Crisis: Participants and Issues,* P. Edward Hales and Lewis W. Snider, eds. (Syracuse, N.Y., 1979), pp. 225–233.

42. On the American involvement in the Litani Operation as well as in the Lebanon War, see Alnwick and Fabyanic, *Warfare in Lebanon,* pp. 1–7, 31–43, 69–94. For a detailed account of the U.S.-Israel relationship, see Samuel W. Lewis, "The United States and Israel: Evolution of an Unwritten Alliance," *Middle East Journal* 53, no. 3 (1999): 364–378.

43. See Ma'oz, *Syria and Israel,* pp. 161–235; Quilliam, *Syria and the New World Order,* p. 155.

44. Elizabeth Picard, *Lebanon, A Shattered Country: Myths and Realities of*

the Wars in Lebanon (1996), pp. 24–28. For an elaborate account of the early Syrian-Lebanese relationship, see also Weinberger, *Syrian Intervention in Lebanon*, pp. 31–60.

45. Moshe Ma'oz, *Asad: The Sphinx of Damascus: A Political Biography* (London, 1988), pp. 127–128.

46. See Quilliam, *Syria and the New World Order*, pp. 134–136.

47. The Syrian invasion of Lebanon was also supported by the Ford administration, which believed that only Syria could stop the Lebanese civil war. See Ma'oz, *Syria and Israel*, pp. 166–167; Quilliam, *Syria and the New World Order*, pp. 134–135.

48. Evron, *War and Intervention in Lebanon*, p. 54.

49. A. Norton, "Lebanon After Ta'if: Is the Civil War Over?" *Middle East Journal* 45, no. 3 (1991): 457–474; F. Nasrallah, "Syria after Ta'if: Lebanon and the Lebanese in Syrian Politics," in E. Kienle, *Contemporary Syria: Liberalization Between Cold War and Cold Peace* (London, 1994), p. 135.

50. See Harris, *Faces of Lebanon*, p. 292. See also F. Nasrallah, "The Treaty of Brotherhood, Co-operation and Co-ordination," in Y. Choueiri, ed., *State and Society in Syria and Lebanon* (Exeter, UK, 1993), p. 105.

51. See Habib C. Malik, "Between Damascus and Jerusalem: Lebanon and Middle East Peace," The Washington Institute for Near East Policy, Policy Paper No. 45, Washington, D.C., 1998, p. 40.

52. Report of the Secretary-General Pursuant to Security Council Resolution 1559, UN Doc. S/2004/777, October 1, 2004, p. 4.

53. See, for instance, Security Council Resolution 501, S/Res/501. Adopted by the Security Council at its 2332nd meeting, held on February 25, 1982.

54. See Winslow, "Between Damascus and Jerusalem," at 291–292; Quilliam, *Syria and the New World Order*, p. 143.

55. See Harris, *Faces of Lebanon*, pp. 123–137.

56. See Quilliam, *Syria and the New World Order*, p. 215.

57. Zvi Barel, "Katyusha in the Range of Understanding," *Ha'aretz*, February 16, 2000, B3 (in Hebrew, translation mine).

58. See Brig. Gen. (Ret.) David Agmon, "The Hezbollah Came Out Reinforced," *Ma'ariv*, April 28, 1996, 1 (in Hebrew, translation mine).

59. Waldman, *Arbitrating Armed Conflict*, pp. 23–26.

60. Shai Feldmann, "Israel's Security Doctrine," in David Tal, ed., *Israel's Routine Security Doctrine: Its Origins and Development 1949–1956* (Be'er She'va, Israel, 1998) (in Hebrew, translation mine); Ariel Levite, *Offense and Defense in Israeli Military Doctrine* (Boulder, Colo., 1990).

61. See, for instance, ILMG Press Statement of November 11, 1997 (32nd meeting); ILMG Press Statement of July 2, 1998 (51st meeting). Statements are on file with the author. All statements were reproduced in Waldman, *Arbitrating Armed Conflict*, pp. 145–298.

62. August Richard Norton, "Hizballah and the Israeli Withdrawal from Southern Lebanon," *Journal of Palestine Studies* 30, no. 1 (2000): 22–35, 29.

63. See ILMG Press Statement of July 13, 1999 (84th meeting).

64. David Rudge, "Israel Boycotts Grapes of Wrath Meeting," *Jerusalem Post,* June 30, 1999, 1.

65. One such case was an incident in which the SLA shelled mortar rounds deliberately into Saida, following the killing of two youngsters, family members of an SLA commander, by a Hezbollah roadside bomb. The shelling was conducted contrary to the IDF's policy, and Israeli settlements paid the price of Hezbollah's retaliation. See ILMG Press statement of August 23, 1997 (25th meeting). During the ILMG deliberations of the incident in Saida, Israel struggled to get the ILMG to point at the SLA itself rather than to Israel as the party responsible for committing the violation. The Syrian and Lebanese delegations strongly objected, and the compromise was in concluding that it was incumbent upon Israel to ensure that similar attacks are not carried out. For a report of this debate, see *BBC Summary of World Broadcasts,* quoting Radio Lebanon, 1530 gmt, August 20, 1997.

66. International judicial tribunals have expressed two different tests: that of "absolute control," articulated by the International Court of Justice in the case of *Nicaragua vs. United States,* and that of "effective control," articulated by the International Criminal Tribunal for the Former Yugoslavia, in the case of *Tadic.* See *Military and Paramilitary Activities (Nicaragua v. US),* 1986 ICJ Rep. 14; *The Prosecutor v. Tadic,* ICTY Judgment, Appeals Chamber, 15 July 1999.

67. Art. 50–51 to Protocol Additional to the Geneva Conventions of August 12, 1949, and Relating to the Protection of Victims of International Armed Conflicts (Protocol I), adopted June 8, 1977, art. 1(4), 1125 UNTS 3, offer a definition of civilians and civilian population and prescribe the protections which should be accorded to them. Article 52(2) gives a broad definition of "military objects," to include "objects which by their nature, location, purpose, or use make an effective contribution to military action and whose total or partial destruction, capture or neutralization, in the circumstances ruling at the time, offer a definite military advantage."

68. See Article 23 of the Hague Regulations in the appendix to the Convention Respecting the Laws and Customs of War on Land, October 18, 1907, 36 Stat. 2277 (hereafter, Hague Regulations).

69. Declaration Renouncing the Use, in Time of War, of Explosive Projectiles Under 400 Grammes Weight, Dec. 11, 1868, 138 Consol. T. S. 297 (1868–1869). Earlier recognition of the principle of distinction was expressed in the Lieber Code during the American Civil War.

70. See also Art. 57(2) to Protocol I, Hague Regulations, which orders the attacker to refrain from launching any attack that may be expected to cause incidental injury and damage to civilian life and objects that would be excessive in relation to the concrete and direct military advantage anticipated.

71. See Dieter Fleck, *The Handbook of Humanitarian Law in Armed Conflicts* (Oxford, 1999), p. 179.

72. Yoram Dinstein, Laws of War (Tel-Aviv, 1983), p. 150 (in Hebrew, translation mine).

73. See Fleck, *The Handbook of Humanitarian Law*, p. 180.

74. On the role of the laws of war as providing only the minimal humanitarian protection, see Edward Kwakwa, *The International Law of Armed Conflict: Personal and Material Fields of Application* (Dordrecht, 1992); see also Leslie C. Green, *The Contemporary Law of Armed Conflict*, 2nd ed. (New York, 2000), p. 229.

75. These included water pipes, trees, animals, broken windows, etc. As for physical injuries, any injury was acknowledged, apart from shock. The Israeli delegation has raised the issue in conjunction with a violation report concerning six civilians in Israel who suffered from shock when a mortar round shelled by the Hezbollah hit their house in the village of Arab El-Aramshe in Israel. See ILMG Press Statement of July 7, 1998 (52nd meeting). The Lebanese delegation refused to acknowledge "shock" as an injury, claiming that Lebanese civilians suffer daily from fear, anxiety, and mental disorders brought about by the Israeli attacks on Lebanon.

76. Evidence of this debate can be found in one press statement, in which the Israeli delegation stated its position while reaffirming "its right to file violation reports whenever it deems necessary within the framework of the April 26 Understanding." See ILMG Press Statement of July 31, 1997 (23rd meeting).

77. See Art. 51(7) and 58(b) of Additional Protocol I, 1977 (see note 67 above).

78. See Letter from the U.S. secretary of state, Warren Christopher, to the Israeli prime minister, Shimon Peres, April 26, 1996, available on the U.S. Embassy in Tel-Aviv Web site, *www.usembassy-israel.org.il* (hereafter, Letter from Christopher to Peres) (accessed 9/25/06).

79. Kwakwa, *The International Law of Armed Conflict*, p. 88. See also Gerald Draper, "The Status of Combatants and the Question of Guerilla Warfare," *British Yearbook of International Law*, vol. 45 (1971), pp. 177–178.

80. "Back to Bombs and Rockets," *Economist*, February 12, 2000.

81. See also interview with Secretary of State Madelene Albright, in which Secretary Albright expressed understanding for the Israeli action and refused to regard it as a "war crime": "Secretary of State Madeleine Albright Talks About Latest Setbacks to Middle East Peace Process," *CNN Worldview*, CNN, February 8, 2000.

82. See interview with Hezbollah's deputy secretary general, Sheikh Naim Kassem, in which he explained that the meaning of Article IV was that Hezbollah was entitled to fight the Israeli occupation of Lebanon, in *Al-Diar*, May 15, 1996.

83. Letter from Christopher to Peres.

84. See, for instance, an account of damages to structures and vehicles, in the village of Kabricha, caused by IDF fire. There was no dispute that the action was defensive. Nevertheless, the ILMG concluded that "even in such situations, combatants are obliged to take every precaution to prevent injury or damage in civilian populated areas and to accept responsibility for their actions." ILMG Press Statement of July 2, 1998 (51st meeting).

85. "Protocol on the Warning Rules For the Israel-Lebanon Monitoring Group," The text of the protocol appears in Waldman, *Arbitrating Armed Conflict,* pp. 129–131.

86. The option of referral to the foreign ministers was invoked when Lebanon brought a complaint on Israeli air force sonic booms over Beirut. As there was no agreement on whether this issue fell within the purview of the Understandings, the group agreed to refer the matter to the "diplomatic channels." See ILMG Press Statement of December 20, 1998 (66th meeting).

87. Articles 1(C)–1(E) and 2 of the Protocol (note 85).

88. Article 3(E) of the Protocol.

89. Articles 3(B) and (C) of the Protocol. In Israel, the Protocol provided that such a mission would be undertaken by the representatives of the United States, France, and Israel; in Lebanon, the chair and cochair were to be accompanied by the Lebanese and Syrian (if so wished) delegates.

90. "Refugees from Abandoned Ship Saved by Israel call on U.N. for Help," *Deutsche Presse-Agentur,* International News, November 1, 1999; David Rudge, "Israel Returns Bodies of Two Hezbollah Gunmen," *Jerusalem Post,* December 29, 1999, 1.

91. One such issue was Israeli aircraft supersonic flights over Beirut. See ILMG Press Statement of December 20, 1998 (66th meeting) and of July 13, 1999 (84th meeting).

92. For an account of the incident in Arab Salim, see ILMG Press Statement of December 17, 1999 (99th meeting).

93. See ILMG Press Statement of August 15, 1996 (2nd meeting): "It is recalled that the work of the Monitoring Group is confidential and for the use of the governments concerned."

94. See Robert Axelrod, "An Evolutionary Approach to Norms," *American Political Science Review* 80 (1986): 1095–1111, 1105; Jon Elster, *The Cement of Society: A Study of Social Order* (Cambridge, 1989).

95. It is partly for this reason that the parties would draft their own press communication to their media, emphasizing the conclusions more favorable to themselves. In Lebanon, the ILMG received tremendous attention, much greater than in Israel or in the other participating countries.

96. Even a decision not to agree (a "he said, she said" format) needed the agreement of all parties.

97. "General on ILMG Role, Meeting with Senior Syrian Officer," June 6, 1997; quoted by Waldman, *Arbitrating Armed Conflict,* p. 114.

98. "Report Views ILMG's Prospects, Achievements," *Al-Nahar,* April 22, 1997; quoted by Waldman, *Arbitrating Armed Conflict,* p. 115.

99. Alan Philips, "Israel's Military Might Cannot Quell Lebanese," *Telegraph,* September 23, 1998, Internet version (no longer available); quoted by Charles W. Spain, Lawrence C. Trost, and Michael G. Vannoni, "Conceptual Monitoring Options for a Southern Lebanon Withdrawal Agreement," Sandia National Laboratories, SAND 2000–0184, Albuquerque, N.Mex., January 2000.

100. One such occasion was the group's meeting following wide-scale clashes in June 1999. The press statement noted that "the Monitoring Group agreed

that the resumption of its work should help to open a new page, with a view to strengthening the implementation of the April Understanding and contributing to a positive environment for broader peace efforts in the region." ILMG Press Statement of July 13, 1999 (85th meeting).

101. See statistical data, Figure 1.

102. ILMG Press Statements of November 6, 1996 (6th meeting), June 9, 1997 (19th meeting), April 7, 1998 (42nd meeting), May 27, 1998 (46th meeting), December 20, 1998 (66th meeting), and April 8, 1999 (75th meeting).

103. See Yoram Dinstein, "Armed Attacks From Within Civilian Centres," *Justice* 9 (1996): 19.

104. See report of interview with Lebanese Prime Minister al-Huss, on Radio Lebanon, Beirut, in which he commented on the M.G.'s composition: "[Al-Huss] noted that its importance lies in the fact that it includes the USA and France, which alternately chair it, and Syria. So, he added, we cannot say that it is solely a Lebanese-Israeli committee" ("Lebanon: Premier Denies Receiving Request to Amend ILMG," BBC *Worldwide Monitoring*, February 11, 2000.)

105. Amos Harel, "Arens Tells IDF to Find New Options for Lebanon," *Ha'aretz*, English edition, *www.haaretzdaily.com*, March 9, 1999 (accessed 8/10/04).

106. Arieh O'Sullivan, Amotz Asa-El, and Danna Harman, "Defense Minister Arens Tells 'Post': Grapes of Wrath Deal Should be Reconsidered," *Jerusalem Post*, March 3, 1999, 1.

107. See Voice of Israel Radio, Jerusalem, "Lebanon: Israel Sets Condition for Resumption of Role in Monitoring Group," BBC *Worldwide Monitoring*, April 16, 2000.

108. In an interview, Ambassador Joseph-Lauren Rapin, who served as the head of the French delegation, admitted that no one believed the ILMG would survive for more than three months; see "Until White Smoke Arises," *Ici France*, no. 4, July–August, 10 (published by the French Embassy, Tel-Aviv, 1998 (in Hebrew, translation mine).

109. In one such case, the question of the legality of Israeli operations in Lebanon, intertwined with the question of the extent of the Israeli responsibility for the SLA actions, arose out of a petition to the Israeli High Court of Justice concerning the El-H'iam detention center in south Lebanon. SLA soldiers ran the infamous detention facility, and there were constant allegations of ill treatment and bad conditions inside it. Several human rights organizations and lawyers appealed to the court to rule that Israel is responsible for the El-H'iam prison and must either order the release of all prisoners or ensure that they are tried in due process and receive adequate conditions during their imprisonment (HCJ 1951/99 *Ramadan v. Minister of Defense*, 2260/00 *Turmus v. Minister of Defense* [unpublished]). The state's position was that Israel did not occupy south Lebanon nor did it fully control the SLA, and therefore the HCJ did not have the authority to intervene. The HCJ largely accepted the state's position that the court does not have the authority to rule on the matter, taking into account, inter alia, that Israel announced its intention to with-

draw from Lebanon in July 2000. The HCJ further demanded some assurances from the state attorneys that Israel would inform the SLA of its position that the safety and well-being of the detainees in El-H'iam should be observed both before and after the Israeli withdrawal. The petitions became moot with the final withdrawal from Lebanon.

110. See Yossi Beilin, *The Guide to the Withdrawal from Lebanon,* (Tel-Aviv, 1998) (in Hebrew); Joel Greenberg, "Mothers' Cry, 'Out of Lebanon,' Rouses Israelis," *New York Times,* September 19, 1997, A4; Ilene R. Prusher, "Israel's Mothers Cry: 'Bring 'Em Home,'" *Christian Science Monitor,* December 31, 1997, 6.

111. Alan Sipress, "U.S. Planning to send Monitors to Mideast," *Washington Post,* July 27, 2001, 24; Herb Keinon and Janine Zacharia, "US Pressing Israel to Begin Counting Period of Quiet," *Jerusalem Post,* July 27, 2001, A.

112. David Rudge, "IAF hits Syrian Radar Station after Hezbollah Attacks," *Jerusalem Post,* April 17, 2001, 3.

113. Alex Fishman, "Hezbollah is Not Collapsing, Damascus is Not in a Hurry," *Yediot Ahronot,* April 19, 1996, 8 (in Hebrew, translation mine).

114. Jaber, *Hezbollah: Born with a Vengeance,* p. 195.

115. Editorial, "Lebanon: Finding Its Own Voice," *Christian Science Monitor,* June 22, 2005, 8.

5. Testing Theory in Practice

1. Eccles. 1: 9–10.

2. Barbara Wertheim Tuchman, *The March of Folly: From Troy to Vietnam* (New York, 1984).

3. Joseph W. Dellapenna, "Foreword: Bringing the Customary International Law of Transboundary Waters Into the Era of Ecology," *International Journal of Global Environmental Issues* 1 (2001): 264.

4. Smruti S. Pattanaik, "Indo-Pak Relations: Need for a Pragmatic Approach," *Strategic Analysis* 23, no. 1 (April 1999): 85–110.

5. Christopher D. Stone, "Common but Differentiated Responsibilities in International Law," 98 *AJIL* 276 (2004).

6. George W. Downs, David M. Rocke, and Peter N. Barsoom, "Is the Good News About Compliance Good News About Cooperation?" *International Organizations* 50 (1996): 379–406. There is an extensive debate in the literature with regard to the political economy school and its claims about compliance with international regimes. Rather than take sides in this debate, I borrow the term "depth of cooperation," as it seems to me a meaningful one, especially in the context of a rivalry.

7. Ibid., p. 385.

8. Yoram Dinstein, "Armed Attacks from within Civilian Centres," *Justice* 9 (1996): 17–20, 19.

9. Kal Raustiala suggests a distinction between "contracts" (legally binding) and "pledges" (legally nonbinding). See Kal Raustiala, "Form and Substance in International Agreements," 99 *AJIL,* 581 (2005). Friedrich

Kratchovil submits that the distinction lies between specific obligations, which are "hard," and those which are of a higher level of abstraction, which are "soft." See Friedrich V. Kratochwil, *Rules, Norms, and Decisions: On the Conditions of Practical and Legal Reasoning of International Relations and Domestic Affairs* (New York, 1989), p. 203. Christine Chinkin argues that the distinction is one that depends on how precise and specific the obligations prescribed by the legal instrument are. See Christine M. Chinkin, "The Challenge of Soft Law: Development and Change in International Law," 38 *International and Comparative Law Quarterly* 850, 851 (1989).

10. A. G. Noorani, "A Treaty to Keep," *Frontline* 19, no. 18 (April 13–26, 2002), available on *www.hinduonnet.com/frontline* (accessed October 13, 2005).

11. M. James Wilkinson, "Moving Beyond Conflict Prevention to Reconciliation: Tackling Greek-Turkish Hostility," in Adel Safty, ed., *Leadership and Conflict Resolution* (Famagusta, Cyprus, 1999), pp. 135–177, 138.

12. Andrew T. Guzman, "The Cost of Credibility: Explaining Resistance to Interstate Dispute Resolution Mechanisms," 31 *Journal of Legal Studies* 303–326 (2002).

13. Kyle Danish, "The New Sovereignty: Compliance with International Regulatory Agreements," 37 *Virginia Journal of International Law* 789–810 (1997).

14. Pattanaik, "Indo-Pak Relations," p. 103.

15. Ayesha Siddiqa-Agha, *Maritime Cooperation between India and Pakistan: Building Confidence at Sea,* Cooperative Monitoring Center, SAND 98-0505/18, Sandia National Laboratories, Albuquerque, N.Mex., 2000.

16. In March 2002, the Israeli Knesset passed a law prohibiting visits by members of Knesset to "enemy states" without prior approval by the minister of the interior or the prime minister. See "New Law Bans Unauthorized MK's Diplomats Travel to Enemy States," *BBC Monitoring International Reports,* March 14, 2002. Movement of Druzes is normally allowed for purposes of marriage, study, or attendance at Syrian leaders' funerals.

17. The term "compliance-pull" is borrowed from Thomas M. Franck, *Fairness in International Law and Institutions* (Oxford, 1995).

18. Qudssia Akhlaque, "India Cannot Scrap Indus Treaty," *Dawn,* May 26, 2002, available on *www.dawn.com* (accessed September 12, 2006).

19. The principle of "community of interests" in navigable rivers was introduced by the Permanent Court of International Justice as early as 1929 in the case of the River Oder. See Case Relating to the Territorial Jurisdiction of the International Commission of the River Oder (United Kingdom, Czechoslovak Republic, Denmark, France, Germany, Sweden and Poland), PCIJ, Series A., Mo. 23. 1 (1929). The Lake Lanoux arbitration case determined that states must consider the interests of other states when planning any works on their part of a transboundary watercourse. See Lake Lanoux Case (France-Spain), Award of November 16, 1957, 12 UN Rep. Int'l Arb. Awards 218 (1957); 24 ILR 101 (1959). A series of domestic cases involv-

ing conflicts over water in federal states was also in place. See the German case of *Wirttemburg and Prussia v. Baden* (1927–1928) Ann. Dig. Pub. Int'l L. Cases 128; and the U.S. case of *New Jersey v. New York,* 283 U.S. 336 (1931). For a more detailed survey of the international and domestic case law on international watercourses, see Patricia Wouters, "Present Status of International Water Law," in Patricia Wouters, ed., *International Water Law: Selected Writings of Professor Charles B. Bourne* (Boston, 1997). Still, there was legal support for the other three theories of transboundary water sharing as well.

20. In 1966 the International Law Association included the Helsinki Rules on International Rivers, in the Report of the 52nd Conference Helsinki, 1966, and in 1986—it adopted the Seoul Rules on International Groundwater, of the 62nd conference, in Seoul, in 1986. More recent conventions are the Convention on the Protection and Use of Transboundary Watercourses and International Lakes, March 17, 1992, 31 ILM 1312 (organized by the United Nations Economic Commission for Europe) and the United Nations Convention on the Law of Non-Navigational Uses of International Watercourses, opened for signature May 21, 1997, 36 ILM 700 (not yet in force).

21. Art 8 of the Berne Declaration on the Procedure to be Followed for the Delimitation of the Continental Shelf by Greece and Turkey. Signed in Berne, November 11, 1976, available on www.turkishgreek.org/Bern.htm (accessed 9/22/06).

22. Article 3(5) to the *Watercourse Convention.* Convention on the Law of Non-Navigational Uses of International Watercourses, 36 ILM 700 (1997).

23. Salman M. A. Salman and Laurence Boisson de Chazournes, "Conclusion," in Salman M. A. Salman and Laurence Boisson de Chazournes, eds., "International Watercourses: Enhancing Cooperation and Managing Conflict," Proceedings of a World Bank Seminar, World Bank Technical Paper no. 414, Washington D.C., 1998, pp. 167–170, 168.

24. Stephen McCaffrey claims that although on the basis of this provision one might have expected India to insist on its long-held position emphasizing territorial sovereignty and freedom of action, its more recent agreements with Bangladesh display a considerable evolvement of the Indian position towards principles of equitable sharing and community of interests. See Stephen C. McCaffrey, *The Law of International Watercourses: Non-Navigational Uses* (Oxford, 2001), p. 250.

25. See Wouters, *International Water Law;* Joseph W. Dellapenna, "Treaties as Instruments for Managing Internationally-Shared Water Resources: Restricted Sovereignty vs. Community of Property," 26 *Case Western. Reserve Journal of International Law* 27–56 (1994). See also Hilal Elver, who claims that "there are international water law agreements that resolved conflict involving the allocation of water for irrigation use in the third millennium B.C. that have a remarkably similar structure to contemporary water allocation agreements." Hilal Elver, *Peaceful Use of International Rivers: The Euphrates and Tigris River Disputes* (New York, 2002), p. 115.

26. Michael Ignatieff, *The Warrior's Honor: Ethnic War and the Modern Conscience* (New York, 1998), p. 158.

27. Ibid., p. 160.

28. W. Michael Reisman, "Stopping Wars and Making Peace," 6 *Tulane Journal of International and Comparative Law* 5–56, 17 (1998).

29. Edward N. Luttwak, "Give War a Chance," *Foreign Affairs* 78 (1999): 36.

Epilogue

1. Anthony Shadid and Scott Wilson, "Hezbollah Raid Opens 2nd Front for Israel," *Washington Post,* July 13, 2006, p. A1.

2. "Lebanese Premier Addresses Nation on Army Deployment, Rebuilding Tasks," BBC Worldwide Monitoring, August 17, 2006.

3. "Lebanese PM's Office Denies Receiving Invitation From Israeli Counterpart," BBC Worldwide Monitoring Report, September 3, 2006.

Index